D0221922

THE
LANAHAN
CASES AND READINGS

IN

Abnormal Behavior

———◄◉►———

KAYLA F. BERNHEIM

is also the author of

Schizophrenia: Symptoms, Causes, and Treatments
(with Richard R. J. Lewine)

The Caring Family: Living with Chronic Mental Illness
(with Richard R. J. Lewine and Caroline T. Beale)

Working with Families of the Mentally Ill
(with Anthony F. Lehman)

THE
LANAHAN
CASES AND READINGS
IN
Abnormal Behavior

———◀o▶———

Kayla F. Bernheim, Ph.D.

LANAHAN PUBLISHERS, INC.

Baltimore

Copyright © 1997 by LANAHAN PUBLISHERS, INC.
All rights reserved.
Printed in the United States of America.

Since this page can not legibly accommodate all copyright notices,
pages 377 through 379 constitute a continuation of this copyright page.

The text of this book was composed in Sabon with display type set in Novarese. Composition by Bytheway Typesetting Services, Inc. Manufacturing by Victor Graphics, Inc. Book design by Justine Burkat Trubey.

ISBN 0-9652687-0-5

LANAHAN PUBLISHERS, INC.
324 Hawthorne Road
Baltimore, MD 21210

1 2 3 4 5 6 7 8 9 0

Contents

————◄o►————

Chapter Four Mood Disorders 89

Cases

Readings

Chapter Five Schizophrenia and Related Psychoses 124

Cases

Readings

Chapter Six   Sexual and Gender Identity Disorders

Cases

Reading

Preface

————◄○►————

This book of cases and readings is designed to be used as an adjunct to basic textbooks in Abnormal Psychology and courses in related fields like Clinical Social Work and Psychiatric Nursing. Observation of individual cases is the backbone of both research and theory building in the study of psychopathology. But most textbook authors have, of necessity, devoted limited space to case material. When they have included case material, there is often little follow-up discussion of the cases. Films and videotapes can offer impressionistic glimpses of abnormality, but only through reading a full case report (or first-person account) and its discussion can students capture the richness of a person's experience over time. We hope that the addition of contemporary readings to this book will generate additional opportunities for classroom discussion.

In my own teaching of Abnormal Psychology, I have often felt that textbooks left me nothing to teach—that lectures were too often rehashes of what was included in the text. *The* LANAHAN *Cases and Readings in Abnormal Behavior* is the book I would have liked to have available. I hope that it will also be used as a primary text by instructors who, like me, wish to begin with the case material as a focal point, using lecture time to discuss research and models of disordered behavior.

The Cases

The cases are all real. They are drawn from my own twenty-two year clinical practice, from colleagues, and from such well-known experts like Hilda Bruch, Judith Rapoport, and Oliver Sacks. Identifying information has been changed, but they are otherwise true-to-life. Because of this, few of the cases are simple and clear-cut, or what one might call perfect-fit textbook cases. Some illustrate the fact that many, if not most, patients have symptoms that justify more than one diagnosis. Others show that not all treatment is effective, and not all cases have happy endings. Most of the cases are about common disorders with common presentations, but a few have been chosen because they are particularly vivid or unusual. Rather than offer a quick sketch, I have tried to include enough detail to generate a picture of a real person confronting real problems. All, I hope, will hold your attention and generate interesting questions about psychological disorders, their causes and treatments. And all, I hope, will remind you that each "case" is really a person, with hopes, fears, and aspirations like the rest of us.

Each case is followed by a brief discussion that not only fully follows up on the case and its treatment, but also provides some basic content that is part of the Abnormal Psychology course. Each discussion is followed by a list of questions designed to stimulate further thought.

The Readings

The readings have been chosen from a variety of sources—professional journals, mental health newsletters, the popular press. Some of the readings on topics from the biopsychosocial model, PTSD, and light therapy to borderline personality disorder and living with mental illness in the family offer up-to-date basic content for the course. Other readings provide an introduction to some of the current controversies in the field, such as the usefulness of psychotherapy, who can best treat ethnic minorities, the validity of repressed memory syndrome, media portrayals of abnormality, and involuntary treatment. I hope that the variety will provide something for everyone.

The Format

The book is organized into two broad sections preceded by a first chapter. This chapter, "The Scope of Abnormality," examines some basic issues in defining abnormality. Each of its two cases tries to get us to think about the boundaries of abnormality. The reading on the "biopsychosocial model" lays out an approach to abnormality that many in the field are currently taking.

The main part of the book, "Part I: The Disorders," comprises nine chapters. They include numerous cases and readings covering the full range of disorders most commonly discussed in Abnormal Psychology courses as they are organized in the Diagnostic and Statistical Manual (DSM-IV).

In addition, for each chapter I have prepared what my publisher calls the LANAHAN NOTES. These are meant to be brief study sections for students. They offer, in outline form, a broad overview of the classification, symptomatology, etiology, and treatment of the basic disorders in Part I. They are general enough to be compatible with the material in virtually any textbook on abnormal psychology. We envision them as being like the notes that students, themselves, might take of lecture or text material.

The last section, "Part II: Abnormality and Society," is made up exclusively of readings, and includes two chapters. One looks specifically at psychotherapy: Does it work? Who should treat whom? Another examines social and legal issues related to abnormal behavior from coverage in the mass media, deinstitutionalization, and involuntary treatment to the formation of national mental health policy.

The Biopsychosocial Model

It is now clear that few, if any, psychological disorders can be fully explained within the rigid boundaries of any one theoretical model. Genetic and biochemical influences on behavior are becoming ever more apparent and the use of psychoactive medications in treatment is becoming ever more widespread. On the other hand, the individuality of human experience, the influence of culture, religion, socioeconomic status, family life, and a host of other factors influence the development, treatment, and outcome of most disorders. In my own Abnormal Psychology course, I attempt to teach students to see psychopathology through a wide lens and to keep the individual who is struggling with the disorder always in view. For this purpose, I have adopted a biopsychosocial view in the case discussions of this book. Informed by the research and clinical literature, I have attempted to balance attention to biological, psychological, and social factors in our examination of the phenomena under study. Discussion questions encourage students to view each case from different perspectives and to blend aspects of different theoretical visions whenever possible.

One final hope: that you will find reading and thinking about these cases as stimulating and instructive as I do in working with my patients, teaching the course, and learning more about the changing and challenging field each day.

Acknowledgments

————◄o►————

I would like to thank my colleagues, Patricia Fitzpatrick Thompson, Ph.D., Lorraine Rocissano, Ph.D., and Stephen Karl, M.S.W., for their contributions of case material. Susannah Bernheim and Caroline Beale made helpful suggestions about both cases and the book's format. Dimitri Papageorgis, Ph.D., of The University of British Columbia and Ann Kaiser Stearns, Ph.D., of Essex Community College both reviewed the manuscript, and their thoughts and ideas on it were most helpful. To my clients who participated actively in shaping their own case histories, and to those who allowed me into their lives, I owe a great deal. I am also appreciative of the careful copyediting performed by Margaret M. Brassil. I am particularly grateful to my publisher, editor, and friend of twenty years, Don Fusting. His support, good humor, ability to compromise, and unfailingly useful editorial advice has been invaluable throughout my writing career. He also makes a mean French toast.

—Kayla F. Bernheim, Ph.D.

THE
LANAHAN
CASES AND READINGS

IN

Abnormal Behavior

CHAPTER ONE

The Scope of Abnormality

————◀o▶————

Behavioral disorders have fascinated humankind from as early as we have written records. References to abnormal behavior and its treatment can be found in the early writings of the Hebrews, Greeks, Egyptians, and Chinese. The Greek physician Hippocrates, writing around 400 B.C., offered a rudimentary classification of mental disorders and suggested that brain pathology, heredity, and environmental factors were all implicated as causal agents.

Still, an exact definition of psychopathology eludes us even today. How do we know that someone is "abnormal?" Do we mean by this that his behavior is simply different? Were this all that was necessary, we would find "genius" in abnormal psychology textbooks. Is psychological misery a sufficient criterion for abnormality? It cannot be, because some people who suffer, like recently bereaved people, are clearly "normal" while other people who don't, like people who derive sexual stimulation from contact with children, would be considered "abnormal" by most of us. Perhaps an individual who engages in maladaptive behavior can be considered abnormal. Clearly, this criterion is relevant, but not sufficient. Consider, for example, a man who robs people for a living. If he is not very smart, he may get caught and go to jail. This behavior is clearly maladaptive, but he is not necessarily mentally ill. Contrast this with another man who works as a bank teller, all the while believing that he is an alien who is waiting for his spaceship to come and take him back to his native planet. His behavior is not noticeably maladaptive, but most of us would agree that he is clearly "abnormal."

In Chapter One, we take up two fundamental questions: First, how do we define abnormality, and second, how do we explain abnormality when we see it. To address the first question we have included two cases, one in which a statistically "abnormal" behavior causes no suffering or apparent maladaptiveness, and the other in which a statistically "normal" reaction involves substantial emotional pain and dysfunction. In struggling with which, if either of them, reflects mental "disorder" you will sharpen your own definition.

As regards the second question, we have included a brief piece illustrating a comprehensive biopsychosocial approach to understanding behavioral disorder. This model integrates the various ways that clinicians and researchers have approached the study of abnormal behavior. It combines elements of medical models, behavioral models, psychological models, and environmental models to create a comprehensive account of the factors that can influence behavior. We will refer back to it often in examining the disorders that comprise the bulk of the book.

1

——————◄o►——————

ABNORMALITY OR ECCENTRICITY? THE CASE OF NEIL CARGILE

NEIL CARGILE IS A SIXTY-FIVE-YEAR-OLD Nashville millionaire. He is a superb pilot, having been trained in Navy jets, who loves to "push the envelope." He has survived so many emergency landings that he carries the nickname, "Crash Cargile." He began flying as a teenager, in a plane he rebuilt out of surplus parts from the Second World War. As an adult, he built a helicopter pad on the grounds of his mansion. He played football at Vanderbilt College, has driven race cars, sailed yachts, and played polo. A daredevil in business as well as pleasure, he has flown crop-dusters and dredged for gold and diamonds in remote parts of the world. Twice married and twice divorced, the father of three grown children, and decidedly heterosexual, Neil Cargile would be the proto-typical "man's man" were it not for one thing: he likes to dress up in women's clothing. He doesn't just dress up in private, either. He often appears at parties and even at restaurants dressed entirely in women's clothes. In an article by John Berendt in *The New Yorker* magazine (Jan 16, 1995), Mr. Cargile is interviewed and his behavior described. Is he abnormal? Does he have a psychological disorder? See what you think.

Neil Cargile grew up a privileged member of Nashville society. Mr. Berendt doesn't say much about Cargile's childhood, except that he was a talented youngster, both intellectually and in working with his hands, and that he always loved to be the center of attention. His father was a successful, conservative businessman, and his mother was a high-society, stay-at-home mom.

He has a brother, a born-again Christian, who is appalled by his cross-dressing. His mother is embarrassed but has been unable to con-vince him to rein in his behavior. His father is dead but when asked what his father would have done if he had seen Cargile in a dress, Cargile replied, "he would have killed me." Cargile's life has been adventurous but not entirely without tragedy: his fourteen-year-old son died of a burst aneurysm in 1970, a few years before the cross-dressing began.

Mr. Cargile first wore women's clothing at an out-of-town Halloween party in the mid-1970s when a few women friends talked him into going to the party as Dolly Parton. He won first prize for his costume. Over the next several years he attended several other costume parties in women's clothes—always out of town. Then, gradually, he began to cross-dress at local private parties, beginning subtly, with a kilt along with a jacket and tie, then adding stockings and high heels to the outfit. Finally, he had a party at his house in which guests were required to come dressed as a member of the opposite sex, and shortly thereafter, he appeared at a local costume party in full drag. After that, to the consternation of his friends and family, he began cross-dressing in public in Nashville itself.

Recently, Cargile has taken to calling himself SheNeil when he goes out in women's clothing. Author Berendt asked him if he felt like a different person when he became SheNeil. He replied "No, I feel like Neil Cargile in a dress."

Cargile seemed to get as much pleasure out of shocking people as in wearing the clothes. He does it, he says, for "fun." Berendt quotes Cargile as saying, "I'm a big showoff. I have a motto: If you aren't doing something different, you aren't doing anything at all. That's the way I've always lived." Still, there were some places Cargile would not go in drag: to church or the local country club. He also attended business meetings dressed in men's clothing, although he sometimes wore pantyhose under his suit and carried a miniskirt and a pair of heels in the car.

At the insistence of his ex-wife, Cargile went to a psychiatrist once about his cross-dressing. After finding out that Cargile was heterosexual, the psychiatrist confided that several of his colleagues cross-dressed too, although in private. Cargile got the impression that the doctor didn't feel there was much wrong with him, and he never returned.

Cargile's current girlfriend affectionately indulges his cross-dressing, helping him select outfits and doing his makeup. His daughter bought him a makeup kit one Christmas. His cross-dressing doesn't seem to have altered his social standing in Nashville, nor his capacity to make business deals.

Thinking About the Case

It is estimated that three to five percent of the male population puts on women's clothes, at least occasionally. It is difficult to access the number of women who cross-dress, since wearing men's clothing is more acceptable and less noticeable for women.

The reasons that men cross-dress vary widely. For some men cross-dressing is a sexual fetish—the clothes themselves cause sexual arousal. For others, the behavior seems to be a relaxation strategy, a way for high-achieving men to get some relief from the demands for aggressive, even ruthless competition to which they perceive themselves subject. In these men, as in Cargile, a female second self emerges in which emotional vulnerability and "softness" can be expressed more freely. Still others were dressed in women's clothing as children by mothers who wanted daughters instead of sons, while others were forced as children to wear clothing of the opposite sex as punishment. For these men, adult cross-dressing is associated with humiliation and poor self-esteem.

While most male cross-dressers are heterosexual and comfortable being men, some are homosexual and a subgroup of these cross-dress as a part of a transsexual syndrome: they wish to be women. Their subjective experience is that they are actually women, mistakenly imprisoned in a male body. (We describe such a case in Chapter Six.)

The meaning of cross-dressing is, at least in part, culturally determined. Anthropologists have found individuals in aboriginal cultures throughout the world (except, curiously, in Europe) who, while masculine in sex, seemed to behave in many ways as women. In these cultures, an institutional role was created for these individuals in which they were neither men nor women. This role varied from culture to culture but could include child-care duties, healing functions, storytelling, or acting as go-betweens in love affairs. The attitude towards these individuals, referred to by anthropologists as "berdache," also varied from society to society. In some they were revered while in others they were reviled. In all these cultures, however, the berdache constituted a third gender, neither male nor female.

Questions to Consider

1. Is Neil Cargile abnormal? Does he have a psychological disorder? Why or why not? Do you think everyone would agree with your assessment? If not, what implications might this disagreement have for the study of abnormal psychology?

2. Would you have a different answer to the first question if

   a. Cargile was poor and homeless rather than wealthy?

   b. Cargile admitted to getting sexual pleasure from the cross-dressing?

   c. Cargile only cross-dressed at costume parties?

   d. Cargile were a woman who dressed in men's clothing?

   What do your answers tell you about the role of context in how we evaluate unusual behaviors?

3. Martin Seligman and David Rosenhan, in their textbook, *Abnormal Psychology*, Third Edition (Norton, 1995), list seven elements that count towards whether we label a person or a behavior abnormal. These are 1) suffering, 2) maladaptiveness, 3) irrationality

and incomprehensibility, 4) unpredictability and loss of control, 5) vividness and unconventionality, 6) observer discomfort, and 7) violation of moral and ideal standards. The more of these elements that are present, the more likely we are to call something abnormal. Which are present in Neil Cargile's behavior? Would you delete or add elements to this list?

4. What can you hypothesize about some possible causes for Cargile's behavior? Do you think it's related to his apparent need to be the center of attention? If so, why might Cargile have chosen cross-dressing as opposed to some other flamboyant behavior? Might it be related to the death of his son? How? Might there be relevant factors in his childhood? In his biological makeup? What sorts of data would you need to help you decide whether your ideas were correct?

2

——◄o►——

A "NORMAL" PSYCHOLOGICAL DISORDER: THE CASE OF MARTIN B.

MARTIN B. WAS A WRECK. Sitting in his doctor's office, disheveled, several days growth of stubble on his face, and fourteen pounds thinner than when he was last in, he looked the very picture of misery. Haltingly, and sobbing softly from time to time, he told his physician (and personal friend) that his wife of twelve years had taken their four-year-old son, along with most of the furniture, and left him ten days previously. For the first two days, he had slept almost all of the time, except when he was at work, where he had continued to function as if nothing had happened. But on the third day, he fell apart. He had been sleeping poorly since, often waking in the middle of the night with a pounding heart and feelings of impending doom. During the day, he couldn't sit still, couldn't concentrate, couldn't eat. For the last three days, he hadn't even been able to go to work. He had begun to drink bourbon each evening "to help him sleep," and had occasionally thought that he might be better off dead. His older brother, seeing Martin's despair, not only insisted that he come to the doctor's office, but accompanied him to ensure that he kept the appointment.

Martin was a thirty-nine-year-old engineer when his wife left. He made a good living, though working long hours to do so. His wife had worked as a dental assistant until their child was born, at which time she quit her job to stay home. He had been proud that he was able to support his family without his wife's financial help.

His wife's leaving had come as a complete surprise to Martin. He felt that he had done everything a husband should do—make a living, take care of the yard and auto maintenance, come home directly from work. He wasn't a heavy drinker nor a womanizer. He didn't abuse his wife in any way; in fact, he loved her devotedly. Her complaints that they didn't communicate, didn't have common interests, didn't have any fun together, he had taken as the sorts of things any wife might say. He had heard them so often that he had learned to tune his wife out when she brought them up. He had been a much more attentive husband and father than his own father had been, and his mother had endured marriage for forty-one years. He felt betrayed and abandoned, humiliated, and enraged . . . and completely defeated.

Martin's physician made three recommendations: first, that Martin stop drinking for at least one month; second, that he take antidepressant medication to help him sleep and to improve his mood; and third, that he get psychotherapy to help him manage the crisis more effectively.

Despite following his doctor's orders, the next several months were rocky ones for Martin. He couldn't stop himself from contacting his wife, despite her repeated request that he do so only if he had some "business" to discuss with her. Her occasional unsolicited calls to him, in which she told him that she really loved him and was sorry about how things had turned out, only fueled the fire and strengthened his resolve to hang on to the hope that they might be reunited. Each time they spoke, he felt anguish as great as he had felt when he first discovered she'd gone. Seeing his son, which he did often, was a mixed blessing. He loved being with him, but it seemed to make the pain of his wife's absence even more intense.

Gradually, however, Martin began to improve. The medication did help him sleep and his appetite improved as well. His lows, while still frequent, weren't as devastating as they had been. Weekly sessions with his therapist were painful but he often felt relieved when he left. In her office he was able to cry without shame. He also began to try to understand what had gone wrong in his marriage and to face the fact that his wife seemed determined to move forward with the divorce. Telling his extended family and his friends at work about the separation, and feeling their support and affection for him, also helped him feel better. His concentration returned, although his zest for his work (or, indeed, for anything) was still missing.

At the end of four months, Martin was still sad, but not despairing. He was still taking the antidepressant although he was uncertain whether it, his therapy, or simply the passage of time, had served to improve his condition. His life consisted of working, visiting with his son, and occasionally seeing his brothers and their families. It was satisfactory, but joyless.

At that point, Martin's therapist suggested that he attend an orientation meeting at a support group for newly single people that existed in his community. For weeks he demurred, saying that he was too busy, that he was satisfied with his life as it was, that his son was his first priority. Finally, though, he acquiesced to his therapist's tenacity and to his own loneliness and attended a meeting. At the orientation, he chatted with a few other anxious newcomers and learned about the organization. Feeling more comfortable than he had expected, he signed up for a six-week introductory "class" in which he and seven other newly separated or widowed people would meet and discuss practical and emotional issues related to being alone. Classes were led by members of the singles' organization who had been in the group awhile, had gone through the orientation themselves, and had received some training in leadership skills. The members of his class quickly became a tight-knit group, carrying on their meetings informally at the local coffee shop, after the class ended each evening. When the class terminated, they kept in touch, forming a sort of extended family for each other.

From this time on, Martin's emotional recovery was fairly rapid. He began to date occasionally and attended social events held by his singles' group. His mood lifted enough so that he was able to discontinue both his medication and psychotherapy over the next six months. At a follow-up session two years later, he was engaged to be remarried and had resumed living a full and happy life.

Thinking About the Case

In the first case in this section, we examined when and under what circumstances behavior that is clearly uncommon should be defined as a "disorder." Neil Cargile's cross-dressing is clearly unconventional and even, for some of us, incomprehensible, but it does not meet the criteria for sexual transvestism since it is not motivated by sexual pleasure, nor, for that matter, any other category in the American Psychiatric Association's *Diagnostic and Statistical Manual*, Fourth Edition (DSM-IV). In the case of Martin B., we are faced with behavior and feelings that we all

understand and that many of us might experience were we to find ourselves in a similar situation. Yet, Martin's "symptoms" qualify him for
two possible DSM diagnoses—major depressive episode and adjustment
disorder with depressed mood. It is ironic that were Martin to respond
with no distress at all, we might consider that less "normal" and even a
but suspect, but he would not be considered to have a psychological
disorder. So perhaps there are situations in which it is "normal" to have
a disorder and "abnormal" not to have one!

On a less confusing note, the case raises two noteworthy treatment
issues. First, most psychological disorders are often treated as Martin's
was—with a combination of approaches. Medication, psychotherapy,
group or family treatment, as well as various environmental manipula-
tions, when used together, can produce a more beneficial effect than any
one used alone. Second, self-help methods, like reading and attending
support groups, can be a useful adjunct to, or in some cases a substitute
for, professional interventions. Today, there are self-help groups for
almost any psychological disorder—substance abuse, pathological gambling, overeating, phobias, schizophrenia, and depression among them.
There are also self-help groups for people in various isolating situations—singles, vertically over-endowed persons, obese people, and relatives of people with illnesses, among others. These groups have the advantages of being inexpensive (often free), nonstigmatizing, and reducing
the sense of isolation that so often accompanies psychological distress. In
addition, they afford an opportunity to learn from people who have
"been there," and who may have developed coping strategies of which
professional helpers are unaware. They are also empowering, since the
subtle power differential between "doctor" and "patient" is absent. Many
people find interacting with peers less threatening than interacting with
authority figures, particularly when self-esteem is already fragile. A reading on the benefits and pitfalls of self-help is included in Chapter Eleven.

Questions to Consider

1. According to Martin Seligman's and David Rosenhan's elements
   of abnormality listed at the end of the previous case (suffering,
   maladaptiveness, irrationality and incomprehensibility, unpredictability and loss of control, vividness and unconventionality, observer discomfort, and violation of moral and ideal standards) is
   Martin B.'s reaction abnormal? Which criteria are met and which
   are not?

2. Who do you think is "more" abnormal, Neil Cargile or Martin B.?
   Why? Which of them do you think has a psychological disorder?

What does this say about your own criteria for "abnormality" and "disorder?"

3. What are some of the biological, psychological, or environmental elements that might predispose an individual to respond to life events, in this case, marital separation, as strongly as Martin B. did? How might these same elements be relevant in distinguishing between those who will recover well from those who will not?

4. Some might argue (as did Martin, in fact, when he spoke to his physician) that it is not Martin B. who is abnormal but his wife. We use the term "mid-life crisis" to describe the emotional state of people who make abrupt, major life changes between the ages of about 35 and 55 for reasons that are not completely clear to the uninvolved observer. What do you think of this argument?

5. Do you think your answer to question 4 might be different if you and the B.'s had come from a culture in which the expectations for men and women in marriage were markedly different? For example, in some cultures marriage represents an economic partnership—"communication" and common interests are not generally expected. What implications might this have for the cultural relativity of psychological diagnosis?

3

———————◀o▶———————

Virtually all textbooks in abnormal behavior have a chapter on models of psychological disorder. Major models covered include the biomedical model, psychological models like the psychodynamic, learning, cognitive, or existential models, and environmental models that focus on the role of family and culture. These discussions often give the impression that one must choose between models — that they are mutually exclusive accounts of human behavior. However, this is not true. Instead, they each look at a different aspect or level of organization of behavior.

In the reading that follows, we illustrate how these models can be integrated so that the insights brought by each can be retained. We will call upon this comprehensive approach to understanding behavior, called the "biopsychosocial model," many times in the case discussions that follow. In doing so, we hope that your own ideas about "why" people behave as they do will be infinitely richer and more complex.

APPROACHING ABNORMALITY:
TODAY'S BIOPSYCHOSOCIAL MODEL

Kayla F. Bernheim

CONSIDER A MIDDLE-AGED WOMAN — let's call her Jeanne — who becomes depressed. She neglects her appearance, sleeps twelve to fourteen hours each day and still feels tired. Her sense of humor disappears, as does her interest in intimacy and sex with her husband or lunch with her friends. She spends most of her time staring into the television set, but if you ask her what she's watching, she can't even tell you the plot of the story. But she hasn't always acted this way. What has caused the change in Jeanne's behavior?

Humankind's interest in understanding the causes of behavioral and emotional disorders dates back to earliest times. The ancient Greeks, who approached problems of abnormality from a purely physical or biological perspective, might have explained Jeanne's depression by assuming that she had a dislodged and wandering uterus or an imbalance in the four humors (bodily fluids) that were presumed to be responsible for mood. In the Middle Ages, when explanations relied more on spiritual models, she might have been thought to be possessed by evil spirits or the victim of "hereditary taint." In Freud's day, when the importance of psychological factors in the development of symptoms became apparent, her life history would have been searched for evidence of trauma—repressed and symbolically revisited in the form of her depression. Each society's approach to understanding disturbed behavior reflects the prevailing science of the day.

Today it is clear that developing causal explanations of behavioral disorders is rarely an "either-or" proposition. While the balance of factors may change from disorder to disorder and from individual to individual, a full explanation must include biological, psychological (including spiritual), and social/environmental influences. Therefore, we no longer ask, for example, "is depression a biological disorder?" but rather "what biological factors may influence the onset, course, and prognosis of depression in this woman?" At the same time, we would be asking "what are the psychological and social factors that may have influenced the development of depression in this woman?"

In 1977, George Engel, an eminent professor of psychiatry and medicine, coined the term "biopsychosocial model" to capture the fact that all illnesses (not just psychological ones) must, as he wrote, "take into account the patient, the social context in which he lives, and the complementary system devised by society to deal with the disruptive effects of illness, that is, the physician role and the health care system." He argued eloquently that the road from a biological or behavioral symptom to patienthood is a long one that meanders through the personal and cultural landscape of both the individual and the clinician who "diagnoses" the problem. To understand what "caused" Jeanne's problem, we would need to know much more about her. Let's look at some of the common biological, psychological, and social influences on behavior and apply them to the changes Jeanne experienced.

Biological Factors

Genetics   Depression, like many other disorders, both behavioral and physical, runs in families. Further, adoption and twin studies, which are able to tease out the relative contribution of heredity and common rearing, provide support for the existence of a genetic predisposition for these disorders. We would not be surprised when we find that Jeanne's mother had periods of deep depression that lasted for several months at a time. During these episodes, Jeanne's aunt would come each day to straighten the house and prepare meals for the family. Upon further inquiry, we learn that Jeanne's brother is a problem drinker. This is interesting, too, since alcoholism and depression often run together in families.

Temperament   Every mother knows that each child is unique from day one of life. Some are sunny and social while others are fussy and shy. Some can fall asleep anywhere and will eat anything. Others seem to need their own beds, a fairly rigid schedule, and lots of predictability. These and other differences which appear to be innate, and have been shown to be relatively stable throughout life, we describe as traits of temperament. Jeanne, we learn, has a shy and somewhat timid temperament. She never had a lot of friends, although she does have two or three close ones who have been friends for many years. Why would this matter? Well, recently, her very best friend moved away. Her youngest child went off to college last year. We can hypothesize that Jeanne's capacity to fill these gaps in her life may have been hampered by her own particular temperament.

Chemical Use   Lots of chemicals have behavioral effects. Among them are lead, nicotine, alcohol, and caffeine, as well as all of the drugs of abuse and many medicines taken for a variety of physical problems. As it turns out, Jeanne is taking propanalol, a medication prescribed to treat high blood pressure. It is also known to cause depression as a side effect in some patients.

Brain Abnormalities   Anything that affects the brain can affect mood and behavior. Brain injury (recent, prenatal, and perinatal) or disturbances in brain biochemistry can contribute to psychological disorders. In fact, the genetic component of depression is almost certainly related to imperfect functioning of the neurotransmitters (chemicals that facilitate nerve function) in the brain, particularly one called serotonin. Since brain imaging techniques, like the C.A.T. scan, which shows the structure of the brain, and the P.E.T. scan, which shows which parts of the brain are functioning at any given time, are so expensive, they are rarely used in cases of depression unless the patient's history is suggestive. Inquiry into Jeanne's history reveals nothing of interest here.

Psychological Factors

Goals, wishes, aspirations, values   Each of us wants something different out of life, and, we may want different things at different times in our lives. We learn that while Jeanne has spent her adult life raising her children and supporting her husband's career, as a young woman, she had wanted to be a writer. Often nowadays she wonders if she has made any useful contribution to society. Is producing honest and thoughtful children enough, or should she have done more?

She has also begun to revisit spiritual questions that she hasn't thought about in years. What is the purpose of life? How must life be lived so that approaching its end will not bring a flood of regrets? Is there a God? If there is, how can she move closer to him/her?

Psychological Defenses   Each of us has acquired some skills in reducing and managing anxiety. Among these are conscious skills, like relaxing or socializing, and unconscious skills, like "discovering" that we really didn't want something that we can't have anyway, or "forgetting" some incident that troubled us. These unconscious skills are called "psychological defenses."

The choice of psychological defenses is an individual matter. Some people rely primarily on denial and repression when they are confronted by anxiety-provoking material, while others are prone to rationalize or intellectualize. Some see themselves at the root of all problems, while others habitually project blame elsewhere for the ills that befall them. Jeanne takes responsibility for things and tends to ruminate a lot. She figures that if she feels lonely or sad, it is her own fault. She feels that she deserves it for being lazy or timid, or just not worthy of more.

Other Psychological Factors   There are many more aspects of who the person is that may be relevant to the development of psychological disorder. Among these are pre-existing self-esteem, ego strength (the ability to make reasoned decisions versus behaving impulsively), the level of insight versus denial, and the phase of development—child, adolescent, young adult, middle-aged adult, elderly adult. Each of these may be protective or risk factors, and each may influence how an underlying biological disorder is expressed in a particular person at a particular time in that person's life.

Social Factors

Family   The family is the carrier of cultural values as well as the inner ring of the concentric circles that make up the person's support network. It is now abundantly clear that what happens within the family can have a powerful impact on an individual's psychological development and on the risk for psychological disorder. We may wonder, for example, what effect Jeanne's mother's depression had on Jeanne's development. We can hypothesize that her mother's emotional unavailability for months at a time might have had a negative impact on Jeanne's developing sense of self worth. We also know that her mother modelled depressed and helpless behavior, which may have affected how Jeanne's own unhappiness is expressed.

Having examined how Jeanne's family of origin might have contributed to her depression, how about the effects of her family of procreation? Jeanne's husband is a hard-working, stolid man. He is reliable and trustworthy, but not very demonstrative. He believes that marriage is a partnership in which the wife's job is to take care of the home. He has, for years, dismissed Jeanne's verbalized longings to take writing courses or to work part-time. We can hypothesize that Jeanne may be harboring buried resentments or wishes to change her situation that her temperament and history have made difficult to express. Perhaps these feelings are relevant to her depression.

Economic Status   Poverty breeds psychological and behavioral disorders. For one thing, it can result in biological factors like malnutrition, which, in turn, can have a negative effect on the development of the brain. In addition, poverty can affect the development of self-concept and the availability of environmental support. For example, it has been shown that people from impoverished backgrounds are more likely to view what happens to them as out of their control. Further, it has also been shown that this belief system is associated with clinical depression. However, poverty is not a relevant factor in Jeanne's case.

Cultural Background   Jeanne, her husband, and both of their families are of Italian, Catholic heritage. Values of fidelity, self-sacrifice, and family are paramount. Fairly rigid gender role definitions are part of the culture. Jeanne's nascent longings for self-expression, fueled by media representations of women working outside the home and pursuing personal goals, find no support in her family, church, or community. We can hypothesize that the conflict between her own, largely private, wishes and the demands of her social environment may play a role in her depression.

Other Social Factors   Again, there are numerous additional social influences. Media images, alluded to above, have a lot to do with what we come to believe about ourselves. The density and quality of our social network is relevant, not only to the development of psychological disorder, but to the likelihood that we will recover successfully. Conflicts or trauma in our social interactions can certainly be precipitants of psychological or behavioral dysfunction. Certainly, major sociopolitical upheavals, like war, can have a major impact on combatants and noncombatants alike.

The above list is only a partial one. No doubt you can think of many more examples of biological, psychological, and social factors in the development of psychological distress and behavioral dysfunction. In Jeanne's case, a combination of genetic predisposition and the possible added physical stressor of the drug, propanalol, combined with a child-hood history of periods of emotional neglect by her mother, an adult-hood marked by prolonged repression of personal aspirations, and a couple of important recent losses propelled her into a profound depression.

In order to be successful, treatment would have to take into account who Jeanne is, how she understands her world, the feelings and behavior of those around her, her social context, and her biological makeup. Would Jeanne be a candidate for a biological therapy like antidepressant medication? Possibly, if she were inclined to understand her disorder as a physical "illness," and if her husband saw it the same way. Otherwise, it's unlikely she would take medication for very long or perceive it to be helpful. Might she benefit from individual psychotherapy of some sort? Yes, if the therapist took into account the cultural and interpersonal constraints within which Jeanne functioned. Exhortation to become more assertive and expressive, for example, might not work or might backfire in this case. Perhaps couple counseling would be preferable. Possibly Jeanne's husband could be helped to be more supportive of Jeanne's need for some self-fulfilling activity, particularly now that the children need her less. Maybe a support group in which Jeanne could discover other women who felt much as she did would be of use. In any case treatment planning would have to be based on a comprehensive biopsychosocial understanding of Jeanne's predicament.

A biopsychosocial model is the basis for genuine understanding of human behavior — both normal and disordered. We will refer to it often in the cases that follow. And the challenge for us is to determine which factors are more influential in each individual case, and which therapies or combinations of therapies will alleviate the suffering and isolation felt by so many individuals.

References

Engel, G. 1977. The need for a new medical model: A challenge for biomedicine. *Science* 196, 129–136.

Part One

THE
DISORDERS

CHAPTER TWO

Anxiety-Based Disorders

————◀○▶————

It is likely that fear is among the most commonly experienced of human emotions. None of us is a stranger to it. The heart pounds, muscles tense, pupils dilate, sweat glands secrete, and one experiences a strong urge to escape. Often, fear is a functional response: if a tiger is at your heels, being afraid motivates running away. However, decades of research have demonstrated that the fear-response pattern is highly conditionable. That is, neutral stimuli can come to elicit fear if they are paired, under certain circumstances, with painful, emotionally charged events. So, a wide variety of non-noxious situations can come to produce dysfunctional fear responses—responses that aren't useful and may, in fact, be harmful. Housecats may resemble tigers in some ways, but running from them isn't necessary and may even prevent you from going where you might otherwise like to be. Yet, some people with phobia react in this very way.

Fear has a specific object. Anxiety, fear's more nebulous cousin, is a feeling of apprehension or dread for which no specific stimulus is apparent. When we are anxious, we are generally unable to say exactly what we are afraid of. Or if we can, we are painfully aware that others do not feel the same way. Like fear, anxiety is a commonly experienced emotion.

When fear or anxiety seem out of proportion to the stimulus, when they cause significant distress or dysfunction in the sufferer, one of the anxiety-based psychological disorders is diagnosed. The DSM-IV lists twelve anxiety disorders. We have chosen three of the most common for inclusion here: agoraphobia, obsessive-compulsive disorder (OCD), and one of the post-traumatic stress disorders (PTSD), rape-trauma syndrome.

The first anxiety disorder concerns a woman who has spent years suffering from panic disorder with agoraphobia, in which attacks of overwhelming fear, seemingly coming out of nowhere, caused her to become virtually housebound. The case is particularly instructive because the woman had several different kinds of therapy before she recovered. It is fascinating because she recovered despite the fact that her history of sexual abuse was never disclosed or discussed in therapy. This patient actually participated in writing up her own story for this volume.

The second case begins with a first-person account of an attack of obsessive-compulsive symptoms in a man whose son also has the disorder. It was reported by Dr. Judith Rapoport, who has been carrying out research on obsessive-compulsive disorder at the National Institute of Mental Health. In this disorder, which usually begins in childhood or adolescence, the individual has repetitive, intrusive, unpleasant thoughts—called obsessive thoughts. These thoughts can bring about enormous anxiety in the individual. To ward them off, the sufferer typically responds by repeatedly engaging in behaviors like cleaning, counting, or checking.

The third case is an example of rape-trauma syndrome, which is, in turn, one kind of post-traumatic stress disorder (PTSD). PTSD can be brought on by any catastrophe or trauma—war, flood, rape, or accident, among them—and is thus extremely common. I have chosen this case because gradual improvement occurred even though no therapy ever took place, leading you (we hope) to speculate on natural sources of healing in our everyday environment and in ourselves.

Two readings are also included in this chapter. The first is a review of three books that have contributed to the "recovered memory" debate. Perhaps you have heard of this controversy about whether it is possible to completely repress (forget) all memory of a traumatic event or series of events from childhood (usually severe physical or sexual abuse) for many years, only to have it resurface in therapy when the person is an adult. Are the memories reported in this context real or "induced" in suggestible people by overzealous therapists? If real, then the symptoms reported by these clients—somatic complaints, phobias, substance abuse, depression, anxiety, and relationship difficulties among them—are actually variants of chronic PTSD.

The second reading also addresses PTSD—this time in the context of war and related catastrophies. The author argues that being present during a catastrophic situation is not enough to induce the disorder. He points to the relevance of a person's belief system, suggesting that those who feel more personal responsibility for bad outcomes will experience more symptoms.

4

————◄◦►————

PANIC AND AGORAPHOBIA:
THE CASE OF SANDY J.

SANDY J. IS A PETITE, lively, forty-three-year-old woman. She has been happily married to the same man for twenty-three years and has two healthy, successful young adult children. She and her husband manage an apartment complex in a small college town in Maryland. She also founded and is still active in an organization that cares for and finds homes for stray cats. Recently, she has been driving a friend, who had been injured, to physical therapy appointments. But for years, she could not drive at all. In fact, she had been virtually housebound. Here's how it happened.

Sandy was one of five children in a two-parent, working-class family. She had a twin brother, two older sisters, and a younger sister. Her father was a machinist who had left school in the tenth grade, and her mother was an office worker who had completed high school. Sandy reports there was heavy drinking, possibly alcoholism, in the males on both sides of her family in her grandparents' generation. Her parents, though, were both teetotalers. She describes her maternal grandfather as emotionally disturbed. She remembers him as being unstable, jealous, and full of insecurities. He panicked easily. She recalls that he was deathly afraid of thunderstorms and used to make the family hide in the basement until they passed over. She says he was both physically and verbally abusive to other family members.

Sandy believes that her parents were good providers but were "distinctly lacking in nurturance." She describes them as "not good at coping with life." Rather, they were "easily overwhelmed" and "seem to me, in retrospect, terribly frightened in just trying to manage life." She describes her father as somewhat distant and her mother as a "wrathful disciplinarian" who went after the children with hairbrushes, flyswatters, and whatever else was handy. Sandy remembers that her mother once broke her sister's nose with a blow of the brush. Sandy feels one key to her later problems may be related to the fact that while her mother often "flew out of control," the children were not allowed to express any anger. She believes she grew up without a role model for the appropriate expression of feelings, and without tools to help her manage her own feelings. The children's anger was managed by insisting they sit absolutely quiet in a chair until they apologized, at which point their mother would refuse to accept the apology and make them sit some more.

Sandy describes herself as a child as shy, introspective, self involved, and often afraid. She remembers being afraid that airplanes would mistake the flat roof of her house for a runway and try to land on it. She became frightened of carbon-monoxide poisoning after a neighborhood girl died while necking with her boyfriend in a parked car. She was most especially afraid of drawing attention to herself by speaking in front of the class at school. Despite this fear, she was able, with encouragement from her parents and teachers, to perform the lead role in the school play as a high school senior.

Sandy's childhood and young adulthood was marred by a number of terrifying sexual experiences which, although remembered, did not seem particularly important to her until years later. From about the age of eight until her early to mid-teens she was regularly molested by neighborhood boys who lived as foster children with a family up the road from her house. None of them had intercourse with her, but they fondled and rubbed up against her to the point of their having orgasms. She can't remember why or when the abuse stopped. However, this was not the end of it.

When she was sixteen, her father kissed her—hard—on the lips when no one else was home. He never did it, or anything like it again, but when she talks about it now, she says, "it took him ten seconds to destroy our relationship." A couple of years later, Sandy lost her virginity through date rape. "What's so bizarre," she says, "is that the relationship went on for six months after that. I can't understand why I let that happen." Over many years, Sandy has told virtually no one except her husband about these experiences, and even he doesn't know about her father. She doesn't know whether her sisters were also molested by the neighbors or sexually approached by her father, although one of her sisters doesn't like her father and no one seems to know why.

Despite her private hardships, Sandy appeared, for a while, a model youngster who was moving successfully through life. She graduated high school and looked forward to college. However, on the first day of her freshman year, her grandmother, "the one I really loved," died suddenly of a heart attack. Her sister came to campus to tell her, and then, unaccountably, she left without Sandy and went back home alone. Sandy attended college orientation and then, by herself, went to the funeral, all in the same week. Freshman year, she recalls, "was doomed to failure." At its end, she took a leave of absence, and went to work.

In October of what would have been her sophomore year, she met her future husband, Donald. By November she was pregnant, and they married in February. Fourteen months after the birth of their first child, they had another. It was then that Sandy had her first panic attack. Out of the blue, and with no apparent precipitant, her heart began to pound intensely. It felt as if it were going to jump right out of her chest. She broke out in a cold sweat and felt as if she were suffocating. She remembers thinking that she was going to die. While that attack abated after several minutes, it was not to be her last. Doctor's visits, tests, and examinations revealed nothing physically wrong, despite her growing apprehensions that she had heart disease, a brain tumor, or a host of other diseases. She became acutely sensitive to every bodily sensation, examining each for cues of disease. Her doctor gave her Valium, an anti-anxiety medication in the benzodiazepine class, which helped some but still the attacks continued and expanded. They seemed to occur most often when in the car—the farther from home, the more likely and the more severe the attack. Gradually, Sandy developed the symptoms of agoraphobia—avoidance of places in which an attack might occur. She began to curtail driving by herself. After an attack occurred in the grocery store, she stopped going to that store. Since she felt safer if Don were around when she had an attack, she stopped going out except when he could accompany her. Within a couple of years, she was completely housebound. She begged Don not to leave the house, and when he had to go, she would go from window to window, trying to keep sight of him for as long as possible. She was distraught until he returned. Don became her only source of safety. The symptoms seemed manageable in his presence, but without him, she felt they would "swallow me up, eradicate me."

Sandy went to a psychiatrist for a few visits, but found them unhelpful. She can't now remember what they spoke about. A year and a half later, as her symptoms worsened, she began treatment with a clinical social worker who seemed to focus on the dynamics of the marriage as the cause of the symptoms. Towards the end of the treatment, the therapist tried some hypnosis, but that didn't seem very useful either. Sandy stayed in treatment about ten months that time.

Finally, after another year had passed, she tried therapy again, this time with a psychologist who took a cognitive approach, helping her identify the thoughts that were leading to her fear, and helping her learn to modify those thoughts in a more realistic direction. For example, she learned to recognize her symptoms as being related to anxiety, rather than illness. She learned to question her belief that fainting or being embarrassed would be catastrophic. She learned to ask herself the question, "what's the worst that can happen?" She learned not to say, in her mind, "I can't stand it," but rather to say "I prefer that it be different."

For the first time, she got a label for the disorder and soon learned that many others suffered from similar symptoms. Reading about agoraphobia, joining a therapeutic support group, and subscribing to a newsletter from a national phobia-support organization helped as well. She began to set behavioral goals for herself and practice them each day. Don was her support person, encouraging her and accompanying her on her practice when necessary. He also consulted with the psychologist from time to time, so that his questions and concerns could be addressed. Sandy says the therapy taught her that she really could make choices for herself, and it helped her to view her "baby steps" towards confronting and mastering her fears as victories. She also feels it was immeasurably helpful to "be viewed with respect [by her therapist] in the midst of a paralyzing disorder" instead of being treated like a "sick" or "weak" patient.

After a couple of years of individual and group therapy, Sandy was functioning at a much higher level. She had resumed driving, although she was still wary of the expressway into the nearby city. She was doing all her local chores—shopping, banking, and the like—by herself. Don was able to go about his business without worrying that she would be unable to do without him. She decided to terminate therapy and continue to work on her own with the "tools" she had been given.

Now, some eight years later, Sandy is virtually symptom free, although she says her progress to this point has been, at times, "inexorably slow." She reports she now has an "absolute feeling of emotional integrity," which is entirely new for her. She has gone back to college and has finished her undergraduate degree. She is immeasurably grateful to her husband and children for their support and believes it significantly aided her recovery. She is also convinced that getting involved with the "kitties" was key, in that it focussed her attention outside of herself and increased her self-esteem. Of therapy, she says, "when I was ill, it seemed my emotional landscape was illuminated by candles, each one lighting only a small portion of the field at a time. On the other hand, therapy was like halogen lighting, wonderful for reading, but almost too bright." Describing the present, she says, "now I have a GE softlight, with a rheostat that's under my control."

Thinking About the Case

This case is illustrative of the typical development of agoraphobia. First come a series of panic attacks. While they often begin during a period of time when the individual is under significant stress, they generally are perceived as coming "out of the blue," with no immediate precipitant at hand. With racing heart, pain in the chest, nausea, dizziness, and a sensation of choking, the sweaty sufferer has the strong sensation that she is having a heart attack or going crazy—in either case, losing control.

The attacks are so painful and so frightening that sufferers are highly motivated to avoid them, so they start to avoid situations in which attacks have occurred, reasoning that there must be something in the situation that stimulated the attack. If an attack occurs in a grocery store, the individual begins to be wary of going shopping in that store. If another occurs there, the person may begin to avoid the store altogether. If an attack then occurs when shopping in a different grocery store, the person may begin to avoid shopping altogether. As you can see, it doesn't take long for the sufferer to develop a "fear of fear." When this happens, attacks begin to occur with increasing frequency in situations in which the person feels unprotected. Examples include being in places where exit without embarrassment is difficult, like church, restaurants, checkout lines, or being some place without a "safe" person, one who could protect the sufferer if something terrible did happen. Desperately, the individual further restricts activities. In the worst cases, like Sandy's, people become virtual prisoners in their own houses.

Sandy's illness occurred at a time when the treatment for agoraphobia was changing. Psychoanalysis and psychodynamically oriented psychotherapy, which had been the treatment of choice for all the anxiety disorders for years, had proven fairly ineffective with panic and agoraphobia, although some professionals still relied heavily on those methods. Some practitioners, like the social worker Sandy saw, were beginning to look for the etiology of the disorder in the social relationships of the patient. For Sandy, the focus on her marital relationship seemed to have quite limited value in modifying her symptoms. At the same time, medical practitioners were researching medicines that could potentially block the panic attacks from occurring. Several of these medications were available at the time Sandy sought treatment, but because of their side effects and her desire to control her own progress, she elected not to take any of them. Still other therapists, like the psychologist, were beginning to use behavioral and cognitive strategies to modify the "fear of fear" and address the avoidance component of the disorder. This approach proved to be most helpful to Sandy.

Most striking about this case is the fact that, although the trauma history was virtually neglected in therapy, Sandy made substantial progress anyway. It is hard to imagine that the sexual abuse she endured did not predispose her in some way to psychological disorder, but it appears that analyzing this aspect of her past was not necessary in order for her symptoms to improve greatly. In retrospect, Sandy believes that she had not been ready to discuss her abuse history at the time of her treatment. Rather, overwhelmed by her symptoms, she apparently had needed to focus directly on reducing her level of dysfunction. Interestingly, she reports that thoughts and memories of the abuse have grown "more vivid" in recent years as she has recovered emotional stability. Perhaps she will find that a course of more exploratory, psychodynamically-oriented psychotherapy aimed at resolving some of her feelings related to the abuse would interest her in the future.

Questions to Consider

1. According to learning theory, agoraphobia combines elements of both classical and instrumental conditioning. Can you identify the components of each in Sandy's case?

2. Some people have panic attacks but never go on to develop agoraphobia. Can you imagine some reasons why this might be?

3. Are there elements in Sandy's history that might particularly predispose her to panic and agoraphobia, as opposed to other psychological disorders? What might these be?

5

——————◄◊►——————

OBSESSIVE-COMPULSIVE DISORDER:
THE CASE OF DR. S.

Dr. S. is a psychologist in his mid-forties. He suffers from obsessive-compulsive disorder (OCD) as do his paternal grandfather, his father, his two brothers, a nephew, and his son. His case is reported in *The Boy Who Couldn't Stop Washing: The Experience and Treatment of Obsessive-Compulsive Disorder*, written by Judith Rapoport, M.D., a clinician-researcher at the National Institute for Mental Health. Here, in his own words, is a description of one of Dr. S.'s OCD attacks.

I'M DRIVING DOWN THE HIGHWAY DOING 55 MPH. I'm on my way to take a final exam. My seat belt is buckled and I'm vigilantly following all the rules of the road. No one is on the highway—not a living soul.

Out of nowhere an Obsessive-Compulsive Disorder (OCD) attack strikes. It's almost magical the way it distorts my perception of reality.

While in reality no one is on the road, I'm intruded with the heinous thought that I *might* have hit someone . . . a human being! God knows where such a fantasy comes from.

I think about this for a second and then say to myself, "That's ridiculous. I didn't hit anybody." Nonetheless, a gnawing anxiety is born. An anxiety I will ultimately not be able to put away until an enormous emotional price has been paid.

I try to make reality chase away this fantasy. I reason, "Well, if I hit someone while driving, I would have *felt* it." This brief trip into reality helps the pain dissipate . . . but only for a second. Why? Because the gnawing anxiety that I really did commit the illusionary accident is growing larger — so is the pain.

The pain is a terrible guilt that I have committed an unthinkable, negligent act. At one level, I know this is ridiculous, but there's a terrible pain in my stomach telling me something quite different.

Again, I try putting to rest this insane thought and that ugly feeling of guilt. "Come on," I think to myself, "this is *really* insane!"

But the awful feeling persists. The anxious pain says to me, *"You Really Did Hit Someone."* The attack is now in full control. Reality no longer has meaning. My sensory system is distorted. I have to get rid of the pain. Checking out this fantasy is the only way I know how.

I start ruminating, "Maybe I did hit someone and didn't realize it . . . Oh my God! I might have killed somebody! I have to go back and check." Checking is the only way to calm the anxiety. It brings me closer to truth somehow. I can't live with the thought that I actually may have killed someone — I have to check it out.

Now I'm sweating . . . literally. I pray this outrageous act of negligence never happened. My fantasies run wild. I desperately hope the jury will be merciful. I'm particularly concerned about whether my parents will be understanding. After all, I'm now a criminal. I must control the anxiety by checking it out. Did it really happen? There's always an infinitesimally small kernel of truth (or potential truth) in all my OC fantasies.

I think to myself, "Rush to check it out. Get rid of the hurt by checking it out. Hurry back to check it out. God, I'll be late for my final exam if I check it out. But I have no choice. Someone could be lying on the road, bloody, close to death." Fantasy is now my only reality. So is my pain.

I've driven five miles further down the road since the attack's onset. I turn the car around and head back to the scene of the mythical mishap. I return to the spot on the road where I "think" it "might" have occurred. Naturally, nothing is there. No police car and no bloodied body. Relieved, I turn around again to get to my exam on time.

Feeling better, I drive for about twenty seconds and then the lingering thoughts and pain start gnawing away again. Only this time they're even more intense. I think, "Maybe I should have pulled *off* the road and checked the side brush where the injured body was thrown and now lies? Maybe I didn't go *far enough* back on the road and the accident occurred a mile farther back."

The pain of my possibly having hurt someone is now so intense that I have no choice—I really see it this way.

I turn the car around a second time and head an extra mile farther down the road to find the corpse. I drive by quickly. Assured that this time I've gone far enough I head back to school to take my exam. But I'm not through yet.

"My God," my attack relentlessly continues, "I didn't get *out* of the car to actually *look* on the side of the road!"

So I turn back a third time. I drive to the part of the highway where I think the accident happened. I park the car on the highway's shoulder. I get out and begin rummaging around in the brush. A police car comes up. I feel like I'm going out of my mind.

The policeman, seeing me thrash through the brush, asks, "What are you doing? Maybe I can help you?"

Well, I'm in a dilemma. I can't say, "Officer, please don't worry. You see, I've got obsessive-compulsive disorder, along with four million other Americans. I'm simply acting out a compulsion with obsessive qualities." I can't even say, "I'm really sick. Please help me." The disease is so insidious and embarrassing that it cannot be admitted to anyone. Anyway, so few really understand it, including myself.

So I tell the officer I was nervous about my exam and pulled off to the roadside to throw up. The policeman gives me a sincere and knowing smile and wishes me well.

But I start thinking again. "Maybe an accident did happen and the body has been cleared off the road. The policeman's here to see if I came back to the scene of the crime. God, maybe I really did hit someone . . . why else would a police car be in the area?" Then I realize he would have asked me about it. But would he, if he was trying to catch me?

I'm so caught up in the anxiety and these awful thoughts that I momentarily forget why I am standing on the side of the road. I'm back on the road again. The anxiety is peaking. Maybe the policeman didn't know about the accident? I should go back and conduct my search more *thoroughly*.

I want to go back and check more . . . but I can't. You see, the police car is tailing me on the highway. I'm now close to hysteria because I honestly believe someone is lying in the brush bleeding to death. Yes . . . the pain makes me believe this. "After all," I reason, "why would the pain be there in the first place?"

I arrive at school late for the exam. I have trouble taking the exam because I can't stop obsessing on the fantasy. The thoughts of the mystical accident keep intruding. Somehow I get through it.

The moment I get out of the exam I'm back on the road checking again. But now I'm checking two things. First that I didn't kill or maim someone and second, that the policeman doesn't catch me checking. After all, if I should be spotted on the roadside rummaging around the brush a second time, how in the world can I possibly explain such an incriminating and aimless action? I'm totally exhausted, but that awful anxiety keeps me checking, though a part of my psyche keeps telling me that this checking behavior is ridiculous, that it serves absolutely no purpose. But, with OCD, there is no other way.

Finally, after repeated checks, I'm able to break the ritual. I head home, dead tired. I know that if I can sleep it off, I'll feel better. Sometimes the pain dissipates through an escape into sleep.

I manage to lie down on my bed—hoping for sleep. But the incident has not totally left me—nor has the anxiety. I think, "If I really did hit someone, there would be a dent in the car's fender."

What I now do is no mystery to anyone. I haul myself up from bed and run out to the garage to check the fenders on the car. First I check the front two fenders, see no damage, and head back to bed. But . . . *did I check it well enough?*

I get up from bed again and now find myself checking the *whole body* of the car. I know this is absurd, but I can't help myself. Finally . . . finally, I disengage and head off to my room to sleep. Before I nod off, my last thought is, "I wonder what I'll check next?"

While some symptoms of OCD may have existed in his childhood, Dr. S.'s disorder began in earnest when he was in his early twenties. He found himself needing to check to make sure that various awful things hadn't occurred—that he hadn't left a light on that might start a fire, that he hadn't poisoned someone with insecticides that he may have touched, that the figures for his research hadn't been incorrectly computed. His doubts were endless and the hours he spent compulsively checking and rechecking seemed equally endless. About one year following the first onset of his illness, Dr. S. consulted a psychiatrist. Together they worked on finding and eliminating any possible emotional source to the illness and in developing ways that Dr. S. could adapt to his symptoms. They paid particular attention to Dr. S.'s angry and aggressive feelings, since many of his compulsions seemed designed to ward off the possibility that he had caused someone harm. Dr. S. also began taking the anti-anxiety medication Valium, which provided minimal relief from the emotional suffering but made him feel tired and gave him headaches.

At about the third year of therapy, Dr. S. experienced a partial remission, as he put it "not perfect, but substantially improved." However, with the birth of his first child, the symptoms returned in force. While he was able to perform his public responsibilities quite well, in private he was consumed by intrusive, frightening thoughts. Everyday tasks took him twice to three times as long to do as they would have taken someone else due to the ritualized checking he had to perform over and over. He felt exhausted, and his wife felt frustrated and sometimes furious with him. Still, with a great deal of motivation and sacrifice, he was able to hide his illness from most people who knew him, although the private toll taken by his obsessions and compulsions was enormous.

After ten years of therapy, Dr. S. begged his psychiatrist to consider a medication trial. The psychiatrist prescribed imipramine, a drug that had been used for many years to treat depression. The medication was gradually increased from 25 mg. to 200 mg. per day. One month after Dr. S. began the 200 mg. dose, his symptoms suddenly receded. While he still had obsessive doubts, they no longer had the force they once had. The overpowering need to act on them had disappeared. The attacks gradually decreased in frequency from daily, to weekly, to monthly. Once the attacks of severe symptoms stabilized at a frequency of once every few months, the medication was gradually reduced to a maintenance dose of 100 mg. For the last several years, Dr. S. has been essentially symptom free. Both his brother and son have also experienced marked relief from their OCD through the use of imipramine.

Thinking About the Case

It is ironic that obsessive-compulsive disorder, which has often been cited to illustrate the psychodynamic principles of altered representation of unconscious wishes, has been the least amenable to change through psychodynamically oriented psychotherapy. As in Dr. S.'s case, years of psychotherapy often left the symptoms essentially unchanged.

Today, neurobiological substrates are presumed to underlie OCD. Using brain imaging techniques, researchers have identified abnormalities in the functioning of the basal ganglia in OCD patients. The basal ganglia is an area of the brain that is related to how individuals organize and respond to information from their senses, and possibly, to how individuals formulate the complex functions of "purposiveness" and "will." Further support for the biological model comes from the fact that OCD is often accompanied by various tic behaviors (brief, spasmodic movements or sounds that are not under the individual's voluntary control), and is often co-diagnosed with Tourette's disorder, in which facial and vocal tics are prominent symptoms. Finally, recent advances in psychopharmacology have given OCD sufferers new hope. Dr. S.'s case is atypical in that imipramine, a tricyclic antidepressant, is not generally helpful for OCD patients. However, a new class of antidepressants, called SSRI's (selective serotonin reuptake inhibitors) is at least somewhat effective for about 70 percent of OCD patients. The very popular antidepressant, Prozac, is an SSRI, as is its newer pharmacological cousin, Paxil, although the drug of choice for OCD is a related compound called Anafranil.

The essentials of modern therapy for OCD include medication, education of the patient and the family about the illness (known as "psycho-education"), and, particularly in cases in which compulsive behaviors play a prominent role in the symptom picture, behavior therapy. The behavioral techniques of modeling, flooding, and response prevention are generally combined. If, for example, the patient is afraid of contamination by germs, the therapist will set up a series of gradual "confrontations" with the alleged "germs." First, the therapist may begin by having the patient watch her smear dirt on herself. Then, the patient will be encouraged to dirty herself, and to tolerate the anxiety that arises when she resists the urge to wash. In effect, the avoidance behavior becomes extinguished as the patient becomes desensitized to the anxiety-producing situation associated with dirt. Note that this is essentially the same as the "exposure therapy" used with phobias, in which the person is encouraged to remain in the phobic situation until the anxiety diminishes.

In practice, behavior therapy is often combined with cognitive-behavioral techniques in which the therapist will help the patient identify and dispute irrational, "catastrophizing" beliefs that contribute to the maintenance of the compulsions. In Dr. S.'s case, this might include helping him recognize that even if his data were incorrectly analyzed (an infinitesimally small possibility), the result would not be catastrophic, but only unpleasant or unfortunate. The therapist might also help Dr. S. develop more rational ideas about the probability of the various events he fears. Supportive therapy, relaxation training, and stress management may also be part of the main pharmacological, educational, and behavioral treatments.

Questions to Consider

1. OCD is often co-diagnosed with depression. What are some reasons why this might be so? Can you devise experiments that might decide which hypothesis is correct?

2. The content of OCD obsessions and compulsions appears not to

be random. Generally, obsessional ideas have to do with aggression, contamination, or sexuality. Compulsions include cleaning, counting, checking, and repeating. What do you make of this? Does it suggest a role for nonbiological factors in the way the illness expresses itself?

6

———————◄◦►———————

POST-TRAUMATIC STRESS DISORDER: THE CASE OF MISS F.

MISS F. WAS A TWENTY-FOUR-YEAR-OLD graduate student in psychology at the University of Pennsylvania. She had been born the eldest of three children in a two-parent, middle-class family. Her father had been married previously and had had a daughter from which he had become gradually estranged. Although he worked long hours and was often way, he doted on Miss F. She grew up a happy and successful child, perhaps a bit bossy to her siblings and friends, but bright and active. During high school she participated in a plethora of school activities, garnered the drama award at high school graduation, and went on to study psychology at the University of Pittsburgh where she worked a part-time job, took honor classes, and graduated Phi Beta Kappa.

Like most graduate students at Penn, she lived in an apartment in West Philadelphia which, like most urban university environs, was not the safest place to live. One early spring evening, while her fiancé, with whom she lived, was out playing bridge, the doorbell rang. Peering through the crack in the door, she saw a young man who appeared to be in his late teens or early twenties. "Is Mr. B. here?" he asked, "he was supposed to tutor me tonight." Mr. B. was an instructor at a nearby college and might, for all she knew, have been providing special assistance to one of his advisees. Miss F. told the young man that Mr. B. must have forgotten the appointment, because he was out playing bridge, and when he asked whether he might leave his phone number, she unlatched the door and let him in. When she returned with a pad and pencil, she found him standing in front of the now latched door, with his right hand in his pocket. Evenly he said, "if you scream, you're dead." At that moment, Miss F. seemed to step into an alternate universe, from which she watched the ensuing events with detached calm, as if she were watching a television show. As he walked her into the bedroom where he raped and sodomized her, she thought clearly about whether she should scream or try to break away. She could hear her upstairs neighbors' stereo playing loudly, so she judged that they were unlikely to hear her if she screamed. She assumed her attacker had a knife in his pocket, and he was certainly larger and stronger than she, so fighting him off seemed hopeless. In the end, she judged that her best chance of staying alive was to submit. When he was finished, he tied her hands behind her back with wires he had ripped off the stereo, took $100 that she had in her purse, told her to count to one hundred before she tried to get out, and warned her that he would come back and kill her if she called the police.

When he left, she lay quietly for some time wondering why he hadn't killed her. She tried to get his face firmly fixed in her mind, because, despite his threat, it never occurred to her not to call the police. Finally, she extricated her hands from the wire cuffs, threw on a robe, went upstairs to her neighbors, and told them she had been raped and robbed. She then called the police, who warned her not to shower until after she'd been examined. She also called her fiancé, and asked him to come home from the bridge game. She seemed so calm and collected that her neighbors were astonished. She only said that she was amazed that she was still alive. She didn't see why her attacker hadn't killed her to prevent his ever being identified. A few minutes later a police detective arrived. He took her to the city hospital where she was examined, treated prophylactically for venereal disease, and seen briefly by a psychiatric resident. He tried to get her to say how angry she was, but all she could say was that it had been a very strange interaction to have with another human being. She didn't feel angry. Actually, she didn't feel anything.

After the examination, the detective came back in to take her home. She asked him to take her to the police station so she could look at mug shots, but he said that she needed some rest and could do it the next day. "No," she said, "I can feel his face slipping out of my mind. I need to do it now. By tomorrow I won't remember what he looked like." "Lots of women feel like that," he said. "If you see him, you'll remember."

Miss F. elected not to return to her apartment right away. That night she and her fiancé went to the home of a professor they knew—a household full of children. She felt she needed to feel "lots of life" around her. A few days later, her apartment was broken into and vandalized. Oddly, this seemed to frighten her more than the assault had. She wanted never to return to the apartment, feeling that she could never be safe there again. Her fiancé went back, packed their belongings, and they moved into a house with some friends.

In the first week or two after the assault, Miss F. talked about it a lot with friends. She told what had happened, explained why she hadn't cried out, and described how oddly detached she had felt. She almost never described the experience as frightening, more often she described it as "odd" or "interesting." She cooperated with the police investigation, even typing out her own statement, because the detective was a much worse typist than she. She had been right, though. She looked at thousands of mug shots and hadn't a clue whether any of the men resembled her attacker. She felt she'd be able to walk by him on the street and not recognize him.

To everyone she knew, she was a picture of mental health. She was able to talk dispassionately about her experience and seemed to be functioning well at her daily routine. However, the feeling of unreality that began at the moment she realized that she was in danger had persisted. She found herself sleeping ten to twelve hours a day, and after some months her fiancé complained that she seemed emotionally unavailable, short-tempered, and distant. While her actual sexual response was unimpaired, she wasn't very interested in sex. She was troubled by occasional nightmares, in which she was walking to her house, aware that she was being followed by someone who was going to hurt her. Always he caught up with her just as she was at the door, fumbling with the lock, and she awoke, terrified. She was generally able to be alone, even at night without difficulty, but sometimes, without warning, as she was walking down the street, if a young man of about the same age and body build as her attacker approached from the opposite direction, her heart began to pound out of her chest, her throat tightened up, and she felt overcome by panic. For months, she replayed the scene at the apartment door over and over in her mind, trying to figure out what she might have done differently, trying to undo what had been done. She felt guilty about not having protected herself better at the same time that she felt proud of having survived, both physically and emotionally.

Miss F. did not receive any formal therapy. But over the first couple of years, she found reasons to tell her story over and over, to muse aloud about her reactions to it, to receive the support of people who were impressed with her ability to talk about it, to feel a sense of mastery, to reassure herself that "that was then, this is now." Gradually, her sleeping and emotional distance abated, as did the nightmares and occasional panic episodes. Now, twenty years later, she speaks of it less, although she can talk about it when appropriate. She finds herself avoiding movies, television shows, books, or plays in which rape plays a part in the plot. On the rare occasions when she thinks about what happened, she distracts herself from the unpleasant memories fairly quickly, but without panic. She is probably more careful than most people when she goes into urban areas, locking her car doors, and staying with other people. She feels she has mostly mastered the experience, but she notices, as she writes this account, a distinct feeling of queasiness in the pit of her stomach.

Thinking About the Case

The classic features of post-traumatic stress disorder are present in this case: intrusive reexperiencing of traumatic feelings and memories, avoidance of stimuli associated with the trauma, numbing of general responsiveness, and symptoms of increased arousal, all lasting longer than one month. One might speculate whether this syndrome, or constellation of symptoms, is a "disorder" at all, in that it is hard to imagine anyone who has experienced a severe trauma not having these symptoms or having them disappear within a month's time. Even if they do disappear within a month's time, the DSM-IV labels the syndrome a disorder (acute stress disorder).

The most salient of Miss F.'s symptoms is emotional numbing. The psychological defenses employed are repression, suppression, and intellectualization. An example of repression is the automatic, involuntary forgetting of the assailant's face that Miss F. experienced. Suppression is voluntary and can be seen in her active avoidance of media presentations which would stimulate recollections of the rape. Intellectualization includes conceptualizing her experiences as a "case," from which she could learn something about human behavior. Defense mechanisms like these, which serve to shield the individual from painful feelings, often are considered pathological by psychodynamic theorists on the grounds that they distort or deny reality. True recovery is thought to be possible only if traumatic memories are reunited with the feelings of terror, guilt, and shame that are presumed to have been present. However, it could be argued that in Miss F.'s case, these powerful defense mechanisms protected her from being overwhelmed initially and led to gradual mastery of the traumatic event.

This case is also interesting in that substantial recovery occurred in the absence of formal therapy of any kind. Researchers and clinicians who study trauma (traumatologists) suggest that telling and retelling the traumatic event in an atmosphere of safety and support can facilitate recovery. While this process is often confined to the therapy room because people may be ashamed or otherwise inhibited from telling their tale to others, it can sometimes take place within the natural support system as well.

Questions to Consider

1. Some people seem to recover from trauma more quickly or more completely than others. What factors might contribute to these differences? What aspects of the person's personality, history, or phase of life might be relevant? What aspects of the traumatic situation or events might be relevant? What aspects of the support network might be relevant?

2. Post-traumatic stress disorder often co-occurs with other psychiatric disorders like depression, substance abuse, eating disorders, and personality disorders. Why might this be so?

3. Researchers are currently studying the possibility that PTSD might have a chronic form in which biological, social and occupational functioning remain impaired ten, twenty, or even thirty years after the trauma occurred. Evidence for this hypothesis comes from the experience of Vietnam-era veterans, many of whom were unable to make an adequate adjustment when they returned to civilian life, and from survivors of childhood abuse, many of whom are diagnosed as having a personality disorder as adults (see "Borderline Personality Disorder: The Case of Roberta F." later in this volume). What are the possible mechanisms through which trauma might have long-term, possibly permanent effects on an individual's functioning?

7

⸺◦⸺

A woman comes into therapy with a vague set of complaints: lack of energy, sadness, self-esteem problems, headaches, and relationship difficulties. With her therapist, she begins to review the story of her life, beginning with her childhood in an alcoholic, stress-filled home. As the weeks go on, her condition deteriorates rather than improves. Therapy sessions focus more and more on trying to fill in the gaps in her memory about her childhood. Finally, one night she has a dream about a small child who is being molested. In the dream, she is rooted to the spot, watching but unable to help. Her therapist tells her that the dream, combined with her inability to recall long periods of her history, makes him strongly suspect she may have been sexually abused as a child. Two sessions later, she reports having had a brief mental "snapshot" of her drunken father fondling her as she lay, pretending to be asleep, in her bed. She is terrified and can't believe that what she "saw" actually happened. Her therapist, however, is completely convinced, and in time, she is, too.

This scenario constitutes what is called a "recovered memory." While some clinicians believe that traumatic memories can, and often are, repressed for years, only popping up in the safe environment of the therapeutic relationship, others, including some memory researchers, think that such complete repression is extremely rare. They feel that over-eager therapists who are looking for abuse everywhere can "plant" memories in receptive clients by suggestion. Since families can be torn apart, sometimes in the courtroom, by allegations of abuse, the extent to which recovered memories are real is important.

In the reading that follows, three books that deal with this topic are reviewed. Whether the review spurs you on to read one or more of the books, it will give you a good idea of the scope of the debate, and the kinds of data that are brought to bear by proponents of each view.

This article first appeared in the Family Therapy Networker *and is copied here with permission.*

THE DEVIL IS IN THE DETAILS:
FACT AND FICTION IN THE
RECOVERED MEMORY DEBATE

Robert Schwarz and Stephen Gilligan

The Myth of Repressed Memory: False Memories and Allegations of Sexual Abuse. By Elizabeth Loftus and Katherine Ketcham.

Unchained Memories: True Stories of Traumatic Memories, Lost and Found. By Lenore Terr.

Suggestions of Abuse: True and False Memories of Childhood Sexual Trauma. By Michael Yapko.

ON SEPTEMBER 22, 1969, a 9-year-old girl, Susan Nason, was discovered brutally murdered near a reservoir in the San Francisco Bay Area. For 20 years, the case was an unsolved mystery. Then a remarkable event occurred: Eileen Franklin Lipsker, Susan's childhood friend, reported that one day while playing with her daughter, she suddenly remembered an awful truth. She had witnessed her father murdering and then burying Susan Nason near the reservoir. An ensuing investigation led to the arrest, trial and conviction of Lipsker's father on the murder charge.

How can a person suffer some horrific trauma, forget about it entirely, and then suddenly remember it years later? Such claims have proliferated not only in psychotherapists' offices over the past few years, but in the courts as well, giving increased urgency to the question: Is there really such a thing as "recovered memory"? If so, how often does it occur? Can some "memories" be partially or wholly false, implanted by zealous therapists or fantasized by disturbed clients? How can therapists distinguish between "true" and "false" memories?

In hopes of gaining clarity on these questions, we turned to three recent books. The first is *The Myth of Repressed Memory: False Memories and Allegations of Sexual Abuse* by Elizabeth Lofts and Katherine Ketcham. Loftus is a noted memory researcher from the University of Washington, a founding board member of the False Memory Syndrome Foundation and a leading expert witness for the defense in litigation against accused perpetrators. The second is *Unchained Memories: True Stories of Traumatic Memories, Lost and Found* by Lenore Terr, a San

Francisco Bay area psychiatrist known for her work on childhood trauma. The third is *Suggestions of Abuse: True and False Memories of Childhood Sexual Trauma* by Michael Yapko, a San Diego psychologist with a background in Ericksonian hypnosis and psychotherapy.

What makes the Loftus and Terr books especially fascinating is that both authors were expert witnesses on opposing sides of the Lipsker case. Terr testified that floods of long-lost memories were triggered in Eileen at one particular moment in which her own daughter looked strikingly similar to Susan Nason. From the opposite camp, Loftus insists that such a traumatic event as seeing a father murder a childhood friend would become indelibly burned into Eileen's memory. In her argument, Loftus cites Terr's own previous work with the children involved in the Chowchilla kidnapping, demonstrating that the children couldn't get the event out of their minds. But while Terr agrees that a single traumatic event would be clearly recalled—she calls this Type I trauma—she believes that a series of traumas—what she calls Type II trauma—will often produce defense mechanisms that prevent the victim from remembering them. A child in the midst of ongoing, repeated trauma, argues Terr, must develop self-hypnotic skills to shield her-or himself from further trauma. These skills are activated at the beginning of a new traumatic event and result in repression, dissociation and splitting.

In the case of Eileen Lipsker, Terr argues that her long-term abuse at the hands of her violent, alcoholic father comprised a Type II trauma, with the murder occurring during the course of a long, brutal sequence of traumatic events. Terr suggests that Lipsker used repressive mechanisms she had already developed to shut out the horrible memory of her friend's murder for 20 years. Once the repression was loosened by the perceptual similarity of her daughter to Susan Nason, however, Lipsker was able to recall the horrible event.

Not so fast, says Elizabeth Loftus, who acknowledges Lipsker's father was alcoholic and sexually abusive. She rejects Eileen Lipsker's "repressed and recovered" memory as false and makes the case that all of the details in her story could have been culled from newspaper accounts 20 years earlier, supporting her argument by citing the various changes and alterations of Lipsker's story that took place during the course of multiple interviews with police and prosecutors.

" . . . Perhaps Eileen's mind created the memory in an attempt to destroy her father's power over her and live the remainder of her life free of fear," writes Loftus. "She was able to punish her father for his cruel, abusive treatment of her family and achieve mastery over her past." In Loftus's assessment, the accused perpetrator becomes the victim of the misguided and even hostile intentions of his daughter.

So whom are we to believe, Terr or Loftus? Who is the real victim—the accuser or the accused? Loftus argues doggedly, but effectively, that memory is notoriously unreliable, subject to so many distorting factors that we really can't know for sure whether anything we remember really happened without objective verification. She shows that we never directly reaccess a memory, as if it were a tape recording; instead, we reconstruct an event from a heterogeneous mix of recollection, extraneous memories, fears, wish, fantasy, social context. For Loftus, all memory is history rewritten and rewritten again.

Unfortunately, Loftus's application of her experimental research to the recovered memory debate is often reckless and misleading. She implies that since much of memory is malleable, nothing within memory is really believable. Most memory research, however, is really about the distortion of details, not central events. A person hit by a car may misremember its color, or the day of the week, but will rarely confuse being hit by a car with, say, falling down a mountain. Even Loftus admits that no experiment has had a false memory for a central detail. Yet she plays the great debating trick of saying that since some memory is likely to be distorted, all memory is likely to be distorted, and no memory of childhood abuse should be believed unless corroborating, objective evidence can be found.

Terr is much more inclined toward sympathetic belief in recovered memories. Her book is comprised of case studies of people whose memories and lives were deeply affected by childhood trauma. Terr rejects Loftus's black-and-white dichotomy between "true" and "false" memories, arguing that the accuracy of a memory may be measured along a wide continuum from wholly true to wholly false. She emphasizes that the report of a true traumatic memory will often be accompanied by symptoms of post-traumatic stress, which itself is often accompanied by the disruption and disassociation of memory.

Reading Terr and Loftus is a jarring reminder of the apparently irreconcilable positions taken by both sides of the false memory debate. We hope Yapko might provide a bridge over the chasm of mutually exclusive "myths." Unfortunately, his book is restricted "primarily to those cases in which allegations of abuse are made on the basis of memories that were recovered through the suggestions of a therapist." His central thesis is that therapists are wittingly or unwittingly causing many clients to erroneously believe that a presenting complaint (such as depression or bulimia) was caused by a childhood trauma of sexual abuse. Yapko doesn't simply criticize incompetent therapy, but says that the explosion of recovered memories is at least partially the result of a "culture of victimization" and lawsuit-happy crybabies who "believe that they are entitled to whatever they want, however unrealistic and irresponsible." . . .

[J]ust how common are repressed or dissociated memories of trauma? A number of studies document these effects, though neither Yapko nor

Loftus gives them much attention. Loftus herself studied female substance abusers in an outpatient treatment program who were interviewed
about their memories of sexual abuse. She found that 19 percent of the
women claimed that they forgot the abuse for some length of time and
only recalled it later. It seems strange that Loftus calls something a myth
that occurs with anything approaching that kind of frequency.

Other studies show a higher incidence rate for amnesia. Judith Herman and Emily Schatzow, for example, found that 28 percent of 53
women in their study had significant memory loss for trauma. Linda
Myers Williams followed up hospital records of girls who had been
sexually molested as children, finding that 17 years after the abuse, 38
percent had no memory of the documented event. Even the FBI has some
data to offer on this question. The American Society of Clinical Hypnosis
(ASCH) report on Hypnosis and Memory cites FBI agent Kenneth Lan-
ning's report on child pornography that showed that many adults who,
as children, had been the subjects of pornographic films had no memories of being in the films.

Yapko and Loftus reject the very idea of repression, and they also
ignore the vast clinical literature on dissociation, which many trauma
researchers see as the main mechanism by which traumatic memories are
kept out of memory. Most trauma experts think that the distinction
between repression and dissociation is important, because dissociative
phenomena dovetail better with the clinical data of trauma. In psychoanalytic thought, repression is conceived as the mechanism that pushes
traumatic memories below an invisible, horizontal barrier in the psyche
separating the upper stratum of consciousness from the lower level of
unconscious processes. The traumatic memories, like sea creatures swim-
ming far below the surface of the water, remain whole and intact, though
invisible and unknown to the surface awareness of the conscious mind.
Dissociation, on the other hand, is visualized as a series of *vertical* barri-
ers in the psyche that segment consciousness into isolated, often mutually
incommunicable, segments of experience.

Discussing the differences between dissociation, repression and an
additional defense mechanism called splitting, Terr maintains that the
child who *represses* an event knows that it happened, but then proceeds
to "forget" it whole. The child who disassociates, on the other hand,
alters his or her consciousness, usually through some form of auto-
hypnotic procedure, so as to be "not home" when the abuse happens.
While being abused, the child may imagine herself a detached observer
looking down from the ceiling, or may go "dead" during the abuse;
these altered states interfere with memory encoding. The dissociative
framework also accounts for the partial, confused and distorted details
of the memories. For example, Eileen Franklin Lipsker first thought that
she was raped by a black man, but later realized that while her father

was abusing her she dissociated by fixating her attention on a Jimmy Hendrix poster.

Of the three authors, only Terr explains how a person might remember a buried trauma after many years. She points out that traumatic memories may emerge in a context of known and dependable safety from the conditions that prompted the necessity to repress. Thus, a person can "suddenly" remember in the security of a therapist's office, or even within the protection of a solid marriage. In addition, there is usually a "cue," similar enough to some aspect of the trauma to reactivate the memory. Often, a survivor's own children become powerful cues to remembering their own childhood trauma.

Neither Yapko nor Loftus suggest the possible occurrence of a person remembering falsely the physical act of rape, while nonetheless having truly experienced a great deal of sexual boundary violation in the home, perhaps via pornography or masturbation or fondling and lewd remarks. Terr is more evenhanded; she presents, for example, a case of a woman who misremembered that her grandfather had sexually abused her, when in fact she was remembering a procedure done to her urethra when she was three by a doctor who looked like her grandfather.

Terr, as well as most other experts in the fields of trauma and memory, criticizes the conclusions drawn from memory research cited by Loftus and Yapko. First, the research typically focuses on nonsignificant details (e.g., the color of a car), which are more easily misremembered than central details (an accident happened). Second, the items used in these experiments are often innocuous and inconsequential (such as a phone ringing or hearing a sound in the night, or asking subjects whether the robber in the movie wore a scarf or not) as compared with the highly emotional and meaningful events involved in childhood sexual abuse. Third, the criteria used for saying that a pseudo-memory was created were often overly literal, thereby inflating their occurrence. For example, in several studies, if a subject was even unsure about the test time, it was scored as the creation of a pseudo-memory. If "science" is to be the standard that we use to judge the debate, the fact is there is little solid evidence that suggestions can create clinically relevant false memories at a significant rate.

But granting even a low incidence of false memories, how might they occur? Both Yapko and Loftus have a ready answer: the therapist is responsible through a combination of personal influence and sheer ignorance. Devoting an entire chapter to the analysis of responses to a questionnaire he gave to therapists about their ideas on hypnosis and memory, Yapko concludes that therapists as a group are woefully ignorant about memory and hypnosis and how they relate to recovery from trauma. It is this widespread lack of knowledge, he suggests, that may account for the creation in therapy of so many false memories.

But both the questionnaire and the analysis of the data collected from it are seriously flawed. Yapko asked therapists to answer questions on a four-point scale: strongly agree, slightly agree, slightly disagree and strongly disagree. In the text of the book, he lumps the groups "slightly" and "strongly agree" together, inflating his statistic on therapist ignorance by about 300 percent. He states that 43 percent of the respondents believed that "if someone does not remember much about his or her childhood, it is most likely because it was somehow traumatic." In the actual data, only 9.4 percent strongly endorse this statement. The other 33 percent agree slightly. Yapko reports that 83 percent of therapists agree with the statement, "Hypnosis seems to counteract the defense mechanism of repression." However, only 28 percent agreed with this statement strongly. In an interview for the journal *Treating Abuse Today*, Yapko stated that he believed therapists were creating the problem; he created a survey to document what he already thought he knew. Yapko found exactly what he was determined to find.

The dominant mechanism in the creation of false memories, according to Loftus and Yapko, is the suggestion and social pressure inherent in the therapeutic message, "Incest is rampant, recovery is possible, and recovered memory therapy can help." Terr points out that false memories may occur more often with therapists who work exclusively with trauma and incest because the client, knowing the therapist's specialty, "expects from the beginning to retrieve memories." Loftus is short on details about the suggestive processes, but Yapko specifically lists them. Therapists lose their neutrality, move too quickly to resolve ambiguity, and pressure clients, directly or indirectly, by insisting that they must remember in order to get better. They focus far too much on the past and not enough on current contexts or future goals, and contaminate memory via suggestion and hypnotic procedures. Terr agrees these clinical errors are possible, but discriminates between correct central information, false details, correct details, but false central information (e.g., client correctly remembers pain in the vaginal area, but falsely concludes or remembers that it must have been caused by father); and completely false memory.

For all the hammering they give "false memory," neither Yapko nor Loftus mention the possibility of it occurring in alleged perpetrators. Where is it written that the adult's memory of the past should be taken as the universal standard of truth and empirical fact? The accused certainly may be lying. But, on the other hand, many perpetrators may actually have false memories of their own innocence. They truly do not remember the abuse for a variety of reasons, including state-dependent memory loss due to alcohol or chemical intoxication, massive denial and dissociation. . . .

Childhood sexual abuse is a pervasive problem in our society, which long went totally unacknowledged even by therapists who should have had a bit more trust in the painful tales of their clients. No amount of backlash or therapist-bashing can undo that fact, but because therapists themselves share a certain culpability in burying the reality of abuse, they must not now lose their capacity for open-ended attention and compassionate discrimination. To do any less not only undermines the profession of therapy, it betrays the real victims of abuse, whether they remember or not.

8

————◄o►————

Many people experience human-made catastrophies—war, concentration camps, rape—or natural disasters—earthquakes, floods—but not all trauma survivors react in the same way. Some seem to recover with minimal residual symptoms, while others may experience prolonged, sometimes life-long emotional and behavioral disability. Aspects of the trauma itself (its duration and intensity, for example), the person who experiences it (including pre-existing mental health), and the recovery environment (availability of crisis counseling or the presence of a strong support system) have all been shown to be relevant to prognosis. In this article, the author uses numerous case examples to illustrate that a particular psychological aspect, namely the extent to which the individual feels personally responsible for some awful consequence, may account, in part, for the difference in reactions between individuals. Do you have any personal experiences that would bear on the author's argument?

PERSONAL RESPONSIBILITY IN TRAUMATIC STRESS REACTIONS

John Russell Smith

INTENSIFIED INTEREST IN THE LONG-TERM reactions of Vietnam veterans was followed by and partly instrumental in the introduction of Post-Traumatic Stress Disorders into the latest edition of *The Diagnostic and Statistical Manual of Mental Disorders.*[1] This interest also sparked renewed comparison of the pattern of reactions of Vietnam veterans to veterans of Australia, Israel and Afghanistan as well as to POWs, Iranian hostages and victims of rape, fire and a range of other catastrophes.

Clinicians are now more readily recognizing and attending to patterns of stress reactions and rediscovering observations noted at the turn of the century by Janet,[2] Freud[3,4] and, thereafter, Lindeman,[5] Adler[6] and others. Insights into survival guilt, the death imprint and psychic numbing—

reactions generated in survivors and clinical observers as well—have enabled clinicians to better understand and develop ameliorating interventions. The rap groups fostered by Shatan,[7] Lifton,[8] and Pincus, dream groups designed by Wilmer,[9,10] guided imagery and behavioral interventions adapted by Keane,[11] hypnotic techniques[12] and family systems interventions,[13] have all enabled victims with powerfully troubling and alienating experience to reach some more peaceful resolution. As clinicians increasingly recognize post-traumatic stress reactions, they are readily recognizing the central symptom patterns and are making attributions about the underlying issues to be resolved in therapy.

Survival guilt has now become commonly accepted and is widely held to be a major factor in reactions following such events as the concrete walkway collapse at the Hyatt Hotel in Kansas City.[14] After the event, clinicians readily began to help people deal with their guilt over having survived while others did not. Survival guilt does not explain, however, why equally severe traumatic stress reactions are generated in emergency medical personnel who treat victims of such disasters. It is often commonly assumed that rescue workers and bystanders are simply overwhelmed by the gruesome and horrible sights which they witness.

With some validity, it is recognized that in most disasters, the more deadly and grisly the event, the greater will be the reactions of the normal witness or survivor. Studies of veterans and other survivors[15-17] consistently support the common observation that the level of exposure and the intensity of catastrophic experience are the best predictors of the intensity of symptoms of stress reaction. Such field studies have consistently affirmed the finding that stress reactions are precipitated in roughly half the victims of intensely traumatic experience. Many factors have been advanced and explored as contributing to the intensity of reactions.[16,18] None of these factors have yet been found, however, to have the predictive power of the intensity and level of exposure to the catastrophic experience itself.

The powerful and often wrenching reactions of clinicians as they begin to listen to the tales of survivors have been explored previously.[19,20] Such reactions in clinicians confirm our common assumption that witnessing such horrible deeds and deaths leave extreme residual traumatic effects. These clinical observations have proved to be valuable tools for understanding and treating such reactions. But, the popularization of the notion of survival guilt and the common assumptions about the impact of witnessing deadly catastrophes may obscure recognition of another factor with a potentially more devastating impact on survivors, participants and witnesses. A focus on the intensity and inherent traumatic quality of the events also subtly encourages clinicians to grade the *quality* of the traumatic event and the reactions it should generate.[21] This focus may encourage clinicians to underestimate traumatic stress reactions in other survivors, participants and witnesses whose catastrophic experience is assumed to be considerably less objectively traumatic than others.

In such cases, a lack of survival guilt and the implicit devaluing of apparently lesser traumatic events contribute to the emphasis, too early and too heavily, on character disorder and predisposition, which, for many years, has obscured the recognition of long term stress reactions. A subtle interaction of all of these factors has clouded recognition of this element in stress reactions (JR Smith, unpublished data, 1981). Attention to a further aspect of catastrophic experience may open an avenue for better understanding the relationship between reactions to normal life stresses and reactions to catastrophe.

Increased clinical experience has led me to focus on the role of personal action and responsibility in catastrophic reactions. This may take the form of perceived personal responsibility for individual actions or for failures to act in the midst of catastrophic conditions, leading to tragic and often deadly consequences. Such a factor of personal responsibility interacts in an exponential fashion with the moral and ethical questions of meaning described so well by other writers.[22–26]

The following case examples illustrate this factor. The first case was related to me by Dr. William Neiderland in a conversation following a New York seminar on the concentration camp syndrome at The New School in April 1976. At the time, while working on the stress disorders proposal for DSM-III, I had been grappling with the paradox over how the *victims* of a catastrophic experience, such as the concentration camps, could manifest nearly identical reactions as those reactions seen in more active *perpetrators* of another disaster, such as the veterans of the American war in Vietnam. It was this case, related by Dr. Neiderland, which drew my attention to the role of personal action.

X, a concentration camp survivor, had been involved for some time in psychotherapy. One day he came to his session with a painting he had recently completed which he gave to the therapist. The painting portrayed a grotesque, demonic figure in a Nazi stormtrooper uniform. Something about the painting disturbed the therapist but it was not until a few days later, when glancing at the painting again, that he realized that the face in the painting belonged to the client. At the next session, the therapist shared his observation with the client. At first, baffled and denying the similarity, X suddenly broke down and began sobbing. X then revealed that, during his imprisonment in the concentration camp, six inmates had escaped one night. Following the escape, as was their policy, the guards selected double the number to be executed as an example to the rest. The following morning, X and the other eleven prisoners slated to die, were marched off in the early morning fog to be shot. As the column of inmates passed the long, open slit trench used by the inmates as a latrine, X slipped out of the column and buried himself in the latrine. After many hours covered in excrement, X found his way back to his compound. There, he discovered that two other companions had been selected and executed in his place.

What struck me about this case was the later evidence of overwhelming personal guilt and unconscious self-punishment which X had carried for so many years, unmitigated in his mind by the circumstances which might have prompted his action for survival.

Lifton[19,24] has described survival guilt as guilt over having survived while others perished. In my experience, such guilt is far more powerful when one's survival is bought at the price of another's life.

Billy N. joined the Marines with his best friend from high school. They served in the same combat unit in Vietnam. One day, while crossing a swollen stream, the rifles over their heads, Billy was in danger of being swept away. His buddy, who had reached the opposite bank, stretched out a hand to help Billy. Billy handed his rifle, muzzle forward, to his buddy and while being hauled from the water, his hand slipped, releasing the trigger, killing his buddy with a round through the chest. Later, back home, Billy first sought treatment because of his wife's complaints about the length of time it took for Billy to drive to and from work, only two towns away. Billy explained that he vaguely always wanted to avoid the town next door where he had grown up; so, he drove an elaborate thirty mile route around it, to and from work. Under questioning, he suddenly remembered that his buddy was buried in a cemetery along the route he would normally have driven to work. Later, after considerable work in therapy, Billy drove to the cemetery, sat in front of his buddy's grave, and, in a lengthy conversation with his long dead friend, asked him for forgiveness.

Even when the personal action leading to dreadful consequences seems to be offset by evidence of dozens of successful, even heroic, actions, the impact of the tragic one appears to distort evaluation of the others.

K was a 33-year-old former Marine who was among the first American Marines in Vietnam. After several ambushes and intense battles which marked the first weeks after his arrival, K found himself trusted and relied upon as the point man because of his childhood, backwoods experience in the South. On several occasions, his instincts and sudden caution had saved the platoon from ambushes and booby traps. K, a scrappy and somewhat delinquent kid in school, relished the trust and responsibility relegated to him for the first time in his life. Later in his tour, while leading his platoon on patrol along the railroad tracks near Chu Lai, K noticed cowchips from water buffalo arranged in a regular pattern between the tracks. Immediately questioning such regularity, which was not his experience with cows at home, he suspected that the cowchips might conceal booby-traps. Halting the platoon, he fanned the men out along either side of the roadbed to avoid the possibility of detonating the booby-traps. Unfortunately, as the platoon passed alongside that section of track a watching North Vietnamese soldier plunged a handmade, remote detonator, exploding a series of mines buried under the cowchips. The explosions immediately killed several of the platoon and wounded several others, including K, ripping the legs off of some men, including an especially beloved black lieutenant.

For 16 years, since that incident, K has avoided recollections of that event only to see them emerge in nightmares and daytime flashbacks. Characteristically, his avoidance of that event and its implications for him have been accompanied by the use of alcohol and drugs, emotional numbness, somatic difficulties and social alienation.

Nor is it always action that is the source of the intrusive thoughts. Failure to act may also precipitate later reactions.

Bobby, another former Marine, first came to my attention because of legal difficulties. It was alleged that he had beaten his wife during sexual activities. During the initial interview, Bobby insisted that, while he had indeed hit his wife, the more common occurrence was that she often beat him in the course of sexual intimacy. When Bobby was asked if he needed to be punished, he replied, "Yes." When asked why, he answered, "Because of Vietnam." When asked if there was a specific incident, Bobby, becoming agitated, spoke of an incident involving a captured female North Vietnamese nurse. Bobby was serving as an advisor to a South Vietnamese Army unit when the prisoner was turned over to them. Bobby stood by while she was raped, tortured, and sodomized, then masturbated, defecated and urinated on. Bobby felt unable to reconcile his failure to act on the impulse to stop the behavior and indicated a secret conflicting impulse to join in.

Conflicting impulses are often at the core of a traumatic episode buried for years.

RD is a 39-year-old former Navy Medical Corpsman. After one tour in Vietnam with the Marines, he was released from active duty into the Reserves and returned to his home town of Baltimore. Due to a shortage of trained corpsman, he was recalled to active duty where he saw intense action during the Tet offensive in 1968.

Out on an operation five days before the end of this second tour, the corpsman's unit got caught in an ambush. Panicked at all the previous close calls he had survived, he hid behind a rock while hearing the cries for "corpsman." For ten years after his discharge, he was haunted by his act of "cowardice." While never speaking of the experience, he nonetheless spent ten years as a veteran counselor rescuing other veterans in bars and flop houses and creating forums for them to talk. RD's deeply held belief that corpsmen and medics risk all for the wounded allowed no room for his conflicting impulse to protect his own life. His belief was bolstered by the high esteem and respect accorded corpsmen and medics for precisely that selflessness.

Quite often, when there is not an initial working through and resolution of traumatic experience, the return to normal functioning forces the working through of the traumatic action to take place at the subconscious level. Thus, in many survivors, the playing out of the traumatic action often takes the form of very concrete undoing, as in the above case. In another case, the clinician may see a veteran who flew aircraft spraying chemical defoliant in Vietnam who denies that the war had any impact on his life, but now works as a chemical safety officer for a major chemical firm. Subconscious undoing of the past "fault," frequently by being intensely involved in directly helping victims similar to those in Vietnam, is a common and effective pattern in medics, corpsmen, doctors, nurses and chaplains for avoiding conscious confrontation with one's own wartime actions. This pattern is especially dramatic in former combat nurses who not only persist in healing roles but often find themselves continuing to function in crisis and emergency situations, where the circumstances of their current positions play out concretely the stresses of their own traumatic war experience. These helping professionals will often devote large amounts of time to counseling others even in groups where they are ostensibly members seeking help. Frequently, only a dramatic episode will trigger the recognition that they also have personal experience which needs to be explored.

M, a Boston nurse who had served in Vietnam, described her current difficulties in a recent interview. She was haunted by troubling thoughts of Vietnam and described her inability to stay in bed at night without the light on. Since her return, she indicated that not a week had gone by without recurrent thoughts about the decisions she had made in Vietnam. She gave the example of one night, when, with a short-handed unit, she became the triage officer whose duty it was to assess the gravity of injuries and then select, given the limited treatment resources, those soldiers with salvageable wounds who would receive treatment, leaving those soldiers too severely wounded to die. As ostensibly neutral non-combatants, despite their vigorous objections, the medical staff was required to treat both Americans and any wounded North Vietnamese prisoners. Torn over an oath to care for all the injured, she followed common practice and selected Americans with even minor injury for treatment while leaving North Vietnamese prisoners, with severe but treatable injuries, to die.

Despite objections, American and North Vietnamese patients were often placed on the same ward. The nursing staff, loyal to their American charges, were often reluctant to care for the Vietnamese. One evening, M volunteered to change dressings on a severely burned Vietnamese for whom no one else would care. As she was changing his bandages and cleaning the wounds, the prisoner suddenly grabbed a pair of scissors and lunged at her. Narrowly escaping, she called for a pair of military guards to "take care of" him. The military guards quickly hustled him off the ward. A short while later, they returned to assure her that he would no longer bother her and that he had been taken care of. She has a recurrent nightmare about this incident.

Because of a recent flashback experience she no longer carries scissors. On this particular day in the operating room, a fellow nurse announced that she was reaching into the pocket of M's uniform for a pair of scissors. As the nurse did so, M panicked, turned and struck the other nurse.

Until her interview, she had never spoken with anyone about the earlier incident. Though highly regarded by her peers, she feels ashamed and inadequate about her performance as a nurse in Vietnam. Afraid to look into the future, she refuses to look at the past, feeling that if she did, she would start crying and never stop.

Blank[27] has noted that such personal traumatic episodes, repressed and unexamined for years, yet still powerfully charged affectively, may result later in an unconscious re-enactment of the episode in vivid concrete detail. Such later recapitulations and undoing of the past personal action in a traumatic incident may be the key to recapturing an integrity which opens a channel to recovery.

T was a 26-year-old former Army infantryman who begged to be permitted to join an ongoing rap group. At his first session, he poured out a terrible tale. T, the squad leader, had stopped the squad's armored personnel carrier (APC) while they broke for lunch. While T and the others ate outside, T had the radioman stay inside the vehicle at the radio. Suddenly, the squad came under attack and the APC was hit with an RPG—rocket powered grenade. T dashed to rescue the radioman but was unable to pry open the door, warped shut by the heat. T was now agonizing in the group over the terrible screams of the dying radioman and his impotence in doing something about it.

In the following weeks, the group learned that T was under pressure at the advertising agency where he worked as a production manager. T was dragging his feet on getting out an airline's ad on their jet fleet. In discussions with the group, it emerged that the entire jet fleet of this airline was composed of a type of plane which had, in the past few years, been involved in a series of crashes resulting from a faulty latch on a cargo door, thereby killing several hundred people. T was unsure whether the expensive modifications recommended by the airplane's manufacturer had been performed on this airline's fleet. The group helped T to finally realize that his reluctance to participate in an ad campaign which might induce people to ride in a potentially unsafe aircraft might be connected to the incident in Vietnam. The group then helped T find a course of action which, with a minimum of confrontation, would lead to the assurance that the modifications had been performed.

While in T's case, exploration of the current situation and a past action of perceived responsibility led to significant improvement in the quality of T's life, long years of denial can result in serious pathology.

LR was a thirty-three year old former Marine. At the time of interview, he was hospitalized with his forty-second admission in a large East Coast VA psychiatric facility. The staff suspected a case of multiple personality since LR referred to himself as Karl and frequently spoke in German on the ward. He had been a particularly troublesome, aggravating and intractable patient, disruptive on the ward and often signing himself out abruptly only to end up at another VA facility somewhere across the country to then be transferred back to the hospital. The staff knew little about LR's military history except that he had been in Vietnam and had read the book, *The Spy Who Came In From the Cold*, on the plane on his way over to Vietnam. During the interview with a consulting psychologist, it was revealed that LR had been a forward observer tasked with calling in artillery fire on enemy positions. After the interview, the consultant read the book, *The Spy*, and realized that the central character was responsible for an ally's fleeing across the no man's land at the Berlin Wall where he was shot. The consultant suggested to the ward staff that LR be placed in a rap group where the possibility be explored that LR might have called in artillery fire on some of his own troops. Fourteen months later, LR broke down in the rap group and revealed that he had mistakenly misdirected artillery fire on an American unit killing and wounding ninety men.

Not all traumas connected to a war or catastrophe happen just to the participants. Lesser traumas can have a great impact even far from the front, and will be connected only later when the participant realizes the import of his actions.

P was a black Army officer in charge of returnees from Vietnam reassigned to Germany. He was responsible for mustering out, with administrative discharges, those Vietnam veterans with poor attitudes who failed to adapt to the regimentation and boredom of non-combat garrison life by using drugs, talking back, or having general "bad attitudes." After his release from the service, even with his excellent education and record, P found himself unable to "get his life together" until he "happened" to find a job where he counseled veterans with less than honorable discharges and helped them to upgrade those discharges and get a fresh start. Though P repeatedly remarked on how satisfying and meaningful he found his work for the first time, it was some time before he recognized the connection to his military experience.

Another example of a minor earlier decision having later impact is illustrated in the demonstration video tape of a sodium amytal interview by Dr. Lawrence Kolb.[28]

X, a black Vietnam veteran is sedated with amytal. At first quiet, he becomes agitated, enraged and tearful as a painful memory of a Vietnam attack is triggered by the playing of a tape of combat sounds. X recounts how a hometown buddy died in his arms after being hit in the attack. Under questioning by Dr. Kolb while crying and angry, X repeats his blame for the death because the admiring buddy followed him into the service despite X's protests.

Having made the observation of the apparent role of personal action and responsibility in war and other major catastrophes, I have come to see it frequently in other situations. I suspect that the consequences of personal choice and action may be part of the reason why we see stress reactions among rescue workers and emergency medical technicians. As these workers race to the aid of victims, as in the Hyatt Regency walkway collapse in Kansas City (1981), these rescue workers make choices about whom to treat first or about moving a steel beam which, in retrospect, may have had tragic consequences for another victim. In a similar way, victims themselves make choices. After grabbing the hand of a spouse and dashing to the left, where a beam collapses on that spouse, the victim will often agonize over wishing he had made the choice to go to the right instead. Furthermore, victims may distort the blame so that they appear to hold themselves more responsible for the death than the accident itself.

In some cases, a distorted notion of personal responsibility may sometimes lead rape victims to blame themselves in a caricature of the old myth of "asking for it."

> MP, a 26-year-old Midwesterner, worked for an antipoverty agency in Tucson. Returning home from work one evening, she was walking the dimly lit streets between the bus stop and her home. Tired from a long day, she neglected to cross to the other side of the street, as she normally did, when she saw a strange man approaching as she passed by a wooded area. When the man grabbed and attacked her, she found herself screaming internally but was stunned to realize that no words came from her mouth. Though she finally managed to wiggle free and escape in terror, four years later she appears to blame and in subtle ways punish herself for the incident, with greater focus on her role than on the rapist's role.

In many victims of catastrophe, the assertion of personal responsibility is an attempt to overcome overwhelming feelings of powerlessness and helplessness in the face of the disaster. Such assertions of responsibility and control, while serving positive ends, may also contain seeds of future turmoil.

Distorted perceptions of responsibility can haunt even families caught in a common traffic accident.

> WS, a surgeon, had been away on one of his frequent professional trips. On his return, he wanted to relieve M, his wife, of the responsibility of watching over their four year old daughter, R, so he planned to spend time with R shopping at a local toy store. En route to the store, WS asked R which of the two popular toy stores she wanted to visit. R chose the further store because it had a greater selection of toys. As the two drove on, WS was reflecting on pressing issues about his work. The car in front stopped short to turn left without signaling and WS's car plowed into the rear, crushing the gas tank and bursting into flames. Despite partially crushing his own skull against the windshield, WS managed to unbuckle, grab his daughter and dash out the passenger side before both cars burned. The driver of the other car escaped but WS was left with head injuries and several cracked ribs. In the hospital, WS worked over his responsibility and what he could have done differently. Meanwhile, his wife was agonizing over the brief spat that they had just before the trip and her guilt over how relieved she had felt "to be rid of" the two of them for a time.
>
> R, appeared to be little affected by the accident, the sight of her father bleeding by the side of the road and the tension and bustle of the hospital emergency room. However, she later revealed, during a play session, how

she was responsible for the accident. On questioning, she said she had been dreaming and thinking about the fact that if only she had chosen to go to the closer store, the accident would never have happened.

Even more ordinary events of everyday life may lead to rumination about personal responsibility and to the pattern of intrusive thought characteristic of stress reactions.

> "I was very upset because, essentially, a guard (Indiana's Isiah Thomas) beat us and that's my position," UNC guard Jimmy Black said of the Tar Heel's championship game loss to Indiana last season. "I felt like I had let the team down and that's what probably bothered me the most. Then I realized it was a team effort and we can't put the blame on anyone.
> "I know I couldn't sleep for about a week afterwards, thinking about what we could have done," Black added, "I want to get my rest this year."
>
> (*Durham Morning Herald*, March 25, 1982)
>
> In later interviews, Jimmy revealed that in the weeks following the basketball loss to Indiana, he had been obsessed by nightmares and daytime intrusive images of Isiah Thomas' various fakes and moves during which he had scored crucial baskets. Jimmy was haunted by self-blame until chats with his teammates convinced him that the team and coaches together bore responsibility rather than he alone.

Another well-known dramatization of the troubling sequelae to perceived personal responsibility for tragedy is the recent book and film *Ordinary People*.[29] The resolution of the son's traumatic stress reaction comes only when, triggered by news of a friend's death, he experiences a flashback and then he and his therapist face his self-blame. Beyond the grief for the loss, he has blamed and punished himself for the drowning even though it was the older brother who let go of their hands clasped across the hull of their capsized boat.

Too great an emphasis on the survival aspects of catastrophic experience may obscure the actions and choices involved in survival. A focus simply on the intensity of stress invariably leads to a grading and evaluation of catastrophic experience which also obscures the painful consequences of action and the subtle choices made under such stressful conditions. While the severity and intensity of stress may be the best predictor of the symptoms of stress reaction, more powerful, longer lasting stresses may just provide more occasion and opportunity for the types of painful choices illustrated in the cases above.

Such expectations about survival and severity of stress and its reactions also contribute to a falsification of experience on the part of the victim. Victims will sometimes fabricate or distort their traumatic experience in order to bring it into line with expectations of the type of stressful encounter which will generate the sympathy and empathetic response they desire.

Consider the following example.

W is a German, Jewish psychologist from the Southwest. During WWII, she spent her early adolescence fleeing and hiding from Nazi persecutors who had shipped her parents to a concentration camp in Poland. Still at large at the end of the war, she found her way to the U.S. with a group of other orphaned Jewish children. Later, when she learned that her parents had survived, W found herself the only one among her peers who had surviving parents. Consumed and confused by the years of panic and trauma, she nonetheless felt guilty and petty about her experience next to her peers who had lost their entire families. Judging her own trauma to be negligible, but jealous of the warmth and care tendered to her orphaned peers, she distorted and exaggerated her own haunted experience to gain the equality of suffering she needed for that sympathy. Only later did she realize the extent to which that compromise had rendered the sympathy counterfeit, when she found herself repeatedly obsessed with tracking the authenticity of the tales of her combat veteran clients.

The extent of the personal blame victims accord themselves and the quality of the moral judgments they pass on their actions influence the course of the recovery process they will follow far more than the objective severity of the stress which individuals undergo. Unexpressed expectations of the judgments others will make (often confirming their own secret and lacerating evaluations) frequently render unexplained and powerful incidents subconscious, emerging only obliquely to wreak havoc with their current lives. Awareness of and openness to exploration of this theme of personal responsibility in traumatic stress may further the resolution of catastrophic reactions as well as open a path of intersection with the mechanisms underlying intense reactions to more common life stresses.

References

1. *Diagnostic and Statistical Manual of Mental Disorders*, ed 3. Washington, American Psychiatric Association, 1980.
2. Janet P: *Psychological Healing*. New York, Arno Press, 1923.
3. Freud S: Psychoanalysis and war neuroses, in Rieff P (ed): *Character and Culture*. New York, Macmillan Publishing Co Inc, 1963.
4. Freud S: Reflections upon war and death, in Rieff P (ed): *Character and Culture*. New York, Macmillan Publishing Co Inc, 1963.
5. Lindemann E: Symptomatology and management of acute grief. *Am J Psychiatry* 1994; 101:141–148.
6. Adler A: Neuropsychiatric complications in victims of Boston's Cocoanut Grove Fire. *JAMA* 1943; 123:1098–1101.
7. Shatan CF: The grief of soldiers — Vietnam combat veterans' self-help movement. *Am J Orthopsychiatry* 1973d; 43:640–653.
8. Lifton RJ: *The Rap Group Experience with Vietnam Veterans*. Subcommittee on Health and Hospitals of the Committee on Veterans Affairs and the Subcommittee on Alcoholism and Narcotics of the Committee on Labor and Public Welfare, United States Senate. Government Printing Office, June, 1971.

9. Wilmer HA: Vietnam and madness: Dreams of veterans. *J Am Acad Psychoanal* 1982; 10:47–65.

10. Wilmer HA: Dream seminar for chronic schizophrenic patients. *Psychiatry* 1982, to be published.

11. Keane TM, Kaloupek DG: Imaginal flooding in the treatment of post-traumatic stress disorder. *J Consult Clin Psychol*, to be published.

12. Brende JO, Benedict BD: The Vietnam combat delayed stress syndrome: Hypnotherapy of dissociative symptoms!" *Am J Clin Hypn* 1980; 23:34–40.

13. Williams C, Williams T: Evaluation and treatment of the family of Vietnam veterans suffering from post-traumatic stress disorder. Presented at the American Psychiatric Association Annual Meeting, Toronto, May 1982.

14. Wilkinson DR: The Hyatt Regency victims—One year later. Kansas City, Missouri, National Public Radio, July 17, 1982.

15. Egendorf A, Kadushin C, Laufer RS, et al: *Legacies of Vietnam: Comparative Adjustment of Veterans and Their Peers*. Veterans Administration, Center for Policy Research. Government Printing Office, 1981.

16. Norris J, Feldman-Summers S: Factors related to psychological impacts of rape on the victim. *J Abnorm Psychol* 1981; 90:562–567.

17. Frye JS, Stockton, R: Discriminant analysis of post-traumatic stress disorders among a group of Vietnam Veterans. *Am J Psychiatry* 1982; 139: 52–56.

18. Helzer JE, Robins LN, Wish E, et al:

Depression in Vietnam veterans and civilian controls. *Am J Psychiatry* 1979; 136:526–529.

19. Lifton RJ: *Death in Life: Survivors of Hiroshima*. New York, Random House Inc, 1968.

20. Haley SA: When the patient reports atrocities. *Arch Gen Psychiatry* 1974; 30:191–196.

21. Smith JR, Parson ER, Haley SA. On health and disorder in Vietnam Veterans: An invited commentary. *Am J Orthopsychiatry*, to be published.

22. Shatan CF: Post-Vietnam Syndrome. *The New York Times*, May 6, 1972, p. 35.

23. Hendin H, Pollinger A. Singer P, et al: Meanings of combat and the development of post-traumatic stress disorder. *Am J Psychiatry* 1981; 138: 1490.

24. Lifton RJ: *Home From the War*. New York, Simon and Schuster Inc, 1973.

25. Marin P: Living in moral pain. *Psychology Today*, 1981; 15(11):68–80.

26. Capps WH: *The Unfinished War: Vietnam and the American Conscience*. Boston, Beacon Press Inc, 1982.

27. Bank AS Jr: The unconscious flashback to the war in Vietnam veterans: Clinical mystery, legal defense, and community problem. *Am J Psychiatry*, to be published.

28. Kolb L: *Sodium Amytal Interviews with Vietnam Veterans*, videotape. Albany, New York, VA Medical Center, 1980.

29. Guest J: *Ordinary People*. New York, Random House Inc, 1976.

LANAHAN NOTES
Anxiety-Based Disorders

———◄○►———

Symptoms of Anxiety:

Physical: pounding heart, sweaty palms, lightheadedness, nausea, shortness of breath, tingling feelings, chills

Cognitive: racing thoughts or mind blank, fear of going crazy, fear of losing control

Behavioral: retreat, avoidance, freezing

Question: Everybody experiences these symptoms. When do they constitute a disorder? Symptoms must be prolonged and markedly interfere with the individual's functioning.

Types:

Panic Disorder—with or without agoraphobia—avoidance of places where an attack might occur

Specific Phobia—fear of some particular situation, such as being in elevators, or object, like snakes, dogs

Social Phobia—fear of being embarrassed in social situations

Obsessive-Compulsive Disorder

Obsessions: repetitive, intrusive, inappropriate ideas or images

Compulsions: repetitive, ritualistic behaviors that the person feels driven to perform

Acute Stress Disorder—trauma-induced anxiety symptoms that last less than a month

Post-Traumatic Stress Disorder—trauma-induced anxiety symptoms that persist past one month

Generalized Anxiety Disorder—at least six months of excessive anxiety and worry

Others—related to medical conditions, substance abuse, or not specified

Who gets Anxiety Disorders:

Anybody. Very common, maybe up to 10 percent of the population.

Women diagnosed somewhat more often than men (particularly phobias).

Note: Display of fear is more acceptable for women than for men societally.

Causes:

Psychodynamic theory: Symptoms are symbolic or partial expressions of unacceptable impulses (generally sexual or aggressive). Repression is fundamental defense.

Note: not empirically studied very often, so validity in doubt.

Behavioral theory: anxiety (classical conditioning and modeling) and avoidance (instrumental conditioning and modeling) are learned.

Cognitive theory: one's distorting or misinterpreting thoughts, images assumptions can produce anxiety.

Biological theory: some anxiety disorders run in families—perhaps the predisposition is (partially) inherited.

Evolutionary ("preparedness") theory: combines behavioral and biological theories (Seligman)—individuals are prepared to learn certain fears.

Treatment—Many Approaches Have Reasonable Success:

Behavioral therapy: good outcome for several anxiety disorders
Some behavioral methods:
    systematic desensitization
    exposure
    flooding
    modeling
    response prevention
    response satiation

Cognitive therapy: targets the irrational ideas that produce anxiety, teaches patient to re-label bodily symptoms. Good results.

Psychodynamic approaches: uncover repressed conflict. Mixed results.

Biological approaches: medications can block panic but some have high addictive potential or annoying side-effects. Usually used in combination with cognitive and/or behavioral approaches.

Self-help techniques: relaxation, meditation, exercise, and support groups can be very useful.

One recent controversy: Can memories of abuse be totally repressed, resulting in psychological symptoms (as Freud and traumatologists assert) or is the opposite true: that traumatic memories are intrusive and persistent (e.g., "flashbacks")? Probably both are possible, with repeated abuse less likely to be totally repressed than single episodes.

CHAPTER THREE

Dissociative and
Somatoform Disorders

———◄o►———

D issociative disorders are among the most fascinating of all the
phenomena we will study. How can it be that a person can be
blind, although his eyesight is normal? How can several "personalities" inhabit a single body? How can a person be "outside" her body,
watching herself behave?

Among those who have attempted to answer these questions was
Sigmund Freud. Freud developed his theories about the psychodynamic
origins of maladaptive behavior from studying the dissociative symptoms
found in young, middle-class Viennese women of his day. His interpretation of their repetitive accounts of childhood abuse as a symbolic account
of their own fantasies and repressed wishes was a critical (and, critics
would say, a terribly erroneous) turning point in the development of
Western theories about abnormality.

In this chapter we have included a case in which the dissociative
disorder is fairly subtle. This is much more common today than the
complete blindness, deafness, and paralysis that Freud encountered in
his time. We have also included a fascinating first-person account of a
psychiatric nurse who has struggled with multiple personality disorder
for many years.

Somatoform disorders are among the most frustrating disorders to
treat. Sufferers usually do not acknowledge that their problems are of
psychological origin, so the basic task of developing a mutually agreed
upon therapeutic agenda becomes a formidable challenge. How do "psychological" problems come to be reflected in "physical" symptoms? We
examine this question with two cases: one in which both physical and
psychological factors contribute to a young woman's pain, and the other
in which unreasonable fear of having a dread disease becomes the focus
for a man's anxieties.

9

DISSOCIATIVE DISORDER:
THE CASE OF MARIE O.

Dissociative symptoms are marked by alterations in the normal, integrated functions of a person's identity, memory, or consciousness. All of us have experienced the phenomenon of awakening from a particularly compelling dream in a state of disorientation and confusion. Where am I? Am I awake or asleep? Some of us have had the experience of watching ourselves behave, as if from a vantage point outside of our own bodies. These are the dissociative experiences of everyday life. When these symptoms are prolonged and interfere with normal functioning, as they do in this case, dissociative disorder is diagnosed.

MARIE O., A SEPARATED FIFTY-FIVE-YEAR-OLD woman, sat rigidly in the high-backed chair in her therapist's office. Her voice had become faint and she spoke very slowly. She seemed to be taking an inordinate amount of time to process questions and formulate answers. When her therapist asked her what she was experiencing, she became completely mute. After ten minutes of silence, she resumed her previous train of thought, as if the bizarre episode had not happened. Patiently, the psychologist commented on these "absences" in a curious, but nonjudgmental way after Marie recovered from them, and gradually the patient was able to describe her experiences.

During those times, Marie explained, she was not in the room. Rather she was on the other side of the door. At times, she was relatively nearby, so that she could hear what was being said, although the sounds were slightly muffled. Sometimes she was far away, as if several football fields separated her from her therapist. At times the distance was so great that she was unable to hear or see anything at all.

Marie explained that being "way back in my head" occurred automatically when she began to experience emotional distress. There, she was calm and safe. Many things could trigger it—being on a bus with teenagers who were loud and mildly menacing, the smell of alcohol on someone's breath, conversations in which a violent or abusive act was mentioned. It had been going on as long as she could remember. Marie understood that these states were not normal, and while she valued the sense of safety they provided, she wished they were more under her control. Her therapist agreed that this would be one of their therapy goals.

As the weeks went by and trust developed in the therapeutic relationship, Marie naturally disclosed more of her history in the sessions. She had only vague memories of her childhood, but what she did remember was enough. She was raised in a devoutly Catholic home. Her only sibling, a younger brother, is now a priest. Her mother managed to go to church daily, despite holding down a full-time job. Marie doesn't have any images of her mother, save those of her praying or leaving the house for work. As she spoke, Marie's therapist noted that the image of Marie's mother putting on her coat had triggered a mild "absence."

Unfortunately, Marie's memories of her father were more vivid. A verbally and physically violent alcoholic, Mr. O. dominated family life with his unpredictable, demanding presence. Mealtimes were grim, frightening affairs in which Mr. O. quizzed the children about biblical passages or lectured them about God, sin, and hellfire. He had almost always had several drinks by the time they sat down to eat. A wrong answer meant no dinner, but sometimes being banished from the table was a blessing in itself. Marie reported experiencing several days of feeling "spacey" following the session in which she first spoke about her father.

Marie describes herself as a shy, obedient child. She was not allowed to participate in school activities and therefore had no real friends, despite being well enough liked by other children. Not surprisingly, she was a pious child, full of guilt and shame about the smallest infraction, error, or untruth.

Sometime during her teenage years, Marie can't remember exactly when, her father began to molest her. While she had never fully repressed these experiences, she had great difficulty describing them in therapy. She was often mute for long periods of time and upon returning seemed disoriented and a bit dazed. She remembered what she had been talking about but experienced a sense of inhibition so strong that she could barely speak. Still, she persevered and gradually recounted what she could. It appeared that her ability to psychologically remove herself had developed as a way to emotionally survive the abuse and continue on with her life in a "normal" way.

By the time the sexual abuse started, Mr. O.'s relationship with his wife had completely soured—they survived in economic partnership together, nothing more. Marie cannot remember them ever laughing, hugging, or even touching—except, of course, when her father got angry and knocked her mother around. Unable to protect her mother, Marie practiced "removing" herself during these situations as well.

Mrs. O. worked second shift, from three P.M. to eleven at night.

Marie's brother was often out of the house, either at sports or church. As a boy, he had much more freedom of movement then she was allowed, even though he was younger, and he used it to keep away from their father whenever possible. Mr. O. got home from work at four, shortly after Marie got home from school. He began drinking immediately, and after four or five beers would come looking for Marie. What began as fondling and deep kissing, ended as mutual masturbation and forced fellatio. Throughout, Mr. O. talked to Marie, sometimes telling her that she was a slut and a whore, at others declaring that he loved her, and at others explaining that he was preparing her for sex with her future husband—teaching her what her duties would be. Marie had been taught to be a dutiful child, and despite knowing that what they were doing was horribly wrong, she was unable to resist her powerful father. She knew her mother would be unable to protect her, and she couldn't imagine what would happen to their family if she let the terrible secret out. She felt that perhaps her father was right: she was the sinful one. Otherwise, why would God allow her to suffer such torture?

Marie solved the problem the way many young women do. She married immediately upon graduating from high school. Her husband was from an enormous and dysfunctional family in which violence was the preferred mode of interaction. Shortly after they married, the couple moved several hundred miles away in order to be closer to her husband's family. While she was initially relieved to be away from her father, she missed her mother and brother and she felt intimidated by her husband's thirteen siblings and their families. Not surprisingly, in the bosom of his own family, Marie's husband's behavior began to deteriorate. Soon he, too, began to slap and push her when he got angry. Like her father, and like his own brothers, his drinking began to increase. Marie, already adept at surviving abuse through dissociating, used these skills to cope with her husband's abusive behavior as well.

A few years into the marriage a tragedy occurred. One day, a neighbor's car broke down in front of their home. Marie asked her husband to come out and help move it off the road. In the course of doing so, he was struck by a passing vehicle and lost an arm. Marie blamed herself for the accident, and her husband seemed willing to allow her to do so. From the time of the accident forward, his drinking and abusiveness escalated without respite. Marie used to believe that he had no control over his temper, but in talking with the therapist, she realized that he never hit her with his prosthesis—the doctor had admonished him to be careful of it, lest it get jammed up into his arm and damage him further.

In any case, Marie's life was harsh. Her husband earned meager wages as a worker on a dairy farm. She found herself raising three children with little money left over for groceries after her husband's hunting equipment and liquor were taken care of. She had begun to take Valium, an antianxiety medication, shortly after the accident. Neither seeing nor asking about the context in which Marie lived, her family physician simply thought that she was "a bundle of nerves" and needed a prescription to calm her.

After a decade or so of trying to balance her mostly grim life with Valium, Marie had a "nervous breakdown." She was unable to stop crying. She felt that insects were crawling all over her. She couldn't eat.

Her husband was characteristically unsupportive. In fact, in his frustration at her inability to function, he beat her and poked at her eyes when she "looked at him funny." However, her daughter, now a young woman, insisted she be taken to the hospital where she was first diagnosed as having a psychotic depression. One of the attending psychiatrists had a different hypothesis. He felt that her overuse of Valium over a long period of time might also have produced her symptoms, and indeed, when she was gradually withdrawn from the Valium, her symptoms lessened and finally disappeared.

Marie found it harder to tolerate the beatings without the Valium. Finally, after her husband cracked three of her ribs, she left him and went to a battered women's shelter. There, she was helped to get a job and find a therapist. She also developed a support system of women who had been through similar experiences and who remained her friends from that time on. By the time she entered therapy, she was working for an elderly woman as a companion. This afforded her room and board and a small living stipend. She had one brief romance but had found that her companion's beer drinking triggered her "absences," so she terminated the relationship.

Marie remained in psychotherapy off and on for about five years. She would go regularly for six months or so, then take a break for some months, returning when a significant life change occurred or when she felt like she wanted to work on a particular issue. In therapy she recounted details of her father's abuse for the first time, affirming out loud that it had really happened. She learned to manage the pain and rage that these experiences provoked in her. She talked about the guilt and shame she had felt and, with her therapist's help, came to realize that she was not responsible for her father's behavior.

Over the course of therapy, the frequency of her dissociative episodes diminished as she became better able to manage the anxiety that caused them. Her sense of herself as "damaged goods" changed to an image of a decent person who had been victimized as a child by circumstances outside of her control. She began to see that as an adult she had personal skills and resources — in short, she was no longer helpless. Her self esteem and ability to care for herself increased. She became more independent, and showed better judgment in managing her affairs. She became more assertive and self-protective.

Marie has not seen her therapist recently, although she sometimes calls her for reassurance, particularly if something has really unsettled her. She has begun "dating" her husband again. Old habits are hard to break, and the romantic prospects for a fifty-five-year-old woman are not wonderful. Things are different now, though. She does not allow her husband to drink when she visits, nor does she tolerate even the most subtle hint of verbally abusive behavior. She especially enjoys having holiday dinners together as a family with him and her children. She says she's happier than she's ever been. Her therapist worries what will happen to her when the woman she is caring for dies. Marie has never really lived alone. But she will cross that bridge when she comes to it.

Thinking About the Case

Dissociative disorders are among the most dramatic psychopathological syndromes, particularly when they occur in the form of multiple personality disorder. We have all been fascinated by *The Three Faces of Eve*, or *Sybil*, or claims by criminals like the "Hillside Strangler" that an alter-ego actually committed the crimes. Some of these cases are so spectacular that observers have wondered whether they might be faked, particularly when strong motivation in the form of reduced culpability or stealing the limelight exists. As a result, professionals have been reluctant to diagnose multiple personality disorder. More recently, though, the possibility of the disorder being more prevalent is being taken more seriously. Whether more cases actually exist, whether clinicians are simply more prone to properly diagnose them, or whether more suggestible clients are feigning them is a matter of some dispute.

Most actual clinical cases of dissociative disorder are, like Marie's, somewhat less dramatic. Commonly, the dissociation is incomplete. Marie had not completely repressed her horrific memories, nor was she a different person when "absent." Nor were the absences total, except in very rare instances. Rather, she often experienced a sense of distance, called "depersonalization," or of functioning as if in a dream ("derealization") that she referred to as feeling "spacey."

Marie's case, like many, has its origins in trauma. It appears that the mind is capable of protecting itself from unmanageable anxiety by blocking out the memories of situations that evoke the terror. For example, one type of dissociative disorder, called "fugue" (for "flight") is diagnosed with some frequency in soldiers exposed to combat. Under the stress of battle, they simply walk away, losing their memories for the war situation, and taking up a new life elsewhere. Often, a person who has been in a fugue state will wake up suddenly, remembering his past life, but not recent events that occurred when in the altered state. For

Marie, her mind "walked away" from extreme distress by blocking her perceptions (hearing and sight) enough to reduce her discomfort to manageable levels.

Not all dissociative experiences are related to trauma, however. Interestingly (and perhaps reassuringly for you at this moment), mild and fleeting episodes of depersonalization are common in adolescents and young adults and appear not to represent a history of chronic trauma or any serious psychopathology. Perhaps as many as 70 percent of young people report brief out-of-body experiences or spells of being in a dreamlike state. These are sometimes precipitated by acute stress, like an illness or accident. Generally, there are no long-term negative outcomes, although in a small minority of cases, these spells can be the precursors of a more chronic dissociative disorder or even a full-blown schizophreniform illness.

Questions to Consider

1. What would psychodynamic theory have to say about why one symptom versus another is chosen in response to the severe and overwhelming anxiety associated with trauma? What would learning theory have to say about it? Might biological or genetic factors be relevant to the issue of symptom selection?

2. What are some reasons why only a subset of children who are severely abused develop dissociative disorders?

10

——◄○►——

PAIN DISORDER: THE CASE OF LISA L.

LISA L. IS A TWENTY-SIX-YEAR-OLD, married mother of three children. She had the first child out of wedlock, when she was not yet eighteen years old. The birth of the second coincided, within weeks, with her marriage at the age of twenty-three. The third is a newborn. Lisa has a history of psychological problems dating back from the time she was a young adolescent. She has had many different diagnoses—the most recent being Pain Disorder. Here is her story.

Lisa is the second of three children. She grew up in a small town where everybody knew everybody. Her older brother was always in trouble as a youngster and suffered a severe break from reality at the age of seventeen. While drug use was certainly a factor, his condition did not seem to improve much when drugs were withdrawn, and he was finally diagnosed with paranoid schizophrenia two years later. He had a difficult decade, with several psychiatric hospitalizations and a stay in a drug rehabilitation center, but he is now fairly stable. He is married and has a job and a child. Lisa's younger sister had some problems with drugs as well—mostly marijuana and amphetamines, but she, too, has "cleaned up her act" in recent years. She is attending college and working part-time.

Lisa's parents seemed to get along well. She also had her grandparents nearby, and was especially close to her maternal grandmother. Despite an apparently warm and supportive family, Lisa was a fearful child. She remembers being afraid of dying from an early age, often calling out to her mother seeking relief from her panic when she awoke in the middle of the night. Thunderstorms scared her, too, as they did her mother and grandmother.

Lisa had difficulty separating from her mother to go to kindergarten and seemed to be ill frequently through her school years. Several years in a row she missed more school than any other student, which prompted her first visit to a psychotherapist when she was twelve and in the sixth grade. Therapy ended at the end of the school year, after about two months of weekly sessions. She seemed to relate well to the therapist, but her school attendance was essentially unchanged. Like many youngsters, Lisa's obedience and attachment to her parents waned markedly as she approached thirteen and fourteen. She began to experiment with marijuana (helpfully supplied by her big brother) and cut school to hang out with friends in the empty field behind the drug store. Her grades, previously beyond reproach, dropped, but not enough to put her in danger of failing. She seemed desperate to fit in with her peers and unsure of herself in social situations.

At the age of fifteen, Lisa lost her virginity to a boy who barely spoke to her afterwards. Devastated, she slept poorly and lost her appetite for several weeks. Her parents, however, seemed unaware that anything was amiss. They had enough on their hands trying to cope with her brother. Several of Lisa's friends noticed that she had lost weight and commented favorably. She then entered a period of restricting her food intake in an attempt to lose ever-increasing amounts of weight. She supplemented this regimen with occasional use of diet pills and laxatives. When she fainted in school, another course of psychotherapy was begun.

This time, Lisa expressed a wish to die side by side with her continuing fear of death. She starved so that people would see that she had the willpower to deprive herself, but she knew that she might die and she didn't care. In fact, she would have been proud of having been able to exhibit the ultimate restraint by dying of starvation. Still, she sometimes awoke in panic, afraid that she, or her mother, or her grandmother would die. Lisa worked with her therapist for the better part of a year, meeting weekly to talk about her feelings of insecurity, her anger at her brother for "driving everybody crazy," and at her parents for focussing all their attention on him. Gradually, her symptoms receded and therapy was discontinued.

Lisa was next seen when her first baby was about four months old. She was still thin, but not taking diet pills or laxatives. She thought she was fat, but tolerated it for the baby's sake since she was breast-feeding. She came to the therapist's office without outside prompting because she was afraid she might hurt her baby, whom she loved dearly.

The thoughts of hurting the baby came suddenly, without warning when she was tired, frustrated, or lonely. Sometimes she imagined how sorry people would feel for her if her baby were injured. Sometimes, she just felt enraged and almost unable to control herself. She described in some detail thoughts of cutting the baby with a knife or tying her, upside down, to a light socket. These thoughts horrified her, she said, although the therapist silently noted that she talked about them with great gusto.

In therapy, Lisa expressed fury at the baby's paternal grandfather who had talked his son out of marrying her when she got pregnant. Now, none of his family would acknowledge the baby as theirs. Her family, shocked at first, had accepted her pregnancy fairly easily. They were still dealing with her brother's continuing hospitalizations, and pregnancy seemed manageable compared to that. Her mother loved the baby and was willing to babysit while she finished high school and later, when she decided to go to college. During the course of this therapy episode, Lisa's baby's pediatrician called the therapist, concerned that Lisa brought the baby to the office more than was necessary. She had been Lisa's pediatrician, too, and voiced the thought that Lisa had tended to use illness to "get attention" and "now, she's doing it through the baby."

Lisa and her therapist met intermittently for several years. During that time, Lisa mostly attended to going to school and raising her daughter. She had virtually no love life. However, she did have one brief relationship, and, as bad luck would have it, contracted herpes.

For most people, herpes is fairly treatable, with long periods of remission interspersed with brief outbreaks of sores, accompanied by some discomfort. For Lisa, however, it was a nightmare. She had outbreak after outbreak, seemingly uncontrollable by medication. The pain worsened continuously until she had to be hospitalized so that she could receive intravenous pain medications. She had pain even without external evidence of sores. Her behavior ranged from lethargic and depressed to agitated and angry. She was short-tempered with her child and unable to continue at college.

Lisa hounded her physicians for pain medicine and voiced suicidal ideas when it was not forthcoming. The doctors were worried that she might become addicted and would need ever increasing dosages to control the pain. Given her history, they also wondered how much of the pain had psychogenic origins, particularly in the absence of visible herpes lesions.

Lisa sought and received second and third medical opinions. She found a neurologist who told her that sometimes herpes affected neural pathways, and thus could lead to a prolonged pain syndrome, although this condition was exceedingly rare. This pronouncement naturally intensified Lisa's anger at her primary care physicians and seemed to increase the stridency and frequency of her demands for medication. Everyone involved had their own opinion about how much of the pain was "real." A course of treatment at a specialized pain center didn't seem to help much. Lisa felt they had nothing to offer her that her psychologist hadn't already taught her.

In the midst of this chaos, Lisa became pregnant by the young man she later married. He was younger than she and eager to take on the responsibilities of a family, although few people who knew him felt he would be capable of such a large undertaking. Lisa knew that pregnancy would be dangerous for her and for the baby. Vaginal delivery would put the child at risk for contracting herpes, so a cesarean section was scheduled. Lisa had debilitating pain throughout her pregnancy, leaving the care of her child and home to her mother and future husband. Somehow, all of them survived and Lisa delivered a healthy son.

Lisa continued to complain of severe pain for the next year, going into the hospital every three or four months for two or three days of intravenous medication and rest. Then, without warning, her mother died. Lisa was actually in the hospital at the time and had to be released on a pass to attend her mother's funeral.

Over the next six months, Lisa found herself literally shocked into health. Her pain, oddly, receded, but her grief was intense. So was her investment in caring for her father, who seemed withdrawn and lifeless. Following a flurry of psychotherapy sessions aimed at working through her profound sense of loss, Lisa terminated them, saying that she had to concentrate on her father, her siblings, and her children, and could no longer spend time focusing on herself. She has not returned to treatment, despite the birth of her third child, which was apparently without incident.

Thinking About the Case

Pain disorder is invariably frustrating for patients, their families, and clinicians. Since the experience of pain is private, subjective, and affected by a host of intrapsychic and interpersonal factors, both diagnosis and treatment can be difficult. Often physicians and patients find themselves at odds about whether and how much psychological factors are contributing to the person's discomfort. Generally, the suggestion that psychotherapy may be beneficial is received by the affected individual as confirmation that the doctor doesn't believe the pain is "real," but instead feels it is "all in my head."

Complicating the problem is the fact that some people do actually fake pain in order to receive some benefit—usually financial in the form of governmental or insurance disability payments. These people are called "malingerers," and they may be hard to distinguish from people who are genuinely experiencing pain. Many thousands of job-related injuries resulting in claims of disabling, chronic pain occur each year. These claims result in millions of dollars worth of lost wages, disability payments, and medical and rehabilitation bills. Generally, the longer the pain has lasted and the more the individual stands to gain from its continuation, the more difficult treatment becomes.

Lisa's case is typical in that the pain has a possible biological basis, but appears to be out of proportion to the physical stimulus. This is the most difficult type of pain problem to diagnose properly. She has some history of having more than the usual amount of illness in childhood, suggestive of the presence of secondary gain in the form of parental attention and nurturance. She has pre-existing psychological problems which indicate that her general strategies for coping with stress are not as good as they might be. Note, too, that this history might predispose a clinician not to take her claims of pain as seriously as those from a patient with less psychiatric history. The very presence of known psychiatric disorder tends to disqualify to some extent the patient's subjective account of symptoms.

What is known about chronic pain sufferers? First, the syndrome often co-exists with depressive disorders and, although to a lesser extent, with anxiety disorders. It is difficult to tell, in these cases, which is the chicken and which is the egg: does the pain cause the depression or vice versa? Second, the susceptibility to suggestion seems to be a predisposing factor in pain disorder, as it is in many of the somatoform disorders. In fact, suggesting that the pain will disappear in a specified period of time is often a useful treatment strategy.

What can we say about Lisa's prognosis? While Lisa's focus of attention shifted from her pain to the emotions and practical problems associated with her mother's death, it is probably safe to say that her symptoms are unlikely to be gone for good. Most psychogenic pain syndromes wax and wane in severity, sometimes with years of symptom-free functioning interspersed with protracted dysfunctionality, but they rarely disappear permanently.

Questions to Consider

1. List all the psychological disorders with which Lisa might have been diagnosed at one point or another. Are any of these DSM-IV Axis II diagnoses? What does the shifting pattern of symptoms suggest to you about psychological distress and dysfunction? Which models would best explain the presence of different disorders over time?

2. What do you make of Lisa's "flight into health" following her mother's death? Would you predict that she would be likely to have further psychological problems in the future? Why or why not? If you think she would be prone to future problems, what might these be? What is the basis for your predictions?

3. How would a psychodynamic therapist explain and treat Lisa's pain? Contrast this to a behavioral approach. Which would you have more confidence in? Might you combine them? Why or why not?

4. If an insurance company were paying you to tell them whether a patient was experiencing genuine, debilitating pain or not, what strategies would you employ to try to answer the question? How confident would you be in your answer?

11

——————◄○►——————

HYPOCHONDRIASIS:
THE CASE OF HARRY P.

HARRY P. WAS CERTAIN THAT he had stomach cancer. The pain in his gut had been almost imperceptible at first, an occasional dull ache or pulling sensation. Then, sneaking up on him gradually over several months, the sharp pains took over. Paralyzed with fear in the face of the dawning certainty that he had cancer, Harry had put off going to the doctor's for months. Finally, he did go. After the inevitable battery of tests—upper and lower gastrointestinal exams, blood tests, and colonoscopy—Harry received a diagnosis that should have been comforting but was not. He didn't have cancer. In fact, he didn't have any organic illness so far as his doctor could tell. What he had, he was told, was "stress."

Harry was incredulous. The pain was real—he wasn't making it up! Of course, he had stress, but no more than other people. His father had died of cancer at age fifty-two, about the same age Harry was now. He was convinced that he, too, had the dread disease. Harry sought a second and then a third medical opinion. Both confirmed the diagnosis, or lack of one, of his own physician. Finally, against his better judgment, but with no better ideas of his own, Harry accepted a referral to a psychologist.

Harry's behavior during his first interview was cooperative, even ingratiating, despite his lack of confidence in psychotherapy and his discomfort with self-disclosure. He answered questions as honestly as he could, but was curiously unable to describe his feelings in relation to situations or events. He could say he felt "bad" or "happy" about something, but he seemed to have no other feeling words in his vocabulary.

Harry impressed the psychologist as a private, emotionally-controlled person who focused his attention on tasks rather than on feelings. He had been employed for virtually his entire twenty-two-year career by the same *Fortune* 500 company, where he had moved up through the ranks to the mid-level supervisory position he now held. He was a loyal and hard-working employee who worked many hours of unpaid overtime and carried a large briefcase full of work home each evening, although he often managed to get through very little of it.

Harry's wife, a nurse, sometimes complained that he worked too many hours and spent too little time with her and his two teenaged children. However, she, too, had a strong work ethic and produced a long list of chores for herself and Harry to accomplish each weekend. Harry didn't spend much time with the kids, he admitted, although he had dutifully participated in scouts when his son joined a pack, and had gone to each and every dance recital in which his daughter had participated. He seemed wistful about how quickly his children had grown and how little he had known them, but he had no idea how to connect with them on a deeper level. He loved his wife and was satisfied with his marriage. He had been a virgin when he married and had never had a close relationship of any kind with any other woman. He felt that his wife was a good "partner," although, of course, there were times when they got on each other's nerves.

Over the first few psychotherapy sessions, Harry related some of his history. He had been the only son of Scandinavian immigrants. He could not remember ever having seen his parents argue. Neither could he remember having seen them hug or kiss. Like Harry, his father had worked for the same company for his entire career. Harry remembers that during the time his father lay dying with cancer, he had expressed the wish to have done more, to have had a wider range of experiences within his lifetime. Sometimes, Harry worries that he will feel this way, too. Harry feels that his parents treated him well, although there was not much warmth in their interactions. In turn, he was a respectful and dutiful son, caring for both his parents until their deaths.

Harry can't remember much about his childhood. He says he was "a regular nerd" throughout school. He got good grades, although he was often quite anxious about his academic performance. He didn't participate in any sports. He had a few friends, but remembers feeling somewhat lonely and isolated. He did not begin to date until college, where he met his wife. They married the summer after graduation. His wife went to work, and Harry worked part-time while he went to graduate school to earn a Masters' degree in business administration. They have both always worked hard and are grateful to have reaped the benefits— a secure living, a lovely home, the ability to send their children to college.

Harry spoke a great deal about his stomach pain and thoughts of cancer in the first few months of therapy. His therapist had to gently refocus him on talking about his sense of isolation and oppression. His supervisor at work, a woman, was known in the agency as a "ballbuster." Harry got along well with her, he thought, but she demanded a great deal and he always felt that he was not quite measuring up to her standards. She had no loyalty to anyone, he reported, and if necessary would "throw me overboard in a minute." Still, he admired her strength and ruthlessness and expressed the wish that he could be more like her.

Gradually, as he became able to talk about the stresses in his life and how he felt about them, his talk of cancer diminished. After nine months, pain-free and no longer worried about dying, he was discharged from the psychologist's care with the admonition to return if symptoms reappeared.

The psychologist didn't hear from Harry for two years, but then he did return, this time having been rushed to the hospital with chest pains. Panicked about the thought that he must have heart disease—again despite negative test results, he was just as skeptical about the value of psychotherapy as he had been the last time, even though he had appeared to benefit from it. He seemed to have unlearned what the therapist had taught him about paying attention to his feelings, allowing himself to experience them, and even talk about them, and giving himself permission to relax and spend some time in "nonproductive" pursuits.

This time, his preoccupation with his health seemed even more severe, interfering with his capacity to pay attention at work and to relate to his wife. He reported sleeping fitfully, losing some weight because of worrying, lacking sexual interest, and feeling overwhelmed and "foggy." The psychologist felt that Harry might be clinically depressed and suggested a consultation with a psychiatrist. Harry agreed and received a prescription for antidepressant medication to be used while he continued in psychotherapy. However, Harry was extremely anxious about what the medication might do to him. During the first week of medical treatment, he called the psychiatrist six times, worried that the medicine was causing one or another physical effect—drowsiness, dizziness, nausea, balance problems, blurry vision, stomach cramps. Despite attempts to cut back on the dosage, Harry was unable to take the medication without extreme agitation. After two-and-a-half weeks, he discontinued it.

Continuing in psychotherapy, Harry made slow but steady progress as he had done the last time. His fear of heart failure began to recede, and he was again able to see these concerns as symptoms of his feeling stressed and isolated. This time, Harry and his therapist decided not to terminate therapy as soon as he was feeling well. Instead, they continued to meet every other week, working on helping Harry learn to identify and talk about his feelings, and to make some significant changes in his lifestyle.

Two significant things happened during this course of therapy. Harry asked for and received a transfer to another job assignment within the company, and he had an affair. The transfer was an undeniably smart move: the new job was less stressful, allowed more creativity and autonomy, and best of all, allowed Harry to work for a different, more supportive supervisor.

The affair was less indisputably positive in its effects. Harry had become more and more aware of the lack of intimate connection in his marriage as therapy had progressed. Yet, he had found himself entirely unable to change the situation. He knew his wife well, he told the psychologist, and she didn't like weakness. She had problems of her own. She wouldn't want to hear about his. She expected him to solve his own troubles. She wouldn't understand. She would tell his secrets to her sister. She would use them against him in an argument. Harry turned aside his therapist's suggestion that he try some marital therapy. Instead, encased in a wall composed of his own preconceptions, Harry began to confide in a co-worker, a woman who was, herself, in an unhappy marriage. Harry felt himself powerfully drawn to this woman, and almost before he knew it, he had arranged to spend a weekend with her, having told his wife that he had to be away on company business.

Harry's feelings after the weekend were decidedly mixed. It had been wonderful, exhilarating. He had never felt that close to anyone, except his therapist (interestingly, also a woman). On the other hand, he felt deeply guilty and embarrassed. If his wife should ever find out, he would be mortified. He wondered how he could have been so stupid as to risk his marriage for an affair that obviously had no future. Over the next several weeks, the balance of his feelings shifted towards the ashamed side. He broke off the relationship with his co-worker and reinvested his energy in his marriage, which seemed to benefit from his renewed interest. After six months more of therapy, aimed at understanding the feelings that led to the affair and finding some more appropriate ways of meeting the needs he was beginning to identify, Harry again felt ready to terminate treatment.

However, this time, the hiatus was even more short-lived. Harry returned to the psychologist's office seven months later, convinced that he had contracted AIDS from his affair. "I was a fool to think I could get away with it," he whispered. "If you play, you pay. Isn't that what they say?" Harry was distraught. He could not bring himself to get a blood test because even if it was negative, he knew he would not believe it. Besides, he was certain that it was going to be positive and he just didn't think he could handle having the actual objective evidence in front of him.

In the psychologist's office, Harry could hardly sit still. He kept poking himself under the arm to feel for swollen glands. His nails were bitten down to the nub and he had clearly lost weight. The only positive note was that this time he had come to the therapist's office himself, without having been referred by his physician. This time he seemed to have some dim awareness that his AIDS obsession might reflect a psychological rather than a physical problem, although this awareness was certainly not fully conscious.

As before, therapy was successful at helping Harry identify the psychological underpinnings of his fears. As he did so, the fears themselves receded. Three months into treatment Harry felt able to ask for an AIDS test, but by this time he felt he no longer needed one. Instead, he added a regimen of exercise and meditation to his daily schedule, and began to attend church, something he had done as a child with his parents, but had given up as an adult. He still had difficulty communicating with his wife, now more than ever because he had to protect his secret. But he was able to share with his therapist how sad and sorry he was to have created this additional block to intimacy. He was also able to see that the affair had had some value for him and that it had not irrevocably damaged his marriage. His black-and-white style of thinking was beginning, slowly, to allow for shades of gray. Harry and his therapist decided, faced with the evidence of his multiple relapses, that ongoing, if less intensive, therapy might be of use. They agreed to meet monthly for the foreseeable future in the hopes that they might be able to head off future problems before they became severely debilitating.

Thinking About the Case

Harry's symptoms are quite typical of hypochondriasis. They are long-standing, but of variable intensity. They worsen in response to stress—in Harry's case, the difficult work situation, the anniversary of his father's death, the guilt over the affair. They are accompanied by a generalized focus on and distress about bodily sensations, as evidenced by Harry's inability to take medication. Harry's personality and style of being in the world are also typical of hypochondriacal patients. He has limited ability to identify and manage his feelings. He even exhibits "alexithymia," an inability to use words describing feelings, which has been shown to increase the susceptibility to somatoform disorders.

Hypochondriasis, while sometimes seen as a syndrome itself, can also occur as a symptom of another disorder, most typically depression, obsessive-compulsive disorder, or panic disorder. Actually, Harry confessed to obsessive-compulsive symptoms when examined closely—he sometimes felt that he had to engage in certain ritualized behaviors, like cleaning the bathtub using three sponges, three dabs of soap, and groups of three swipes at a time, so that his son would be protected from harm. These thoughts were so much a part of him and engaging in the rituals caused him so little distress that he hadn't thought to mention it himself.

Harry also had symptoms of depression, at least at some times. The psychologist noted over the years that Harry's symptoms tended to worsen in fall and improve in spring. Some people have seasonally sensitive depression, thus strengthening the hypothesis that perhaps Harry was clinically depressed. Interestingly, some of the same medications that are used to treat depression are also used to treat obsessive-compulsive

problems, so Harry may have benefitted doubly if he could have tolerated the medication that the psychiatrist had prescribed.

Historically, most explanations of hypochondriasis and other somatoform disorders have been psychodynamic. According to this model, the
physical symptoms and fear of illness provide a focus for anxiety which
is actually caused by an unconscious conflict revolving around unacceptable impulses. The presence of alexithymia in many patients suggests,
instead, a communicative rather than a defensive function for the symptoms. According to the communicative model, emotions that cannot be
expressed in words are expressed in physical symptoms. The fear of
AIDS, for example, can be seen as an expression of guilt and remorse
over Harry's affair, emotions to which he has little access and little
ability to express in other ways.

Questions to Consider

1. If the fear of AIDS has symbolic meaning for Harry, might the
   other two diseases he thought he had also have meaning? What
   might they mean?

2. What features of a person's biology or personal history might
   make him or her susceptible to somatizing disorders?

3. What kind of theory might explain why talking about feelings
   generally relieves hypochondriacal concerns? How might silence
   affect the body's functions?

4. Does learning theory have anything useful to say about the origins,
   maintenance, or treatment of hypochondriasis?

5. What might therapists of different theoretical orientations do
   when Harry expresses thoughts about having an affair? What
   would you do if you were the therapist? Why? What does this tell
   you about the values you hold about the psychotherapy process?

12

———————◄○►———————

Multiple personality disorder seems such an exotic disorder. It's hard to imagine anyone who has it functioning in everyday life. The anonymous nurse in this reading describes how she managed at work and at home despite her occasionally having several distinct personalities. She also talks poignantly about how the stigma and skepticism associated with multiple personality disorder affects her.

LIVING AND WORKING WITH MPD

Anonymous

*The sad part about being a multiple
is that no one knows.*

In the fall of 1984, when I was 39 years old, I went into therapy for symptoms of depression. For years I suffered ghastly outbursts of anger. They came so fast that I only could be stunned by the words coming from my mouth. I had a violent side and a hateful nature. I was unable to make decisions. I had been a "good girl" growing up, however, and never gave my parents a moment of trouble. From where was this behavior coming?

The day before I began therapy, I had no idea that there was more of me than I was aware. I had no idea I would be seeing a psychiatrist for the next 9 years for supervision of my medication, and that I would soon meet the therapist who would start me on the path to self-discovery. I knew only that there was something terribly wrong with me. I was not like other people; I was miserable.

After 2 years of therapy fraught with emotional pain and upheaval, I was stuck in a desolate place where I could move neither backward nor forward. Although my therapist was nurturing, she was unaware of my dissociation. I began again with a second therapist, a psychotherapist (PhD) specializing in sexual issues. It was this therapist who after a year made the diagnosis of multiple personality disorder (MPD). Thus began the long, difficult treatment process . . . the search . . . the journey into sorrow.

Painful Years

Growing Up   Looking back, I can see that I was not comfortable when alone with men, and I made sure that situation rarely occurred. The few dates I had in high school resulted in sweaty palms and anxiety attacks. I could not bear the thought of being near anyone of the opposite sex, and holding hands was out of the question. It was not worth it. It was difficult, and much too frightening.

As a young teenager I became preoccupied with religious beliefs. There was a deep-seated feeling that I was a bad person, yet I was not aware of ever doing anything wrong. To compensate, I became pious. I meditated, sang in the church choir, read the Bible, and prayed daily. I hoped that although I failed at being good, trying would count for something. I was lost in a great, dark pit.

Nursing School   I had suicidal thoughts while in nurses' training. Many times I despondently stood on the roof of my dormitory, seven floors up, and considered jumping. I had no idea why I wanted to jump—it did not make sense. I had friends among my classmates, but none was close. I was forgetful; my math skills stopped developing in the 4th grade. As a result, I had difficulties in some of my nursing classes.

Family Life   After graduation, I gathered my courage and married a handicapped man introduced to me by a friend. I loved him and he was "safe." He was a gentle person with a sparkle in his eyes and a positive attitude toward life. His physical limitations made it possible for me to approach him without feeling threatened.

The first year of our marriage, I went into a sudden rage—without warning—and threw the Christmas gifts given to us by our families into the garbage can on Christmas Eve. I threw them, smashed them, and screamed at my husband—I was beside myself, not knowing why I was doing what I was doing. I was horrified as he sat watching in disbelief.

We became foster parents. Part of me loved it; part of me hated it. Friends said, "There is a special place in heaven for you"—I thought hell was more like it. What they did not know was that at times I lost control and physically abused the children. I hated myself for doing this—but no matter how hard I tried, I could not stop. How was I to know that it was not actually me?

I had no idea when I might "lose it." One alter would decide, "This is the last child. I HATE KIDS! You're CRAZY and shouldn't be doing this." Another alter would lovingly accept the children and anticipate their arrival. Still another would pray for forgiveness and ask God to let the children forget the cruelty. I would rock them one day and then hit them the next. Why was I so different inside?

My internal struggle continued as child alters fought with my own children, screaming at and hitting them. I heard myself shout that I hated them and that they were not mine. They stood staring at me with huge round eyes. Part of me cringed and hurt for them. One alter cursed loudly. Alarm bells clanged. Babies wailed in my head. Internal arguing went on during the nights. Insults from within pelted me.

My husband became my "daddy." One alter married him; others hated him. I could not bear for him to look at me during sex, so I hid my face under a pillow in shame.

Career   I am a certified clinical psychiatric nurse and have worked the past 10 years on acute crisis stabilization units. It was important that I function on the job; not only to help my family financially, but also to pay for therapy. In the beginning of therapy, working became my focus; for this I developed an alter who went to work for me. She was industrious and well liked by co-workers and patients.

Getting to work was often difficult because I would lie in bed unable to get up. My body felt eight sizes too big and too heavy to move. Inside, little girls would sigh, tired of being in bed. They wanted to play outdoors. One of them would get me up and most times appropriately dressed for work.

When my key slid into the door of my unit, a "switch" immediately took place and my working alter would be there—smiling and ready to begin. My work alter loved her work. She was gentle and sensitive to those in her care. She was especially perceptive to persons with MPD. She recognized their "switching" and acknowledged each alter with respect.

Working with inpatient MPD patients can be emotionally draining for a "normal" nurse. Working with MPD patients while having MPD is extremely draining. In my situation, most of our MPD clients had the same physician that I did. When he came onto the unit I cringed and headed for the medicine room and hid in acute embarrassment. I studiously avoided charting on his patients and felt much shame.

During office visits, he reassured me that I was an excellent nurse. His patients did well with me and they felt that they could trust me.

It was difficult to have therapists treat MPD clients on the unit; some of them knew I was in therapy for MPD. Nevertheless, we worked together, in and out of seclusion rooms, and during "Amytal interviews" with their clients. Two of these therapists saw me, as a client, for psychiatric assessment and verification of my MPD diagnosis. The situation felt unreal.

At work MPD patients often triggered switches in myself. There was strong countertransference toward their child alters. My work alter was strong and no one guessed my distress. If I got overinvolved, and I sometimes did, my peers smiled and said I was a wonderful, caring person. Other staff members instinctively came to me for advice, not always knowing how to talk to alters. I pointed out switches and, for those nurses who were interested, I encouraged developing a trusting relationship between patient and nurse.

At the end of the 8-hour work shift a reverse occurred. When I turned the key in my car's ignition, a depressed, confused person—an empty shell—would drive home and go to bed exhausted and relieved that another day was done. In my head I heard plaintive cries of, "Mommy . . . mommy! Oh God . . . Oh God! I want to die!"

I knew I could not hurt myself in ways that would show because I had to continue working and appear normal. When the need to cut came, an aggressive alter named *Abusive* drew blood from my arm. In my room with the door locked, I splashed the blood, warm and sticky, onto art paper; when it dried I projected pictures onto it. The pictures were of ghoulish men torturing little girls; little girls with mouths open in silent screams, trying to get away. Like wisps of smoke, figures of little girls rose from the screaming children; alarm etched on their faces.

I cut my feet with a utility knife to punish myself for being such a miserable excuse for a human being. At work my feet hurt. Bandages and ointment covered the cuts. I wore socks to my therapist's office and would not permit her to see my feet.

If my co-workers had any suspicions about me, then they did not voice them. It is a wonder they did not; I thought my MPD was obvious. One year I received a teddy bear in a Christmas gift exchange—with the sheepish explanation, "When I saw it, I thought of you." I was amazed and pleased with the giver's perception.

I was forgetful. I blanked out in the middle of conversations with my colleagues at the desk. I would flicker in and out, catching bits and pieces of social chatter. I became a master of changing the subject. I covered my memory lapses by making jokes about how forgetful I was. I remembered details of MPD clients from one admission to the next, however. I remembered the names and characteristics of their alters, and they remembered me.

Therapy

Denial   As months of therapy slowly turned into years, I continued to deny the diagnosis of MPD. It could not be right. I had no memories. I was resistant to treatment. Some alters felt threatened and were hostile toward my therapist. The babies were scared . . . she was trying to "get inside" and she wanted to make them cry. Angry alters wanted to vandalize her office. "WE DON'T CRY!" they yelled. In my dreams they threw books on the floor and shattered her glass doors.

I was evasive. I intellectualized. Fortunately, my therapist refused to give up. Of particular value to me was her patience and ability to talk me through my doubts. My confusion was immense at times and, as a result, I must have tried to quit therapy 100 times. To my chagrin, however, I found myself back in my therapist's office each time.

I was encouraged to read — and read I did. I read everything I could find about dissociative disorders. When I forgot what I read I read it again . . . and again. Contrary to the belief that reading about MPD encourages MPD symptoms, I read to compare myself with textbook MPD cases and prove that I did not have MPD. I treated myself to day-long workshops on MPD and other dissociative disorders, earning many continuing education credits. I was privileged to have heard lectures by such renowned experts in the field as Dr. F. W. Putnam and Dr. Roberta Sacks.

Realizing the Truth   Studying helped me to confront the truth. The MPD diagnosis fit. I wrote; I kept journals. Alters wrote and drew pictures. They fussed, fumed, and fought.

Having MPD hurts. It makes one feel shameful and exposed. Memories are confusing and doubts are many. There is pain, despair, panic, and hiding. Resistance is difficult to overcome. It feels "crazy." Everything feels out of control. Having MPD made my thoughts spin round and round. My body jerked at night, leaving me feeling like I had been kicked in the stomach. My heart raced and my limbs ached.

I learned, through recurring pictures in my mind, what happened to me. These pictures, or memories, were of unhappy little girls, frozen in time, in pain and isolation. In the beginning I did not know what these memories were. As I learned — through trancing and hypnosis — I experienced abreactions, body memories, weight loss, weight gain, crying, resistance to crying, and the odd feeling of standing beside myself while listening to my voice speak.

Among the most frightening experiences was being unable to move . . . not an eye, not a finger . . . while another alter was out, usually a child, crying. Inside, my heart pounded and I screamed for my therapist, "Get me out! Please, please get me out!" When I "came out" my face was drenched with tears. During "real" time I was constantly bombarded by feelings and behaviors that I had little control over. This situation was ongoing in therapy and at home, while I continued to work. I truly was split. Work was my refuge and the source of my sanity.

Although I worked, I was lonely. I confided in two non-nursing friends and watched them back away because of a lack of understanding. This response reinforced my "don't trust anyone" stance. For several years, however, I wanted to trust a fellow nurse with my struggle with

MPD. Some of my alters wanted to come out to be with her. Sometimes they did, briefly, and she never knew. She was amazingly comfortable to be around. I had a shy teenage alter who adored her and envied her for her free spirit and honesty.

I worked with this nurse closely for years. I dropped hints, venturing out slowly; fear kept me from fully revealing myself to her. I finally told her and we both cried. She believed me and did not think that I was crazy. She is now my dear friend, and she guards my secret.

A Turning Point   The opportunity arose for me to join a group of women who were recovering from MPD. A kind and "safe" therapist facilitated the group. She created a protected environment in which she watched over us carefully. With uncanny perception and sensitivity she and the others helped me to accept my dissociated selves and believe in myself. Before joining, I made certain that I knew none of the others and they knew nothing of me. I was afraid because of my occupation as a psychiatric nurse.

It was a growing time and a relief to have a safe place to dissociate. Dissociating with others like myself at last! I have great admiration for the women in this group for displaying their courage and willingness to face their unknown terrors. They are intelligent and sensitive; I love them and have a permanent place in my heart for them. I thank them for sharing themselves with me. I was, and still am, deeply touched by them.

Now that I am integrated, I realize that I have come to love all my alters and grieve their loss. Each of them protected me over the years. They creatively kept me from losing my mind. They took the abuse for me. They hid for me, ran for me, became numb for me, and provided refuge for me. They married for me, had children for me, and got me through nurses' training.

All the alters wanted to be validated and they were. Each was listened to by my therapist. Each was heard. Each was loved and accepted. After the telling and the feeling, the anger went away—and each one said goodbye. I am proud of myself for completing this difficult task.

The Help of Others

I thank my beloved therapist, without whom I would not be free today. She gave me my life—and even more importantly, she helped me salvage my soul. She held me when I cried. She covered me when I felt naked. She listened to cries of, "I am real . . . I am real!" She was patient. She never wavered in her belief in me. Babies sat at her feet and held the hem of her dress. Alters who in sheer frustration banged their heads on her table and struggled with her found out she cared. She was strong and kept boundaries clear. Through visualization she brought color into their dark world, covered them with healing colors of the rainbow, and opened windows to outside. She was gentle; she comforted me and treated me with compassion. I learned a great deal from her during therapy.

I also want to thank my doctor for his support and assurance that I "wasn't crazy," when I felt otherwise. He was understanding of my predicament.

What can I say about my family? For 25 years my husband loved and supported me—no matter how dreadful my behavior was. He was both father and mother to our children when I could not be there for them. He cooked, cleaned, and went to school programs and conferences. Though hurt and confused, he helped the children deal with their hurt and confusion. He was, and is, my solid rock.

I also am fortunate to have an older sister who was vital to my acceptance of myself as an MPD sufferer. Her memory of events, people, and places verified my scattered memories, as the pieces of the puzzle fell together in a perfect fit. She was, and still is, supportive of me.

Skepticism and Injustice

I hope some day to come out of hiding and reveal who I am. As long as I have to keep it secret that I once had MPD, I will be hiding. I fear that I would lose my job were my secret known. I would be labeled, UNSTABLE . . . *Do Not Hire!*

The skepticism of co-workers prevents me from revealing my history. Recently, a colleague said to me, "Integration doesn't work. Multiples always come apart at the first sign of trouble." I looked at her disappointed, and thought, I am an integrated multiple. I worked 9 years at becoming whole. It is people like you who make it impossible for multiples to be open.

Unfortunately, I have seen much injustice done to individuals with MPD in the mental health field. I have seen disbelief, skepticism, misunderstanding, lack of knowledge, and hostility. I have been saddened by witnessing ineffective electroconvulsive therapy, misdiagnosis, undermedication, and overmedication. The terms *multiple personality disorder* and *borderline personality disorder* often are used interchangeably.

I have heard such comments as, "They're borderline . . . "; "She just wants attention . . . "; "Therapists create multiples, they are a status symbol . . . "; and "It's the 'in' diagnosis." These statements cause disbelief, confusion, and hurt. Such comments reinforce the resistance and denial that we fight so hard to overcome.

I personally can vouch that most persons with MPD think that they are "making up" the alters. They are not trying to be "in." We try to conceal our symptoms. We try to appear normal. We struggle every day with doubt and denial—many times right up to integration.

Please do not judge us. Every person with MPD is different. We are your friends and neighbors. We have different life experiences, and different doctors and therapists. We have different families, different support systems, and different abilities to cope.

Although I do not have the education or credentials to teach about MPD, I do have personal insight into the disorder. I have shared some of my experiences and feelings of having had MPD while working as a psychiatric nurse. Although I am whole, I continue to recover from MPD. I say *continue* because I will be recovering for the rest of my life.

LANAHAN NOTES

Somatoform, Dissociative, and Factitious Disorders

——◦——

It is estimated that 30 percent to 80 percent of patients who visit primary care physicians complain of symptoms not fully explained by a medical condition.

Per capita cost for health care for individuals having somatoform disorders is up to nine times the national average for health care.

These disorders illustrate an intimate relationship between psychological and physical well being.

SOMATOFORM DISORDERS

Definition:

1. physical symptoms or complaints

    or

2. loss or alterations in physical functioning

    or

3. pain

} that cannot be explained fully by a known physical or neurological condition and are not under voluntary control.

— generally, there is positive evidence that psychological factors are related to the symptoms.

— sometimes, but not always, the patient appears indifferent to the diminution in functioning.

— sometimes a physical condition is present, but is not serious enough to explain the symptoms.

— often difficult to distinguish from a) real medical problems, b) faking.

Types of Somatoform Disorders:

Somatization Disorder (Briquet's Syndrome): many physical symptoms occur, beginning before the age of thirty, which results in a more or less chronic impairment in functioning.

Undifferentiated Somatoform Disorder: one or more physical complaints that creates a significant impairment in functioning.

Conversion Disorder: symptoms or deficits affecting voluntary motor or sensory function (like ambulation, sight, or sound).

Pain Disorder: pain is unrelated to or apparently out of proportion to a medical condition.

Body Dysmorphic Disorder: preoccupation with an imagined or objectively minor defect in appearance.

Hypochondriasis: belief that one has a serious disease based upon a misinterpretation of bodily symptoms.

Somatoform Disorder not otherwise specified: all other somatoform symptoms, for example, pseudocyesis (false pregnancy).

Who gets these disorders? Diagnosed more often in women than men (perhaps the sick role is more allowable for women).

Causes:

Genetic: tends to run in families; also runs in families with antisocial or substance abuse disorders; also associated with anxiety/depression disorders.

Environmental: sometimes associated with severe trauma (for example, sexual abuse); childhood experience with pain or illness is a risk factor (modeling); operant conditioning; "sick role."

Treatment:

Attempt to get patients to become more aware of underlying emotions/conflict.

Teach family physicians how to manage them better (this has been shown to reduce costs).

Note: Somatoform Disorders tend to be chronic and difficult to change.

DISSOCIATIVE DISORDERS

Definition: alteration or loss of

1. consciousness
        or
2. memory   unrelated to medical condition.
        or
3. identity

Types of Dissociative Disorder:

Dissociative Amnesia: inability to recall important information, generally of a traumatic or stressful nature.

Dissociative Fugue: sudden travel to a distant place with accompanying amnesia (confusion about identity or the assumption of a new identity may be involved).

Dissociative Identity Disorder: presence of one or more completely separate identities or personalities within the individual.

Depersonalization Disorder: Persistent or recurrent episodes of feeling detached from one's body or mental processes without loss of reality testing.

Dissociative Disorder not otherwise specified: other dissociative syndromes.

Causes:

Almost exclusively related to severe stress or trauma.

Basis of much of Freud's theories about neurosis: symptoms as a way of managing unbearable anxiety.

Biopsychosocial model: new specialty called "traumatology"

1. biological factors, like suggestibility, may play a role in the choice of symptoms.
2. trauma may produce a permanent change in autonomic functioning in some individuals, leading to a more chronic course for trauma-induced disorders.
3. learning theory—learned helplessness may explain predisposing vulnerability to the effects of trauma; modeling and serendipitous experiences (like discovering that being ill brings maternal affection) may also be relevant.

Treatment:

Psychodynamic: explore underlying conflicts in attempt to reduce the necessity for symptoms.

Cognitive: review and rework deficits in self-esteem and changes in view of self and others associated with trauma.

Medications: sometimes helpful in combatting anxiety and depression.

Prognosis:

Guarded. Treatment is long-term. Improved functioning but not "cure" is the rule.

FACTITIOUS DISORDER (MUNCHHAUSEN SYNDROME)

Definition:

—an individual intentionally feigns psychological or physical signs and symptoms in order to derive the emotional benefits inherent in the sick role.

—may result in multiple hospitalizations and even surgeries

—distinguished from malingering (faking illness) by having psychological rather than economic goals (Note: malingering is not a psychological disorder).

—responds poorly to treatment; psychodynamic orientation most common.

Controversies:

—How much conscious control does the individual have over symptoms? The line between somatization disorders, factitious disorders, true dissociation, and malingering is often difficult to ascertain. (Some clinicians don't believe that multiple personality disorder even exists.)

—Is trauma a necessary precondition for dissociation?

—Is the use of hypnosis in the diagnosis and treatment of dissociative disorders appropriate given that studies clearly indicate that highly hypnotizable individuals are prone to developing false as well as real memories while in the hypnotic state?

CHAPTER FOUR

Mood Disorders

————◀o▶————

Next to anxiety, sadness is probably the most common human emotion. None of us escapes loss in our lives, and loss inevitably leads to sadness. But when does sadness, a normal feeling, shade into depression, a clinical condition? The DSM-IV answers this question by specifying that mood disorders must be of sufficient duration and intensity that they cause significant subjective distress or dysfunction in one or more of life's roles (relationships, work, school).

Depression is an all-encompassing condition. Its accompanying physical symptoms include changes in sleep, appetite, activity level, and the ability to experience pleasure. Cognitive changes include thinking of the present as bleak and the future as hopeless. The past seems marred by errors that one is helpless to rectify. Concentration and motivation are impaired. Emotional changes include despair, emptiness, and often guilt. Social changes include socializing less and feeling short-tempered and ill at ease. It is no wonder that depression is associated with an elevated risk of suicide.

The good news is that depression is often self-limiting and is, in most cases, a highly treatable condition. Both biological and psychological interventions have been shown to be effective in ameliorating the symptoms of depression and in preventing relapse.

In this chapter, we look at two cases that illustrate how stage of life may be relevant to the development of depression. One case (#13) discusses the treatment of an elderly man and his wife, each of whom is diagnosed with depression. The other case (#15) examines depression in a teenager. This second case is also interesting because it illustrates the important role that cultural factors can play in both the onset of psychological disturbance and in its treatment. We have also included a case in which the depressive disorder is recurrent and appears to have strong biological as well as environmental roots. Finally, we present a case of bipolar disorder in which depression alternates with an abnormally elevated mood called "mania." This young woman was treated many years ago when long-term institutionalization rather than community-based treatment was more prevalent. Read in conjunction with readings later in the book (#52, #53, and #54), it raises some interesting issues about changes in treatment philosophy over time.

When have chosen two readings for this chapter. The first is a brief update on seasonal depression and the use of bright light as therapy. The second examines some of the surprising cognitive differences in depressed versus normal people.

13

————◄○►————

SITUATIONAL DEPRESSION IN THE ELDERLY: THE CASE OF MR. A.

MR. A. IS A SEVENTY-SIX-YEAR-OLD married father of three. He grew up the oldest son of immigrant parents in a large East Coast city. Under his parents' stern and watchful eye, he did well both academically and in schoolyard sports and graduated from high school at sixteen, then going on the road to learn the sales trade with his uncle. He married at nineteen and fathered a son, but the marriage did not survive his almost constant absence and single-minded focus on making money. He and his wife divorced after three years. For some years he kept in touch with his son, but squabbles with his ex-wife over money and visitation gradually eroded his emotional ability to stay involved. His ex-wife wanted him out of their son's life and finally she got her way.

Mr. A.'s apprenticeship with his uncle was interrupted by a three-year stint in the Navy during World War II. He was at sea in the Pacific for most of that time. He recalls playing lots of poker on board the ship and making friends with the cooks and bakers so that he ate as well as the officers. With his poker winnings, he paid other sailors to do his laundry, make his bed, and even, occasionally, take his watch. Still, he was always at his place during battles and earned an honorable discharge at the war's end.

Mr. A.'s self-confidence and charm made him a natural salesman. It didn't take long, upon his return from the service, to develop his own business. Over the next forty years, he made (and occasionally lost) lots of money, married his secretary and fathered two more children, joined a country club, and generally lived the good life.

He did not, of course, escape his share of heartache. He went bankrupt twice (but bounced back quickly), his parents died—first his father, and then his mother less than six months later. His second marriage, relatively happy for the first decade, gradually disintegrated over the next twenty years into one in which bickering and sniping outweighed loving and communicating. His wife complained that he was totally self-centered and had an unreasonable temper. He felt she nagged, belittled, and blamed him. His wife often thought of leaving him, but, having two children and no independent source of income, she stayed, resentfully, in the marriage.

Mr. A. was without diagnosable mental health problems until a series of catastrophes befell him in his seventy-third year. It began with his falling one day. His wife felt that his complaints of weakness in his leg were "in his head," but after the third fall, spinal stenosis, a narrowing of the spinal openings through which nerves pass, was diagnosed and surgery recommended. Mr. A. had every possible complication of surgery. His pacemaker (installed some years before following coronary bypass surgery) failed immediately after the incision was made so the surgery had to be aborted and a new pacemaker inserted. He developed a potentially dangerous blood clot in his leg. He suffered a post-surgical psychosis in which he thought that the doctors were engaged in a plot to sell drugs. In a panic, he tried to tear out his intravenous tube and had to be sedated. His diabetes, previously under fairly good control, became unstable and several times he went into insulin shock. His wound failed to heal properly and had to be reopened, cleaned out, and reclosed. This involved days of painful packing of the open wound. Every time it appeared that he had stabilized, something else happened.

In the midst of all of this, an unrelated event made his medical problems seem minor in comparison. Mrs. A., having gone to her husband's office to clean it out and prepare it for subletting, found a loveletter written to Mr. A. by a woman acquaintance. Confronting him with this, she discovered that he had had an affair with this woman. She could never get clear exactly when and for how long the affair had lasted, but what she learned was enough to devastate her.

Mr. A.'s presumed fidelity was the one trait that had allowed Mrs. A. to remain attached to him over the years, despite what she felt were his serious flaws. At least, she reasoned, he was faithful to her. With this presumption shattered, she had nothing left. For days she refused to visit him or speak with him on the telephone. She decided that he probably had had other affairs and had visited prostitutes during his years of traveling. Whether this was true or not, her pain was intense. She cried continuously and told the hospital social workers that she would not bring him home from the hospital. But since Mr. A.'s financial condition did not make him eligible for Medicaid, and with nursing home costs being what they were, she really had no choice. She brought him home, and took care of him in stoney silence. Over the next two years, Mr. A.'s medical condition deteriorated gradually. His heart had been severely stressed by the traumas he had recently survived, and he was hospitalized several times in acute heart failure. Each time, he lost weight—and strength. His back surgery, ironically, had come too late to prevent nerve damage, and he was not able to regain much use of his leg, despite physical therapy. Finally, wheelchair bound and demoralized, he was placed in a nursing home, much to Mrs. A.'s relief and Mr. A.'s chagrin.

By this time, Mrs. A., having entered psychotherapy herself, had come to some peace about Mr. A.'s infidelity. She was no longer enraged at him, but neither did she feel love or loyalty towards him. She was, however, loyal to her own sense of duty and continued to provide some caretaking for Mr. A. She supervised his care at the nursing home, visited him almost daily, and brought him whatever he needed. She engaged him in casual conversation as best she could but her coldness was unmistakable.

Mr. A. was a much changed man. Having been voluble, social, and optimistic all his life, he was now silent, withdrawn, and depressed. He took all his meals in his room and refused to participate in any therapeutic or social activities at the nursing home. He complained bitterly that the nursing aides treated him disrespectfully and that the food was intolerable. He cried easily and spent his days staring, unseeing, at the television. He neither told nor laughed at jokes. He was unable to engage in conversation of any kind. He continued to lose weight even after he recovered from the acute heart failure. He seemed prepared to die in that life offered no pleasure.

Mr. A.'s physician at the nursing home recognized the signs of depression. While Mr. A.'s family thought his behavior was normal for an old, sick, disappointed man, the doctor felt that his mood might improve if he were treated with an antidepressant medication. Within ten days after treatment was begun, his appetite began to improve, and he stopped complaining about the food. A week later, he allowed himself to be talked into eating in the communal dining room where he found a table of men who became his regular mealtime companions. Gradually, his sense of humor returned. So did his ability to charm. He went from being the bane of the staff's existence, to being one of their favorites. He got to know them, joked with them, wheedled special favors from time to time. One of the nursing aides took to sharing her "garlic chicken," his favorite Chinese food, with him whenever she got it. He began to act more like his old self—optimistic and gregarious. He was appreciative for what his wife had done for him. In his optimism, he even talked himself into believing that she really stilled loved him and that, in time, she would forgive him. It appeared that whatever life would be left to him, despite his limitations, he would live with gusto and zest.

Thinking About the Case

Depression in the elderly is often undiagnosed. Like Mr. A.'s family, we tend to think that people who are old, limited, and who have suffered losses and setbacks must necessarily feel sad and demoralized. Anybody who has to suffer the indignities and loss of freedom of living in a nursing home would be depressed, we reason. Anybody whose wife now despised him after fifty years of marriage would be depressed.

As this case illustrates, "it ain't necessarily so." Brain biochemistry may be an important intervening variable. It is likely that external events affect the relative balance of neurotransmitters in the brain, which then affects mood. With treatment, the nursing home food tasted better, the nursing staff were perceived as more friendly, and even Mr. A.'s wife seemed more loving to him. His longstanding emotional resilience, his ability to make the best out of any situation, was restored.

Could psychotherapy have produced the same result? Perhaps. The literature is equivocal about the comparative benefits of antidepressant medication versus psychotherapy. Two forms of psychotherapy in particular have been shown to be effective in treating depression: interpersonal psychotherapy, which focuses on the critical relationships in the person's life, and cognitive psychotherapy, which works on changing the distorted thinking patterns often exhibited by depressed people. Other forms have not been systematically tested, but may also be effective. Mrs. A. was treated with psychotherapy and improved significantly over the two years she was in therapy. She didn't achieve the sunny optimism of Mr. A., but then, she'd never had it before.

It's likely that some people respond better to psychotherapy and others to pharmacological interventions. Psychological-mindedness, ability to form a trusting therapeutic relationship, and a model of symptoms that lends itself to "the talking cure" are probably prerequisites for achieving a good psychotherapy result. Some people distrust and fear medicines, which would also make them candidates for a psychotherapeutic approach. Others don't have the patience for psychotherapy, don't wish to or can't share their feelings with another person, don't have very good capacity for insight, or believe that medication will cure them. These people would be good candidates for pharmacological treatment.

In practice, many people who are depressed receive both psychotherapy and medication, since we do not yet have any real way of knowing who will benefit from what. While most of these improve significantly, the relative benefits of combined treatment compared with single treatment have not been scientifically sorted out.

Questions to Consider

1. If you became depressed, what sort of treatment would you be inclined to seek out? Why would you choose that treatment over the alternatives?

2. Learned helplessness is a model of depression on which much of cognitive therapy is based. How would the model apply to Mr. A.'s experiences? What kind of therapeutic intervention would be dictated by this model?

3. Depression is diagnosed much more frequently in women than in men. What are some reasons why this might be so?

14

———◄◦►———

RECURRENT MAJOR DEPRESSION: THE CASE OF HANNAH H.

HANNAH H. IS A VIBRANT, GREGARIOUS fifty-two-year-old naturalized American citizen. She was born in Hungary towards the end of World War II. Her parents divorced when she was a baby and she was raised, primarily, by her mother and grandmother, although her mother did remarry when Hannah was eight. Hannah did not know who her biological father was until she was eleven, when her mother confessed that a man who had functioned as a family friend and sort of "uncle" to Hannah was actually her father.

Hannah's mother, Mrs. P., was a prominent woman in the business community in the city where they lived. She had a good bit of money and Hannah went to the best schools and dressed in the best clothes. On the surface, her life seemed serene. However, appearances can be deceiving. Hannah's mother was a difficult, demanding, and judgmental woman. She controlled Hannah's every move, never allowing her an independent thought or movement. She berated her daughter constantly for being fat, stupid, ugly, or selfish. No matter what Hannah tried to do to please her mother, nothing worked.

But this was not the worst of it. Mrs. P. had a serious mental illness in which she had recurrent bouts of suicidal and homicidal feelings. Hannah vividly remembers an incident that occurred when she was about five or six in which her mother was holding her hand as she walked them both into the river near their home, apparently planning to drown them both. Hannah remembers her mother saying, "It's alright, it won't hurt, it will be very peaceful." She remembers crying and struggling, saying, "I don't want to die, mother, please don't." She doesn't remember why her mother stopped, but she thinks it was because she remained upset and wouldn't calm down. In those days mental illness carried even more of a stigma than it does today, so Mrs. P.'s family attempted to cover up her illness rather than seek treatment, although Hannah remembers that her mother did spend some time in a sanatorium at some point during Hannah's childhood. She can't remember exactly when or for how long, though.

Hannah's misery was not exclusively in the hands of her mother. When she was ten, her stepfather began to undress and fondle her when no one was around. He went upstairs into her room at night, while her mother and grandmother sat reading or crocheting in the living room, and exposed himself to her forcing her to rub his penis until he ejaculated. After about a year of this, Hannah worked up the nerve to tell her mother, who became hysterical and swore she would divorce him. However, after confronting her husband, she became enraged at Hannah and accused her of behaving seductively. She stayed married but saw to it that Hannah was never alone with her stepfather again. Oddly, though, Hannah felt less protected than ostracized.

While this account makes it sound as if Hannah's childhood was an unremitting disaster, this is not so. She had an unusually loving and trusting relationship with her grandmother. Even though she was Mrs. P.'s mother, Hannah's grandmother could not have been more different in temperament and behavior. She was there to comfort Hannah after her mother or stepfather had verbally or physically abused her. They laughed together and played together. From her grandmother she learned how to keep house, and how to love another person. Her grandmother always tried to keep Hannah connected to her mother by making excuses for her or urging Hannah to forgive and forget. Hannah believes that her grandmother's presence saved her life, both emotionally and in reality.

Hannah also had a good life at school. While a bit shy, she was a good student and well like by both teachers and peers. Her outward success was about the only thing in which her mother took any pride, so Hannah strove as hard as she could. She felt that if only she could be a better student, a better daughter, a better person, then her mother would be able to love her.

Nobody in the community ever reacted to the abuse Hannah suffered at home. She believes people must have known about it because she often came to school with bruises on her face and arms from her mother's beatings. In those days, she says, people minded their own business, and what parents did to children was a private matter.

From age ten or eleven on, Hannah suffered from symptoms of panic disorder. These were characterized by difficulty breathing, pain in the chest, and lightheadedness. She was terrified of dying. Gradually these attacks, which lasted from minutes to hours, became more frequent and longer in duration. Despite her suffering with these symptoms for years, she was never taken for treatment.

Not surprisingly, Hannah married young. At nineteen, she married a young man who turned out to be physically abusive. She had two daughters from that marriage, and after she divorced him, her husband dropped out of sight. A year later, Hannah met and soon married a young American soldier stationed in Hungary. He seemed kind and considerate, and, best of all, he planned to take her and her daughters back to the States to live. This marriage has lasted twenty-five years, although it, too, was not without its share of troubles.

Mr. H., Hannah's second husband, had a violent temper, as had her mother, stepfather, and first husband. In the early years of their marriage, he beat, choked, and shoved her whenever she displeased him. When she cowered or tried to run or hide, he beat her worse. She says he seemed to enjoy her terror. The beatings only stopped when Hannah began therapy and, with the help of her therapist, decided to call the police when her husband attacked her. She had him jailed once, which, though it infuriated him, stopped him from laying hands on her again. She also stopped cowering. Instead, she learned to hold her ground and tell him that if he touched her, he would go to jail. Apparently, he learned that she meant it.

Why did she stay? Hannah says she didn't find what she was living with particularly odd. She had always been beaten. Besides, her husband was a good provider, often fun to be with, and he treated her two girls exactly like the three children they subsequently had together. In fact, he was a wonderful father to all of the children. She loved him, and she felt fairly certain that he loved her as well.

Hannah first requested mental health treatment when she was thirty-six years old. She sought treatment for her panic symptoms and was seen for a few sessions. She had a few more sessions for the same problem when she was forty. Then, three years later, following the birth of her fifth child, she suffered a serious post-partum depression. Her mood gradually worsened, she had difficulty sleeping, and she was horrified to find herself thinking of killing the baby. Because of the concern that she might hurt her child, Hannah was hospitalized in a psychiatric unit of a general hospital for about two weeks. There she was treated with antidepressant medication as well as individual and group psychotherapy. Her thoughts of harming her new son receded, and she continued to do well with medication and outpatient psychotherapy. Two years after this episode, Hannah's therapist left the mental health center. Hannah had difficulty attaching to the new therapist that had been assigned to her. Since she had felt well for some time, she gradually stopped going to the center and taking her medication.

Hannah remained essentially symptom-free for three more years when, in the midst of some family turmoil, she began to again display the symptoms of depression: early morning awakening, lack of interest in her appearance or her usual activities of daily living, and the reappearance of suicidal and homicidal thoughts—again directed towards her son, whom she adored. In a panic, she called her primary care physician who prescribed Prozac, one of the newer antidepressant drugs, and referred her for psychotherapy. Her therapist requested a consultation from a psychiatrist, reasoning that a psychiatrist's involvement would be necessary if hospitalization should become necessary. The therapist also wanted to see whether, in view of Hannah's history of relapse, lithium carbonate should be added to the medication regimen. This medication has been found to be effective in treating bipolar disorder (previously known as manic-depressive illness), and seems to prevent relapse in a substantial number of patients. The psychiatrist agreed the lithium carbonate might be useful and this was prescribed by the primary care physician.

While her depression continued for some time, Hannah's suicidal and homicidal thoughts disappeared when she began taking the antidepressant again, so she was able to avoid hospitalization during this episode of illness. A month later she was essentially symptom free. Her depression appeared to have lifted. She reported sleeping well, having increased energy, experiencing a return of her sexual drive (often diminished during depression), and rediscovering her sense of humor. If anything, she appeared mildly elated, causing her therapist to worry that she might develop a manic episode, as sometimes happened with people who have an underlying bipolar disorder not yet diagnosed.

This did not come to pass, though, and Hannah's mood has ranged from mildly depressed to normal ever since. She stopped taking lithium carbonate about one year after she started, because she felt it made her somewhat lethargic and sleepy. In addition, she suffered from annoying diarrhea as a side effect. She understood that she ran some risk of relapse, but decided that the benefits of the medication were uncertain while the side effects were known and unpleasant. She did, however, elect to remain on the Prozac given the clear and convincing evidence that it relieved her depression. She was particularly fearful that her homicidal thoughts would return without medication, and these were so horrifying to her that she would do anything to stop them.

Hannah also elected to remain in psychotherapy, essentially indefinitely. She sees her therapist approximately twice a month, and they discuss the various stresses in her life—problems with or concerns about the children or her husband, unresolved feelings about her mother, who is still alive in Hungary, upset feelings brought about by television shows or some news event related to child abuse or neglect. They also monitor carefully how she is sleeping and how her energy level is, because they know from experience that problems in either of these areas can be warning signs of impending relapse. They are working on two fronts at once: they hope to increase her psychological resistance to environmental stress, and to intervene earlier, should she begin to suffer a relapse. Hannah has not only survived, she is a loving and protective mother, a loyal and devoted friend, and a productive citizen of the community. She demonstrates the resilience of the human spirit, the redemptive value of the care and protection of even one loving adult in the life of a child, and the benefits conferred by modern mental health treatment.

Thinking About the Case

Hannah's case is not unusual in its multiplicity of diagnoses and pathways to illness. Hannah's primary diagnosis is recurrent depression, characterized by saddened mood, lack of energy and initiative, inability to take pleasure in previously enjoyed activities, oversleeping, and suicidal thoughts. These are hallmark symptoms of the disorder. The homicidal thoughts are somewhat unusual, particularly because they were not experienced as consistent with her depressed mood — "life is so awful that my son would be better off without it." Rather, they were experienced as intrusive, unwanted, compelling ideas, more in the nature of a compulsion. One could have been led to diagnose her as having obsessive-compulsive disorder, but, the bulk of the symptoms supported the diagnosis of depression.

Hannah also suffered from panic disorder, although she doesn't have the symptoms at present. She does have symptoms of post-traumatic stress disorder, characterized primarily by nightmares about being held against her will by her mother, and by her strong avoidance of and emotional overreaction to stimuli associated with child abuse. Thus, she has at least three mental health diagnoses. Research indicates that each of these three disorders may share some neural pathways in the brain (primarily involving the neurotransmitter serotonin), so Hannah's symptoms may all be related to a common disturbance.

It appears that Hannah's medication provides some protection against depression. It may also be of value in treating the panic symptoms. The post-traumatic symptoms seem relatively unaffected and are treated more by the support that psychotherapy has to offer. They seem to come and go, depending upon whether her children have contact with their grandmother, thus stimulating her thinking about her own childhood.

This case also has material for both nature and nurture supporters. Hannah appears to have symptoms similar to those her mother had. This may indicate a genetic predisposition, although since she was raised by her mother, modeling may play some role. The onset of depression was post-partum, so hormonal forces may be implicated. Women undergo massive hormonal changes after childbirth. Naturally, the traumatic aspects of her childhood could be expected to have contributed to her psychological distress.

Rather than choose between heredity and environment, the widely accepted "diathesis-stress model" allows us to combine features of both. According to this model, mental illness occurs in people who have a built-in genetic or constitutional vulnerability combined with environmental stress of some kind. Whether the vulnerability (the "diathesis") must be specific for a particular illness, or whether the stressor must be of a specific kind for a particular illness is, as yet, unknown. According to this model, Hannah inherited a predisposition to develop depression with suicidal and homicidal features from her mother. In the face of her stressful childhood, combined with the hormonal, physical and emotional stresses of having a new baby, the predisposition manifested itself. The model states that both the diathesis and the stress are necessary for the illness to occur. It is likely that some individuals have a very strong predisposition to illness, such that little if any stress is necessary. Others may have a weaker predisposition, requiring extraordinary stress to trigger an episode of illness. Hannah appears to have had a hefty dose of each.

The prognosis for depression is variable. About one-third of patients seem to recover from a single episode of depression without any long-term effects. Another third recover well, but relapse after some time has passed. The last third, appear to experience only a partial recovery, struggling with a milder form of the disorder on a more chronic basis. Hannah appears to fall within the second group, recovering well, but prone to relapse.

Questions to Consider

1. The question of whether adult mental health disorders can be prevented by early intervention is being studied by researchers world-wide. Do you think Hannah's depression could have been prevented by mental health intervention earlier in her life? Why or why not? If your answer is "yes," what sorts of interventions would you have wanted to see done?

2. Post-partum depression is usually thought to have at least a par-

tially hormonal etiology. Can you think of some psychological reasons why a woman might become depressed following the birth of a baby?

3. Apply the diathesis-stress model to your own life. Do you have familial predispositions for depression or other psychological disorders? Have you experienced relevant stressors? If you answer is yes to either of these questions, what steps might you take to reduce your risk?

15

——————◄o►——————

DEPRESSION IN AN AFRICAN–AMERICAN TEENAGER: THE CASE OF TAKISHA LANDRY

THE CASE PRESENTED HERE IS FROM "Dealing With Cross-Cultural Issues in Clinical Practice," a book chapter written by Harriet Lefley, Ph.D., in P.A. Keller, and S. R. Heyman, (eds.), *Innovations in Clinical Practice: A Sourcebook* (Sarasota, FL: Professional Resource Exchange, 1991). It is included here, with Dr. Lefley's introduction, comments, and treatment plan, to illustrate the role that cultural and socioeconomic factors can play in the diagnosis and management of psychological problems. After you read the case, but before you read the "Comments" section, stop and consider how you might conceptualize Takisha's problems, and what you might do to resolve them. Then, compare your ideas with Dr. Lefley's in the following case:

Two critical errors emerge in therapy with persons who are culturally different not only in racial/ethnic background, but also in socioeconomic status. One is the misinterpretation of behavioral cues that are linked to specific cultural values. The other is the tendency to impose unwarranted psychodynamic meanings on some basic realities of living at or just above the poverty line. These are exemplified in the following case example. It is presented in some depth to show patterns of cultural misinterpretation, reassessment of need, and treatment planning geared toward empowering both parent and child while restoring psychological stability to an economically stressed family system.

Takisha Landry (a pseudonym), a female, African-American, 12-year-old sixth grader, was referred to the school counselor for evaluation. Previously a fine student, Takisha's grades had slipped in the last year, and she was now in danger of repeating sixth grade while her peers moved on to a higher level. During the past 4 months she had seemed tired, preoccupied, and increasingly depressed. The counselor tested her on the WISC and obtained a Full Scale IQ score of 118. She denied any trouble at home.

Takisha's mother came to school for a conference and indicated she was not aware of any trouble at home, did not see particular changes in Takisha's behavior, but was concerned to learn that her child's school performance was decreasing. When Takisha and her mother met together with the counselor, Mrs. Landry spoke sharply to Takisha and ordered her in no uncertain terms to shape up in school or she would be punished. Takisha looked down at her hands and said nothing. The counselor observed that there was not eye or body contact between the two, no touching or overt affection. Takisha, she noted, seemed either afraid of her mother or distant from her; she addressed her only as "yes ma'am" and "no ma'am." Later, however, when Takisha returned to class, Mrs. Landry asked to speak privately with the counselor. She seemed genuinely puzzled and concerned. Takisha was a good child, dependable, honest, and a great help to her. The mother wanted Takisha to finish school and go to college. She would do anything she could to help.

Takisha was referred to a child guidance clinic for psychotherapy. Because of her previously fine school performance, which indicated a high level of intelligence and motivation for learning, she was considered a good candidate for psychotherapy and was assigned to a young psychology intern from a midwestern white Protestant background. Mrs. Landry received a letter asking her to come in for a preliminary conference. She called the clinic and asked to reschedule an 11:00 A.M. conference to an earlier hour; her voice seemed harassed and short-tempered. When she spoke with the interviewer, she again could recall nothing that would explain Takisha's behavior, was annoyed at the questions, and finally said sharply it was the clinic's job to "fix Takisha up," because raising children was just too hard. She was very disturbed that the clinic had scheduled Takisha's sessions for just after school, saying she didn't know what she would do with the younger children, but that she would try to arrange for a neighbor to take care of them as long as it was for only a few weeks or so.

In the first three sessions Takisha was depressed and spoke in soft, reluctant monosyllables, but the following story came out. She was the main caregiver for her three younger brothers and sisters, aged 5 to 8. Their father had left long ago. They lived in the projects, and in addition to picking up each of the children from their various schools and walking them home, Takisha was required to prepare their meals, monitor them, and keep them from playing outside because it was too dangerous. She also had to do laundry and housework. The children wanted to play outside and were getting increasingly harder to handle. Their mother was always away from home working, because she refused to be on welfare. About 6 months ago, a man had moved in with them, but he stayed only briefly, maybe a few months.

The therapist thought Takisha's depression was tied into that particular time frame—to the man's coming and leaving. He questioned gently about abuse, particularly sexual abuse, but Takisha denied any. Ultimately it came out that, following the man's departure, Takisha's mother had taken a second job; she worked from 3:00 P.M. to 11:00 P.M. as a hospital aide, then went on a midnight to 8:00 A.M. shift at an all-night restaurant. It was only after four sessions that the therapist began to understand why the mother had seemed so short-tempered about the clinic's scheduling of appointments for herself and her daughter—schedules that were for the convenience of the clinic rather than responsive to Mrs. Landry's needs for sleep and her job responsibilities as a breadwinner. The enormity of Takisha's role as a parental child, whose tasks extended from early morning to night, from getting the children up to putting them to bed, also began to take on significance. The therapist thought that the only time the mother seemed to assume her proper parental role was on Sundays, when the family spent the entire day and evening in church.

The therapist still thought that strained relations between mother and daughter were at the root of Takisha's depression. The mother was viewed as harsh and demanding, insensitive to Takisha's needs as a child, and emotionally distant. All of this went into the case record. Takisha was approaching puberty and had had no life as a child. The treatment goal was to remove the yoke of parental child, to allow her time to study, and to give her some play experience with children her own age. To accomplish this, the therapist hoped to validate Takisha's separation from her parenting role by counteracting her need for maternal approval. He would substitute unconditional positive regard within the therapeutic alliance. He gently normalized: "Sometimes we all get mad at our parents, at the things they expect of us." Takisha looked startled. He continued: "I used to get angry at my mother all the time. I was just about your age when I realized that parents don't know everything!" But instead of responding, Takisha looked terrified. The therapist decided there was really something profoundly disturbing going on between Takisha and her mother. However, the more he tried to explore this, the more withdrawn and depressed Takisha became, and after six sessions they seemed to be getting nowhere.

Comments

Given the therapist's perceptions, a psychodynamically oriented treatment approach is doomed to failure because the "insight" he is seeking is based on incorrect premises. First, let us consider some realities of cultural life in the lower income African-American community. The sharpness heard in Mrs. Landry's admonitions to her daughter, and the child's seeming passivity, are culturally normative in ghetto life. For centuries, beginning with the harsh realities of slavery, children have learned to accept the withholding of praise and the strictures to behave obediently—often reinforcing submissiveness and passivity with elders—that were essential for survival in earlier times. Children learned to accept these parental behaviors without missing the underlying love and approval that are typically invisible to cultural outsiders. The passive response does not mask anger, but indicates acceptance of culturally normative parent-child interactions and perhaps a tacit understanding of the meaning of the behavior. A child's avoidance of eye contact with an adult still connotes respect, in American Indian as well as in African-American cultures. Lack of tactile contact between a mother and 12-year-old daughter does not in any way indicate that affection is missing; as a baby, Takisha was undoubtedly cuddled and held on the laps of numerous adults. But hugging in front of strangers is not commonly done.

Finally, criticism of one's mother is unacceptable in its overt form, in both black and Hispanic lower income life. This is such a powerful tool for insult and metaphor that it has become transmuted into an art form in ghetto life: games such as "playing the dozens" are based on insults to another's mother. The most penetrating attack on another person's integrity comes through insulting his or her mother. In the black community, for a child to acquiesce in criticism of his or her mother is called "flying in the face of God." It defies the most powerful of cultural taboos, and can be harmful to subject and object. It is inappropriate for an adult authority figure to give a child permission to express anger toward the mother. In some belief systems, anger can harm the mother and in some cases even cause her death. Nor is depression always the obverse side of object-related anger; in this particular case, a child is trapped in an impossible situation, and this is reason enough for her dysphoria.

Treatment Plan

This particular case calls for involving the mother in a collaborative role in treatment planning. From a structural viewpoint, the mother's authority should be reinforced and redirected, not undermined. There is no reason to think the underpinnings of this case are psychodynamic conflict between mother and daughter; it is rather a matter of reality needs, cultural expectations, and the daughter's approaching the age of puberty when the burdens are becoming overwhelming.

. . . The therapist cannot and should not remove the parental role in a family where this is necessary for survival. Rather, the therapist helps redistribute the burden by alerting the family to alternative resources. In Takisha's case, the best therapeutic option is to work with the mother in solving the problem. Mrs. Landry realizes her daughter has no life; she just cannot see her way out of the situation. The therapist works with the mother and children to draw on the social network of available helpers. A relative, neighbor, or friend, perhaps available before but unsolicited, is now asked to help out. If necessary, the family's pastor and church are enlisted. The therapist works with the school to assign special help, perhaps a tutor. A specified amount of time is set aside for Takisha to do her homework, and a specified number of hours to spend on her own or with friends. The younger children are assigned tasks. The therapist praises Mrs. Landry for her hard work in keeping the family together—it is legitimate praise—joins with Takisha in admiring her mother, and joins with the mother in admiring Takisha's contribution to the family. Finally, since Takisha is nearing puberty, the therapist may give the mother instruction and reading materials so she can share with Takisha the functional aspects of menstruation and prepare her for her approaching role as a woman. In this process the mother's directive role is reinforced, mother-daughter bonding is reinforced, and Takisha is endowed with a more adult female identity that will legitimate and ease her needed role as a caregiver to the young.

Thinking About the Case

Depression is, by far, the most common psychological problem of adolescence. Takisha exhibited its most prominent symptoms, dejected mood and lack of pleasure in previously enjoyed activities (called "anhedonia"), as well as decreased concentration, lethargy, and declining school performance.

This case illustrates the importance of considering the context in which a disorder is manifested, both in terms of understanding the causes of the disorder and in planning treatment. Models of mental illness are not culture-free. Freud's view of neurosis developed out of his experiences with middle-class women in late nineteenth-century Vienna. Skinner's view that reinforcement is the primary (if not only) factor in the development and maintenance of behavior comes out of the radical environmentalism of mid-twentieth-century America. The current emphasis on biological bases of behavioral disorders is, no doubt, related to technological developments in brain-imaging equipment as well as to ongoing turf battles between the medical establishment and non-medical mental health practitioners. In attempting to understand any individual case, it is useful to be aware of one's own biases and to keep an open mind with respect to alternative perspectives. The perspective of the patient (in medical terminology) or client (in non-medical language) is particularly important. Studies indicate that feeling understood may be the primary feature of a successful therapeutic relationship. Interventions which are based on models that are substantially different from that of the person being treated are unlikely to be successful.

Questions to Consider

1. If you have encountered Martin Seligman's Learned Helplessness model of depression in your text or lectures, what might it say about Takisha's problems?

2. Does this case make an argument for matching patients and therapists along cultural dimensions? Why or why not? What about same sex versus opposite sex therapist/patient matches? Are the arguments the same?

3. Suicide is the third leading cause of death among adolescents (behind accidents and homicides). But the rate is substantially lower for African Americans than for Caucasians. Why might this be so? There is also a difference between males and females, with males completing suicide more than twice as often as females. Why might this be so?

4. The rate of suicide in adolescents has increased over 200 percent since the 1950s? Why might this be so? What could be done about this?

16

——◀o▶——

BIPOLAR DISORDER:
THE CASE OF NOREEN W.

THE CASE REPORTED HERE is more than twenty years old. While it had an eventually positive outcome, years of the patient's life were consumed by her illness. Had she been diagnosed today, her prognosis would be greatly improved. This case illustrates both changes in treatment and the vagaries of diagnostic fads and fashions.

Noreen was nineteen years old when she first became a resident of the state hospital. As it turned out, she was to live there, off and on, for over seven years. Her first admission was occasioned by an episode in which she was discovered dancing naked outside the church where her parents had been founding members. Had she been first spotted by church members, she would have been taken home where her parents would have tried, no doubt unsuccessfully, to calm her, to get her to eat something or to rest. Instead, she was noticed by a police officer cruising by. He took her to the hospital for evaluation, and she was admitted that same day.

During the evaluation, Noreen spoke rapidly, shifting topics every few sentences, seemingly unable to maintain a single stream of thought. Her mood was labile, ranging from laughter to agitation to anger. One moment she would be shouting obscenities at the admissions officer, the next she would be seductively pleading with him to take her to his home. She was unable to sit still. She paced about the interview room and at one point suddenly burst into song, causing even the doctor to break into a giggle. Noreen told the doctor that she was planning a career on the stage. She said that her family did not understand her, that they were plotting to keep her prisoner so that she could not go to New York as she had planned.

Noreen's parents provided additional data when they arrived at the hospital a few hours after Noreen's admission. Apparently, she had been a model youngster, quiet and well behaved until about fourteen months previously. She began to develop a certain moodiness that her parents found distressing, but thought was probably typical of her age. At times she was withdrawn and listless, at others more outgoing than usual, seemingly tirelessly engaged in countless school and church-related activities.

Of more concern to her parents was her developing interest in young men. From time to time, she seemed especially keen on getting male attention, and there had been frequent arguments of late about what she wore and how she behaved in public. Since the church the family belonged to was quite conservative, her flirting was particularly embarrassing for the W.'s. They could also ill afford the money she spent on clothes. She had even "borrowed" her mother's credit card and come back from the store with over five hundred dollars worth of clothing, most of it entirely inappropriate for her to wear. Mrs. W. was able to return the clothes, although not without difficulty.

The W.'s were entirely at their wits' end. They had been told by their minister that Noreen was possessed by the devil, and the congregation had been praying for her regularly for some months. Everybody's patience was running thin, and Noreen was in danger of being removed from the congregation which would, in essence, mean that she would be disowned by her family.

Mr. and Mrs. W. were quite wary of the hospital. They considered Noreen's problem to be a spiritual one, not a medical one. They did not wish her to have intimate contact with the secular world. Besides, then as now, state hospital admission carried with it a permanent stigma. Still, they were exhausted and fresh out of ideas about how to contain, let alone help, Noreen. They were even a bit afraid of her, they admitted reluctantly. Twice recently she had tried to hit her mother, and her father had to physically intervene.

Noreen's diagnosis on admission was schizophrenia, paranoid type. Her anger, her disorganization, the inappropriateness of her emotions, and the apparent presence of delusional ideas all contributed to this formulation. Indeed, the great majority of patients admitted to the state hospital in those years were diagnosed with schizophrenia.

Noreen was treated with an antipsychotic medication, and after a couple of weeks, she seemed more like her quiet, compliant self. She appeared genuinely embarrassed and contrite about her inappropriate behavior. She felt so ashamed that she did not know how she would be able to return to her community and face her family, friends, and neighbors. Gradually, over the course of the next few weeks, she fell into a depression, which seemed to the hospital staff to be a reaction to her previously psychotic behavior. She cried frequently and was full of self-recrimination and remorse.

The hospital had a full working farm at which she could spend some time, a pool and bowling alley, a hairdresser, a canteen, a used clothes center, occupational therapy, and movies. Noreen was so immobilized by guilt and shame that she was unable to make much use of the hospital's activities. Staff had to lock her out of the dormitory in the morning and press her to do even the most mundane of personal chores for herself, like showering and dressing.

Gradually, over the next several months with a compassionate thera-pist and support from other staff, Noreen's depression lifted. As her psychotic thinking seemed to be under control, Noreen was discharged to her family's care. They, however, were hesitant to take her back. Without her, their home life had returned to some semblance of normal-ity, and they were just beginning to overcome the discomfort they felt around the minister and others in the church congregation who had seemed silently to blame them for Noreen's bizarre behavior. They had seen little of her while she had been hospitalized since the staff felt that their visits were potentially upsetting to her, and they had had virtually no contact with her doctor, her therapist, or others involved with her care. They didn't know what her diagnosis was or what they could do to prevent her from having further difficulties.

To make matters worse, the Noreen they were presented with was a far cry from the Noreen they had raised. This Noreen was twenty pounds heavier, moved slowly, and seemed uncharacteristically subdued and tentative. Still, she was docile and seemingly eager to do anything she could to regain their trust and respect.

When she left the hospital, Noreen was scheduled for a visit to the local outpatient mental health center one month after her discharge and given a month's supply of medication. However, within a week Noreen had stopped taking her medication. She felt it made her sleepy and heavy and fuzzy in the head. She had only taken it in the hospital because she had had no choice. Her parents agreed with her decision—the side effects of the medication were all too apparent, while the benefits, if there were any, were subtle and harder for them to detect. They felt that, with their support and that of the congregation, Noreen would turn over a new leaf. The church was going to give her one more chance, and Noreen was determined to use it well.

All did go well, for a while. About six months after her discharge, Noreen was readmitted, this time having cut her wrists in an attempt to kill herself. At the admission interview, Noreen was nearly mute. She did convey that she believed herself to be damned by God for sins too numer-ous and too horrendous to recount. She heard God's voice telling her that she had to die by her own hand as expiation. In this way, she could keep her family safe from harm.

Safe in the hospital, away from the judgmental eyes of family and friends, and placed on an antidepressant medication, along with the antipsychotic that had been prescribed during her first hospitalization, Noreen gradually recovered from this episode. Again, she was returned home, this time more demoralized and doubtful of her chances to suc-ceed than before.

Over the next several years, this pattern was repeated five more times. Sometimes Noreen was suicidally depressed, sometimes she was filled with bizarre and grandiose plans. There were times in between when she seemed like her old self, but these were fleeting. Always, she was diag-nosed, with hardly a second thought, as having schizophrenia—until her seventh hospitalization.

During the years that Noreen was in care, standards for diagnosing schizophrenia had gradually changed. It had been known for some time that schizophrenia was diagnosed far more often in the United States than in Western European nations where patients with similar symptoms were being diagnosed as having affective disorders: depression or bipolar disorder (then known as manic-depressive illness). In the state hospital where Noreen was being treated, psychiatric interns were being trained in the admissions unit. Their lack of experience and expertise was bal-anced by their knowledge of the most current research findings and by their capacity for viewing problems with few preconceptions. One of these young interns suggested that perhaps Noreen really had manic-depression and might benefit from lithium carbonate—a relatively new medication that was proving itself to be helpful specifically for this disor-der. As you might have guessed by now, he was right. When Noreen was treated with lithium at the proper dose (as measured by blood levels), her mood stabilized, her delusional ideas subsided, and her behavior returned to normal. More important, the lithium had a prophylactic effect: it prevented further episodes of either mania or depression.

It took several more years for Noreen to really recover. Once, she stopped taking her lithium to see what would happen—what happened was a manic episode. This proved to her and to her family that she really did need the medicine. She stayed in therapy for some time, trying to work through what the illness had done to her life. She had virtually lost seven years. Socially, academically, and psychologically, she had fallen behind her peers. She felt she had to prove herself to everyone, but the illness had eroded her confidence that she could succeed at anything. She kept worrying that she would get sick again. She had been told that stress could precipitate an episode, even with the lithium, so she wasn't sure what she could attempt and what she shouldn't try.

Still, as they say, time heals. As Noreen went through the subsequent years, without serious setbacks, she gradually regained her confidence as she gained the respect of those around her.

Thinking About the Case

A patient like Noreen would be treated much differently today than she was twenty years ago. Now, the diagnosis of bipolar disorder, once called manic-depression, would likely be made much more quickly. While a manic episode and an acute episode of schizophrenia share may features—among them delusional thinking, grandiose ideas, possible hal-lucinations, inappropriate emotions, particularly irritability, pressured or rambling speech, and distractibility—clinicians are far more sensitive to the timing of psychotic episodes, and the individual's level of functioning in between in making diagnoses. Noreen's alternating periods of manic elation with profound depression are consistent with a diagnosis of bipolar disorder. An individual with schizophrenia would be less likely to experience such marked shifts in mood, and would be likely to continue to have some symptoms, even between acute episodes.

Of course, even a diagnosis of bipolar disorder is not always clear. Some individuals have very mild depressions or manic episodes, so that the cycling of mood is not always readily apparent. Still others seem to have genuinely schizophrenic symptoms, even between episodes. For these we have the diagnosis "schizoaffective," referring to a disorder midway between bipolar disorder and schizophrenia.

Despite our advances in diagnostic clarity, we still get "stuck" in diagnostic ruts from time to time—a diagnosis once made is unlikely to be changed even in the face of new data. We simply organize the data differently now than we did twenty years ago. We will organize it in yet a different way twenty years hence.

The role of the state hospital has changed enormously in these last twenty years. When Noreen was ill, state hospital residence for long periods, sometimes life-long, was the norm for young people who developed serious mental illness. We had far fewer effective treatments and a dearth of supervised therapeutic living environments in the community. Now, Noreen would be treated episodically in the psychiatric unit of a full-service hospital. Her stays would likely be fairly brief, a few weeks at most, while medication was stabilized. At discharge she would have other options besides returning home to her family. These would include group homes and supervised apartment living. Much of her therapy would take place on an outpatient basis.

Deinstitutionalization, the movement responsible for these changes, has not been without its drawbacks. A substantial percentage of the homeless population suffers from serious and persistent mental illness. This group remains on the street because under the law, they can not be hospitalized against their will unless they represent an immediate danger to themselves or others. Community mental health facilities are neither plentiful nor aggressive in reaching out to those who do not seek treatment on their own. Many patients who have been discharged from inpatient care "fall through the cracks" once they are on their own. They fail to keep their appointments, stop taking their medications, and drift onto the streets, or into harm's way. Still, the development of community-based alternatives to inpatient treatment allows newly-diagnosed patients to engage in treatment without shredding the fabric of their lives. Social connections and skills in community living can be better preserved.

Another way in which modern treatment focuses on preserving natural supports involves viewing families as partners in treatment. Today, Noreen's parents would be provided with information about her diagnosis and treatment. They would be invited to treatment planning meetings. They might be referred to a family education or support group for additional help. State hospital treatment tended to isolate and stigmatize families, often leading to their withdrawal from the treatment system and from their loved one who was ill. Families still sometimes complain about lack of communication with mental health professionals and about insensitive clinicians who make them feel guilty and incompetent, but these complaints have diminished greatly in recent years.

Questions to Consider

1. Imagine yourself as Noreen's younger sister or brother. What effect do you think her abnormal behavior would have on your life as a preteen, a teenager, and as a young adult? What feelings might you have about her? About yourself?

2. Some patients with bipolar disorder are resistant to taking medication that controls their abnormal moods. Aside from the possible presence of distressing side effects, what are some other reasons why this might be so?

3. Psychoanalytic explanations for bipolar disorder suggest that manic episodes constitute a defense against depression. What sorts of data might help you decide whether this hypothesis is true?

4. Many people with bipolar disorder are treated, like Noreen was, involuntarily. In trying to balance individual civil liberties, protection of people who are not thinking clearly, and society's right to be protected from potentially harmful people, what criteria do you think should be met before a person could legally be treated against his or her will?

17

——◀◦▶——

Many people have some change in mood and behavior during the winter months. We tend to eat and sleep more, to exercise less, and to feel sluggish and weighed down. For some, these charges are abnormally severe. The DSM-IV recognizes the reality of what has come to be called "seasonal affective disorder" (SAD) by allowing mood disorders to be described with the specifier "with seasonal pattern."

Dr. Norman Rosenthal, a psychiatrist at the National Institute of Mental Health in Washington, D.C., has written a book called Winter Blues: Seasonal Affective Disorder — What It Is and How to Overcome It *(New York: Guilford, 1993). In this reading, from* The Harvard Mental Health Letter *he outlines what is known about why SAD occurs.*

LIGHT AND BIOLOGICAL
RHYTHMS IN PSYCHIATRY

Norman E. Rosenthal

ABOUT 20 YEARS AGO, researchers began to suggest that disturbances in biological rhythms might be a cause of human psychiatric disorders, especially those of mood. Since that time, understanding of the subject has advanced greatly, especially with the discovery of seasonal affective disorder (SAD), a type of depression that occurs in winter and responds to treatment with bright light.

Mood is affected by two types of biological rhythm, the circadian and the seasonal. In people isolated from environmental cues, circadian cycles run about 24.5 hours; exposure to normal daylight and darkness sets them at 24 hours. The circadian process most thoroughly studied in human beings involves the secretion of the hormone melatonin by the pineal gland, at the base of the brain. This gland is controlled by the suprachiasmatic nuclei (SCN) of the hypothalamus, a region of the brain that serves as the body's clock. Nerves lead directly from the retina of the eye to this region. Melatonin secretion occurs mainly at night, and sufficiently bright light suppresses it. Depending on the time of exposure, light can move the cycle of melatonin secretion and other circadian rhythms either to an earlier time (phase advance) or to a later time (phase delay). Light also affects the amount of daily change in melatonin secretion.

In organisms ranging from algae to mammals, hormone secretion and other rhythms are regulated by two internal clocks, one that marks the timing of dusk and another that marks the timing of dawn. In human beings the effects of these internal clocks are disguised by use of artificial light to extend the day. When a person is exposed to prolonged darkness, more melatonin is secreted for a longer time, body temperature declines at night, and the pattern of sleep EEG (brain waves) is altered.

The daylight tracking system governs many seasonal rhythms that serve as a cue for adaptive biological changes in animals. Melatonin secretion influences such seasonal adaptations as breeding capacity in sheep, the color of a weasel's coat, and the growth of antlers in caribou. The biological function of daylight tracking in human beings is unknown, but SAD may be one consequence of its failure. This disorder is clearly related to seasonal rhythms in animals. Like certain small mammals, people with SAD often gain weight in winter, and they sometimes say they wish they could hibernate.

My colleagues and I have effectively treated SAD by exposing patients to bright light for several hours a day. Despite this success, we have not been able to show that symptoms of SAD are related to the amount, duration, or pattern of melatonin secretion. Bright light is apparently no more effective at night than during the day, when little melatonin is secreted. The drug atenolol prevents the secretion of melatonin but usually has no effect on SAD. When melatonin is given to patients who have recovered after light treatment, they tend to oversleep and gain weight, but do not become depressed again. However, some patients given propranolol, another drug that suppresses melatonin, have improved and then become depressed again when switched to a placebo.

Off Beat

An alternative to the melatonin theory is that SAD results from abnormal delays in several circadian rhythms. If this is correct, light therapy should be effective in the early morning but not in the evening, since early morning light advances circadian rhythms and evening light only further delays them. But in most experiments light therapy works at either time. Although there is some evidence that patients with SAD have delayed circadian rhythms, depressive symptoms do not improve more in the patients who circadian rhythms change most. Nor is there any evidence that patients with SAD have unusually flat rhythms, or that their symptoms improve when the amplitude of the rhythms increases.

My colleagues and I are now exploring the effects of a winter decline in the brain's synthesis and release of the neurotransmitter serotonin. This decline occurs in most people but may be especially severe in patients with SAD. Many nerve cells that use serotonin are located in the SCN, and animal experiments suggest that bright light raises the concentration of serotonin. Patients with SAD respond abnormally to certain drugs that enhance the effects of the neurotransmitter, and bright light therapy normalizes those responses.

In many depressed people (not only those with SAD) circadian rhythms such as those governing body temperature, REM or dreaming sleep, and secretion of the adrenal hormone cortisol are abnormally advanced in relation to the timing of sleep. Some investigators have suggested that, as a result, biological processes normally confined to waking hours occur during sleep instead. If this theory is correct, it should be helpful for depressed patients to rise early so that cortisol secretion and body temperature will not start to increase before they are awake. Unfortunately, sleep deprivation seems to improve symptoms of depression only for a day or two. The same effect on circadian rhythms can be achieved without loss of sleep by going to sleep as well as waking up earlier. A few uncontrolled studies suggest that a policy of early to bed and early to rise does have some beneficial effect on depression.

The sleep-timing theory implies that non-seasonal depressions can also be treated with light therapy. Only a few experiments have tested this proposition. In one case bright white light had some effect on non-seasonal depression and dim red light had none when the treatments were administered in the evening every day for a week. Another study found that two hours of bright morning light had some effect (dim light had none) on non-seasonal depressions that had not responded to antidepressant drugs. In this study the response took several weeks, about the same time it takes for antidepressant drugs to work. Patients with SAD usually respond to light in a few days.

Shed New Light

Another disorder sometimes blamed on a mismatch between circadian rhythms and the timing of sleep is premenstrual syndrome, or late luteal phase disorder. Melatonin secretion starts early at night in women with this disorder, and light therapy seems to help some of them, although controlled studies have not been able to demonstrate the effect. But bright light may be useful in treating the disorders known as delayed sleep phase syndrome (going to sleep and waking too late) and advanced sleep phase syndrome (going to sleep and waking too early). Morning light helps patients with delayed sleep phases, and evening light (in combination with restricted morning light) helps those with advanced sleep phases. Evening light may also be useful for ordinary insomnia.

Light has been used to treat the symptoms caused by the abnormal daily schedules of jet travelers and night workers. But this can be tricky, since inappropriate timing may shift circadian rhythms in the wrong direction. Melatonin, which has different and often opposite effects on these rhythms, has been successfully used in treating jet lag. A combination of light therapy and melatonin may eventually turn out to be most effective.

The recent discoveries about circadian and seasonal rhythms have considerably improved our understanding of psychiatric disorders, and new applications are on the way; for example, understanding the genetic basis of circadian rhythms in animals may provide clues to the hereditary component of mood disorders. Much has been learned in only 15 years of research on biological rhythms, and this impressive rate of discovery should continue.

18

—————◄o►—————

People who perceive reality correctly have better mental health, right? Wrong! Dr. Lauren B. Alloy presents some fascinating findings indicating that being too accurate in your appraisal of yourself might be associated with depression. What light might this research shed on Freud's theory of psychological defenses? What implications might it have for cognitive psychotherapy?

DEPRESSIVE REALISM:
SADDER BUT WISER?

Lauren B. Alloy

IN HIS SATIRICAL WORK "The Devil's Dictionary," the 19th century American writer Ambrose Bierce defined a pessimist as "a person who sees the world as it is." The mental health professions, not endorsing this cynical wit, have usually regarded pessimism as one hallmark of a major mental disorder—depression. Many people are inclined to believe that unrealistic negative thinking is not only a symptom but a cause of depression. We have a tendency to regard people in their ordinary moods as rational information processors, relatively free of systematic bias and distorted judgments.

But Ambrose Bierce may be right. Much research suggests that when they are not depressed, people are highly vulnerable to illusions, including unrealistic optimism, overestimation of themselves, and an exaggerated sense of their capacity to control events. The same research indicates that depressed people's perceptions and judgments are often less biased.

In one of the earliest of these studies, Lyn Abramson and I asked depressed and non-depressed people to judge how much they could control the outcome of an experiment. We systematically varied the actual degree of control as well as the frequency and nature (good or bad) of the outcome. People who were not depressed tended to believe wrongly that they were responsible for good results but not for bad ones; other studies have confirmed this bias. Depressed people might have been expected to show the opposite bias, but they did not; we consistently found that they were accurate judges of their capacity to control events.

Many other studies of depressed persons—children, college students, and older adults—confirm this even-handedness. Experiments also show that depressed people are better than average at predicting events in their own lives, especially misfortunes. The subjects in most of these experiments were only moderately depressed, but it is not clear that even severely depressed people are unrealistically pessimistic. The evidence is mixed; some studies have found that even patients hospitalized for depression are quite realistic.

Social Studies

Depressive realism and non-depressive illusions are also evident in social situations. One study found that mentally healthy people and psychiatric patients who are not depressed rate their own social competence much higher than objective observers do. Depressed patients, on the other hand, agree with the observers. There is also substantial evidence that depressed people are better at evaluating the impression they make on others, and numerous studies show that depressed mothers report their children's behavior more accurately than average.

These results are provocative. They contradict both the intuitions of common sense and the theoretical assumption that mental health should be associated with a high capacity to perceive and test reality. The phenomenon of depressive realism also presents a serious challenge to cognitive theories of depression, which have become increasingly popular in the last 20 years. If depressed people already view themselves realistically, their thought patterns hardly seem to need the correction that cognitive therapists propose to supply. In fact, there is good evidence that cognitive therapy works, but it may work by training patients to construct illusions—a conclusion that cognitive therapists could find unwelcome.

The study of depressive realism may serve as a bridge between clinical and experimental psychology. Unlike, say, neuropsychologists or students of visual perception, clinical psychologists and psychiatrists have rarely studied abnormal functioning to develop theories about normal psychology. Yet an understanding of depressive realism may allow us to see the adaptive functions of optimistic bias in normal human thinking.

One clue is the discovery of situations in which depressed people are not so realistic. Studies consistently find that most people, although they succumb to optimistic illusions about themselves, are fairly unbiased in judging others. In depression it is the other way around. For example, we have found that depressed subjects are more likely to believe wrongly that others have the power to influence a good experimental outcome. In one study researchers asked college students and psychiatric patients, some depressed and others not, to say whether a roll of two dice would have a "successful" outcome—defined as a 2, 3, 4, 9, 10, 11, or 12 (a 44% chance). When subjects rolled the dice themselves, depressed people made better guesses. When experimenters rolled the dice, non-depressed subjects (both college students and psychiatric patients) guessed more accurately. Other research indicates that it is easier to recall a description of your own personality if you are depressed, but easier to recall a description of someone else's personality if you are not depressed.

A Good Judge

This difference may be important to the understanding of both depression and normal mood. One process underlying depression appears to be self-directed attention—a concern with one's own thoughts, feelings, behavior, and appearance rather than with the external world. It goes almost without saying that people are better at absorbing information about matters to which they pay close attention. Experiments show that depressed people are more highly self-focused than others, and an increase in self-directed attention reproduces many characteristic features of depression, including, naturally, the ability to give better reports about oneself. People who are not depressed make better judgments about others because they are less highly self-focused.

In an experiment testing this effect, my colleagues and I asked depressed and non-depressed subjects to judge their personal responsibility for an uncontrollable but advantageous outcome and a controllable but disappointing outcome. In ordinary conditions depression made for more accurate judgments. But when we heightened self-focus by asking subjects to face a mirror while answering the questions, people who were not depressed became better judges. We then proceeded to decrease self-focus by introducing a distraction—a recorded voice reading letters of the alphabet at random. Now depressed people became more like the others, overestimating their responsibility for uncontrollable but satisfying outcomes and underestimating their responsibility for controllable but unhappy outcomes.

Are people more realistic about themselves because the are depressed, or more vulnerable to depression because they are more realistic? Our experiments suggest that it works both ways. When we made non-depressed subjects feel temporarily depressed and depressed subjects feel temporarily elated, their susceptibility to illusions of control was reversed. But we have also found that people with a strong optimistic bias are less vulnerable to depression under stress. After performing a task designed to measure illusions of control, the college students in our experiment were asked to solve problems that had no answers. They were questioned about their mood immediately before and after the inevitable frustration and failure. At this time and a month later, they also filled out a standard checklist of depressive symptoms, the Beck Depression Inventory. The second time they also listed unfortunate experiences they had had in the previous month.

Reality Check

The students who were most realistic about their capacity for control on the original task also showed more symptoms of depression after they failed to solve the insoluble problems, and more depression after a given number of misfortunes in the following month. Students with strong illusions of control on the original task did not become more depressed when they failed to solve the problems, and they showed few signs of depression a month later even when they had been under stress. Thus depression and realism appear to be interdependent. Optimistic illusions, normal or elated mood, and a sense of well-being apparently constitute a self-perpetuating adaptive system. Its functions may include resilience under stress, heightened capacity for persistence, and decreased vulnerability to illness.

At least one clinician recognized long ago that the maladaptive features of depression might result from the loss of normal, healthy personal illusions. Sigmund Freud wrote in his famous essay, "Mourning and Melancholia":

"When in his [the depressive's] heightened self-criticism he describes himself as petty, egoistic, dishonest, lacking in independence, one whose sole aim has been to hide the weakness of his own nature, it may be so far as we know, that he has come pretty near to understanding himself; we only wonder why a man has to be ill before he can be accessible to a truth of this kind."

LANAHAN NOTES
Mood Disorders

——◄○►——

Question: What is normal sadness or elation versus depression or mania?

Many people suffer some sadness or intense elation: How do we distinguish these individuals from those who are clinically depressed or manic (mood disorder)?

Indications of a Mood Disorder:

—person's emotional reaction is greatly out of proportion to the events causing the reaction.

—person's daily functioning is impaired.

DEPRESSIVE DISORDER VS. BIPOLAR DISORDER

What's the difference between Depressive Disorder and Bipolar Disorder?

Depressive Disorder—characterized by negative changes in

Mood: sad, tearful, unable to experience pleasure

Physiology: changes in sleep patterns, appetite, weight, energy, and activity level

Cognition: diminished concentration, indecisiveness, feelings of worthlessness and guilt, and thoughts of death and suicide

Biopolar Disorder—characterized by the presence of distinct phases of mania and depression.

The manic symptoms:

abnormally elevated, expansive, or irritable mood

changes in physiology—decreased need for sleep, increased mental and physical energy

skewed cognitions—inflated self-image, unrealistic plans, poor judgment, racing thoughts, distractibility, and impulsivity

Note: It is sometimes hard to distinguish mania from schizophrenic symptoms.

DEPRESSIVE DISORDERS

The DSM-IV Categories Under Depressive Disorders:

Single episode

Recurrent: when previous episodes have existed

Dysthmia: a more chronic, but less severe form of depression that has lasted for at least two years.

Not otherwise specified, i.e., depressions that do not meet criteria for more specific syndromes.

Who Gets Major Depressive Disorder?

3–5 percent of the population

Women twice as likely as men, but considered a controversial statistic.

Causes of Major Depressive Disorder — Biopsychosocial Model

Biological contribution: genetics — depression runs in families as possible biochemical defect.

Behavioral-cognitive contribution:

1. Patients learn that they have no control over their situation, therefore they get depressed: learned helplessness theory.
2. Depressed individuals tend to have distorted thoughts (cognitions) out of sync with actual experience.

Depressed behavior may be modeled from parent.

Environmental contribution:

1. Childhood loss may predispose to adult depression.

Treatment:

Drugs that affect the brain's biochemistry can help alleviate the depressed mood:

1. Tricyclics act on the level of the neurotransmitter, serotonin
2. MAO inhibitors, though dangerous when certain foods (cheese, red wine) are consumed
3. Selective serotonin re-uptake blockers (SSRIs)

Interpersonal psychotherapy: helps the person handle relationship issues better.

Cognitive therapy: can "re-order" the client's thoughts.

Behavioral therapy: rewards clients for small, then larger positive actions, thereby giving them a gradually increasing sense of control over their situations.

Electroconvulsive therapy (ECT): sometimes used to relieve very serious depressions that cannot wait for drug and behavioral-cognitive therapies to work (sometimes several weeks).

Marital or family therapy: helpful if the depression seems to evolve more from interpersonal factors or has interpersonal effects.

Light therapy: a new therapy; has had some success with a special kind of depression:

Seasonal Affective Disorder (SAD), in which people—particularly those who live where there are fewer hours of sunlight—get depressive symptoms at certain times of the year (winter). Light therapy actually initiates a chemical change in the body.

Note on therapy evaluation: Drugs, interpersonal psychotherapy, and cognitive therapy treatments have all been shown effective in large, controlled clinical trials undertaken by NIMH.

BIPOLAR DISORDER

The Major DSM-IV Categories Under Bipolar Disorder:

Biopolar I Disorder: diagnosed when mania or both mania and depression are present.

Biopolar II Disorder: diagnosed when there are recurrent major depressive episodes interspersed with hypomanic (mildly manic) episodes.

Cyclothymia: mild mood swings

Who Gets Bipolar Disorder?

1 percent of the population
no sex difference
individuals usually in their twenties
runs in families: likely strong genetic and biochemical basis

Treatment:

Drugs

Antidepressants, anticonvulsants, and antipsychotic drugs: used to treat actual symptoms.

Lithium carbonate: can reduce the frequency and severity of mood swings, but blood levels must be closely monitored.

Psychotherapy: helps patients and families deal with the practicalities of living with bipolar disorder.

CHAPTER FIVE

Schizophrenia and Related Psychoses

————◄◦►————

Most of us rely on our ability to distinguish what is real from what is not. We know the difference between our thoughts and others' voices, between our fantasies and real lives. Only in our dreams do we get a hint of what it feels like to experience the world as a person with a psychotic condition might—as bizarre, fragmented, incomprehensible.

The disorders covered in this chapter are some, but not all, of the conditions in which the sufferer cannot, at least at times, tell what is real. He or she may hear, see, smell, touch, or taste things in the absence of appropriate sensory stimulation. Or the sufferer may have thoughts or ideas that don't match reality—perhaps the radio is sending him special messages, or maybe she thinks the psychology professor is really a CIA agent sent to spy on certain students in the class.

Historically, the psychoses have been separated diagnostically into those with known organic origins from those without. Drug abuse, brain injury, and various medical conditions can induce psychotic symptoms. A case later in the book (#29) describes a young man who developed a brief psychosis as a consequence of drug use. But these syndromes are not the focus of this chapter. Instead, we deal here with the group of disorders that used to be called the "functional psychoses," meaning that specific organic origins could not be found. Included are schizophrenia as well as "functional" delusional disorders.

Schizophrenia is by far the most disabling, and most stigmatizing of all the psychological disorders. People think of schizophrenia as being "split personality" which it is not. Return to an earlier reading (#12) for a description of dissociative identity disorder, previously called multiple personality disorder—that is "split personality." People think of individuals with schizophrenia as being invariably dangerous, which they are not. In fact, they are more likely to be victimized than victimizer. People think of schizophrenia as being caused by faulty parenting, which it is not. While the environment (not just the parents) can play a role in the timing and prognosis of psychotic episodes, biochemical factors have also been implicated in the etiology of the disease. People think of schizophrenia as being rare, which it is not. Instead, schizophrenia is one of the most common and expensive of all psychological disorders. It is diagnosed in as many as one out of every hundred Americans (but striking twice as often in Scandinavia and four times as often in western Ireland, for reasons as yet unknown). This means that over two million people in the United States are diagnosed with schizophrenia, at a cost to society estimated between ten and twenty billion dollars a year in treatment costs, disability and welfare payments, and lost wages. And, since schizophrenia tends to strike in late adolescence or early young adulthood, the emotional costs to individuals and families who must give up or at least adjust their hopes, dreams, and aspirations are incalculable.

In this chapter, we include two cases. The first looks at the course of treatment for a young man who developed fairly typical symptoms of schizophrenia. The second case is fascinating in that a man's longstanding delusional disorder is only discovered and diagnosed in the context of his daughter's mental health treatment.

We have also included two readings. The first is a first-person account, originally published in the prestigious *Schizophrenia Bulletin*. In it, a patient describes how she handles the symptoms of her illness. Only lately have the views and insights of patients been sought by the treatment community as rehabilitation is coming to be viewed as a collaborative process rather than as a medical procedure that one person performs on another. The second reading is a brief report by researcher Courtenay Harding, whose work on the long-term outcome of schizophrenia has helped to dispel one other myth about schizophrenia—namely that its course is inevitably downhill. The real prognosis is substantially more hopeful than that.

19

————◄o►————

SCHIZOPHRENIA IN A YOUNG ADULT:
THE CASE OF STEVE M.

STEVE M.'S TROUBLES BEGAN when he was a nineteen-year-old college freshman. He was a handsome and engaging young man, the second in a family of four boys. Steve's high school career had been, by any measure, successful and satisfying. He had earned letters in both football and track, had served as co-editor of the student newspaper, and had been elected president of his senior class. With high grades and SAT scores, Steve earned a place in one of the finest colleges.

Still, Steve's early life was not without tragedy. When he was four, his mother, who had had a long history of troubled behavior, committed suicide by hanging herself in the attic. Only Steve and his younger brothers were home at the time, and they found her body when they woke up from their afternoon nap. Steve's father, an attorney, struggled valiantly to provide both financially and emotionally for his traumatized sons, but, in truth, he had been severely shaken himself. Already accustomed to a cocktail in the evening after work, he began to drink more heavily after the loss of his wife and, even though he remarried four years later, he became a quiet, withdrawn alcoholic. His new wife found herself in complete charge of the household and threw herself into the task with diligence. She was determined to make up to the children and their father for the loss the family had incurred. She believed firmly that with devotion and time, she could heal the wounds. Sure enough, the children seemed to thrive under her loving and watchful eye. She was impressed by how they seemed to bounce back from the loss of their mother. If their father was still distant and uninvolved, at least he worked steadily and provided an income which allowed her to tend to the needs of the family. Mr. M. clearly loved the children, but he interacted with them only intermittently, and then with wry, intellectualized banter.

Steve did well the first semester at college, although he came home frequently to visit his girlfriend and to see his parents. He wished he could find a way to relate more genuinely to his father, but had long since accepted that this was unlikely to happen. Occasionally they fished together, or discussed the course material he was studying in philosophy, but for emotional support he always went to his stepmother.

At the beginning of the second semester, Steve's girlfriend, with whom he had been going steady since junior year of high school, broke up with him. He appeared to take the news reasonably well and began staying at school on weekends in order to begin to date. Still, in private, he found himself lonely and miserable. He really didn't know how to ask women out and didn't seem to have the knack for flirting or reading their nonverbal signals.

One day, while studying in his room, Steve had a strange sensation. He felt an ominous presence of some sort, a premonition that something dangerous was afoot. The feeling stayed with him for some hours and then it passed, but a few days later, in the cafeteria, he felt it again. This time, he looked around, and saw a knot of students across the room who seemed to be looking at him and smiling. He thought he heard one of them say, "he's queer." He couldn't understand why they would think such a thing about him—they didn't even know him. Visibly upset, he left quickly and went back to his room.

Later that week, in psychology class, his professor referred to a laboratory experiment, and suddenly Steve had a flash of insight. He understood that he, himself, was the subject of the experiment, and that his professor was trying to warn him that he was in danger. Still, he didn't know what kind of experiment he was in, nor why he had been chosen. As the class conversation continued, he began to detect hidden meaning in the remarks of the male students. The female students seemed blithely unaware of the plot against him.

Over the next week, Steve became increasingly vigilant, and increasingly agitated. He heard hints about the experiment in the songs broadcast by the student radio station. His preoccupation was so severe that he was unable to study effectively. His sleep was fitful and restless. His appetite was nonexistent—in truth, he was afraid to eat in the cafeteria, because he was beginning to feel that the food he was served had been laced with chemicals related to the experiment. He noticed that people would invariably stop what they were doing and give him strange looks as he passed them in the hall. Even his good friends began to shun him. Sometimes, in desperation, he tried to ask for help by code—using the first letter of each word he said to mean something else, but the few people he still trusted didn't seem to understand.

Finally, terrified and desperate, he decided to contact the professor who had tried to warn him. He looked up his home address in the campus directory and then, at two A.M., when no one would suspect him of being out, he broke into the professor's bedroom crying and pleading for help. The professor, who couldn't understand anything Steve was saying, was badly frightened. While trying to calm Steve, he called the campus police who took Steve to the emergency room of the local hospital for a psychiatric evaluation. Within hours, Steve was admitted to the hospital's psychiatric wing where he was administered a sedative, so that he could get some rest, and an antipsychotic medication, which, it was hoped, would lessen his delusions.

Steve was hospitalized for two-and-a-half weeks. During that time he was given medication on a daily basis. He also participated in individual therapy and group therapy. In these settings he discussed his loneliness and his grief at losing his girlfriend. He developed some plans for meeting girls and did some role playing to rehearse how he might start conversations. At the same time, his parents had a consultation with the hospital social worker, who provided a tentative diagnosis—schizophreniform disorder. This meant that Steve had a psychotic break that might signal the beginning of schizophrenia, but only time would tell. They had many questions about whether Steve should return to school, how long he would have to take medication, and what his prognosis might be, and the social worker tried to answer them as best he could. Still, they felt his answers had been frighteningly vague.

Gradually, Steve's delusions began to recede. His mood brightened and he started to take better care of himself. By the end of his hospitalization, he wondered where he could have gotten all those "crazy ideas." He was embarrassed, but eager to return to school and pick up where he'd left off. Despite the recommendation of the treatment team that he take a few courses at first rather than a full load, Steve chose to resume his formerly busy schedule. He did agree, however, to continue taking the medication to treat the chemical imbalance he was told he had, despite the fact that it made him feel sleepy and somewhat "fuzzy" in the head. He also agreed to attend follow-up appointments at the local mental health clinic.

As it happens, Steve didn't keep his promises for long. He did return to school and tried hard to do what he had practiced in the hospital. He was finding it difficult, though, particularly since everyone appeared to know he had been in the psychiatric wing. His concentration seemed impaired, and he found that he had trouble following conversations. At the end of each day he was exhausted, and socializing seemed more trouble than it was worth.

He didn't like going to the mental health center, either. The waiting room was full of people who seemed "out of it." Most of them were a lot older than he was, too. The psychiatrist spent only a couple of minutes with him, asking him the same questions each time. She seemed pleasant enough but, in truth, not very interested. Steve didn't see why he had to take medicine that made him feel worse than he felt normally, nor why he had to go to a place where nothing therapeutic seemed to happen. After two months he stopped doing either, although he felt it best not to tell his parents about his decision. He knew they would worry, but he felt sure he could "make it" on his own.

For the next few weeks, Steve felt substantially better. His mind felt clearer and he had a lot more energy. His parents commented on how good he looked when they saw him, which wasn't frequently since he was determined to develop a social life at school. He pushed himself hard to ask young women out, and he had a date virtually every other night. This meant a lot of late night study sessions, since he wasn't willing to give up the high grades he was used to.

One evening a few months later, while studying, Steve again felt the familiar feeling of foreboding. This time, he distinctly heard someone say, "you think you've fooled us. You're queer." He looked around, but he was alone. He opened the door to the hall, but it, too, looked empty. From the other end of the hall, he heard, "he's a pig, look at him," but again, no one was there. Suddenly, he realized that the experiment he had feared had occurred while he was in the hospital. A transmitter had been implanted in his head through which he was receiving these messages. Someone wanted to drive him crazy!

Without waiting to put on shoes or socks, Steve ran out of the dormitory and down the street. He planned to confront the doctors in the hospital about what they had done. He ran the two miles to the hospital, threw open the emergency room doors, and tackled the first man in a lab coat he saw. Within an hour he was readmitted to the psychiatric wing.

Steve's diagnosis was changed to paranoid schizophrenia. This time it took longer for the voices and the delusions to recede. Larger doses of medication were needed. When he began to feel better, the doctor cautioned him that he had a formidable illness, a "chemical imbalance in the brain," and that his knowledgeable cooperation with treatment was essential to his remaining well. Rather than return to school immediately, he was advised to attend a day treatment center at the hospital for a few months.

Steve was badly shaken. He didn't know what he had done wrong. He couldn't really believe that there was something the matter with his brain. The idea that he couldn't trust his ears or his thoughts was terrifying. Besides, he retained a lingering fear that the plot was real and the doctors were lying to him. Still, his mother had been dreadfully ill. Maybe he was destined to follow in her footsteps. This was the most frightening thought of all.

It is now five years later. Steve has been hospitalized three more times. Each time he had stopped his medication, twice believing himself well and once, just tired of the whole thing. In between hospitalizations, he has spent some time in the day treatment program and some time taking classes at college. He still struggles with determining what is real and what is not, but he has learned that he can check this out with people he trusts, principally his stepmother, brother, and father. His self-esteem has been badly shaken, and he no longer has a clear idea what he might reasonably hope to accomplish in his life. Some days, just getting dressed and out of his apartment (which he now shares with two other young men from the day treatment program) is a monumental achievement.

Nonetheless, some gains have been made. Steve has developed a long-term therapy relationship with a psychologist from the clinic who he sees once a week (in addition to his medication checks with the psychiatrist). Together they confront the very real challenges that his illness and the stigma attached to it pose. He is learning to set short-term goals and to modify his expectations without altogether giving up hope. His parents, through the parent-support group they have joined, are learning to do the same. Steve has learned, through trial and error, that he needs the medication to keep the irrational ideas and the voices at bay. He doesn't like the side effects of muscle stiffness and diminished clarity of thinking, but he has decided that they are the lesser of two evils. The day treatment program provides practice in socializing and classes in stress management and in independent living. He doesn't feel he really belongs there, but he doesn't feel at home on campus either. His life, though nothing like what he and his family had envisioned for him a decade before, holds possibilities for mastery and satisfaction. Still, the illusion of security is gone forever.

Thinking About the Case

Approximately one out of every hundred persons develops schizophrenia in which the core features include loss of contact with reality as manifested by delusions, hallucinations, or gross disorganization, as well as severe dysfunction in virtually all areas of life. Like Steve, most of the sufferers become ill when they are in their late adolescent or young adult years. While the illness strikes men and women equally as often, women tend to develop the disorder, on average, ten years later than men. Schizophrenia is known in all cultures throughout the world and has been around for as long as we have written records available. Interestingly, its prognosis is somewhat better in less developed cultures than in the Western world.

Just fifty years ago, Steve might have spent the majority of his adult life in a mental hospital. As a result of more effective treatment methods and a treatment philosophy that emphasizes community-based care, most people with schizophrenia can now expect to spend only a small fraction of their time in inpatient care. A host of outpatient services have been designed to assist people with major mental illnesses to live as independently as possible. These include supervised housing alternatives, like community residences that might house eight or more recovering people in a house supervised around the clock by trained counselors, or smaller apartments like the one Steve lived in, with counselors who drop by on a regular basis and are available by phone anytime. Vocational training programs, shared jobs, special college programs, and sheltered workshops (which provide fairly simple, repetitive tasks and a very low wage) are designed to offer a range of occupational alternatives, depending upon the individual's ability to concentrate and motivation to work. Various psychotherapies, including individual, group, and family treatment are also part of most treatment plans. But the backbone of the plan, for the great majority of sufferers, is medication. While not without side effects, the antipsychotic medications, of which there are more than two dozen, provide a level of control over symptoms that is not otherwise available. Most patients could not function nearly as well, if at all, without them. New antipsychotic medicines are constantly under development and coming to market. And most patients need to take them for many years because, as Steve discovered, symptoms generally return when medication is stopped.

The short-term prognosis for schizophrenia is quite variable, but generally fairly grave. While some people seem to recover uneventfully, most, like Steve, find that their lives are profoundly changed. The cognitive and social deficits associated with schizophrenia make one's progress through the life tasks of early adulthood very challenging. For example, the inability to filter out extraneous stimuli makes attending to social or occupational tasks exceedingly difficult. Residual paranoia and distrust can interfere with developing relationships. The stigma and assault on one's sense of self engendered by having experienced a psychotic episode can erode a person's ability to function independently. Multiple hospitalizations are common, and goals generally need to be revised downward.

Interestingly, data are emerging to suggest that the long-term prognosis (twenty years and more) might be substantially better. Several studies, carried out in different countries, have indicated that well over half of study subjects who had been gravely ill with schizophrenia as young adults were functioning fairly well in their sixties and beyond. Many of these subjects had experienced prolonged hospitalizations which could be expected to further impair their ability to function in the community, but even these seemed to fare well in their later years. Still, schizophrenia is one of the most seriously disabling of all psychiatric conditions. Wasting thousands of lives and costing millions of dollars each year in lost wages and treatment costs, it is worthy of substantial attention in terms of public health research priorities.

Questions to Consider

1. What were the possible contributions of nature and nurture to the development of Steve's illness?
2. What do you imagine it might be like to return to campus after

going through what Steve went through? What might you worry about? How might these worries affect your recovery prospects? What might your friends do that would be helpful to you? What could you do that would be helpful to yourself?

3. What hypotheses might you entertain to explain why the short-term prognosis for schizophrenia is far worse than the long-term prognosis? Can you design a study or experiment that could test one or more of your ideas?

4. What are some reasons why the age of risk of developing schizophrenia is different for women than for men? Consider both biological and social possibilities.

5. While schizophrenia is distributed equitably by gender, the same is not true for social class. Schizophrenia tends to be diagnosed far more often in the lower social classes than in the upper ones. Why might this be so?

20

————◄○►————

DELUSIONAL DISORDER:
THE CASE OF MR. P.

LIFE IS SOMETIMES NOT what it seems. This is certainly the case for delusional patients. They have sensations or ideas that to them seem perfectly real, but for us, their ideas have only the slightest relationship to reality. In their work, therapists and researchers may also confront a surprising reality from time to time. Consider the case of Mr. P. and his daughter, Sarah, in which the patient is not the person who is ill.

Sarah was fifteen when she was brought to the mental health clinic by her parents, Mr. and Mrs. P. Apparently, she had been running away from home every few months for the past year and a half. Her parents were totally puzzled as Sarah had been a sweet and obedient child, apparently well-adjusted in every way. Even now, she continued to do well in school, had many friends, and seemed generally happy, but still she ran away—sometimes to friends' houses, sometimes to her aunt's in a neighboring state, sometimes to hide in the woods until hunger over-took her and she came home again.

Sarah was not able to shed much light on her motives for running away. She just wasn't comfortable at home, she said, but she couldn't say why. She denied the presence of family conflict or abuse. A mental status examination and clinical interview revealed no evidence of depression, psychosis, or any other mental disorder. The therapist, nonetheless, asked Sarah to return to the clinic for a few more counseling sessions as clearly something was going on. She agreed.

Because her mother was working, Sarah's father brought her to the next session. After another pleasant, but unilluminating hour with Sarah, the therapist spoke with Mr. P., to see if he might have any insight into Sarah's problem.

Serendipity plays an occasional role in psychotherapy. In this case, Sarah's "problem" became more defined when the therapist, thinking only to make a connection with Mr. P., happened to ask him something about his job. He replied that he had recently changed jobs. Why? Well, apparently he had had some trouble at his previous place of employment where he had worked for eighteen years. He had left that job because of some conflict with the union leadership there. The conflict had been so severe, he reported, that union officials were still persecuting him. In fact, he whispered, they had implanted a minute radio receiver in his head through which they transmitted all manner of disgusting messages to him. Specifically, these messages told him to sexually molest various women, including his daughter.

Mr. P. became increasingly agitated as he spoke. The union had surrounded him with agents that tempted him. For example, a secretary at work persistently leaned over the filing cabinet in a way that suggested he was supposed to rape her. He, however, was onto their game and had resisted all of their efforts to get him to engage in these despicable behaviors. They had targeted him years ago, but he had been strong enough to ignore their behavior and to continue to work until he was able to get a new job at the same rate of pay. After all, he had a family to support.

Needless to say, the therapist was taken aback by Mr. P.'s ideas. When Mrs. P. brought Sarah in for the next session, the therapist told her what her husband had said and was surprised to find that she knew all about his delusions. She reported that she had long since stopped trying to talk him out of them, since her experience had been that he had only gotten more agitated when they discussed it. It was better, she had discovered, to gently change the subject after sympathizing with how difficult the situation must be for him. She reported that he had never behaved inappropriately, had never missed work, had never even spoken about his odd ideas to anyone other than to herself as far as she knew.

Mrs. P. and the therapist brainstormed a bit about what could be done about the situation. Sarah's discomfort at home was now totally comprehensible. They both agreed that she was probably sensing Mr. P.'s agitation, and probably even the sexual feelings he had towards her. But since he had never acted on these feelings, Sarah wasn't consciously aware of what was making her uncomfortable. The therapist advised Mrs. P. that psychotherapy was unlikely to have an impact on Mr. P.'s delusions, but that antipsychotic medication might. The problem was that since he was unaware that he was ill, he was unlikely to agree to take medication. Still, they decided to give it a try. The therapist called him back in and suggested that since Sarah's running away, combined with his new job, was clearly putting a lot of stress on him, he might want to take some medication to help him feel calmer. He seemed quite resistant, but agreed to think about it and talk it over with his wife for a week. Since Mr. P. had not acted on his delusional ideas, the therapist felt it was physically safe to let Sarah remain home while he and Mrs. P. tried to enact the treatment plan, so a session was scheduled for a few days later.

At the next session, Mrs. P. reported that her husband had continued to refuse to consider taking medicine, no matter how she had tried to convince him of its value. Since he had committed no crime and did not appear to constitute an immediate threat to anyone, involuntary treatment was not possible. Together, Mrs. P. and the therapist agreed that an alternative placement for Sarah had to be found, since she was clearly being emotionally damaged by her father's illness. Mrs. P. shared with Sarah, in the therapist's office, what she knew about Mr. P.'s illness, and the therapist filled in the gaps by explaining his diagnosis and prognosis. With her mother's help, and oddly, with her father's agreement, Sarah went to live with her mother's sister for the remainder of her high school career. She saw her parents frequently, but avoided spending time alone with her father. The family was lost to follow up, so there is no way of knowing whether Mr. P. ever received treatment or got over his bizarre ideas.

Thinking About the Case

This case presents a diagnostic puzzle. The DSM-IV criteria for delusional disorder specify that the delusion must be nonbizarre, involving situations that could occur in real life, such as being followed or deceived by a spouse. While "being poisoned" is included in the examples, Mr. P.'s conviction that an electrode had been implanted in his brain was clearly bizarre by almost any definition. On the other hand, Mr. P. did not suffer the characteristically severe and diffuse functional deficits that are typical of schizophrenia, nor the diffuse distrust and suspicion of the person with paranoid personality disorder. He seemed to be perfectly normal, except when the topic of his previous job came up. Most clinicians, I think, would diagnose him as having a delusional disorder.

Sadly, this type of problem is quite resistant to treatment. Psychotherapy generally is markedly ineffective. A good example of this can be found in a book called *The Three Christs of Ypsilanti*. The author, Martin Rokeach, a social psychologist, brought together at Ypsilanti State Hospital in Michigan three men, each of whom believed himself to be Jesus Christ. Rokeach hoped that being confronted with each other might shake the men's delusions. However, each man simply modified or held fast to his delusion. One, for example, decided that there were various levels of Christ and that he was the highest level.

Some clinicians have tried a variant of Rokeach's idea, in which they attempt to engage the patient's rational faculties to confront paradoxes between his beliefs and reality, but they have generally had quite limited success. Medications are sometimes helpful in reducing the delusional ideas, but, like Mr. P., most people with delusional disorder are reluctant to take them because they have no insight that they are ill.

Questions to Consider

1. If you had a belief system that you knew to be at extreme variance with the beliefs of your friends and family, how do you think it would affect you? What do you make of Mr. P.'s ability to behave so normally in situations in which his delusions are not activated?

2. What do you think are the ethical issues involved in talking about Mr. P. being his back to his wife and daughter? Would you have handled the case differently? How?

21

——————◄o►——————

The Schizophrenia Bulletin, *a scholarly journal published by the National Institute of Mental Health, has for some years now solicited first-person accounts from patients and family members in recognition that understanding the person is equally important to understanding the disease. In the reading that follows, we have the rare opportunity to learn firsthand what it is like to live with the symptoms of schizophrenia on a day-to-day basis. In it a woman describes how she copes with her illness. Take note of the personal strengths that she brought to bear on the challenges she faced.*

FIRST-PERSON ACCOUNT:

BEHIND THE MASK:

A FUNCTIONAL SCHIZOPHRENIC COPES

Anonymous

A LITTLE KNOWLEDGE, people say, is a dangerous thing. My problems first started when I decided to go back to college at the age of 27. My education and exposure to different lifestyles led to discontent with my life and especially my marriage. After taking a psychology course, I recognized signs of stress in myself and went for help to a school psychologist. He advised me to take some weeks away from home and consider a divorce. However, at the end of that time, I was convinced that I could not support myself alone and resigning myself to what seemed a problematic marriage; I came home in despair. It was on this ride home that I first heard messages over the car radio that I was sure were meant for me. I thought my old boyfriend was sending the messages.

That summer I had a very negative perception of my husband. In reflecting back on it, I realize that this did not have much basis in reality. There were quite a number of times that he tried positively to mend the relationship, but I didn't recognize it then. I attributed it to my state of mind. I began to relate incidents that were totally unrelated. A friend of mine talked about my neighbor suing a large company. A week later, the neighbor's daughter, who taught a summer class at college, defended the neighbor's right to sue. I thought it more than coincidence. I felt these two were part of a group of people who were probing my reactions in the process of gathering information about me. I felt that the world was beginning to revolve around me.

In the fall, I threw myself into schoolwork to drown out the unhappiness. I was taking 16 credits, working full time in my business which was a day-care center, and taking care of my children in the absence of their father. He was working out of town and came home on weekends. This load was to cause a major breakdown, though no one noticed my illness, including myself, for 9 months.

During that school term, certain remarks made by my professors led me to the conclusion that they were all working to rescue me from what they thought was an abusive marriage. And I, contrarily, was convinced that I wanted to stay married. I realized that I loved my husband and needed his love in return. This perception of what I thought was going on caused me to feel a great deal of fear and insecurity. I felt particularly influenced by a foreign language instructor. Because of my loneliness due to my negative feelings toward my husband and his absence, I had transferred my emotional feelings to this man and was prey to a full-blown infatuation which intensified into a very real moral battle within myself.

I was convinced that this professor and I had a private means of communication and, because of this, interpreted most of what he said in class as personally relating to me. Sometimes the things I heard in class were bizarre and had no relation to the class purpose. One time the professor asked the room at large, "So your husband used to be a minister?" I had not divulged that information to him, but because I had recently told my babysitter that, I felt the incident was more than coincidence. I felt that there was a large network of people finding out about me, watching me on the street for some unknown reason. This feeling of lack of privacy soon grew into thinking my house was bugged, a fear I would have off and on for the next 8 years. The bizarre and illogical statements I heard people make were later dismissed as auditory hallucinations. They seemed very real to me, however.

On one occasion, I saw a personal experience of mine written on the blackboard in French and English. I had dropped a history class because I had gone to a party instead of to a required class and so missed an important test I could not make up. All this was written on the board. I did not recognize it as a hallucination at that time. These things caused me considerable anguish, but I continued to act as normal as I could for fear that any bizarre behavior would cause me to lose my job. I did not talk about these things, so the only noticeable signs of my illness were that I became silent and withdrawn, not my usual ebullient and smiling self. I did not think I was sick, but that these things were being done to me. I was still able to function, though I remember getting lunch ready very slowly as if working in molasses, each move an effort. However, my ability to study and write were not impaired because I got A's and B's for that semester.

By Christmas I heard an actor call me a liar over the T.V., and I felt sure the media also knew about me. I was displaying considerable insecurity and fear, which caused my husband to quit his job and come home to look after me. However, my job became even more important to me then, and I continued to work though I quit college for a time. I continued to have recurring cycles of delusion and normality. I felt the language teacher was still conveying messages to me through the radio and would spend hours tuned to it. I found messages from my husband in the way things were arranged on the dresser or on the bookshelf. When I went to the store, I bought things that symbolically meant something else to me; each fruit, flavor, or color had a meaning that tied in with my delusion. For example, I would not buy Trix cereal, because it was associated with prostitution in my mind, but I bought a lot of Cheerios to make my day happier. The world of delusion soon became a world of imagined depravities that were a torment to my moralistic mind. I felt I was the only sane person in the world gone crazy.

Finally, my sleeplessness and delusions led to an inability to function at all. That spring I was supposed to go on a trip. I drove aimlessly around town, afraid to leave, calling my husband frantically and speaking of the fears that bound me. I was hospitalized for 7 days after a checkup by my doctor, and I was referred to a psychiatrist.

Though the Navane he prescribed did help me function again, and I regained my trust in people and my smile, the delusions were always in the background. My husband and children wrapped me in arms of love and acceptance, taking on household duties so I would not be stressed. I continued to hold down my job, after a short rest, but still lived in two worlds. The psychiatrist never asked me about my delusional world, so I never talked about it. Actually, the psychiatrist did not tell me the extent of my illness, only saying that I had a chemical imbalance for which I needed pills. While this gave me the confidence to resume my job and normal living, it also allowed me to believe my delusional world was real. When I finally did some research on my own about the chemical dopamine, he told me I was schizophreniform. After my second acute episode 2 years later, he told me this illness was for life. At this time I joined a very nurturing civic theater drama group. This increased my confidence and memory skills preparatory to going back to college. In the last 3 years, I have returned to college part time while working, and have been successful.

The world of delusion and symbols is as real to me as the normal world. When coincidences happen or people speak in a strange way, I am very likely to take what they say as applying to my delusional world even though I do not usually act on those delusions. Most of the time I see my delusional world superimposed on the real world. At times, the network of people who watch me seem to be benevolent. At other times, I feel controlled and manipulated by my delusion and become so afraid and tormented that I have considered suicide or running away from home to escape. I still have trouble with making up symbols that I compulsively act on to appease my inner needs. For example, when I need to be close to my grandfather, I buy blackberries.

Several years ago, I had visual images of gross, sexual, or obscene images floated in front of my eyes when I least expected them. This mortified me, especially as I thought others could see these images of mine. The experiences really unnerved me until my therapist gave me Theodore Rubin's *Compassion and Self-Hate* (1975) to read. I learned to like myself and accept myself in spite of the ugly tricks my mind plays. Now I do not claim these images—I laugh at them and they go away. They haven't bothered me much since then.

This winter, I was acutely sick for the third time with 7 sleepless nights. I continued to work even though I was convinced that my work was part of an extrasensory perception (ESP) project designed to make me a teacher of ESP. All the remarks the children and other teachers made were integrated into and reinforced by my delusion. However, I continued to behave in a very conservative and rational manner, purposely avoiding behavior that might brand me as different. The abundance of sensory input during this time made the delusions run wild and added to the cumulative effect of the delusions. I wonder now if I wouldn't have been better off to have taken time off from work and waited until the added medication took effect. Perhaps, I could have avoided the sensory input which seemed to have intensified the construction of delusions.

Now, 3 months later, I am free from the delusions for the first time in many years. I find I am able to fight the delusional thinking better by discussing it with people. It also helps me to hear other patients in my Emotions Anonymous (E.A.) group talk about their delusions, because then I realize that I am sick and not the victim of some plot. My illness has caused me to grow in my inner self to discover who I really am with the help of my therapist. There are many unsung heroes and heroines behind the scenes in this saga of mine. I have not been in this battle alone. My family and relatives have offered financial and emotional support throughout my illness. I have a widespread circle of nurturing friends in church, E.A., the civic theater, work, and college. The acceptance I have found gives me courage and fulfills my life in a way no fantasy can. When my delusions threaten to turn to paranoia, I remember my friends and dare to trust, to reach out, and to be vulnerable.

Reference

Rubin, T.I. *Compassion and Self-Hate: An Alternative to Despair.* New York: David McKay Co., Inc., 1975.

22

——————◄o►——————

Emil Kraepelin (1856–1926), a German psychiatrist frequently referred to as the "father of psychiatry," coined the first term for the syndrome we now call schizophrenia. He called it "dementia praecox" which means "premature mental deterioration." The name itself implies the prognosis; Kraepelin and virtually all clinicians who followed him felt that the illness was progressive and the outcome was almost invariably very poor, even though a few studies had questioned this assumption. However, when Dr. Courtenay M. Harding, a nurse and researcher at Yale University, and her colleagues studied a group of patients from the back wards of Vermont's only state mental hospital, her findings shook the professional community. It is now thought that the outcome of schizophrenia may be much more variable than had previously been thought. In many cases, it can be thought of as a prolonged, but not a life-long disorder. Read below and see why.

THE OUTCOME OF SCHIZOPHRENIA

Courtenay M. Harding, Ph.D.

FREDERICK L. AND CATHERINE S. are clients at a community mental health center. Mr. L., 27, now lives in a shelter for the homeless; he has had episodes of schizophrenia and alcohol abuse for ten years. Ms. S. is

32 and lives in a board-and-care home on Social Security disability payments. She has had episodes of schizophrenia for seven years and can do only occasional volunteer work. Mr. L. often fails to follow his treatment plan and take the medications prescribed for him. His clinician sees him as a dull, colorless person who will always live on the fringes of society. Ms. S.'s flamboyance and escapades have so exasperated the people caring for her that she has been diagnosed as a borderline personality.

The professionals who treat these patients doubt that they will recover or even significantly improve; they hope only for stabilization and maintenance. Yet recent long-term studies show improvement even in some schizophrenic patients who seem to be hopelessly ill. Why does clinical experience apparently contradict this research? The answer has many implications for the understanding of schizophrenia, the care of schizophrenic patients, and the training of professionals who treat them.

Clinicians see a stream of chronically ill patients who need more than antipsychotic drugs and psychosocial treatment; their lives are in total disarray. They need food, clothing, shelter, and treatment for physical illnesses. They often require help in obtaining a source of income and dealing with personal and legal problems. Many clinicians find that their caseloads are too large and their training is insufficient to deal with these patients. The paperwork is burdensome. There is no payment for extra time spent on ancillary activities. Clinicians often feel overwhelmed, and find it hard to believe that these patients could even improve, much less recover.

But the vision of clinicians is obscured by the atmosphere of constant crisis and seeming hopelessness. They are so busy that they rarely have time to think about patients they are no longer seeing. They often assume that these patients are in someone else's care or living in decrepit hotels. Recovered patients hardly ever call their former therapists and say "Hi, this is Joe. I just wanted you to know that I finally got my life together, married Jane, and found a decent job. Thanks for all the help you gave me." Working without such feedback creates a persistent bias in clinical perspective.

Over Fifty Percent Improve

The earliest studies gave a discouraging impression of the long-term outcome in schizophrenia, because they included only hospitalized patients. For a more accurate picture, researchers should follow the lives of patients both in and out of treatment. In the last two decades there have been five such studies, including more than 1300 subjects. Every study has shown that half or more of people hospitalized for chronic schizophrenia recover or significantly improve over a period of 20 years or more.

The first of these studies was conducted at Burghölzli Hospital in Zürich by Manfred Bleuler, the son of Eugen Bleuler, who gave schizophrenia its name. Bleuler chose 208 patients in 1942–43 and followed them for an average of 23 years. Fifty-three to 66 percent significantly improved or recovered; one recovery occurred after 40 years.

Luc Ciompi and Christian Muller, working at the psychiatric hospital in Lausanne, Switzerland, considered all patients ever admitted there who were over 65 by 1963. They then chose a representative sample, interviewed them, and studied their psychiatric records. It was the longest outcome study ever conducted: the average time between the first admission to the hospital and the interview was 37 years. Forty-nine to 57 percent of the former patients had recovered or significantly improved by the early 1960s.

Another study was conducted by Gerd Huber and his colleagues at the University Psychiatric Hospital in Bonn, Germany. Of 758 patients admitted from 1945 to 1959, 502 were followed for an average of 22 years. Interviews and psychiatric records indicated that 53 to 57 percent recovered or significantly improved in psychological and social functioning.

Ming Tsuang and his colleagues at the University of Iowa Psychiatric Hospital studied 186 schizophrenic patients admitted between 1934 and 1944. The average follow-up time was 35 years, and the follow-up interviews were conducted by people who did not know the original diagnoses. Forty-six percent of the patients were found to be significantly improved or recovered.

Back Wards Patients Also Improve

My colleagues and I have recently completed a study of 269 patients who once lived on the back wards of Vermont's only state mental hospital. At the time they were chosen for the study, they had been disabled for an average of 10 years and hospitalized for an average of 6 years. They were followed from the early 1950s to the early 1980s. From 1955 on, they participated in a model rehabilitation program, first in association with the hospital and then in the community as a planned deinstitutionalization effort. When they were interviewed in 1965, 70 percent lived outside the hospital, and only 10 percent had remained in the hospital for the entire decade. At that time most had some form of sheltered employment, and their care still required a heavy expenditure of time, effort, and money.

In the early 1980s researchers who did not know the original diagnoses once again interviewed the former patients and people who knew them. One hundred sixty-eight were still alive, and half to two-thirds of them were considerably improved or recovered. They had been rehospitalized an average of twice during the 30 years. Twenty-six percent were employed, 33 percent unemployed, and 26 percent retired; others were housewives or volunteer workers. Half lived in independent housing and 40 percent in boarding homes. Half were single, 19 percent married, and a quarter divorced or separated. On a scale rating psychological and social functioning, two-thirds scored at a level indicating that, although they had some mild symptoms, most untrained persons would not consider them mentally ill. Women were generally doing better than men.

Because the definition of schizophrenia current in the 1950s was broader than the one in use today, it might include more people likely to recover. For that reason we studied separately the patients who would have been regarded as schizophrenic by present standards as well. Those who fit that definition had improved as much as the others. By the early 1980s, 68 percent had no symptoms of schizophrenia, and 45 percent had no psychiatric symptoms. Eighty-four percent were supposed to be taking antipsychotic drugs (mainly in low doses), but interviews revealed that only a quarter always took the drugs and half did not use them at all.

Some Functions Undisturbed

Except at the height of psychosis, schizophrenia rarely disturbs functioning in all domains equally. We found that some former patients were able to work, establish friendships and act as responsible citizens despite delusions and hallucinations. They said they had learned not to talk about these symptoms and had found ways to control them. Other patients could care for themselves and make friends but did not work, sometimes because of disability payments, the unavailability of jobs, or medication side effects such as blurred vision and involuntary movements. We need to acknowledge these complexities in choosing treatment programs and educating mental health professionals.

For anyone who expected to see constant gradual deterioration, these five studies were a great surprise. In urban Europe, in Iowa, and in rural Vermont the results were similar. What do these results tell us about the treatment of patients like Frederick L. and Catherine S.?

First, clinicians should reconsider their pessimism about the long-term prognosis of schizophrenia. Patients often recover the capacity to care for themselves and participate in society. Symptoms, both positive (such as delusions and hallucinations) and negative (such as apathy or withdrawal) often subside. Clinicians should avoid suggesting to patients that they will never recover, will deteriorate, or will have to take antipsy-chotic drugs for the rest of their lives. That betrays hope and discourages self-healing. Instead, mental health professionals could show through their words, actions, and attitudes that recovery is possible; patients are more likely to improve if they believe they can.

We should also reconsider the practice of describing schizophrenia as if it had only two forms: acute, with a rapid resolution, and chronic, with continual recurrence and gradual deterioration. Most patients would be better described by an intermediate term. The existing systems for diagnosing schizophrenia are not very useful in predicting long-term outcome: more attention might be paid to the differences among people who are labeled schizophrenic. Some researchers have proposed substi-tuting "person with prolonged psychiatric illness" for "schizophrenic pa-tient." Furthermore, the time spent in treatment is only part of the lives of these people. It would make sense to think of treatment as "walking along part of the path" with them. That clinical perspective would en-courage patients to clarify who they are, what they want to do, and when they want to do it. It would relieve the pressure for rapid improve-ment and allow both patients and clinicians to cope more realistically with fluctuating symptoms.

Outcome Unpredictable

Many patients, of course, do not improve. Some succumb to a particu-larly severe form of the illness. Others receive inadequate treatment or lack opportunities for returning to society. Still others are prevented from changing their lives by the side effects of medications, the stigmatiz-ing label of mental illness, personality disorders, or the demoralizing effects of prolonged institutionalization. But no one can know in advance which patients will improve and which will not. We and other research-ers have recorded history after history of patients who, after years of sitting in the day room of a hospital watching television, get on their feet and make new lives for themselves—as much to their own as to their therapists' surprise. Mental health care could be reorganized to provide long-term options in the light of these variations.

Some signs traditionally thought to predict outcome in schizophrenia are the state of a patient's mental health and social functioning before the first psychotic episode, the age at which it occurs, the sex of the patient, the presence of negative symptoms, and the degree of inherited vulnerability. According to long-term research, these account for about 25 percent of the difference in outcome between one patient and another. Other influences become more important as time passes: the presence or absence of a personality disorder, the patient's ability to find ways to cope with symptoms, the availability of social support and opportunities for rehabilitation when symptoms improve.

Under the present system most clinicians, families, and patients are already resigned to low expectations by the time the symptoms of the illness begin to lift. Recovery would be more likely if mental health programs treated all patients as if they might recover. Legislators should be urged to enact long-range budgets: 15- to 20-year instead of 2- to 5-year plans. Bright young mental health professionals should be encouraged to work with these difficult but surprisingly rewarding patients. And we should develop research strategies to determine which treatments are best for which patients in the various phases of prolonged psychiatric illness.

LANAHAN NOTES
Schizophrenia and Other Psychotic Disorders

————◦►————

SCHIZOPHRENIA

Definition—a disorder (or group of disorders) characterized by:

1. delusions (false ideas)
2. hallucinations (false perceptions)
3. gross disorganization in thinking and behavior
4. severe deficits in social and/or occupational functioning.
5. duration of at least six months (otherwise schizophreniform disorder)

Note: Not the same as "split personality"—the split here is between fantasy and reality, and/or between thinking processes and feeling processes.

Subtypes:

Paranoid: delusions or frequent auditory hallucinations and the absence of gross disorganization

Disorganized: severely disorganized language, cognition, and behavior

Catatonic: peculiarities of voluntary movement—complete stillness and/or frenzied, purposeless behavior, or stereotyped, bizarre speech or behavior

Undifferentiated: none of the first three can be applied.

Residual: acute symptoms have subsided but functioning is still greatly impaired.

Who Gets Schizophrenia?

One percent of the general population

Has existed for as long as we have records, and in every culture.

Equal occurrence in males and females (although age of onset is later for females)

Occurs in late adolescence or early adulthood.

Note: Among the most severely impairing and persistent of all psychological disorders. Even with treatment, many sufferers are substantially impaired for many years.

Causes — Biopsychosocial (also known as "diathesis-stress") model:

Biological: Genetic substrate has been demonstrated. Abnormalities in brain neurochemistry or neuroanatomy likely (particularly neurotransmitter, dopamine).

Environmental:

1. Stresses (e.g., tasks associated with late adolescence) play a role in predisposed individuals.
2. Family environment: *Not* shown to be cause, but may be relevant to chances for recovery (research on "expressed emotion").

Psychological: How the person reacts to having the disorder can affect recovery potential.

Treatment — also follows biopsychosocial model:

Medication: to reduce psychotic symptoms

Education about the illness for the patient and family

Supportive psychotherapy: helps the person develop coping skills; reduces depression/hopelessness.

Behavioral therapy: increase motivation, teach skills.

Rehabilitative services: sheltered living and working environments, and vocational and social skills training

Prognosis

Variable depending upon:

the severity of the illness

responsiveness to medication and other treatments

the perseverence and personality of the individual

level of family and community support available

— Periods of stability interspersed with relapses and rehospitalization are common.

— Permanent institutionalization is now rare.

OTHER PSYCHOTIC DISORDERS

Schizophreniform Disorder: symptoms of schizophrenia but brief duration, may be re-diagnosed as schizophrenia if symptoms endure or return.

Schizoaffective Disorder: schizophrenia with disordered mood

Delusional Disorder: nonbizarre delusions in the absence of other symptoms of schizophrenia

Brief Psychotic Disorder: symptoms present for less than one month with return to full functioning.

Shared Psychotic Disorder: two or more people share a delusion

Medically-Related Psychoses: induced by disease or ingested substances.

Controversies — schizophrenia and society:

Has deinstitutionalization of schizophrenic individuals helped or hurt them? Increased freedom vs. increased homelessness.

When is involuntary treatment appropriate?

Are psychotic individuals legally (and morally) responsible?

CHAPTER SIX

Sexual and Gender
Identity Disorders

————◀◎▶————

Our sexuality is probably the most value-laden of human behaviors. Bound up as it is in social mores, religious values, dating and mating, and self-image, it is a powerful producer of psychic pleasure and pain. While most people experience some transitory sexual problems at various times in their lives, when these problems are long-standing or severe, a sexual disorder is diagnosed.

The scientific study of sexuality dates back only to the mid-1880s. However, substantial progress in understanding the variants, both normal and abnormal, of human sexuality has been made since then. For example, masturbation, once considered to be both abnormal and harmful, is now known to be widely prevalent and apparently harmless. The notion that women had two separate kinds of orgasms, vaginal and clitoral, has been disproved.

While Freud and other psychodynamic theorists spent a great deal of energy exploring human sexuality, learning theory has also made major contributions to the understanding and, in some cases, successful treatment of sexual problems. Keep in mind, though, that no study of sexuality can proceed without reference to the cultural context in which it occurs, since what is considered normal sexual behavior can change dramatically.

The DSM-IV lists three types of problems in its section on sexual and gender identity disorders. The first set of diagnoses includes all of the sexual dysfunction problems—lack of desire, desire without arousal, and orgasmic difficulties. The second includes the paraphilias—attraction to an inappropriate sexual object or behavior. The third, gender identity disorder, refers to a strong and persistent cross-gender identification.

In this chapter, we have included one case of sexual dysfunction, two of paraphilia, and one of gender identity disorder. We have also included a theoretical piece that examines the intergenerational contribution to sexual abuse of children.

23

——————◄○►——————

FEMALE ORGASMIC DISORDER:
THE CASE OF SUSAN C.

SUSAN C. IS A THIRTY-EIGHT-YEAR-OLD woman who likes to look like she's nineteen. She wears her blond hair in two ponytails, and sports short shorts and midriff-baring tops in the summertime. On entering her therapist's office, she characteristically curls up on the chair, dropping her shoes to the floor as she comes in.

Susan came for therapy because she was upset over her relationship with her boyfriend, a married man with whom she had been sexually involved for a little over a year. Recently, she related, he seemed preoccupied and distant. He no longer wanted to hear the details of her day. His quick calls just to tell her that he loved her had decreased in frequency. Worst of all, he seemed to be delaying leaving his wife, which he had promised to do from almost the beginning of the affair.

Susan had been having trouble sleeping, had lost her appetite, and was losing weight from her already thin frame. She was barely able to concentrate at her job as a bank teller and found herself breaking into tears for virtually no reason—sometimes more than once a day.

Over the first few therapy sessions, Susan related some of her family history. She was the middle child of three. She had an older sister and a younger brother. Both of her parents had been heavy drinkers. They quarreled frequently, although nonviolently, and didn't seem to have much energy left over to apply to their relationships with their children. At least this is how Susan saw it. She said that her sister thought that Susan was overly sensitive and that their parents had done a good job. In any case, her parents divorced when she was thirteen. Her father quickly found a new girlfriend (who, perhaps, had been in the picture before the breakup) and was remarried within six months of the divorce. He had two more children from that union. Susan's mother did not remarry. Instead, she seemed to withdraw further into the bottle and the television. Susan's sister was married and seemed reasonably happy. She and Susan often failed to see eye to eye on things and weren't close. Susan's brother was a heavy drinker and had difficulty holding jobs. He hadn't married, although he did have a son whom he rarely saw.

Susan herself had been married twice. She had two teenage children from her first marriage to an alcoholic and verbally abusive man. Following her divorce after six years of marriage, she had married a man who was very different—older, gentle, responsible. She became bored with him after a few years, and they, too, were divorced. She had raised her children essentially alone after that, dating from time to time but not having a sustained relationship until she met her present lover on the tennis court. She felt that he was the genuine love of her life—the man she was destined to be with. Her life revolved around pleasing him. She waited by the phone for him to call and refused all invitations if she thought he might want to be with her. Often, she cruised by his house or place of business to see if his truck was there. She was obsessively and insistently interested in his every thought and movement.

While Susan's presenting problem was not specifically sexual, it emerged during the course of therapy that Susan had never had an orgasm while with a man. For her, sex was an opportunity to demonstrate her prowess and desirability. She took great pleasure in being hugged and cuddled. She adored being told that she was a wonderful lover and that her lover could not live without her. She thought about making love constantly, but found herself strangely removed during the act itself. Sheepishly, she told her therapist that she only had orgasms occasionally—and then by a method that was so embarrassing she could barely speak about it. Apparently, she had discovered quite by accident years ago that rubbing up against a door jamb could produce an orgasm. Oddly, she had never figured out (or perhaps she was too inhibited to try) that other methods might work as well. So, for almost twenty years, sex with men was for show, while she engaged in her private practice when physical need became overwhelming (often following a visit by her lover when she had become aroused but not satiated). Needless to say, she had become quite expert at faking orgasms (many of them, in fact) with her sexual partners.

Despite her profound shame, Susan was relieved that she had spoken with her therapist about sexuality. She agreed that this was an area on which she wanted to work. Initially, Susan's therapist did two things: first, she asked Susan to read a book on women's sexuality and to begin to experiment with other masturbatory techniques for attaining orgasm. Second, she began helping Susan identify the blocks to being more honest in her sexual relationships.

Susan soon realized that she felt profoundly inadequate, except in her ability to attract and seduce men. If she were less than the siren she pretended to be, perhaps no man would want to be with her—and then she would be worth nothing indeed. Susan realized these feelings had been with her for a very long time, and she linked them to her father's emotional unavailability, despite her desperate attempts as a child to gain his love and approval. Trying to take a candid look at herself, Susan was able to identify some of her positive traits which included loyalty, a sense of humor, keen intelligence, lots of energy, and a wide range of interests. She was able to acknowledge, at least in principle, that men might be attracted to these qualities, in addition to her showy sexuality. Additionally, she asked herself for the first time whether a man who was only interested in her (often faked) sexuality was really worth keeping.

Susan did not feel that she could take the risk of confiding in her boyfriend that her orgasms had been faked and that she had been so focused on his sexual pleasure that she had neglected any attention to her own. However, she did agree to begin to pay attention to her own physical sensations during lovemaking. This led to the discovery that when she did so, her own natural responses, which included verbalizations and body movements, heightened her lover's ardor. After a few weeks of actually experiencing sex, rather than simply going through the motions as she had been, Susan had an orgasm while her boyfriend was engaging in oral sex. Over the next several months, she had additional orgasms, some during mutual masturbation, and some during intercourse with additional manual stimulation. While, like may women, Susan did not have orgasms during intercourse alone, she was more than satisfied with her sexual responsiveness. She reported no longer feeling like a "fake" and a "freak."

Ironically, the more sexually responsive and confident she became, the less Susan felt dependent on her lover's admiration. Therapy continued its exploration of Susan's intense need for approval and adoration. Almost a year after therapy started, Susan terminated her affair. Not long after, she also terminated therapy, resolved to seek a more suitable partner and to widen her focus to include other sources of pleasure and self esteem: friends, family, sports, and finishing her college undergraduate degree. She had come to grips with her parents' limitations, grieved their inability to be as attentive as she had wished them to be, and ceased to hope that they might some day change. This process had caused her some sadness, but it resulted in a greater sense of peace and freedom.

Thinking About the Case

Susan's orgasmic disorder occurred in a wider context which included her family history, her ideas about herself and others, and cultural notions about gender relationships. In this, her case is typical of virtually all of the sexual dysfunctions. Note that Susan could have been given multiple diagnoses including adjustment disorder with depressed mood (clinically significant symptoms of depression in the face of an identifiable stressor), and, possibly, histrionic personality disorder (a pattern of excessive emotionality and attention-seeking).

The case is also fairly typical in that the sexual disorder is not the presenting problem but, instead, emerges during the course of treatment. It is common for people to be ambivalent about discussing sexual concerns with a stranger. Gaining confidence in the therapist is a prerequisite for self-disclosure. In addition, the sexual concern is often not the most pressing problem. Susan was more concerned initially about possibly losing her boyfriend than she was about her orgasmic dysfunction.

Susan's therapy was truly biopsychosocial in nature. The reading and masturbation assignments were designed to give Susan a fuller understanding of the physiological aspects of arousal and orgasm. Cognitive therapy techniques were used in helping Susan question her assumption that she only had value as a sexual object. Clearly, this work was informed by an understanding of how women are socialized by the culture to think of themselves in certain ways. However, cultural expectations are interpreted through the family (as well as through television, literature and other sources). A psychodynamic perspective led to the exploration of the familial roots of some of Susan's ideas about herself. While these various schools of therapy seem quite distinct in principle, they are often used together in practice, as they were in Susan's case. Most therapists practice a kind of therapeutic pragmatism, using whatever might be helpful, rather than a therapeutic purism, relying solely on one technique. Research has not yet shed any scientific light on whether such pragmatism actually increases the chances for success, although studies have shown that experienced therapists from different schools behave more similarly than do inexperienced therapists. Apparently, clinical wisdom supports therapeutic pragmatism.

Questions to Consider

1. In this case, the therapy went beyond the presenting complaint. Do you agree with the therapist's decision to do so? Why or why not? What factors would you consider in reaching such a decision yourself?

2. Sex and gender, while different, are intimately connected. How did gender role expectations affect the development of sexual disorder symptoms in Susan?

3. Can you diagram this case (US, CS, UR, CR) as a learning theorist would?

4. Most psychodynamic explanations of mental disorder tend to focus on the mother-child relationship, yet this case seems to suggest that a child's relationship with the father might also be important. What are the ways in which a mother's and father's influences

might be different, but important? Are these differences also related to gender roles?

5. This case illustrates that therapeutic pragmatism rather than therapeutic purism reigns in the day-to-day world of psychotherapy. What implications does this have for theory and for research?

24

——◀◦▶——

SEXUAL MASOCHISM: THE CASE
OF THE ANONYMOUS CALLER

AT MANY COMMUNITY MENTAL health centers where several clinicians might be working together, each clinician takes turns being "on call" for telephone calls and for people who walk in off the street without an appointment. On one such day, a receptionist at one of these centers buzzed the therapist on call about a caller who wanted to speak with "one of the doctors." The following is that therapist's own report of the telephone conversation.

"This is Dr. Frank. How can I help you?" I began.

"What I want to know is, is it abnormal to want to be . . . well . . . you know, spanked?" asked the male caller.

"Well, I need a little more information before I can answer your question. Can you tell me a bit more about it?"

"It's kind of embarrassing to talk about. . . . I like to be, like, spanked, during sex and I want to know if it's crazy or anything."

"Why has it become a problem for you right at this time?" I asked.

"Because my wife won't do it anymore. She says it's crazy and I should get help. I figure it's not hurting anybody, so it's O.K., you know? Still, I guess it is kind of weird. I want to know if she's right. Am I crazy?"

Carefully, I began, "What you're describing is called 'sexual masochism.' Statistically, it's abnormal, but so is being six-foot-four. Humans engage in a wide range of sexual behaviors. Some are more common than others. Odd sexual behaviors are only considered disorders when they cause significant problems for the person or those around him. What's normal or abnormal is less important than what works for you and your partner. How long have you been married?"

"Just about seven years. We get along pretty well, except for arguing about this." The caller must have been feeling more comfortable, because he went on. "You know, I know just how this started. I must have been about ten or eleven. I went to Catholic school. When you misbehaved, they were allowed to punish you . . . you know, physically. They had one nun there, Sister Catherine, who used to take you into the broom closet, take your pants down, put you across her lap, and hit you on the butt with a switch a couple of times. I don't know, I guess it was kind of a turn-on, you know? Lying on her lap, with my butt hanging out. I remember I'd get, you know . . . erections. Boy, I sure got into a lot of trouble the year she was my teacher!"

"Yes," I said, "that's often how these attractions develop. Some behavior or object, in your case, being spanked, is linked with sexual pleasure in childhood or early adolescence, and the association remains strong right into adulthood."

"Can you change it or is it permanent?" he asked.

"That's a good question. In general, old habits are hard to change, and habits associated with sexual pleasure seem particularly hard to change. The method that seems to work best is called "behavior therapy,' and it would involve pairing the spanking with something unpleasant like electric shocks or nausea or masturbating to the point of discomfort so that the spanking-pleasure link would be broken. Tell me, are you capable of becoming sexually aroused and enjoying sex without getting spanked?"

"Oh, yeah. I don't need it, really. I just like it, is all . . . although sometimes I imagine myself getting spanked when my wife won't do it."

"Well, then, since it's uncomfortable for your wife, maybe you could just choose to do without the actual behavior. You could keep the fantasy part if you like. Not many of us get absolutely everything we'd like in a real-life sexual relationship. Or, perhaps with some marital counseling, she might decide she could do it once in a while, just as a gift to you. If you do decide to do without, you could try some 'at home' behavioral techniques that might help to reduce your craving for getting spanked."

"What would that be like?"

"Well, it would involve using your imagination in a somewhat different way from the way you are using it now. It works like this: You find a quiet spot, develop a picture in your mind of getting spanked, just the way you like it, and then, when you begin to get aroused, you would substitute a picture of something you really dislike or are frightened of."

"What, you mean like getting punched in the face or put down in front of a whole bunch of people?"

"Exactly! See how that feels when you say it?"

"Yeah, creepy."

"Right," I said. "Creepy and pleasurable don't go together very well, do they?"

"I'll say they don't," he said emphatically.

"After you get good at developing the images, you'd begin to practice them when you find yourself thinking about getting spanked when you're with your wife. You'd also want to practice developing a wider range of erotic thoughts and images to use when you're making love so you'll have something to substitute for your spanking fantasies."

"So," I concluded, "what can we do for you? Would you like to come in for some behavioral therapy? Would you like to bring your wife in for some marital counseling so we could all talk about this together and maybe bring a little more harmony into your sexual relationship? Would you like to come in by yourself, just to talk it all over?"

"Nope," he said after a pause. "I don't think I need to do any of those things right now. I'm going to talk to my wife about what you said and see what she thinks. I'm glad to know I'm not crazy—that's all I really wanted to know. Thanks for your time."

The conversation ended here—the caller was never heard from again.

Thinking About the Case

Sexual masochism is one of the paraphilias—disorders in which sexual arousal is attached to unusual and/or inappropriate objects or behaviors. Note that strong urges or fantasies are enough to qualify for the disorder, even without the actual behavior, as long as the urges or fantasies have lasted at least six months, are intense and recurrent, and cause significant distress or dysfunction. This leaves a great deal of room for subjective judgment in the diagnostic process. An individual with intense masochistic fantasies who never acted them out but was greatly distressed by them would qualify for a diagnosis, while the caller in this case would probably not have been diagnosable as long as his wife was a willing partner, because the criterion of distress or dysfunction would not have been met. Still most of us would consider the caller to be the more "maladjusted" of the two.

Most research supports a learning theory explanation of the development of paraphilias as follows:

Unconditioned Stimulus (US) ————————▶ Unconditioned Response (UR)
(genital stimulation)   (sexual arousal)

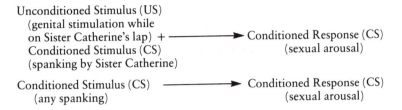

Unconditioned Stimulus (US)
(genital stimulation while
on Sister Catherine's lap) + ————————► Conditioned Response (CS)
Conditioned Stimulus (CS)   (sexual arousal)
(spanking by Sister Catherine)

Conditioned Stimulus (CS)   ————————► Conditioned Response (CS)
(any spanking)   (sexual arousal)

The same principles suggest how the disorder might be treated. Aversion therapy, including the imaginal kind suggested to the anonymous caller, is generally the treatment of choice. In actual treatment, the caller might be subjected to electric shock or chemical nauseants as he becomes aroused in response to masochistic stimuli, either supplied by the therapist in the form of tapes, movies, or readings, or self-produced in the form of fantasy. This procedure, in which sexual arousal in response to deviant stimuli is paired with aversive unconditioned stimuli is called "covert sensitization." A related technique, called "masturbatory satiation" might also be used. In this procedure, the caller would be asked to masturbate for a period of time, perhaps a half hour, following orgasm while continuing to fantasize about being spanked. Since masturbation after orgasm is unpleasant and uncomfortable, this would effectively pair an aversive US with the behavior to be extinguished. We diagram the treatment as follows:

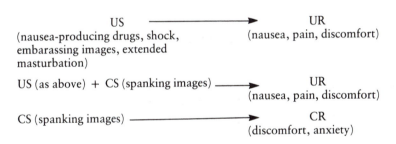

US ————————————► UR
(nausea-producing drugs, shock,   (nausea, pain, discomfort)
embarassing images, extended
masturbation)

US (as above) + CS (spanking images) ————► UR
                                            (nausea, pain, discomfort)

CS (spanking images) ————————————► CR
                                            (discomfort, anxiety)

In order to strengthen the bond between non-spanking fantasies and sexual arousal, "orgasmic reconditioning" might be employed. The caller would be asked to masturbate, while narrating his fantasies aloud. As he reached climax he would substitute a more acceptable scene for the masochistic fantasy. Note that this was also suggested in the telephone call. We can diagram this as follow:

US (impending climax) ————————► UR (sexual pleasure)

US (impending climax) + ————————► UR (sexual pleasure)
CS (appropriate sexual fantasies)

CS (appropriate sexual fantasies) ————► CR (sexual pleasure)

While we have no way of knowing whether this is true for the anonymous caller, many individuals with paraphilias lack social skills that would allow them to develop and practice more normal ways of interacting. They are often described as shy and withdrawn. In these cases, the paraphilia substitutes for, rather than accompanies, normal sexual behavior. Therefore, behavioral treatment directed specifically at the paraphilia might be accompanied by social skills training and therapy designed to increase self-esteem and self-confidence. In any case, treatment success is generally modest with many individuals dropping out of treatment or reverting to old ways once treatment has been completed.

Questions to Consider

1. Except for sadomasochism, the paraphilias occur almost exclusively in men. Why might this be so?

2. What does learning theory have to say about why the paraphilias are so persistent and resistant to change?

3. Does psychodynamic theory have anything useful to say about the paraphilias? Can it be applied to the case of the anonymous caller? Might it help explain why not all of the children spanked by Sister Catherine developed a masochistic paraphilia?

25

———◄o►———

PEDOPHILIA: THE CASE OF JAMES Q.

JAMES Q. IS A FORTY-TWO-YEAR-OLD single man who is presently incarcerated in state prison, having been sentenced to seven-to-twenty years for sexual abuse of children. He is known to have sexually fondled and pornographically photographed at least six children, but it is possible that he abused up to a hundred or more others. Until his arrest, he lived quietly in a small New England town, where he worked as a university groundskeeper. As a prisoner, he still lives quietly, keeping to himself and tending to the two decorative flower beds just inside the prison's gates.

James, the younger of two children, was raised in a middle-class household. His father, a plumber, was a heavy weekend drinker who was emotionally removed from the family. His mother stayed at home until all of the children were in school. Later, she worked as a clerk in a local shop. She was a quiet woman whose pasttimes were mostly crafts activities which she did in the company of her two sisters. She was especially proud of the handmade quilts she had made for each of her children and for each of her nieces and nephews.

While James' older sister was a good student, he was not. He had trouble learning to read and write and, in second grade, he was classified as intellectually "slow" and provided with special services that continued through his school career. He was not particularly athletic, so fitting in with other youngsters was somewhat difficult. In fifth grade, he learned to play the drum, which allowed him to participate in the marching band and afforded him some sense of acceptance at school.

James always seemed more comfortable with younger children, and his primary playmates were his two younger cousins. His first sexual experience was also with these cousins. When he was eleven, and they were five and seven, he convinced them to take off their clothes and let him fondle their penises. Within a few more contacts, he had taught them to stroke his penis to ejaculation. Shortly thereafter, his mother caught him and his cousins in the process of disrobing. She was horrified and strongly reprimanded him. Later that evening his father delivered a brief lecture on sexuality. Its primary message was that sex was to be saved for marriage. While it was normal for young men to have "urges," his father said, these had to be suppressed. In the meantime, vigorous physical exercise and occasional cold showers were the treatment advocated by Mr. Q., as they had been advocated to him (albeit unsuccessfully) by his own father a generation before.

Mr. and Mrs. Q. argued for several days over whether any additional intervention was warranted. Mrs. Q. wanted to seek a mental health evaluation for James, but Mr. Q. was adamantly opposed, saying that his son's behavior had been nothing more than childhood curiosity about sexuality. After several discussions in which Mrs. Q. was tearful and distraught, and Mr. Q. was angry and defensive, a compromise was reached—James was taken to the parish priest for a frank conversation.

Apparently, eternal life in hell was not an adequate deterrent for James. Despite his attempts to control himself, he found himself masturbating several times a week, always with fantasies of sexual acts with children in his mind. While he did not actually touch a child for the next ten years, he was never free of the wish to do so.

During that decade, James moved through and out of high school. He had graduated in a special program that spent half the day on academic subjects and the other half on a vocational skill. There he learned enough about landscaping and gardening to be taken on as an assistant grounds-keeper at the local college. He started working there part-time when he was a junior in high school and accepted a full-time job upon graduation.

James had not developed much of a peer support network in school and had few friends when he graduated. Being shy and socially insecure, he had never really dated, although he had managed to get a date for the senior prom. During that date, he made an awkward attempt at sexual contact but was firmly rebuffed. Three months later, however, he had intercourse with a young woman he met at a bar. He saw her sporadically for the next fourteen months, had intercourse with her several more times, but each time he found himself thinking about watching and touching nude children. The relationship ended when the young woman began to complain about James' apparent lack of real devotion to her, evident in the inconsistency of his contact and his unwillingness to engage in social activities with her. Her increasing demands, in concert with his feelings of guilt about engaging in intercourse before marriage, resulted in his ceasing to call her.

Meanwhile, James was fairly happy in his work. His one additional source of pride, success, and social contact was through church, where he had remained active in youth bible study and community service. At age twenty-one he volunteered to teach a Sunday School class of second and third graders. This proved to be his undoing because, before long, he was unable to resist the lure of being surrounded by young children.

James' pedophilic fantasies increased in frequency and intensity until, one day, he fondled a little boy while helping him on with his snowsuit. The boy's lack of objection seemed to James a sign that what he was doing was not really harmful. He rationalized that the children seemed to like him very much and the his sexual attentions caused them pleasure, not pain. Besides, he was introducing them to sexuality in a low-key, low-anxiety way. He remembered how anxious and guilt-ridden his one age-appropriate heterosexual relationship had been, and felt that he was doing the children a genuine service through his attentions.

Despite these rationalizations, James knew that if he were caught, his life would be effectively over. Therefore, he tried hard to resist his urges to fondle children. He took to visiting prostitutes from time to time, but found their attentions unsatisfying. They were too seductive, too worldly, too aggressive. In truth, they made him uncomfortable. Occasionally, he tried to date someone from the college, but was rarely successful. Students ignored him and staff members tended to have their own boyfriends or husbands. Besides, his awkwardness seemed to put women off. During his twenties, James' encounters with children were rare, but not entirely nonexistent.

When he was thirty-two, his mother died. James was surprised by the pain and loneliness he felt. While he had not thought himself close to his mother, she had been closely woven into the fabric of his life. He now felt bereft and adrift without her. His needs for companionship and emotional succor increased, and again, he turned to children from his church-related activities to meet these needs. Over time, he developed a little "club" in which he would invite youngsters over to his apartment for pizza and videos. Needless to say, the videos he showed the children had gradually increasing sexual content. He organized "games" that followed the videos—games in which mutual touching and exploring of genitalia were the primary activities. Photographs of the games were used to determine the "winners" at each session. The club was very elite—and secrecy was emphasized at all of the meetings. Still, it is astonishing that James' games went on for eight years before one of the children told his parents what was happening. That parent went to the police, and the house of cards quickly collapsed. While only a few of the parents allowed their children to participate in the court process, James' conviction was easily obtained.

While in prison, James participates in a sexual offenders' treatment group that meets weekly in the office of the prison psychologist. Attending the group is voluntary, although it is widely known that participation is virtually mandatory for prisoners who wish to be paroled. The group is strongly confrontational in orientation. Members are encouraged to point out rationalizations and other distortions in thinking when they hear them from other members. The men are encouraged to take responsibility for their behavior and to develop some understanding of the effect of their behavior on their victims. Several of the men were themselves victimized as children. They are encouraged to share their experiences with other group members, both to increase members' empathy for victims of sexual abuse and to help these men identify how the abuse they suffered predisposed them to abusing others. James participates actively in the group, but there is no way of telling whether the treatment is effective, so long as James is still in jail. His prospects for release any time soon are not good.

Thinking About the Case

Between one-quarter and one-third of adults report having been sexually approached by an adult when they were children. While the number of pedophiles is probably fairly small, each can have dozens, even hundreds of victims. James' case is fairly typical of one type of pedophile—those whose behavior represents a deviant sexual arousal pattern. Another type seems to engage in pedophilic behavior as a regressive response to some life stressor or loss. These individuals may prefer adult sexual objects most of the time but turn to a child object when the adult is emotionally or physically absent. Incestuous behavior is often of this latter type, although some people who sexually abuse their own children have a primarily pedophilic orientation and also abuse children outside the family as well.

In order for pedophilia to be diagnosed, the sexual object must be prepubescent (generally younger than thirteen). Sexual abuse of older teenagers is also common, both within and outside of the family, but is not diagnosed as pedophilia. Generally, perpetrators are known to the victims as family members or friends. Many, like James, are drawn to situations in which they can develop a relationship of trust with children.

Pedophiles are much more likely to be seductive, like James, than violent. They tend to rationalize their behavior as being instructive or valued by the children they abuse. In addition, actual penetration is rare, occurring in less than ten percent of the cases. Manual or oral sexual contact is much more the norm. While some pedophiles prefer either girls or boys, many abuse children of both sexes.

Pedophilia is now known to have longstanding and often quite serious repercussions for the children involved. Among the adult disorders associated with childhood sexual abuse are depression, anxiety, eating disorders, substance abuse disorders, somatization disorders, dissociative disorders, and personality disorders. As you have probably already noted, many of the cases reported in this book have sexual abuse as one of the precursors of emotional disorder. Therefore, the successful treatment (and, ultimately, prevention) of sexual abuse constitutes an urgent public health goal.

Unfortunately, treatment is still rare and even more rarely an unqualified success. Pedophiles, like others with paraphilias, generally do not submit to treatment voluntarily, and most prisons do not have a pedophilia treatment program. Further, as we have seen, the treatment of paraphilias is only modestly successful at best. Still, some model programs do exist. They generally use a combination of behavioral techniques like aversion therapy, experiential methods aimed at increasing empathy—for example, role-playing and writing letters of apology to victims—and psychotherapy aimed at increasing self-esteem, social efficacy, and self-understanding. Experts in the area are unanimous in suggesting that long-term, possibly life-long, supervision and follow-up is essential if recidivism is to be prevented.

Questions to Consider

1. Do you think that a man who sexually abuses his thirteen-year-old stepdaughter, but no other children, might have a different prognosis than James? Why?

2. Sexually-abusing adults have often been sexually abused themselves as children. Why might this be so? What theoretical model best encompasses your explanation?

3. What do you think of the use of drugs that suppress the production of the male hormone, testosterone (thereby diminishing sexual arousal and the ability to get an erection) as a treatment for pedophilia? What are the ethical issues involved? What are the legal (civil rights) issues involved? Under what circumstances, if any, would you approve of its use?

4. Mandatory reporting of child abuse to social service authorities by clinicians to whom it is revealed is now the norm in virtually all jurisdictions. What are the pros and cons of this mandate, in your opinion? Do you think the requirement should be the same if the abuse is disclosed by the abuser or by the victim? Why, or why not?

5. Do you think a child would be affected differently by sexual abuse if the perpetrator is a neighborhood acquaintance rather than a family member? Why or why not? What other factors might affect how severe the consequences of the abuse are for the victim?

6. Would you endorse a behavioral or a psychodynamic explanation for the development of James' pedophilia? What aspects of the case description lend themselves to your hypothesis? Do you need additional information? If so, what do you wish had been included?

26

——◄o►——

GENDER IDENTITY DISORDER IN
A YOUNG CHILD: THE CASE OF BILLY B.

BILLY WAS THE MIDDLE of three boys. He looked like his brothers—fair-skinned, blue-eyed, and stocky—but there the resemblance ended. Although an assortment of toys was available to him, Billy, from as early as his parents can remember, ignored the trucks and cars, and guns and hammers in favor of dolls. While his older brother went flying around the house, dressed as an "Indian" and whooping it up, Billy, at two-and-a-half, sat quietly in the corner dressing and feeding one of his "babies." He eschewed rough-and-tumble play, preferring, instead, to follow his mother around while she went about her household routine. She also found him to be especially "sensitive" and in need of more gentle disciplining than her other sons. He would burst into tears at a harsh word from her and rarely need the "time-out" punishments that seemed a part of daily life with his brothers.

By three-and-a-half, Billy had started his collection of Barbie dolls. His only playmate was the child next door, a girl of about the same age as he. Arriving at her house, he would run directly to her bedroom and spend the next several hours trying on all of her clothes. Together they would produce a "fashion show" for whatever parent was around, with Billy wearing his friend's clothes while she wore her mother's. Like most children, Billy and his friend spent a lot of time in fantasy play, but he always insisted on being a girl in their role-playing. Sometimes they would argue about who got to be the "princess." Her suggestions that he could play the part of the "prince" were met with stony resistance.

His friend's mother found the obsessive, driven quality of his behavior disturbing, commenting, "it's as if he were possessed by the desire to try on every dress." His parents didn't know what to think. His mother was worried about his preference for traditionally feminine types of play, but her gentle attempts to redirect him were met with strong resistance or even tantrums. Motivated to raise nonsexist children in an atmosphere that downplayed traditional gender roles, she was hesitant to stifle his natural proclivities or damage his self-esteem by excessive criticism. When Billy asked her, as he often did while parading around in his friend's clothes, "don't I look pretty?" she would tell him, with much misgiving, that he did, indeed.

His father was much more upset by Billy's single-minded interest in things feminine. Following a period of denial, he became increasingly agitated in Billy's presence, alternating between ignoring him and screaming at him to "knock if off and act like a boy." He tried spending more time alone with Billy doing "guy stuff," but these outings were usually disappointing for both father and son. In the toy store, Billy wanted to look at Barbie outfits, while his father wanted to look at the sports section. Billy was bored and distracted playing catch, and when his dad asked what he'd like to do next, he invited his father to a tea party. Mr. B. tried to participate in his son's play, but it made him uncomfortable and frustrated.

A real parenting challenge came when Billy began to refuse to take off his friend's clothes when it was time to come home from her house. He threw such a fit that his mother, to calm his obviously real and palpable distress, finally let him wear the dress home, where he wore it all evening, much to his father's consternation, and insisted on going to bed in it that night. After several months of constant battling and anguish, Mrs. B., over her husband's vociferous objections, bought Billy his own dress. This did not end their struggles, however, since Billy also wanted to wear barrettes in his hair, his friend's shoes (which were too small and hurt his feet), and her underwear.

By the age of five, Billy was voicing the clear wish to be a girl. At his fifth birthday party he told his mother, "I always thought that when I was this many (holding up five fingers) I would like being a boy, but I don't." She had observed him many times standing in front of the mirror, exclaiming that he was ugly, but that when he grew up he was "gonna be a pretty lady." He had no boy friends in nursery school, but the girls liked him just fine. He fit right into their play, and they treated him as if he were one of them.

At the time he entered school, his parents made several changes. First, they set limits on his cross-dressing. He was allowed to wear a girl's nightshirt and tights to bed and to wear girls' slippers, but otherwise had to dress in boys' clothes. His mom and her neighbor agreed that the children would be allowed to dress in adult's clothes for "dress-up," but that Billy would no longer be allowed to wear his friend's clothes. In fact her bedroom was off-limits.

In addition, the B.'s enrolled Billy in a local ballet class that was run by a husband and wife team. They felt that this might give him a socially appropriate outlet for his feminine interests. They also hoped that the male ballet teacher would offer Billy a model for how to integrate the masculine and feminine sides of himself. Billy loved ballet and didn't seem to mind at all being the only boy in the class. He did throw a bit of a fit when the other students got to wear a tu-tu and he didn't, but he seemed to get past this and settle into the class well.

Finally, at the urging of their neighbor, they agreed to have Billy evaluated by a child psychiatrist. The psychiatrist saw Billy alone for several sessions, took a family and personal history from his parents, and saw the family together once. His pronouncement was that Billy was the worst case of transsexualism that he had ever seen, and that the fault lay in a disturbed mother-child relationship. Mrs. B. was devastated. With a family history of depression and alcoholism, she felt that she herself had been raised "in the original dysfunctional family." She had had problems with depression herself from time to time and was primed and ready to believe that Billy's problems were somehow her fault. Her husband, though, was having none of it. He rose to her defense, stating his belief that Billy had been like this almost since birth, that his wife had remarkable patience and wisdom in handling his "differentness," and that he wanted a second opinion.

The B.'s searched around until they found a program that specialized in gender identity disorders at the local university. Billy was accepted into the program where he had individual psychotherapy on a weekly basis for about a year. Therapy failed to produce any profound changes, although Billy seemed to accept limits on his cross-dressing with a great deal less struggle as time went on. In kindergarten and first grade he did well academically and behaved in a way which did not get him singled out for ridicule by his classmates, although he had no real friends.

Now eight years old, Billy still plays with his Barbies and avoids more typically "boy" activities. He has found the computer, though, which now occupies much of his free time. It is also a conduit to a relationship with his father. Together they explore the Internet and play computer games. Billy's gender cross-identification has become somewhat of a non-issue in the family. "Bill is just Bill," his parents say. They understand from their consultations with the therapists at the university that he is unlikely to change. They assume that he will be homosexual and have prepared themselves to love and accept him regardless. Bill's mom says she finds him easier to manage in some ways than her other two sons. He shares her interests and is content to hang around with her, while his brothers seem to need to be entertained in a more active way. Bill's dad has moved past anger and frustration to sadness and resignation. He sees a tough and possibly lonely road ahead for Billy, but he considers the situation to be "an act of God," and one that must be accepted with grace and forbearance.

Thinking About the Case

Gender identity disorder, also known as transsexualism, is diagnosed in individuals who feel trapped in a body of the wrong gender. It is a rare disorder, occurring in about one in 100,000 people. It is distinguishable from transvestism in which clothing of the opposite sex is worn for erotic or playful reasons, but in which the individual is fully identified with his or her own gender. Nor is it synonymous with homosexuality. While most transsexuals are sexually attracted to members of their own gender, some are not.

Billy's case is quite typical in that the disorder appears startlingly early, with fixed cross-gender identification in place by the age of three or four. It is diagnosed much more often in males than in females, although it should be noted that cross-dressing and other cross-gender behavior is much more available and socially acceptable for women than for men, so perhaps there are many undiagnosed cases. It is a chronic condition, yielding to no psycho- or behavioral therapy.

The early onset and immutable nature of gender identity disorder have led investigators to conclude that some hormonal disturbance that occurs some time in the second to fourth month of pregnancy is responsible for this fascinating but heartbreaking condition. In the early fetus, both male and female internal organs are present until, in male fetuses, two masculinizing hormones are secreted from the testes. These hormones affect the subsequent development of sexual organs as well as having psychological effects on the brain — in effect, masculinizing the brain. In transsexuals, it appears that, for as yet unknown reasons, organ development proceeds normally, but the masculinizing of the brain does not. While familial and social factors also play a role in the development of sexual identity, these later influences appear to reinforce or disturb a core identity that is established well before birth.

It is difficult to overstate the anguish felt by transsexuals. Many become profoundly depressed and even suicidal. Some mutilate their own genitals. Almost always, disturbances of personality develop as they try to adapt to the demands and the stigma to which they are subject from an early age.

Until recently, despair was the certain future from those afflicted. However, within the past several decades, advances in medical knowledge and techniques have made the possibility of sex reassignment through hormonal and surgical procedures a viable alternative. Typically, an individual who wishes to have the surgery is required to undergo a careful psychological evaluation to ensure that the apparent gender identity disorder is not secondary to another disorder (like schizophrenia for instance). The psychological health and resilience of the person are also assessed. Then he or she is required to live in the new gender role for a period of several years while hormone therapy is begun. This may entail a change of name, dress, and sometimes even occupation. Finally, genital surgery is undertaken. For male to female sex reassignment, this involves transforming the penis into a vagina. For female to male reassignment, the procedure is more complicated and involves multiple surgeries over several years to remove the breasts and ovaries, and sometimes, to build a penis. Since the penis cannot become erect, a prosthetic device must be used for intercourse.

The outcome of sex reassignment surgery is variable. Probably half or more of patients have a favorable outcome, reporting improvement in their sense of well-being and overall satisfaction with life. However, a substantial minority experience fairly serious surgical complications or feel that their life has been altered in negative ways. Perhaps it will be possible some day to identify and correct the fetal hormonal disturbance so that gender identity disorder can be prevented.

Questions to Consider

1. Close your eyes and imagine, for a few minutes, what it would be like to be forced to wear the clothing of and to act like a member of the opposite sex. If you feel really courageous, try it for a day. What changes occurred in your mood, self-esteem, and ability to engage in everyday tasks and relate to others? What might it be like to have this be your permanent lot in life?

2. As we move from sexual identity, through sexual orientation, sexual interest, and sexual behavior, we appear to move along a continuum from biological to environmental/experiential influences. Can you construct a coherent biopsychosocial model that describes the development of adult sexuality?

27

——————◄o►——————

Since sexual abuse sometimes runs in families, with perpetrators having been themselves abused as children, attempts have been made to formulate theories of how this familial transmission takes place. See if you can interpret the ideas in the reading that follows from various vantage points: cognitive, psychodynamic, interpersonal, and behavioral. What are some ways that you could imagine intervening effectively in the W.A.R. cycle?

A CONCEPTUAL FRAMEWORK FOR UNDERSTANDING SEXUAL ABUSE: THE W.A.R. CYCLE

S. L. Ingersoll and S. O. Patton

RAY HELFER INTRODUCED the W.A.R. Cycle in his work, *The Diagnostic Process and Treatment Programs*, in 1977. Since that time, it has become one of the classic conceptual tools used for gaining understanding of and insight into the family dynamics that foster physical, emotional, and sexual abuse and neglect. (See figure.)

W.A.R. stands for the World of Abnormal Rearing. Helfer traces a pattern wherein individuals reared in the W.A.R. cycle often seek self-fulfillment through extra-familial relationships, escaping from their abusive family of origin through untimely marriage or pregnancy in an attempt to fill the unsatisfied needs of childhood. The child-turned-parent transfers to the next-generation child unrealistic expectations for meeting the needs of the parent. In an effort to satisfy the parent's need to be taken care of, the child reverses roles with the parent. The child is unable to satisfy the parent's expectations, and the parents become frustrated and abuse the child as punishment, which is a learned response from the parent's childhood experience. As a result, the child develops a lack of trust in people, isolates himself or herself for protection against

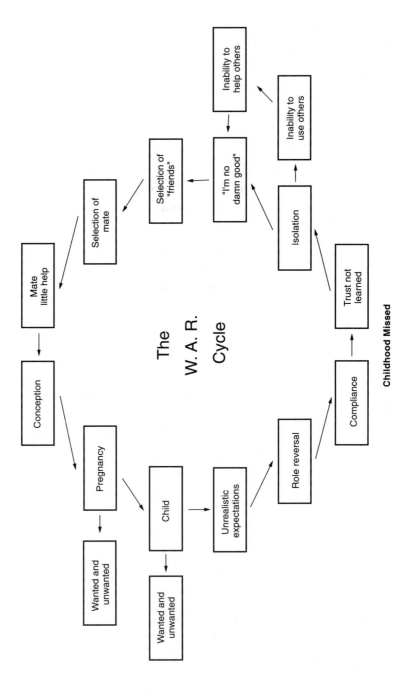

The
W. A. R.
Cycle

Childhood Missed

The War Cycle by Ray Helfer, from the Diagnostic Process and Treatment Programs, U. S. Dept. of Health, Education, and Welfare, Office of Human Developement Services (DHEW Pub. # OHDS 77-30069), 1977.

shame, is robbed of normal child development in deference to parenting the parent, and develops a self-concept of "bad kid," "flawed," or "different." Into adulthood, the abused or neglected child has a hard time making friends due to the burden of internalized shame, and low self-esteem, and arrested development. In search of a way out, the child makes one or more untimely choices of mates in attempts to escape the oppressive expectations and abuses of the parent and to satisfy his or her own unmet needs. The female child is likely to impulsively conceive a child, anticipating that in the infant she will finally have a warm, cuddly little one to lavish her love upon, to "raise better than her parents raised her," who will love her unconditionally in return. But the unrelenting dependency of an infant, the temper tantrums of childhood, and the overwhelming responsibilities of parenthood frustrate that expectation of unconditional love. The parent, unable to deal appropriately with her own pain, places unrealistic expectations on the child, setting the whole cycle into repetition. Unless intervention occurs, this cycle is likely to continue repeating from generation to generation. In the case of sexual abuse, it follows logically that what one learns from one's own experience, one is likely to repeat with one's own children, especially in times of stress. So the child victim becomes the adult perpetrator, responding to stress and pain in the same dysfunctional way his or her parents did.

To better illustrate the W.A.R. Cycle, lets look at a case:

Duane, a sixteen-year-old boy, first came to see me after he fondled his three-year-old brother. Duane was visibly upset, and said he needed help because of what he had done. With total lack of affect, he related his story of abuse (in nondescript details) and told me that he had seen a counselor in another state for about six weeks, right after the disclosure of the abuse. He stated that he thought he "had it together" then, but now he wasn't so sure; he was frightened by his own feelings and behavior. For fourteen weeks, Duane and I talked about his own abuse at the hand of his stepfather, which started when he was three (note the age pattern) and continued until he disclosed it at fourteen. Duane's stepfather had abused drugs and alcohol, becoming physically abusive, and then "making it up to Duane" through sexual abuse. Eventually the stepfather began allowing friends to "use" Duane, and the threats became more and more violent if the "secret" was ever revealed. Since Duane's Mom worked the 11:00 A.M. to 7:00 P.M. shift, Duane never knew when his Dad would "throw a party." Eventually, the abusive situation became so severe that Duane ended up in the hospital, where he finally felt safe enough to disclose. Throughout the disclosure process, Duane was unable to express any emotion. When asked how he felt, he would say "I don't know." This continued for fourteen weeks until finally, in the middle of a Monopoly game (we played games as part of therapy because Duane had never had any constructive playful experience and said he didn't really have any close friends and was afraid to make friends because he "didn't even know how to play a game"), he started to choke and sobbed uncontrollably: the emotional dam had finally broken. As therapy progressed it became evident that Duane was caught up in the W.A.R. cycle. He finally told me he was intimately involved with a fourteen-year-old girl; neither was using protection against conception because they "wanted a baby." He had been caring for his two younger brothers for years and wanted a family of his own. Looking back at family history, Duane had started to abuse his brother as he had been abused. His mother's history revealed that she conceived Duane out of wedlock when she was fifteen years old. She had come from a physically and emotionally abusive home and her father was alcoholic. When Duane was born, she developed some very unrealistic goals for herself, and eventually for Duane as well. She looked to Duane to "father" the two younger boys and to give her the unconditional love that she had been seeking for so long. Now Duane was looking for a way out—for someone who could love him for who he was and for someone to call his own. Duane's mother, unable to get her needs met, charged her son with responsibility for meeting them without consideration for his needs. In turn, Duane, physically and emotionally damaged, and with unmet needs of his own, dragged his emotional baggage into an untimely union, charging his yet unborn child with the task of meeting his overwhelming needs.

And so it goes; the W.A.R. Cycle repeats itself, sometimes for generations.

LANAHAN NOTES
Sexual and Gender Identity Disorders

——◄o►——

SEXUAL DYSFUNCTIONS—DIFFICULTIES
IN SEXUAL PERFORMANCE

Sexual Desire Disorders: a lack of desire for, or even an aversion to sex

Sexual Arousal Disorders: inability to attain or maintain sexual arousal

Orgasmic Disorders: orgasm is inhibited, delayed, or premature.

Sexual Pain Disorders: generalized pain or spasms of the vagina interfere with intercourse.

Substance-Induced Sexual Dysfunction: ingestion of alcohol, cannabis, or some other substance interferes with sexual functioning.

Note: Diagnosis of all of these conditions must take into account the age and context of the person's life and must reflect marked distress or interpersonal difficulty.

Causes:

Often best explained by learning theory: performance anxiety

Psychodynamic perspective: unresolved childhood conflicts about sexuality; sexuality and self-definition closely connected

Interpersonal context also relevant: sexual problems often reflect other relational problems like poor communication, power issues, anger.

Cultural and religious issues may also be implicated.

Treatment—moderately successful:

Masters and Johnson: early pioneers in treating with progressive, step-by-step behavioral assignments—methods still in use today

Cognitive therapy examines dysfunctional beliefs about sexuality.

Note: Generally done in couples' context using combination of behavioral, cognitive, interpersonal, and psychodynamic principles.

PARAPHILIAS—SEXUAL DESIRE DIRECTED AT INAPPROPRIATE OBJECTS OR BEHAVIORS

Sexual Masochism: becoming aroused while being humiliated or hurt

Sexual Sadism: becoming aroused while humiliating or hurting someone else

Exhibitionism: becoming aroused by exposing one's genitals to others

Fetishism: becoming aroused in response to nonliving objects like women's undergarments

Frotteurism: becoming aroused by touching or rubbing up against a nonconsenting person

Pedophilia: sexual attraction to prepubescent children

Transvestic Fetishism: cross-dressing for the purpose of sexual arousal

Voyeurism: peeping-Tom syndrome

Not otherwise specified

Note: Actual behavior is not required for diagnosis—strong urges or fantasies meet the criteria if they cause significant distress or dysfunction.

Question: Many people have paraphiliac fantasies. What is normal? How strong do the fantasies have to be to qualify as abnormal? Who does the judging? (Homosexuality was once listed as a paraphilia, but is now not considered a disorder—is this "medical" or "societal" judgment?)

Causes:

Almost always learned through classical conditioning.

Treatment:

Strongly behavioral with some attention to self-esteem and other psychodynamic issues

Attempt to replace inappropriate object with more appropriate one through re-training procedures

Use of punishments controversial (aversion therapy)

Poor effectiveness—many dropouts, relapses

Question: How should society manage sexual offenders since treatment results are so poor? Lengthy incarceration? Life-long supervision? Chemical castration?

GENDER IDENTITY DISORDER — INDIVIDUAL
IDENTIFIES WITH THE OPPOSITE GENDER

Very rare disorder

May have biological roots (chemical imbalance while in the womb).

Learning and modeling — possibly relevant

Sex-reassignment surgery — mixed results in terms of satisfaction

CHAPTER SEVEN

Substance Abuse
and Eating Disorders

————◄O►————

It may seen odd, at first, to find substance use disorders and eating disorders in the same chapter since the DSM-IV lists them as separate categories. Yet, these and certain other behaviors, like gambling or pedophilia, for example, all share several properties that we call "addictive." First, they involve loss of self-control. Second, those afflicted continue the behavior in the face of clearly adverse consequences. Third, these disorders appear to reflect a compulsion or an irresistible need to engage in the behavior in question. Fourth, they show "tolerance," which is the need for increasingly larger amounts of the behavior or substance over time. While there is currently no single umbrella DSM category for addictive behavior, perhaps we will see one in DSM-V.

Substance abuse is arguably the number one health problem in most Western societies. Alcohol- and cigarette-related morbidity and mortality are enormous. Alcohol, for example, is now the third leading cause of death in the United States trailing only coronary heart disease and cancer, a substantial percentage of which is related to cigarette smoking. The DSM-IV distinguishes between substance use disorders, which include abuse and dependence, and substance-induced disorders, which can include intoxication, withdrawal, delirium, dementia, psychosis, depression, and anxiety, as well as sexual and sleep dysfunction.

Included in this chapter are two substance abuse disorders. In the first, alcohol abuse shades into dependence and is treated successfully. In the second, mixed-substance-abuse results in a psychotic episode, or "bad trip." Both cases are fairly common.

In the area of eating disorders, we have included a case presentation taken from a book by Hilda Bruch, one of the earliest clinician/theoreticians to investigate anorexia nervosa, "the starvation disease."

We have also included three readings. The first focuses on the topic of "controlled drinking." For many years, it had been thought that total abstinence was the only sensible treatment goal for substance-dependent individuals. Alcoholics Anonymous is based on this model, as are most treatment programs. Recently, however, several studies have suggested that some of these individuals can achieve moderate, controlled social drinking.

We have also included a short story, which, although not actually a first-person account, is written by a clinician who has worked with bulimic patients. It is a vivid and realistic portrayal of a bulimic "attack." Finally, we have included a reading that draws some additional parallels between eating disorders and substance abuse disorders.

28

————◄o►————

EMERGING ALCOHOLISM:
THE CASE OF SIMON S.

SIMON S., A FORTY-TWO-YEAR-OLD attorney was brought, somewhat reluctantly, to therapy by his wife of seventeen years, Carla. The couple
were having increasingly painful arguments over the last year or two,
and while neither was considering leaving the marriage, they both felt
that they needed help in communicating more effectively with each other.

Carla took responsibility for her share of the problem. She thought
she might be having a "midlife crisis" in which her lifelong defense of
"clamming up" when she was disappointed or angry was breaking down.
She found herself nagging and arguing and feeling resentful much of the
time. She wondered, too, whether perimenopausal hormonal changes
might not be relevant as well. Her complaints about Simon included his
not being as "accepting" of her parents as she would have liked, his not
spending enough time with the children (two pre-teen daughters), his
overcommitment to spending time at a lake property that had been part
of his family for several generations, and his lack of help with household
chores.

Simon did not dispute these charges. For his part, he wished Carla, a
teacher, would not become so preoccupied with school and the children
that she neglected to spend time with him. They didn't have as much sex
as he would have liked, nor as much "down time." Mostly, though, it
seemed as if Simon would have been happy if Carla hadn't been so
unhappy. He described her as a "terrific teacher and mother," felt "in-
credibly lucky to be married to her," and thought that, in general, she
was "just great." He was perplexed by her growing dissatisfaction with
him and seemed genuinely to want to work on the problem.

Both Carla and Simon had had previous mental health treatment.
Carla, three years previously, had purposely lost one hundred pounds.
In conjunction with her diet, she underwent regular psychotherapy in
which she explored issues related to self-image, subtle societal messages
about weight and self-worth, and familial patterns of relating around
food. Her parents, farmers, were both alive. She also had two older
brothers, one of whom still lived at home and seemed to function at a
marginal level. The other was married and, from all appearances, suc-

cessful. Carla maintained a close relationship with her parents, particularly her father, and she felt that her husband was jealous of that relationship. She also played the mediator between her brothers when they quarrelled.

Simon had a history of clinical depression for which he had been treated with both psychotherapy and antidepressant medications, although he had had neither for several years. Only his mother was still alive, his father having died three years earlier. He had an older brother who had a serious drinking problem. His maternal grandfather and maternal uncle were also alcoholics. Simon, himself, reported "occasionally" drinking to drunkenness. Carla voiced concern that the frequency of these episodes seemed to be increasing lately. Depression also ran in his mother's side of the family.

At the second session, Carla again raised her concerns about Simon's drinking. She reported that their daughters and his mother were also concerned. Simon acknowledged that he might, perhaps, have a "small problem" in that once he began to drink, he couldn't seem to stop. He would decide to have one beer, and it would turn into a six-pack. One glass of wine would turn into a full bottle. He also acknowledged drinking alone sometimes, generally while working in his basement shop. Drinking beer while he worked helped him relax. Carla pointed out that Simon also drank during periods when he was taking antidepressant medication, despite the doctor's admonishment that he should not.

The tone of this conversation was exploratory and respectful rather than confrontative. By the end of the session, Simon had agreed to maintain sobriety for one month to see what this might teach him about the role alcohol played in his life.

In the session one month later, Simon admitted that he had been unable to keep his abstinence pledge. He had had alcohol at a party. In addition, Carla revealed that she had found Valium tablets for which Simon had no prescription. Valium is a medication used to treat anxiety and muscle spasms. It is cross-addictive with alcohol and commonly abused by people who also abuse alcohol.

Carla was angry and disappointed. Both reported that their relationship had gotten bleaker, with a virtual absence of loving behaviors on either of their parts. Simon agreed to consider accepting a referral to the local alcoholism treatment agency. He also agreed to consider attending Alcoholics Anonymous. However, he had serious concerns about both these routes. As a professional in the community, he had a certain reputation to uphold. If word got out that he was receiving treatment for alcohol abuse, his authority and the respect he was granted would certainly diminish. He still felt that he could successfully abstain from drinking without outside help. Carla agreed that he should have the opportunity to try again, and they spent the rest of that session and the next several working on ways to improve their communication and increase the level of trust and affection between them.

At each session, Simon's drinking behaviors and feelings were examined, at least briefly. He began to realize that, even though he had not been drinking recently, he continued to have strong cravings for alcohol. He had "made it" through Thanksgiving without a drink, but felt that he was "not out of the woods." Gradually, it dawned on him that the struggle with alcohol was going to be a protracted, possibly life-long one.

Carla confessed that she had told their physician, who was also a personal friend, that Simon was working to overcome a drinking problem. Simon was dismayed, and talked movingly about his sense of shame and the stigma he felt. How could he look his friend in the eye, knowing that his friend now knew how "weak" he was? The therapist, with Carla's input, helped Simon to confront the truth—that many of his friends and relatives knew that he drank too much. He was particularly horrified when he learned from his wife that their daughters had been frightened and worried about his drinking. At the end of this session, Simon agreed to do two things: First, he would talk to his daughters about his drinking and assure them that he was going to work hard to stop, and second, he was going to speak with a colleague who had been attending Alcoholics Anonymous regularly since getting caught driving while intoxicated.

Over the next several sessions, held at monthly intervals, Simon remained abstinent, but he procrastinated about talking to his colleague. Carla admitted that one of the reasons she hated his spending time at the lake was because she knew that he and his brother would be drinking virtually the whole time they were there together. The lake property and the presence of his brother were both strong stimuli for drinking. By the next session, Simon had confronted his brother about their mutual drinking problems, but had received virtually no response. The couple continued to work on understanding each other's needs and feelings.

Six months into therapy, Simon had a major slip—he got drunk while home alone with one of his daughters. He was horrified and ashamed. Much to his relief, Carla handled the matter calmly. She told him that she knew how hard maintaining sobriety had been for him, that he had done better than she had expected him to, and that she felt he needed some assistance. He gratefully agreed to seek alcohol counseling. At the end of the session, they both rated the quality of their relationship as a seven or eight on a ten-point scale.

It took four more months, and one more episode of drinking, for Simon to overcome his resistance enough to actually make an appointment for evaluation at the alcohol treatment service. He had been gardening and had found an old, open bottle of wine on the back porch. Impulsively, he drank it.

Simon decided to seek treatment in a neighboring county so he would be less likely to run into friends and associates. At the suggestion of the alcoholism counselor by whom he had been evaluated, and with the support of his marriage therapist and his wife, he elected to attend outpatient group treatment three times a week for six weeks. This experience rapidly expanded his knowledge and ability to talk about his alcoholism. Carla attended several family meetings, in which the role of the spouse and other family members in rehabilitation was discussed.

At the insistence of his substance abuse counselor, Simon agreed to begin attending Alcoholics Anonymous meetings, and finally made contact with his colleague, who brought him to the first meeting. There, he heard about other people's experiences with alcohol and about strategies for preventing relapse. He learned that negative emotional states like "tired, hungry and lonely" were triggers for drinking. He learned that he had to avoid "people, places and things" that he had come to associate with drinking. He confronted the risk that being at the lake with his brother presented to him, and decided he would always take one of his children (or his wife) with him, and that he would promise that child that he would not drink. He felt sad at the loss of private time with his brother, but he knew that he would be unlikely to maintain sobriety in that context. He began to identify the social anxiety that had always plagued him, and that had been relieved so successfully by alcohol. He began to practice using social skills sober, and tolerated the discomfort that accompanied the practice.

Through all of this, Simon relied heavily on Carla's support and respect. For her part, she reported that their relationship had been substantially improved by Simon's abstinence. They continued to work on communicating their appreciation for each other, and on making space for each other's "passions"—Carla's for teaching and Simon's for gardening and the lake. They continue to attend monthly marital therapy sessions and may decide to do so for several years. They think of it as a sort of "insurance policy" against slipping back into old patterns of relating. Simon continues in Alcoholics Anonymous, and in biweekly individual counseling for his alcoholism. He expects to stay connected with AA indefinitely, perhaps for life.

Thinking About the Case

Alcohol is clearly the most serious drug of abuse in the United States and Western Europe. Excessive drinking is responsible for untold misery and cost at both the individual and societal level. Of the possibly ten million problem drinkers in the United States today, only one million are receiving treatment. Further, treatment is far from foolproof. Studies suggest that at age sixty-five, about one-third of problem drinkers are dead or disabled, one-third have successfully abstained or are drinking socially, and one-third are still trying to quit. Alcohol abuse is often accompanied by a number of other psychological disorders, including depression, anxiety, and antisocial personality disorder. Generally, the greater the level of overall psychopathology, the poorer the prognosis.

The case of Simon S. gives the lie to the commonly held belief that an alcoholic must hit bottom before he or she can begin to recover. While Simon's marriage and relationship with his children were beginning to be affected by his alcohol use, his occupational functioning and social relationships were, as yet, relatively unimpaired. Still, he was able to acknowledge that his drinking was becoming problematic and, after some additional evidence was brought to bear, he took steps that helped him to arrest the problem.

It is more common for people who abuse or are dependent on alcohol or other substances to be overwhelmed by "denial," an unconscious psychological defense mechanism that prevents the individual from accurately evaluating the meaning and consequences of his or her behavior. Examples of denial include the following: "I'm not an alcoholic—I only drink beer, never the hard stuff"; "I never drink before five o'clock in the afternoon"; "I could stop whenever I wanted to, but I don't want to"; "I never drive when I'm drinking, so I can't be an alcoholic." While there is some evidence of the presence of denial in Simon's case (for example, he needed several episodes of unwanted drinking to get him into treatment), his therapist and wife were able to break through relatively easily. Alcoholism is thought to be a progressive disorder, with the quantity consumed, tolerance to its effects, and denial increasing over time. Generally then, the earlier the intervention is made, the more likely it will be to work.

The course of Simon's ascent into sobriety is quite typical. Relapses are common, so that Alcoholics Anonymous teaches that one can be a "recovering" alcoholic but never a "recovered" one. Therapy aims to reduce the risk of relapse by identifying the circumstances or feelings that might predispose the individual to drink, and by teaching the person strategies for avoiding or managing those situations without drinking. For example, after Simon drank the open bottle of wine, he and Carla decided to make a sweep of the house, garage, and grounds to make sure that all bottles were gone. His decision to take one of his children to the lake with him, and his working on his social anxiety in therapy, are also relapse prevention strategies.

It is generally thought that working with the family of individuals with drinking problems can be crucial to their recovery prospects. Over time, family members may have accommodated to the drinking by trying to reduce the negative consequences of it. For example, a spouse might call the person's workplace to say he or she was ill, when in fact, drunkenness was the real problem. Or, the spouse might minimize the drinking when talking to friends or family, or nag incessantly about drinking which may raise the level of stress in the household and lead to increased, rather than decreased, alcohol consumption. These behaviors are called "co-dependent," meaning that the spouse has developed drinking-related behaviors just like the alcoholic. Children of alcoholic parents are, of course, also affected. Research suggests that they are at increased risk for a host of psychological problems as adolescents and adults. Therefore, one of the components of treatment aims to minimize the deleterious effects of alcohol abuse on the family system.

To date, no one treatment method has been shown to be obviously superior to another. Simon's case is typical in that a combination of interventions is used: marital therapy, individual psychotherapy, group treatment, and self-help in the form of Alcoholics Anonymous.

There are two serious controversies in the field of alcoholism treatment. First, it has long been held that abstinence is the only sensible therapy goal for an individual with alcoholism. However, recent research suggests that a sub-group of people who have a history of addictive drinking can achieve moderate, controlled social drinking. Many clinicians in the treatment community think such a notion is dangerous in that it may encourage alcoholics to remain in "denial." The second, related, controversy concerns whether alcoholism is even a "disease." If it is, then individuals with alcoholism are entitled to the rights and privileges of the sick role, for example, time off from work with pay when the "illness" makes work impossible. But some people think of alcoholism as a moral rather than a medical problem. This disagreement is unlikely to be resolved any time soon.

Questions to Consider

1. Why did Simon develop a drinking problem? What does your answer say about which model(s) you rely on to explain this disorder?

2. The line between alcoholism and alcohol abuse is a fine one and not all clinicians draw that line in the same place. Consider the criteria for substance abuse versus those for substance dependence. Does Simon's use meet the criteria for alcohol dependence, or might he be better thought of as a substance abuser?

3. Consider the drinking habits of your friends. Which of them might be at risk of developing a drinking problem? Why? Consider your own drinking habits in the same way.

4. When people drink too much, they generally experience dizziness, nausea, vomiting, and a headache. The next day they may suffer from a hangover, not to mention the negative consequences of their drinking-related behavior. How, then, would a behaviorist explain the development of compulsive drinking?

5. Do you think alcoholism and other problems of impulse-control, like pathological gambling, are truly "diseases?" Why or why not? What, if any data, would make you change your view?

29

——————◄○►——————

MIXED SUBSTANCE ABUSE:
THE CASE OF MIGUEL S.

MIGUEL S. WOKE TO FIND himself tied to a bed. Both his wrists and his ankles were lightly but securely bound with fabric straps. His head hurt and at first he was dazed and confused. Looking around, he ascertained that he was in a hospital—faint sounds from a far-off public-address system drifted into the sun-lit, double-bedded room. Before he could respond to the rising panic he was beginning to feel, Miguel noticed that the call button was placed near his right hand, where he could reach it. Soon after pressing it, a nurse came in and began to untie his restraints as she told him what had happened.

Apparently, Miguel had been admitted to the hospital the night before. He had been dropped off at the emergency room by a carful of "friends" who hadn't stayed around long enough to offer any information or to see that he was okay. He was dressed in blue jeans and a t-shirt, but he stood out from the rest of the people waiting for care because he was covered from head to toe with stripes and blobs of what appeared to be oil-based paint.

Alone and clearly very agitated, Miguel couldn't sit still. Instead, he had created quite a stir, pacing and hollering, "they're after us; they're following us." When asked who the "us" referred to, he had responded, "me . . . us, all of us, we're breaking apart and they're after us." Alternately paralyzed with fear and lashing out in a rage, he had been unable to speak coherently or to maintain his attention for more than a minute at a time. Every sound startled him and sometimes he stared fixedly at the emergency room door, as if he were seeing something horrible. Unable to calm him or to figure out initially what was wrong with him, the emergency room physician had ordered that Miguel be restrained, admitted, and tranquilized. It had required one policeman and two orderlies to carry out the physician's directives.

As the nurse spoke to him, Miguel began to remember bits and pieces of the evening, although most of what she told him about the emergency room was news to him. He had been smoking pot and drinking wine with his college housemates and their girlfriends. At some point, several of them had decided to drop some acid. Miguel's trip had begun in a pretty mellow way. An art major, he had been sketching and listening to music, when the urge to paint a wall-sized mural came over him. He went to his room and began to mix paints and spread them on the wall. The paints seemed to shimmer and pulse as he applied them in wide swaths to the large, empty space. He could hear the beat of the music through the floor of his room and he felt that the paint and music were moving in the same rhythm. He began to feel very certain that this painting would be his master work—that it would portray the unity of the universe and that, somehow, when people looked at it, the paints would move and they would hear music as he did while he painted.

As he thought about unity, Miguel realized that he and his painting were one and he felt the need to remove artificial boundaries. So he took off all of his clothes and began to paint himself with the same paint he had been using on the walls.

At some point, one of his housemates wandered by and was, of course, struck by the sight of Miguel, naked and furiously painting. At first he thought it was pretty funny, and called several of the others to come watch the artist at work. However, Miguel's response to his girlfriend's attempts to get him to put on some shorts alarmed everybody. He turned toward her, made the sign of the cross and spoke a few words that weren't English . . . and didn't seem to be Spanish, his first language, either. His emotional tone was angry, even threatening, and when he turned back to his painting with total singlemindedness, his friends didn't know what to do next. One of his housemates tried jokingly to cajole him into stopping for a while. Another brought him a cup of coffee which Miguel threw at the wall, using his hands to mix it into the paint. His friends decided to take definitive action when he urinated on the wall, again using his hands to mix the urine into the paint and coffee mixture. Knowing that calling the police or an ambulance would get them busted for sure, they overpowered their friend, threw some clothes on him, and took him to the emergency room of the nearest hospital.

Miguel was terrified and confused. His friends, he thought, must have been able to see that he was on the verge of making a huge break-through—why would they want to stop him? Perhaps they were not really his friends after all, but imposters who meant to see that the world would not be saved by his work. If so, they would certainly want to kill him. They must be taking him someplace to kill him. Screaming for help and lashing out, he nonetheless found himself inside the hospital door and the rest, as they say, was history.

Miguel was the third child in a family of six siblings. His father, a Mexican immigrant had married his mother, a non-Hispanic, when she was just eighteen. She was already pregnant with Miguel's older sister, Maria, at the time of their union. Mr. S. worked construction jobs in the summer and brought in unemployment money in the winter. Mrs. S. worked in a local factory, sewing women's clothing. The S.'s marriage was not an ideal one. They fought frequently and loudly—mostly about Mr. S.'s drinking and womanizing, and about Mrs. S.'s nagging and complaining. Sometimes Mr. S. would stay away for several days on end. Other times, Mrs. S. would take the children to her parents' house, where they spent most of their after-school time anyway, until her husband came to get her, all flowers and sweet talk.

Still, the family unit was strong in certain ways. Both parents were strict disciplinarians. Miguel and his siblings were expected to do well in school, to be respectful and polite to their elders, to do chores without complaining, to attend church each Sunday, and to obey their parents without question. The S.'s believed strongly that their children could do better than they had done in life, and they meant to see that it happened. In addition, Mrs. S.'s parents and siblings provided a ready-made support network for the children, while Mr. S.'s family members were all in Mexico City. Babysitters and playmates were always available, as were adults to listen to Miguel's problems. Mrs. S.'s family didn't exactly approve of Mr. S.'s ethnicity or behavior, though, and sometimes they let the children know it. Miguel always felt uncomfortable when that happened. He didn't know whether to defend his father or keep quiet. After all, he was part Mexican too, and anyway, his father was his father.

Miguel was thought of as pretty normal. His grades were good enough to keep his parents off his back, and he was a talented soccer player throughout junior and senior high school. He was gregarious and likable and had many friends. He was also attractive to the girls in his group. In fact, he began having sex when he was twelve, the same year he began using marijuana. Smoking marijuana and having sex were portals to adulthood among the young men who were his friends. Miguel was proud to have been accepted into the brotherhood of older guys and strove to emulate their fearlessness and machismo. Although he knew that his father would beat him if his drug use and promiscuity were discovered, he felt that secretly, his father would be proud, too.

By the time Miguel went to college, he was a regular marijuana and alcohol user. It wasn't difficult to find other students who had developed the same habits in high school. Naturally, they became his friends. While he seemed to be able to drink and smoke marijuana with little effect on his school performance, he saved cocaine and LSD use for weekends when the workload wasn't too heavy. He also dabbled in amphetamines and barbiturates—mostly to help him stay awake to study and then to sleep. This, then, was Miguel's pattern of substance use at the time of his hospitalization.

Miguel's hospital stay was brief. Showing no further signs of confusion or unrealistic ideas, but having produced a urine sample full of positive indicators for drugs, Miguel was discharged after two days with a referral to an outpatient drug abuse treatment program. The doctor had sort of blackmailed him into going by telling him that if he did not follow through on the referral, his parents would be notified of the true reason for his hospitalization. It seems that Miguel had told them that he had had a bad case of flu.

The drug counselor met with Miguel and took a very careful history of his drug use. Miguel didn't really want to believe that he was addicted to alcohol and marijuana, but he had been pretty frightened by "going off the wall." While he told the counselor that he would stop using all mind-altering substances, in his own mind he only resolved to stop using acid. He began to attend the campus group of Alcoholics Anonymous, which was filled with other multidrug users like himself, and learned to spout the party line—abstinence "one day at a time." And he did, indeed, remain abstinent—for about three weeks.

Miguel hadn't changed who his friends were, nor had his friends changed their drug-use behavior. They agreed with Miguel that maybe he shouldn't use LSD, but he had seemed to handle drinking and marijuana just fine. They felt uncomfortable being stoned while he looked on, sober, and they encouraged him to join in. It didn't take much encouragement to convince him. He didn't use much the first night, or even the next. But by the next weekend, he felt safe in getting high for real. Only this time, he had a mini-version of the "breakdown" that had originally led to his hospitalization. He began to feel that his friends had malevolent intentions towards him, that perhaps they had laced the pot with LSD or cocaine. Maybe they were even plotting with the police to get him busted. Their laughter seemed to him forced—even false. They appeared to be staring at him in an odd way. Miguel went to his room, locked himself in, and stayed there until morning.

When he awoke, he called his drug counselor and made an appointment. This latest episode had made it clear to him that drugs were "messing with my head," as he put it. Now he had some questions: would smoking marijuana always result in a "bad trip?" Had he done some permanent damage to his brain? What if he just drank alcohol and stayed off the other drugs? Could he smoke marijuana again if he waited longer before trying it the next time? The counselor suggested that Miguel engage in an experiment in which he would cease to use all drugs, including alcohol, for one month. They would then discuss the results of the experiment together. Miguel agreed.

A month later Miguel was back in the counselor's office. He had stuck to his word and had made a number of discoveries. First, he felt better about himself. His mind was clearer and studying was easier. He had also begun to play on the intercollegiate volleyball team. He loved the exertion, and he was beginning to make friends with the other young men and women on the team. The downside, though, was that his relationship with his old friends had become strained. He still hung out with them, but being straight for a whole evening in the company of people who were stoned was pretty boring. Their silly laughter annoyed him, and their single-minded pursuit of getting "wasted" seemed senseless. As he spoke, Miguel had an insight: talking in this way about his friends had made him feel oddly guilty, and he stumbled upon the feeling that somehow he was betraying his father by doing so. This led to a fairly extended discussion (the first, as it would turn out, of many) about his father's drinking and its effect on Miguel's family.

Miguel continued to experiment with using alcohol and marijuana over the next year or so, but, at the same time, he continued in counseling and in AA. His substance use dwindled to very occasional use and finally stopped after eighteen months. His circle of friends had changed, too. He now hung out with a "dry" crowd—some were his friends from AA, and some from volleyball. On follow-up, at his graduation from college, Miguel was still abstinent and now identified himself as a "recovering" substance abuser.

Thinking About the Case

Miguel would have qualified for a number of diagnoses: hallucinogen-induced psychosis with delusions, cannabis-induced psychosis, alcohol abuse, cannabis abuse, hallucinogen abuse, and possibly cocaine abuse. Miguel's two psychotic episodes are fairly typical of those experienced by some drug users. Symptoms include paranoia, hallucinations, delusions, and sometimes delirium. These problems typically resolve on their own as the level of psychoactive chemical in the body diminishes. Therefore, treatment involves simply keeping the person comfortable and safe. While substance-induced psychoses can mimic schizophrenia and mania symptomatically, their brief duration sets them apart. The diagnostic picture is cloudier for a small group of individuals who develop psychoses in response to drug use but do not appear to get thoroughly better on their own. Many of these people probably have an underlying psychotic process that was precipitated, rather than caused, by substance use. For these patients, treatment with antipsychotic medications and re-evaluation of expectations may be in order.

Polysubstance abuse like Miguel's is common among young people in today's society. While alcohol and marijuana are staples in the drug culture, amphetamines, cocaine, hallucinogens, barbiturates, amyl nitrate, and other designer drugs tend to come and go as fads and supply change over time.

This case illuminates the various factors that are relevant in the etiology of problematic substance use. The family history of alcoholism may indicate the presence of a genetic predisposition to substance use problems. Parental modeling may also be at work, as Miguel grew up in an environment in which the adult male was a heavy drug (alcohol) user. The "macho" culture which was exemplified in his father's behavior, and which was emulated by young males as he grew up, supported heavy substance use as an indication of manhood. This was probably supported by images presented in the larger culture in which some of the more visible sports heroes and movie stars are known to use a variety of drugs with little, if any, negative effect on their popularity or income-producing potential.

The case also indicates a fairly typical course of treatment, although of course, not all people who abuse drugs improve. Miguel, at first, denied that he had a problem, even in the face of the frightening psychosis he experienced. His first attempt at getting straight and sober was not a very serious one. Once his motivation level increased, because of another "bad trip," he still had to make numerous social changes to support his new lifestyle. Alcoholics Anonymous calls this process changing "people, places, and things." Miguel made new friends and went to AA meetings and volleyball practices rather than bars and off-campus apartments, and he spent his time in different activities than he had before. He also had to explore the ideas he had had about substance use and about what it took to be a man. He was forced to embark on a journey of self-discovery that went far beyond his use of drugs and alcohol. As you can see, this is a fairly extensive process that requires commitment of time and energy, as well as motivation to change.

We should note that insight-oriented psychotherapy, in the absence of sufficient sobriety, is generally ineffective. Most psychotherapists, once they identify a substance-abuse problem in a patient, require that the person be active in substance abuse treatment and be generally abstemious in order for psychotherapy to proceed. If relapse occurs, therapy may be suspended for a time so that energy can be focused on regaining sobriety, or the psychotherapy may continue but be focused exclusively on regaining sobriety for some period of time.

Alcoholics Anonymous has another motto: "One day at a time." Substance abuse often has a chronic course, with periods of abstinence punctuated by periods of renewed use — sometimes referred to as "falling off the wagon," or having "slipped" or "relapsed." Twelve-step programs like AA teach participants never to take their sobriety for granted since relapse can occur in the blink of an eye. Miguel's sobriety at the end of college is a good prognostic sign, but by no means a guarantee of future sobriety. While there is considerable debate about whether lifelong participation in some sort of "treatment" is required for the maintenance of sobriety, it is generally agreed that ongoing vigilance about emotional and environmental risk factors for renewed substance use is necessary.

Questions to Consider

1. Do you think that polysubstance use like Miguel's would be easier or harder to treat than use of only one drug, like alcohol? Why or why not?

2. Twelve-step programs like Alcoholics Anonymous teach that "a drug is a drug is a drug." By this they mean that if you have a problem with any substance, you must quit using all other mind-altering substances (except, apparently, for nicotine and caffeine) as well. Do you agree with this? Why or why not? Are you basing your answers on scientific data, your own experience, or that of your friends?

3. While there are things in Miguel's background that might have predisposed him to substance abuse problems, there are also things that would suggest that he has a fairly good prognosis. What are they?

4. Family involvement is often helpful in the treatment of substance abuse. What do you think might be the effects of involving Miguel's family in his treatment? What might be the benefits? Are there any possible drawbacks? How would you decide how to proceed?

5. Do you think that Miguel's parents deserve to know about his substance abuse problem? Does he have rights to privacy? When, if ever, should these be breached?

30

——————◄○►——————

ANOREXIA NERVOSA: THE CASE OF GAIL

Hilda Bruch, M.D., a psychiatrist, was one of the first clinician-researchers to study eating disorders. Her case descriptions remain among the most vivid and powerful available. The case she relates here from *Eating Disorders*, (Basic Books, 1973), illustrates the incredible power struggle that anorexia can provoke between the patient and other family members. While the case is thirty-five years old, it is still fresh. Gail would not now be treated with extended inpatient hospitalization, but her prognosis would still be considered quite grave. Here's her case:

The case history I am going to present may sound to some of you like a dramatic exaggeration. It is not. On the contrary, I regret that my literary ability is not adequate to convey the full flavor of the grotesque atmosphere of mutual coercion and violence that surrounded the whole development of the patient whom I shall call Gail. She entered the New York State Psychiatric Institute in October, 1959, at the age of 20. Gail was a slim, well-groomed and fashionably dressed young lady. Her doctor had made arrangements for hospitalization several weeks earlier but Gail had refused to sign the application for voluntary admission. Her weight was 96 lbs, a sacred figure to which she had rigidly clung for the past 4 or 5 years. And thereby hangs the tale—how she had managed to maintain her weight.

Up to the age of 13 she had been plump, a fate for which she blamed her parents. Her weight had reached nearly 140 lbs and had earned her the nickname of Two-Ton Tilly. When Tilly was 11 years old the parents had sought help at a child guidance clinic because she was unmanageable at home. There was no improvement during a year of treatment of mother and child, and a boarding school with treatment facilities was recommended. Tilly went there under violent protest, saying her parents wanted to get rid of her. At the school she felt terrified and would not dare eat anything. Her fear of eating was so great that she thought if she took as little as a glass of water she might get out of hand and become even fatter. Instead a miracle happened—she began to grow thinner. When the weight loss became visible, she decided also to get rid of the much-ridiculed name Tilly, and choose for herself a new name, Gail. She continued to protest against being at the boarding school, talked about running away and wanted to go home. The parents finally gave in to her protestations, feeling guilty about the accusation of having gotten rid of her and believing her promise of better behavior. She came back weighing 96 lbs and was determined not to get fat again.

Her absolute insistence on remaining at this magic weight of 96 lbs led to her dominating the household with enforced rituals. Her parents were forced to shop three times a day because she would not permit food in the home between meals. Any food left over after a meal had to be thrown away, since she feared that she might succumb to the compulsion of eating it and thereby spoil her magic weight. She entered high school and obtained very good grades by studying religiously. In order to study she had to have absolute quiet around the home and her parents were not allowed to be there when she worked. The parents were unable to cope with the situation. They again sought psychiatric help and Gail consented to see a psychiatrist, though on her terms.

Things went along this way, with many outbursts of violence, until Gail's graduation from high school. She did not want her parents to come to the graduation and refused to get tickets for them. The mother insisted they would go just the same; Gail asked: "How? How?" When the mother refused to tell, Gail became more and more frantic in her questioning and finally grabbed a pair of scissors and attacked her mother, threatening to kill her. The mother ran out of the house to the father's store; they called the police and Gail was taken to a city hospital. She was cowed by the hospital experience and returned home with the best intentions but then was unable to control herself. She stayed at a private hospital for six months where she was kept quiet with medication; no effort at psychotherapy was made. After her return home she saw a psychiatrist regularly and became very dependent on him. She also began to work and was out of the home a good deal. For a year and a half she kept jobs as a salesgirl, lasting in any one place approximately three or four months.

Throughout this period her behavior at home was unchanged, and she still controlled the family with her demand for a restricted diet. The father suggested that now that she was earning money she should have an apartment of her own. Gail's response was: "You can't get rid of me that easily." She quit her job and just stayed home. Her behavior was so violent that within two months her parents moved out into a furnished room, the address of which they kept a strict secret. Even now, after Gail has been in the hospital for over a year, they have not moved back to their old apartment. The mother does not dare to live there; it reminds her of her daughter's violence with every piece of furniture and fixture marred and half destroyed from these battles. In fits of anger Gail had carved initials into the furniture, and the bed-room door was covered with hammer marks made when Gail had tried to invade her parents' room after they had locked themselves in in desperation. After the upholstery had been destroyed the mother had bought slipcovers but Gail had cut them into ribbons. She also had torn down the shades and drapes from the windows. The parents had put up with all this because Gail's psychiatrist implored them to be patient. The parents said that the doctor had complied with Gail's request not to talk about certain topics, for instance, the word *food* was absolutely forbidden. He also urged the parents never to talk about food, but just to obey the patient.

Gail only left the apartment to go to her doctor's office three times a week. She also had the privilege of phoning him whenever she felt anxious. Otherwise she kept entirely to herself, except for phoning the parents at the store to give them orders. This stage of affairs lasted one and a half years, the parents coming in three times a day and bringing her prepared food. This food had to be the exact amount that would keep Gail from gaining weight. If she gained as much as half a pound she would create a violent scene.

It became apparent that not only was no progress being made but that the whole situation had deteriorated, and Gail became more and more withdrawn. But she absolutely refused to enter the hospital as a voluntary patient. This was just one more of her parents' schemes to get rid of her. Things stayed in this stalemate until one day the mother reacted to her violence and began shouting and throwing things. This was so terrifying to Gail that she consented to hospitalization. "I did not know what was happening to my mother." She felt she must have done something wrong because she had caused this terrible outburst and felt she was no longer in control of her mother.

During the first few months at the hospital the effort to keep her weight under control remained her chief preoccupation. Since people in the hospital did not submit to her dietary demands, this was a strenuous task. She had brought her own scale and weighed herself every day and did not eat if she had gained an ounce. Things changed when an attractive young male patient spoke to her. This indicated to Gail that he was going to fall in love with her. She set out to accom-plish this with all her manipulative skills, with the result that he fled and openly rebuffed her. Even now, many months later, she is indig-nant and bewildered that he did not want to love her even though she was at the perfect weight of 96 lbs and could be glamorous whenever she wanted. Actually she dressed up or was well-groomed only a few times during their brief relationship. Then she became conspicuously sloppy, expecting that since he knew she could be well-dressed if she wanted to be, he should admire her beauty even when she was dirty and neglected. Immediately after this rebuff she began to gain weight rapidly, reaching 150 lbs, within 2 or 3 months. She dressed now in maternity clothes with the expressed intent of creating the impression of being pregnant. This to her was less shameful and aroused less guilt than appearing fat. The idea of intercourse and pregnancy, however, was revolting to her. If it were not painful she would have had her uterus removed, just to be safe.

I became familiar with Gail only after her first physician had left this hospital. She had greeted her new physician with a sarcastic outburst: "I hate you already. You can never be Dr. X. I can see with one look that you are inexperienced, impervious and do not know much psychiatry." These accusations persisted through several treatment sessions. Her new doctor felt discouraged, and with justification. In spite of therapeutic efforts for eight or ten years, including one year at the Psychiatric Institute, the course had been downhill. He asked for help in evaluating the situation, for supervision if it was felt that anything could be done.

In reviewing the previous treatment approaches it became apparent that they had been conducted according to the principle of avoiding past errors, be it that of the parents or the previous psychiatrist, and of confronting the patient with her manipulative behavior and power struggle. The underlying conceptual delusions about herself and all human relatedness had *not* been recognized and therefore had remained unexplored and uncorrected. Actually Gail was unusually clear on this point—but the significance of her frequent statements had been missed. In a conference together with her parents she burst out: "I tried to remake my parents all through my life. I wanted to put them in a different role, make them warm and understanding so that they could raise me better. It is their fault that I am not a good child. What I am now, my parents have created. I'm the product of their creation. The reason that people don't like me is because I am no good; but that is because my parents did not know how to raise me. It is all their fault." There was a note of despair when she added: "Don't they see how much I suffer, don't they see how unhappy I am about being a brat, always fighting and arguing." Being thin was one way of being something in her own right, not quite her parents' product. They always had pushed food on her and wanted her to be fat. Now she is quite heavy and she is infuriated when her father greets her: "Oh, you look so much better now."

The patient was quite concrete in her assumptions (and her parents shared her delusion) that a child remains the parents' property and creation. The mother had been very devoted and attached to a little niece, Gail's five-year-old cousin. She had adored this child, a cuddly and plump baby. When Gail was born, the mother was dreadfully disappointed because her baby was long and stringy, not plump at all. She set out to change her into this dream child and it became her desperate life's work to make her skinny child plump and pleasant.

The result was this tragedy of mutual blame and guilt. I have called the interaction of this family the Frankenstein Theme. The daughter, conceived of as her parents' creation, had turned monster-like against her creators, but appearances notwithstanding, basically not in aggression, but in a desperate effort to change her parents so that they would undo their errors and recreate her in a better mold. The deep conviction of her own helplessness was vividly acted out in the dieting arrangement, which in turn must be conceived of as a consequence of her inability to recognize correctly hunger or satiation; hence the urgency with which she demanded control over her own bodily needs through the parents.

It is too soon to say whether this new orientation toward her problems will be successful. There has been a decided change in her attitude toward treatment; there seems to be a glimmer of hope that she can become a better person without having to change her parents first. I have reported on this patient, although I have many others whom I know more intimately, because she expressed with startling and dramatic directness what I have come to recognize as crucial issues in many patients with serious eating disorders, namely *the basic delusion of not having an identity of their own*, of not even owning their body and its sensations, with the *specific inability of recognizing hunger as a sign of nutritional need*. Whatever we know about regulatory centers in the midbrain, these patients act as if for them the regulation for food intake was outside their own bodies.

Thinking About the Case

Anorexia and the companion disorder bulimia are dangerous conditions that can cause emaciation, loss of menstruation, and possibly death from cardiac abnormalities. They occur almost exclusively in girls and women, with onset generally between the ages of twelve and twenty-five.

The central feature of anorexia is an extreme fear of obesity coupled with the often absurd complaint that one is fat. While some anorexics, like Gail, restrict their food intake, others induce vomiting or take laxatives to remove whatever calories they have ingested. Anorexia is often associated with other psychological disorders, including depression, anxiety, post-traumatic stress disorders, substance abuse, and personality disorders.

Bruch's interpretation of this case is psychoanalytic in orientation. Disturbed mother–child interactions during the early years of life were presumed to cause Gail's disturbed behavior decades later. Most modern researchers agree with Bruch that family dynamics play a role in the development of eating disorders, and that anorexia tends to occur in young women who, for some reason, lack a sense of power and autonomy in their lives. However, factors other than disturbed family relationships can contribute to this sense of disempowerment—for example, a substantial percentage of anorexics and bulimics have been sexually abused. Others may find their lives careening out of control because they have taken on too much and approach tasks too perfectionistically. Researchers are also discovering that there might be a genetic contribution as well.

In addition, anorexia is a disease of plenty: it is virtually unknown in impoverished societies. Western culture incorporates extreme thinness into its notion of female beauty and success. As the old adage has it, "You can't be thin enough or rich enough." While few women can look like the models in fashion magazines (among whom, not surprisingly, there is a high rate of anorexic behavior) many are brainwashed into believing that they should. No doubt cultural notions are relevant to overall rates of eating disorders.

In any case, anorexia is often difficult to treat. Many women, even those who are seriously emaciated, deny that they have a problem. Such a woman proclaims that she has a right to weigh whatever she likes and that others should stop trying to control her. Besides, she says, she is still fat, as anyone who is telling the truth would agree. When others tell her she looks sick, she often feels triumphant, thinking that they mean that she looks thin. When she feels ill, she may paradoxically rejoice, because that means that she is achieving her goal.

Long-term psychotherapy is often indicated in the treatment of anorexia. Cognitive-behavioral strategies like helping the anorexic to identify and change distorted cognitions about food intake, weight, and body shape may be combined with stress management training. Exploration of family dynamics, self-image, and issues of autonomy are also included. Antidepressant medication helps some people, but is virtually never enough on its own. Both family therapy and group therapy also have a role in the treatment of eating disorders, as does brief hospitalization when the patient's health is failing rapidly. Still, anorexia is often intractable, with a mortality rate that is estimated to be from five to fifteen percent.

Questions to Consider

1. As we have noted, anorexia is a disorder of plenty: it occurs most often in wealthy countries and among middle- and upper-class populations. Why might this be so?

2. Studies reveal that anorexic women often describe their mothers in unflattering terms: excessively dominant, intrusive, and overbearing. Does this constitute evidence for a psychodynamic view of the disorder? What other explanations are possible?

3. Research indicates that African American teenagers are less focused on thinness as a central attribute of beauty. These girls are less dissatisfied with their bodies than are white girls, and attribute sexual attractiveness more to personality traits than to physical ones. Why might this be so? What effect might this have on their overall mental health? On their vulnerability to anorexia?

4. Can you design a study to figure out whether anorexia is really an affective disorder (like depression)? What data might convince you that such a hypothesis had merit?

5. Have you known anyone whom you suspected of having an eating disorder? If so, what did you do about it? How did your intervention turn out?

31

————◄○►————

Virtually all clinical substance abuse programs are based on the idea that problematic substance use represents the first stage of an addiction. In turn, addiction is thought to be a progressive disease for which abstinence is the only proper treatment goal. Users' requests for help learning to moderate their substance use pattern are turned away as being based on "denial" of the disease and impossible to fulfill. However, some recent research suggests that moderation may be a possible goal for a select group of users, and some programs are beginning to work on eliminating problematic use rather than all use. The Newsweek *excerpt below examines this controversy. We have also included a box listing the "twelve steps," principles of belief and behavior that form the cornerstone of Alcoholics Anonymous and Narcotic Anonymous programs. As you read, consider the benefits and pitfalls of conceptualizing addiction as a disease process.*

HALF STEPS VS. TWELVE STEPS

Staff, *Newsweek*

ON EVERY TUESDAY EVENING A MODEST room in a church annex in Ann Arbor, Mich., stirs with the business of repairing broken lives. Alcohol has licked each of the eight or so people gathered here more than once. So they have turned to each other in this circle of chairs and affection to try a program of reform. But this is not a meeting of Alcoholics Anonymous. In fact, few in this support group, who, like AA members, wish to remain anonymous, call themselves alcoholics. This is Moderation Management, or MM. Instead of hearing alcoholics support each other's vows to never drink again, MM members listen to "Ralph," who for decades eased his daily commute from the suburbs with booze. Now, he wants not to abstain completely, but just to drink less. "Betty," a housewife, says she used to drink a bottle of wine nightly. "Now I drink a fraction of that." The gathering nods.

For roughly 60 years, Alcoholics Anonymous and similar programs

New Rules for Sobriety

Like Alcoholics Anonymous with its 12 steps, Moderation Management has steps, guidelines and limits.

MM Limits

- *Do not drink every day*: MM suggests that you do not drink more than three or four days per week.
- *For women*: Do not drink more than three drinks on any day, and no more than nine drinks per week.
- *For men*: Do not drink more than four drinks on any day, and no more than 14 drinks per week.

Source: Moderate Drinking by Audrey Kishline

have dominated therapeutic thinking, treating alcoholism not as a behavior but as a disease—insisting on abstinence. But a growing number of moderation programs across the country are challenging that model. Moderation advocates distinguish between "chronic drinkers," who are "severely dependent on alcohol," and who have long histories of substance abuse, and "problem drinkers," whose bouts with alcohol have lasted five years or less and do not suffer physical withdrawal when they abstain. Proponents of moderation contend that problem drinkers can still maintain careers and families—and they can learn to manage their drinking without eliminating it entirely. Moderation supporters acknowledge that their approach isn't for everyone. But they also cite studies, including one by the American Society of Addictive Medicine, indicating that problem drinkers outnumber hard-core alcoholics four to one.

Most moderation programs have codes of conduct much like AA's 12 steps—but without spiritual references. Drink/Link, a seven-year-old program in Northern California, teaches people not to drink more than one drink an hour. MM suggests abstinence for three or four days a week. Practically all of the programs insist that problem drinkers begin with alcohol-free periods of 30 to 90 days. At the University of Washington in Seattle, researchers are preaching "harm reduction." Using a mock bar and nonalcoholic beer, students are taught that some of drinking's effects, like slurred speech, can be psychosomatic—you expect to feel drunk, and you do. So, students are told, they don't need to drink that much to have a good time.

Some problem drinkers, especially those who fail at cutting back, use moderation as a road to abstinence. Albuquerque, N.M., psychologist Reid Hester says this slower process of kicking the habit is called "warm turkey." Success rates for moderation programs are hard to determine. Research in Canada showed that after a year about 50 percent of those

The Twelve Steps of Alcoholics Anonymous

1. We admitted we were powerless over alcohol—that our lives had become unmanageable.
2. Came to believe that a Power greater than ourselves could restore us to sanity.
3. Made a decision to turn our will and our lives over to the care of God *as we understood Him*.
4. Made a searching and fearless moral inventory of ourselves.
5. Admitted to God, to ourselves, and to another human being the exact nature of our wrongs.
6. Were entirely ready to have God remove all these defects of character.
7. Humbly asked Him to remove our shortcomings.
8. Made a list of all persons we had harmed, and became willing to make amends to them all.
9. Made direct amends to such people wherever possible, except when to do so would injure them or others.
10. Continued to take personal inventory and when we were wrong promptly admitted it.
11. Sought through prayer and meditation to improve our conscious contact with God, *as we understood Him*, praying only for knowledge of His will for us and the power to carry that out.
12. Having had a spiritual awakening as the result of these steps, we tried to carry this message to alcoholics, and to practice these principles in all our affairs.

Source: The Twelve Steps are reprinted with permission of Alcoholics Anonymous World Services, Inc. Permission to reprint the Twelve Steps does not mean that A.A. has reviewed or approved the contents of this publication, nor that A.A. agrees with the views expressed herein. A.A. is a program of recovery from alcoholism *only*—use of the Twelve Steps in connection with programs and activities which are patterned after A.A., but which address other problems, or in any other non-A.A. context, does not imply otherwise.

using moderation were drinking within its guidelines, but critics ask whether these programs will be effective over the long haul. Many participants say they now live normal lives without being stigmatized. "The monkey fell off my back when I realized that I wasn't an alcoholic, that I wasn't out of control," says Audrey Kishline, who founded Moderation Management and wrote a new book, "Moderate Drinking: The New Option for Problem Drinkers." Kishline says that many European countries widely use moderation. In the United States evidence mounts that one treatment model may not fit all. A 1994 publication of the National Institute on Alcohol Abuse and Alcoholism says that "moderate drinking may be an acceptable goal" for some drinkers with a "relatively mild" problem.

The stakes are high in this emotional clash of philosophies: there are some 15 million alcoholics and problem drinkers in the United States.

To Kevin, a recovering alcoholic from Chicago, all the moderation talk is a "kind of rationalization to keep drunks drinking. If I could drink like that, I wouldn't have the problem." Many who treat alcoholics are equally skeptical of what they see as a dangerous delusion. Paul Wood, president of the National Council on Alcoholism and Drug Dependence, worries that alcoholics might get wind of the moderation message and tumble off the wagon. "Every alcoholic's great dream," he says, "is to be a moderate drinker again." For most experts, AA's "one day at a time" still beats moderation's one drink at a time.

32

———◄o►———

Bulimia is a painful disorder in which the individual feels compelled to eat huge amounts of food at a time. The binge is typically followed by intense feelings of guilt, self-loathing, and disgust, which lead the sufferer to purge the food, either by vomiting or by taking laxatives in large doses. The following short story, first published in The Family Therapy Networker *and is copied here with permission, paints a vivid picture of what it feels like to be overcome by a bulimic "attack." Does it remind you at all of the OCD "attack" described earlier in "The Case of Dr. S." (#5)?*

PLANET BULIMIA

Susan E. Gordon

I SIT IN CLASS KNOWING I'LL DO IT. I don't care about the miracles of cellular biology. I don't care about Mrs. Helms's chalk marks on the board. I care about frozen yogurt. I think how cool it is. Cold. The sweet and the sour. Vanilla raspberry swirl with brownies—rich, dark, evil brownies. The urge is growing. It starts in the pit of my stomach and spreads like a fungus until I can feel it in every limb of my body, every inch of my soul.

I look down at my notes and realize there are none. The clock ticks on: five more minutes until freedom. I get A's in all my other classes, but this final period kills me. I can't stay focused at the end of the day. Do I want sweet or salty? Or both? I crave the bland and greasy taste of french fries, steaming hot and rough with salt, though definitely the yogurt first.

"How do you feel?" That familiar voice echoes in my skull.

Oh, Dee! I love you so much. Don't waste your time on me; I'll never get better. Every Wednesday after school I sit in your office, in your big, comfortable chair. I listen to you, I talk, I try so hard to feel. I even hear your voice, over and over, in my head.

"How do you feel?"

I feel ugly.

"How do you feel?"

I feel fat.

"How do you *feel*?"

I feel angry because I don't want to feel ugly and fat, and angrier because I don't want you, Dee, to see my ugliness and fatness. I wish you were my mother and not just my therapist. I would give up everything to be lost in your hug forever.

I feel the heat of tears behind my eyelids. Mrs. Helms is drawing a circle on the board. No, Lara, don't cry. Not here, not in biology.

"How do you feel?"

I don't feel; I don't feel; I don't feel; I HATE THIS!

"You feel hateful?"

I feel inadequate, abnormal, outside normal life. I lived normal life Friday night, Saturday and Sunday. Cross-country meet after school Friday. Made excellent time, two seconds ahead of my record. Had breakfast Saturday morning with Dad: orange juice, two poached eggs, dry toast. He brought the paper with him, said he was proud of my time at the all-Cal meet. Went to the football game Saturday with Darren and Dana, and Jason's party Saturday night. Beer and a short of vodka behind the house with Darren. Darren's hands all over me. Sunday morning, Nordstrom's with Jenny, charging new black shoes, my reward to myself for going 57 hours without vomiting. Getting through Friday definitely made Saturday and Sunday easier, but I had to stay with people all the time. Normal life, real life, life on Planet Earth is a completely different reality.

"How did it feel?" Dee will ask me on Wednesday.

It didn't feel natural or comfortable. It felt desperate—like gripping white knuckles, like holding my breath. I felt like an outsider looking in. An alien visitor on a time-limited trek. Today proved that—up bright and early and back on Planet Bulimia, in my own private orbit.

"Lara Dey!" Mrs. Helms's voice jolts me briefly back to earth. I look up from my blank notepad and try to remember what she asked.

"Endoplasmic reticulum?" I venture a guess. Disgusted, Mrs. Helms turns away, calls on Gina Miller. I feel a rush of heat crawl up my neck and spread across my forehead. I want a shake with the french fries, cold and sweet on my tongue. I want to drink it with a straw. Gina Miller is talking about cell structure, shaking back her shiny brown hair. I notice the gold hoops in her ears.

Last season, she cornered me in the locker room, just before an eight-mile run. She stood there in her nylon shorts and running bra and looked me right in the eyes. "Lara Dey, I heard you're into scarf and barf," she said. I'll never forget the harshness of her voice. She was brushing back her hair. She was the most popular girl on the team. She's pretty, with long legs and nice clothes, but she packs a few extra pounds and I can run faster. I remember telling myself, "She's just jealous . . . she's fat and jealous." I remember wanting to be anyone else but me.

"What?" I said loudly. "What are you *talking* about?" I wondered how she knew, but I didn't let it show. "You're full of shit," I said. Fuck Gina Miller.

I push my empty notepad to the corner of my desk. God, oh god! Do I have any money? Panic floods me. Did I leave my wallet on the kitchen table? I unzip my backpack pocket and thumb through it as I strain to remember my morning routine. Damn! No wallet. My heart beats faster and my face flushes. No longer aware of the class or the room around me, I dig through every pocket of my backpack. Two quarters, three, and some dimes. A loose dollar in one pocket, and a few more quarters. Ah—Mom's bank card. She'll never notice. I'm okay.

BZHZHZHZHZH. The bell honks like a foghorn. It marks the beginning of the race, the race against time and fat. Taste buds ready—on your mark, get set, go!

I shove things into my pack and practically run out the door. I want to get out of here with no complications.

"Lara!" It's Dana. I pretend not to hear. "Lara Dey!" I look over my shoulder. "Oh, hi, Dana." I attempt to make it brief. Just a quick hello, I'm in a hurry with things to do, places to go, porcelain gods to pray to. But Dana catches up to me. I look at her pretty blond hair—almost white and delicately curled. How lucky she is not to be trapped on Planet Bulimia, not to feel the tar in her belly.

The tar is always there. I can't remember a time when it wasn't; black sludge weighing me down and nothing will make it go away. And though I hate vomiting, I want to vomit up the tar. I always think that maybe I'll get it out next time, but it just stays there and grows.

"Lara, those shoes are darling." I look down at my new black shoes with silver buckles. Fifty-seven hours without vomiting. Eight months of therapy and I'm rewarding myself for 57 hours. Disgusting. My longest abstinence ever was last spring, for a week. Dad said, "Go for two." He has no comprehension. Dana is struggling to keep up with me, but something won't let me slow down, won't let me help her with her big stack of books. The hallway is closing in on me and the parking lot seems so far away.

I try to think of something nice to say to her without sounding too corny.

"I like your shoes, too." How lame!

"Thanks . . . Hey, do you want to come over to my dad's house to study? I've got the keys to his car." She wants to impress you with his convertible. She wants to be in and she thinks you're her ticket.

"Uh," I hesitate, "now?" We pass a glass case full of student paintings. They're so bright and new they make me ache inside. How many times have I wanted to stop and look? Instead, I hurry on. I'll save that for my next visit to Planet Earth.

"Yeah." Dana looks so hopeful I could cry.

"I'd love to, Dana, but I can't. I have a dentist appointment." A dentist appointment? Come on! Even you can do better than that!

"I can take you and we'll go to my house from there." She's almost pleading.

I feel so anxious I could fall over. I'd love to ride in her dad's car, and I do need to study, but the monster inside me is saying, "EAT! EAT!" The monster always wins.

"I promised my mom I'd drive her to the car dealership—she's getting her brakes fixed. What about later tonight?"

"Yeah, sure." Her voice fades. Damn, Dana, can't you see? It's not you, it's me.

"Really, Dana, I would really love to later on. How about six o'clock?" Now I'm the hopeful one.

"O–kay, Lara Dey." She says it in rhythm, smiling again. "I'll pick you up at six."

"Great, that'll be great." I'm thinking I'll be recovered by then. "See ya then, Dana, I've got to run."

I feel faint with hunger. Or is it anger? Does anyone else in this hallway hurt like I do? What do I feel, Dee? I don't know where I fit in and I don't know what I feel. I'm numb *and* I'm raging. The rage feels so big and so venomous, I have to hold it inside. I don't think anyone understands what it's like. Dee might. At least her voice is always with me. "How do you feel?"

The parking lot seems too far away, so I stop at a campus vending machine. Sixty-five cents, an apple fritter. Greasy, sweet. Greasy-sweet. Crunchy and soft. Munch, munch, munch. I realize that I'm eating fast and like an animal. Has anyone noticed? Of course not—they're on Planet Earth, laughing and talking and living. I take another bite and enter oblivion.

I find three quarters under the seat of my car and a dollar jammed into the ashtray. Under the dollar is a picture of me two summers ago, jumping off a diving board at our cabin on Lake Tahoe. "What I get from the bathing suit pictures," said Mom, "is that a few pounds off wouldn't hurt." I was 14 and I weighed 120 pounds. My upper arms were fat, my face round. My legs looked like tree trunks. I keep the picture in the car to remind me. I never want to weigh that much again. It took a lot of work to get down to 110. I should feel good about my accomplishment, so why do I always give in and eat? Maybe I'd feel better if I got down to the double digits. Then I'd have room to gain a few pounds. I shove the ashtray closed. Fuck it. The adrenalin is pumping. I don't put on my seat belt, just slam the car into reverse, pop the gear forward, and take off. "Frozen yogurt" flashes across my brain in crimson neon. Half a block from school, I brake for a group of band geeks in the crosswalk with their instruments and matching red jackets. I sit waiting, pumping the brakes. Inside, I'm crying, wishing I was the one walking hand in hand with a boyfriend, or sharing jokes with a girlfriend. I can save that for Planet Earth. I can't reward myself for what I'm about to do now. I'm not worth it. Not even worth wearing a seat belt.

Dad would kill me if he knew my reckless ways. He's always been so protective of his little daughter. But my Dad doesn't know me, doesn't see me, doesn't help me. Once, last year, a police officer stopped me when I was in the middle of a binge. I had sticky frosting all over my hands and shirt and steering wheel. I felt like a caged animal under a spotlight, trapped, cornered. I wanted to tell him, "You have to care about yourself to wear a seat belt." I thought my heart would explode in my chest. I wonder if he even noticed the pink cardboard cake box, ripped open on the seat beside me, the finger marks dug into the lemon custard frosting. But he just ticketed me.

In line at Yogurt World, jingling the coins in my pocket, I look down and realize, to my horror, that I have apple fritter crumbs all down the front of my sweater. Attempting to look nonchalant, I brush them to the floor. When my turn finally comes, I ask for a taste of banana, though I know what I want: two small vanilla and raspberry swirls, one with brownie toppings, one with M&M's. To go. "With spoons and napkins," I say, as if I'm sharing it with someone. "And two chocolate chip cookies."

In the car, I start spooning it in. I love the way it feels melting down my throat. I catch a glimpse of myself in the rear-view mirror and realize I'm doing it again. I've lost my grip, again. I can never hold my breath for long. How can *not doing* something be so difficult? I didn't binge for lunch. As if that is a noble thing. Lara Dey. You're so weak, so full of excuses.

Oh, Dee, I'm sorry. Oh, Mommy, I'm so, so sorry. Oh, Daddy, I'd rather die than have you see me like this. If I could just stop eating, everything would be okay. Why am I so hopelessly out of control? My parents say they love me. I'm the best runner on the team. I'm thin, I have friends, I have clothes, Daddy even bought me my own car. I should be happy with my life. Lara Dey, what the hell is your problem? I don't feel loved. I feel regarded, put up with, sometimes even respected, but rarely, rarely loved. Again, I feel the heat of tears behind my eyelids. No! I squeeze my jaw and keep eating. No, no, no, no, NO!

Last summer, I went to an Overeaters Anonymous meeting in Santa Monica, an hour and a half away in traffic. I can't believe I even went, but my mother tore the announcement out of the paper and left it on my bed; she thought it might help me with my "problem," the problem she doesn't like to put into real, ugly words.

"Do you cry a lot?" The speaker was a young girl, pretty. She called herself a "recovering bulimic."

I pondered that for a minute.

"No," I said. "I used to, a long time ago, when I was little." I'd been vomiting then for six years.

"You'd cry a lot more if you stopped vomiting." She sounded almost angry. I wanted to hit her, strangle her. I hated the way she said "vomit," as if it was a mortal sin. I hated that she could stop vomiting without blowing up to 300 pounds. I hated that she was pretty and superior. My plastic spoon scrapes against the styrofoam, getting the last melting curl of yogurt. Dee says almost the same thing every Wednesday.

"You eat to protect yourself from your feelings," she said, last time. "Every time you binge, you're stuffing down feelings."

I clench my jaw and take a long, deep breath. I will not cry. I throw the empty yogurt cup on the floor of the car and take the lid off the second one. I fish around in my pocket. Fifty cents left. Good. Enough for a vanilla creme doughnut. I spoon more yogurt into my mouth and shove cookie in around the edges. I start up the car. I don't taste them any more. I no longer feel the cool smoothness down my throat. They're just there to occupy the monster until I can get to the doughnut shop.

I feel sick as I think about the monster, big and black, lurking in my gut. I can feel his greedy hands reaching up from the top of my stomach. Tired of yogurt, he cries for doughnuts, lots and lots of doughnuts.

I open the door of the doughnut shop and get hit by the familiar smell of hot grease. The doughnuts in the case seem to sparkle. I want them all—the rows of ridged, round old-fashioneds, their crystals of sugar catching the light; the apple fritters so much bigger than the ones at school; the dusty, filled doughnuts—fat, soft, powdered purses injected full of sticky jellies, custards and vanilla cremes. Thirty-eight cents. "One vanilla creme to go, and how much are those little cookies?"

"Forty cents." The donut woman is cold and aloof. Her stomach bulges against her white uniform, smeared with jelly. Her breasts sag. Fat bitch. I'm glad I'm not in her shoes.

I look at the two quarters in my hand. "Oh, just the doughnut, then."

There's a sad-looking man sitting at the counter, eating soup and drinking coffee. I smiled at him when I walked in. "I'll buy her the cookie," he says. "Give her the cookie."

The fat robot looks at me. I look at her. I look at the sad man, "Oh, that's okay," I say with a laugh, embarrassed.

"No, here." He thumbs through his pocket. "Here's 40 cents, right here. It's okay." He sets the money on the counter and turns to me. "I don't want anything—I just want to buy you the cookie and then you can go."

I take the cookie and thank him. I remember an old movie about a teenaged alcoholic who sells her body for some liquor. I wonder if I could get so desperate. I feel as if I could. I think about the sad man and where the cookie will end up, and I feel sad, myself.

In my car, I lock all the doors and tear into the doughnut with my front teeth. The creme squishes onto my tongue and palate, rich, buttery, heavenly. Powdered sugar covers my sweater and the two front seats.

At the ATM, I get $40 out of Mom's checking account. She'll never miss it, never even notice. My mind races as I shove the cookie in my mouth. What next? French fries, salty, greasy french fries and maybe a burger—dead cow. I never eat dead cow for real, or butter. Those are strictly binge foods.

On my way to McDonalds, I stop at a 7-Eleven and enter the store in a daze. What do I want? There's a new macadamia nut chocolate chip cookie by the checkstand. That's it. I reach for it. The old man behind the counter glares at me. "Don't even try those," he says. "You don't need another bad habit."

I feel blood rush to my ears. I should kick myself for coming here so often and swear to never come again, although I doubt my own resolve. I take the cookie and pay him for it. I bolt back to my car feeling like a real loser. What an asshole. I think how ironic it is that my parents, educated at Harvard and Wellesley, have no idea about me. They pay for my therapy, but it's the old man in the 7-Eleven who has me figured out.

I eat without realizing I'm eating. At McDonald's, I go to the drive-thru window. Big Mac, regular fries, apple pie, vanilla shake. What else? The girl hands me the crisp, white bags. I head to Baskin-Robbins, scarfing all the way. In the rear-view mirror, I see my reflection with ketchup and dressing all over my chin. I hope no one else sees me, but I think sometimes they do. How do I feel, Dee? Cut off from the human race.

At Baskin-Robbins, the Chinese girl blinks at me and asks in her broken English, "Double scoop, choc-chip?" She sees me every day. She thinks she has me figured out. Get a real job. It's not my fault you spend your life scooping ice cream. I swallow hard and try to keep my balance.

"Uh, no. A medium, hand-packed, half Chewy Gooey Chocolate, half Caramel Chocolate Crunch." I'm sure they make up the names just to humiliate people like me. She hands me the bag. I pay and run out of the store.

I have to hurry home now and eat the ice cream before all this food turns to fat. I feel it churning in my stomach and mixing with the deadly, black tar.

No one is home. No one is ever home.

I eat the ice cream in front of the TV, like a zombie. When I was younger and a latchkey child, I'd sometimes lose my key on the playground and I would have to sit outside for hours waiting for mom to get home from work. That was before I started doing this. I remember yearning for a mommy to be home and take care of me. I still yearn for a mommy, but not my mommy. She doesn't see me. She only sees what she wants me to be. I'm daddy's girl, but I hide my tar from him, too. I hide behind my good grades, my cross-country trophies, my masquerade on Planet Earth. It's easy, since I only see him once or twice a week. Dee is the only one who really wants to know me, but I try to be perfect for her, too.

My stomach hurts. It's pushed out against my jeans. My head aches. No point in raiding the kitchen: I can't fit in another bite.

I stand up and head toward the bathroom. The worst is yet to come. Okay, Lara Dey, barf, puke, spew, ralph, blow chunks. Upchuck. Mom always says upchuck. That's what she said when she found a pile of my vomit in the back yard from those nights when I was scared she would hear me in the bathroom. That's what she said when she made my first appointment with Dee. Upchuck sounds so cute. But then, Mom likes everything cute and happy. I wish Dee could make her say "vomit."

I lean over and the ice cream comes up easily: rich, dark, cool, almost as cool as it was going down. I wonder what I look like vomiting. How does Dee envision me—down on my knees or standing up and leaning over? I stand up. I used to get down on my knees, years and years ago.

People at OA meetings talk about getting down on their knees and praying to God. Where are you, God? I know you're there somewhere, I just don't know where to find you. I don't even know how to find you. Oh well, keep going. Get it all out. Relive your sins.

The vomiting is getting harder. Big masses of bread and potato stick in my throat and make me choke. I have to use my hand: three fingers now. In the old days I could use one or two. Sometimes I feel so desperate to get it out that I could stick my whole arm down my throat and rip out my stomach.

My teeth scrape the back of my hand. I want to stop, I want to climb under my electric blanket and hibernate. Come on, Lara. You put it there, you get it out. I flush the toilet and wash my hands, rinse out my mouth. I shudder, the way I did Saturday when Darren and I did shots of vodka. Time for round two.

I drink down some water and wait a minute for it to mix around, loosen up the tar. Puke, Lara, puke. Get it out while you can. Up comes more ice cream, white and runny. The vanilla shake? Vanilla creme? The doughnut sticks in my throat. It's all mixed up with the hamburger and apple pie. Keep going, Lara, work back to the yogurt, back to the cookies. Thick, black sludge—cough—chocolate and tar. Come on, Lara, turn your insides out, try to feel pure.

All I really want is to feel pure.

Almost done now, a little more water and push, heave. Spill your guts, Lara Dey. Show us your tar. Show us what you're made of. Back comes the sweet and sour, now mostly sour. Up comes the bile, brown and acidic, full of digestive juices.

Back to the sink, wash hands, rinse mouth, look myself in the eyes. My eyes are red, bloodshot and watery. My whole face is puffy and pink. There are toothmarks on the back of my hand.

I wipe down the toilet and flush two more times just to be sure. Shit Lara, you did it again. You're ugly. Dee will know the minute you walk into her office. I remember what Dee told me: "Every time you think something negative, turn it around." Okay, Dee. I'm not ugly. I'm okay. Tomorrow will be a brand new day. I run a hand across my abdomen. It's flat again, hip bone to hip bone. Next week, when Dad comes to watch me run, I'll be lean and strong. This summer at the lake, Mom can take all the pictures she wants. She won't be able to say a word. I pat my face with cool water and step on the scale just to be sure: a hundred and nine pounds.

33

————◀o▶————

Not only do eating disorders and substance abuse share some of the features of addiction, they not infrequently co-occur in the same patient. In this reading, Dr. Joan Ellen Zweben speculates about why this overlap exists and provides some suggestions about treatment issues.

EATING DISORDERS AND SUBSTANCE ABUSE

Joan Ellen Zweben, Ph.D.

CLINICIANS INVOLVED IN SUBSTANCE abuse treatment have been aware for some time that women with alcohol or other drug abuse problems also frequently suffer from eating disorders. Some of the similarities, such as feelings of shame, need to hide the behavior, and the compulsive quality have led to speculations of an underlying common dynamic, and possibly to common organic predisposing factors. The treatment challenge is complex: One does not have the luxury of postponing the exploration of anxiety-producing issues until abstinence (sobriety) is well secured. Eating disorders are health threatening and sometimes life threatening, and are frequently closely connected with the alcohol or other drug abuse pattern. . . .

Eating Disorders: Sociocultural Perspectives

Bodily functions have perhaps always been an arena in which human feelings and conflicts are expressed (Erikson 1950; Fenichel 1945). Although eating behaviors have received increasing attention over the past 15 years, there is ample reason to think that eating disorders have moved in and out of prominence throughout history (Boskind-White & White, 1986; Strober 1986; Schwartz, Thompson & Johnson 1985; Bruch

1973). Weight concerns are pervasive among American women today, and obesity is stigmatized, particularly in higher socioeconomic groups (Streigel-Moore, Silberstein & Rodin 1986). Over the past several decades, one can trace a clear shift in societal preference toward thinner and thinner women. This is reflected in the changing measurements for what is termed, "symbolically ideal groups of women," such as Miss America contestants and Playboy Bunnies (Garner et al. 1980). Root, Fallon and Friedrich (1986) pointed out that in 1978 the weight of the winner of the Miss America pageant was 78 percent of the average weight for women according to the actuarial charts, making her almost qualify for a *Diagnostic and Statistical Manual (DSM-III)* (American Psychiatric Association 1980) diagnosis of anorectic (75% of body weight).

Contradiction is apparent within the culture: The "Vogue-Playboy dichotomy" represents one ideal for the epitome in fashion and another standard for sexual attractiveness (Bennett & Gurin 1982). What does it mean that contemporary society, which is bombarded with diverse images of abundance, fosters a thinner and thinner ideal for women? It is hardly surprising that disturbed eating behaviors become increasingly apparent, and specialized treatment programs are rapidly proliferating.

Eating Disorders and Substance Abuse

The literature on eating disorders has frequently noted an apparently high incidence of alcohol abuse—and to a lesser extent other drug problems—either coexisting with or preceding the treatment attempt for an eating disorder. Studies and clinical discussions exploring the close connection between eating disorders and substance abuse in more detail are just now starting to appear.

Mitchell and colleagues (1985) reported that over one third of their bulimic patients described a history of problems with alcohol or other drugs, and most indicated substantial social impairment as well. Hatsukami and colleagues (1982) compared bulimics with women who had alcohol or other drug problems and reported similar Minnesota Multiphasic Personality Inventory (MMPI) profiles, and distribution of MMPI code types. Weiss and Ebert (1983) reported that bulimic patients demonstrated higher levels of psychopathology and impulsive behavior, and a history of more suicide attempts, psychiatric hospitalization, episodes of stealing, and problems with drug use. Johnson and Berndt (1983) studied the life adjustment of bulimic patients and found it to be significantly poorer in all areas than that of a normal community sample, and that it was most similar to that of a comparison group of alcoholic women.

Brisman and Siegel (1984) viewed the crossover of addictions as a manifestation of symptom substitution, with the central issue being a failure of the maintenance of self-regulatory functioning. They examined bulimia and substance abuse within the framework of ego growth, with a particular focus on developmental deficits and compensatory actions. Additionally, they noted parallel treatment strategies: identification of triggers; development of alternative coping strategies; use of peer support groups; and exploration of underlying issues.

Rand, Lawlor and Kuldau (1986) questioned 10 women who had both an eating disorder and a history of alcohol abuse about their food and alcohol consumption, and about their perceptions of related events. These women reported that the emotions associated with eating binges were quite similar to those associated with heavy alcohol use: anger, anxiety, boredom and depression. Half considered their problems with food and alcohol to be essentially the same. However, when the exact relationship between the eating behavior and alcohol use was explored, variability was found. Some women drank and binged at the same time, others alternated heavy drinking with eating binging, others reported that the compulsion to binge-purge became more intense when they stopped drinking or using other drugs. It appears that the eating behaviors are enmeshed with the substance abuse, but the nature of the relationship varies.

Systematic inquiries about the drug use of clients with eating disorders are still rare, but they are starting to appear. Jonas and Gold (1986a) administered structured diagnostic interviews to 259 consecutive callers to 800-Cocaine (the national cocaine hotline) who met *DSM-III* criteria for cocaine abuse. Using the *DSM-III* criteria for eating disorders, they identified individuals who had at some time met the criteria for anorexia nervosa and bulimia. They examined the frequency and duration of binging and purging behavior, and obtained information on drug habits and the influence of drug use on eating patterns. In their sample, 22 percent met the *DSM-III* criteria for bulimia, seven percent met the criteria for both anorexia nervosa and bulimia, and two percent met the criteria for anorexia nervosa alone.

Among cocaine users without an eating disorder diagnosis, 82 percent binged twice a month or less. Among those who at some time in their lives met the criteria for bulimia, 60 percent had a history of binging at least once a week. Jonas and Gold (1986a) concluded that patients with eating disorders should be questioned about and possibly tested for drug use, and that cocaine patients be screened for eating disorders. Abnormalities in eating patterns should not be attributed to drug involvement alone. The nature of the link is unknown. Jonas and Gold stated that "perhaps eating disorders and substance abuse have a third disorder in common, such as affective disorder. Alternatively, the propensity to addictive and compulsive behaviors may be expressed as the abuse of food or drugs."

Eating Disorders and Affective Illness

Several authors have explored the possibility that substance abuse, eating disorders and depression are a sufficiently common symptom cluster to suggest a common base. Affective illness has been described by numerous authors in a subset of substance abuse clients (Mirin 1984; Schuckit 1983).

Lee and Rush (1985) indicated that 52 percent of their bulimic subjects (by *DSM-III* diagnosis) reported a personal history of affective disorder, and in 59 percent of their first-degree relatives. Those subjects with first-degree relatives with drug dependence, alcoholism or depression had an earlier onset of bulimia than those without such relatives. These authors speculated that bulimia may be symptomatically or pathologically related to depression.

Hatsukami et al. (1984) used *DSM-III* criteria to identify bulimic women with affective disorder and alcohol or other drug abuse. In this sample (N = 108), 43.5 percent had a history of affective disorder and 18.5 percent had a history of alcohol or other drug abuse. Approximately 56 percent of the bulimia patents scored within the moderate to severe range of depression on the Beck Depression Inventory.

Although most authors lean toward the view that the link is more than coincidental, Viesselman and Roig (1985) presented data suggesting that eating disorders are unique disorders and not variants of affective disorder or alcoholism. They divided their sample into categories of bulimia (binge eating, dieting), bulimarexia (bulimic symptoms, including self-induced vomiting or use of cathartics and/or diuretics), and anorexia nervosa. The incidence of major depression was very high in the sample (80%). However, the patients differed in terms of the family histories of eating disorders, but not in terms of alcoholism or depression. This study poses problems of interpretation in that it used slightly different criteria and procedures for diagnosis than is characteristic of the other studies. In terms of treatment, their main conclusion does not differ essentially from those of others: Eating disorders are entities in their own right and require a specialized treatment approach.

Diagnosis

There are several ways in which eating disorders may manifest themselves in the substance abusing population. They may coexist, with women presenting at alcohol and other drug abuse treatment facilities who also have current eating disturbances. They may be part of a pattern of symptom substitution; eating disorder specialists note that previous alcohol or other drug abuse is frequently reported by their clients seeking treatment, but there appears to be no current abuse. Inasmuch as most mental health therapists are not trained in how to determine if there is a substance abuse problem, it is likely that many current problems are missed. And finally, substance abuse problems are frequently reported in the family members of clients with eating disorders.

There are a number of ways in which disturbed eating behaviors are intertwined with substance abuse problems. From the late 1940's to the late 1970's, many women were put on amphetamine combinations to suppress their appetites, and may date their involvement with stimulants (and other drugs) to that time. Anorexics report being drawn to cocaine because it makes them not want to eat, and gives an enhanced sense of power. Since cocaine is an appetite suppressant and chronic users are often quite thin, the possibility of a coexisting eating disorder is frequently overlooked. Some bulimics report being attracted to heroin because it makes them vomit. For them, the vomiting behavior may then become a conditioned association to heroin use, and must be addressed early in substance abuse treatment. Other women use alcohol to mediate the panic states that accompany the binging and vomiting. Still others substitute alcohol to gain the release experienced with the bulimia; for them, being intoxicated replaces the relief of abandoning controls that they once gained from binge eating.

Eating disorders are regarded by clients as being at least as shameful as alcoholism or other drug abuse problems. These problems frequently remain hidden even from therapists, especially when the client is not asked directly. One client appeared for an assessment of whether or not she was an alcoholic, and described using alcohol to cope with the anxiety that accompanied vomiting. She had labeled herself bulimic for some time, but had avoided any group activities focused on eating disorders. After attending an Overeaters Anonymous (OA) meeting in which several bulimic women spoke, she concluded that she was primarily bulimic, but was hoping for a diagnosis of alcoholism because it was somehow more acceptable. . . .

Bulimia   Bulimia is characterized by episodes of binge-eating, alternating with periods of little or no food intake. Binge episodes are pursued in isolation and are usually followed by depressive feelings and low self-esteem. Self-induced vomiting or laxative abuse is frequently employed to prevent weight gain or facilitate weight loss. Most of these individuals are preoccupied with their weight (Mitchell, Pyle & Eckert 1985). . . .

Anorexia Nervosa   Anorexia nervosa is often considered to be the most serious of the eating disorders, with mortality rates reported between six to nine percent (Hsu 1980). Such individuals go to great extremes in order to lose weight. This may include drastically reducing caloric intake, incessant exercise, hyperactivity, binge-purge cycles, and use of laxatives, diet pills or diuretics. An obsessive preoccupation with food is characteristic, and eating behaviors themselves may be very bizarre (Norman 1984). Some authors use the subtype bulimic anorectic to describe those individuals with a persistent binge-purge pattern, and restrictive anorectics (or restrictors) to designate the pure dieters (Herzog & Copeland 1985). . . .

In her classic work on eating disorders, Bruch (1973) distinguished between primary anorexia nervosa and disorders that appear similar but are nonetheless distinct. She summarized the characteristic features as a pursuit of thinness in the struggle for independent identity, delusional denial of thinness, preoccupation with food, hyperactivity, and striving for perfection. She distinguished these patients from those who suffer from psychogenic malnutrition, which has a variety of causes, and the atypical group. The latter complain about their weight loss, do not want to stay thin or value it only secondarily as a means of coercing others. They may desire to stay sick in order to stay in the dependent role, in contrast to the struggle for an independent identify that characterizes the primary group. . . . [1]

Dynamic Considerations   Looking retrospectively at individual and family dynamics, dysfunctional characteristics can be seen, but nothing that clearly distinguishes eating disorders from other kinds of symptomatology. It is thus useful to view an eating disorder as a heterogeneous entity representing a final common pathway of a number of etiological factors: ego, psychological, familial, organic and cultural (Schwartz, Thompson & Johnson, 1985). In each individual case, one or another factor or factors will appear more predominant. In certain patients, the influence of family dynamics may be so powerful and so specific that the woman would likely have developed an eating disorder in any time and place. In others, contemporary cultural factors clearly play a key role, as in the case of the woman who "learns" to vomit from her sorority sisters and discontinues the practice after graduation. . . .

The overall treatment strategies for both eating disorders and substance abuse have many commonalities: education on health consequences of the disorder and the nature of the recovery process as an essential part of treatment; a combination of behavioral and dynamic approaches; a recognition of the importance of engaging the family in treatment and modifying dysfunctional patterns; and an endorsement of self-help groups as a useful activity (Herzog & Copeland, 1985; Brisman & Siegel 1984). . . .

Conclusion

It is both exciting to tackle a new area and dismaying to know that knowledge and understanding are growing so fast that opinions fondly held today will prove embarrassing in just a few years. Historically, the gulf between substance abuse treatment and mental health treatment has been excessively wide. Eating disorders pose a more general problem of the need to integrate the two: how to determine the severity; how do they interact; and what is the most effective method of intervention. Certainly the growing recognition of the need to address eating disorders within drug abuse treatment programs will prove to be a challenge to clinical skills and creativity.

Notes

1. A comprehensive screening tool called the Bulimia and Related Eating Disorders Screen (BREDS) can be found in *Bulimia: A Systems Approach to Treatment*, edited by M. P. Root, P. Fallon and W. Friedrich (New York: W. W. Norton, 1986).

Acknowledgments

The author wishes to thank the following people who shared their ideas and clinical impressions: Peter Banys, M.D.; Rosemary Bower, Ph.D.; Fran Krieger, Ph.D.; Haven Logan, Ph.D.; Marta Obuchowsky; Maria Root, Ph.D.; Avis Rumney, M.A., M.F.C.C.; David E. Smith, M.D.; and Jody Yeary, M.S., M.F.C.C.

References

Alibrandi, L. 1978. The folk psychotherapy of Alcoholics Anonymous. In: Zimberg, S.; Wallace, J. & Blume S. (Eds.). *Practical Approaches to Alcoholism Psychotherapy*. New York: Plenum.

American Psychiatric Association Task force on Nomenclature and Statistics. 1980. *Diagnostic and Statistical Manual of Mental Disorders (DSM-III)*. 3rd. ed. Washington, D.C.: American Psychiatric Association.

Bennett, W. & Gurin, J. 1982. The century of the svelte. *Harvard Magazine* March–April: 56A–56H.

Boskind-White, M. & White, W. C. 1986. Bulimarexia: A historical-sociocultural perspective. In: Brownell, K. D. & Foreyt, J. P. (Eds.). *Handbook of Eating Disorders: Physiology, Psychology, and Treatment of Obesity, Anorexia and Bulimia*. New York: Basic Books.

Brisman, J. & Siegel, M. 1984. Bulimia and alcoholism: Two sides of the same coin? *Journal of Substance Abuse Treatment* Vol. 1: 113–118.

Bruch, H. 1973. *Eating Disorders*. New York: Basic Books.

Copeland, P. M. 1985. Neuroendocrine aspects of eating disorders. In: Emmett, S. W. (Ed.), *Theory and Treatment of Anorexia Nervosa and Bulimia: Biomedical, Sociocultural, and Psychological Perspectives*. New York: Brunner/Mazel.

Dwyer, J. 1985. Nutritional aspects of anorexia nervosa and bulimia. In: Emmett, S. W. (Ed.). *Theory and Treatment of Anorexia Nervosa and Bulimia: Biomedical, Sociocultural, and Psychological Perspectives*. New York: Brunner/Mazel.

Erikson, E. 1950. *Childhood and Society*. New York: W. W. Norton.

Fenichel, O. 1945. *The Psychoanalytic Theory of Neurosis*. New York: W. W. Norton.

Garner, D. M.; Garfinkel, P. E.; Schwartz, D. & Thompson, M. 1980. Cultural expectations of thinness in women. *Psychological Reports* Vol. 47: 483–491.

Garner, D. M. & Isaacs, P. 1986. The fundamentals of psychotherapy for anorexia nervosa and bulimia nervosa. In: Keller, P. A. & Ritt, L. G. (Eds.). *Innovations in Clinical Practice: A Source Book*. Sarasota, Florida: Professional Resource Exchange.

Glassman, A. H. & Walsh, B. T. 1983. Link between bulimia and depression unclear (letter to the editor). *Journal of Clinical Psychopharmacology* Vol. 3(3): 203.

Hatsukami, D.; Eckert, E.; Mitchell, J. E. & Pyle, R. 1984. Affective disorder and substance abuse in women with bulimia. *Psychological Medicine* Vol. 14(3): 701–704.

Hatsukami, D.; Owen, P.; Pyle, R. & Mitchell, J. 1982. Similarities and differences on the MMPI between women with bulimia and women with alcohol or drug abuse problems. *Addictive Behaviors* Vol. 7(4): 435–439.

Herzog, D. & Copeland, P. 1985. Medical progress—eating disorders. *New England Journal of Medicine* Vol. 313(5): 295–303.

Hsu, L. 1980. Outcome of anorexia nervosa: A review of the literature (1954–1978). *Archives of General Psychiatry* Vol. 37: 1041–1046.

Johnson, C. & Berndt, D. 1983. Preliminary investigation of bulimia and life adjustment. *American Journal of Psychiatry* Vol. 140(6): 774–777.

Johnson, C. & Pure, D. 1986. Assessment of bulimia: A multidimensional model. In: Brownell, K. D. & Foreyt, J. P. (Eds.). *Handbook of Eating Disorders: Physiology, Psychology, and Treatment of Obesity, Anorexia and Bulimia*. New York: Basic Books.

Jonas, J. & Gold, M. 1986a. Cocaine abuse and eating disorders. *Lancet* Vol. 1: 390.

Jonas, J. & Gold, M. 1986b. Naltrexone in the treatment of bulimia. Paper presented as New Research (NR 25), at the American Psychological Association Conference, Washington, D.C.

Lacey, J. 1983. Bulimia nervosa, binge eating, and psychogenic vomiting: A controlled treatment study and long term outcome. *British Medical Journal* Vol. 286(6378): 1609–1613.

Lee, N. & Rush, A. 1985. Bulimia and depression. *Journal of Affective Disorders* Vol. 9(3): 231–238.

Mirin, S. (Ed.). 1984. *Substance Abuse and Psychopathology*. Washington, D.C.: American Psychiatric Press.

Mitchell, J.; Hatsukami, D.; Eckert, E. & Pyle, R. 1985. Characteristics of 275 patients with bulimia. *American Journal of Psychiatry* Vol. 142(4): 482–485.

Mitchell, J.; Pyle, R. & Eckert, E. 1985. Bulimia. In: Hales, R. E. & Frances, A. J. (Eds.). *American Psychiatric Association Annual Review*, Vol. 4. Washington, D.C.: American Psychiatric Press.

Norman, K. 1984. Eating disorders. In: Goldman, H. H. (Ed.). *Review of General Psychiatry*, Los Altos, California: Lange Publications.

Pope, H. & Hudson, J. 1986. Antidepressant drug therapy for bulimia: Current status. *Journal of Clinical Psychiatry* Vol. 47(7): 339–345.

Rand, C. S. W.; Lawlor, B. & Kuldau, J. 1986. Patterns of food and alcohol consumption in a group of bulimic women. *Bulletin of the Society of Psychologists in Addictive Behaviors* Vol. 5(2–3): 95–104.

Root, M. P.; Fallon, P. & Friedrich, W. (Eds.). 1986. *Bulimia: A Systems Approach to Treatment*. New York: W. W. Norton.

Schuckit, M. 1983. Alcoholism and other psychiatric disorders. *Hospital and Community Psychiatry* Vol. 34(11): 1022–1026.

Schwartz, D.; Thompson, M. & Johnson, C. 1985. Anorexia nervosa and bulimia: The sociocultural context. In: Emmett, S. W. (Ed.). *Theory and Treatment of Anorexia Nervosa and Bulimia: Biomedical, Sociocultural, and Psychological Perspectives*. New York: Brunner/Mazel.

Striegel-Moore, R.; Silberstein, L. & Rodin, J. 1986. Toward an understanding of risk factors for bulimia. *American Psychologist* Vol. 41(3): 246–263.

Strober, M. 1986. Anorexia nervosa: History and psychological concepts. In: Brownell, K. D. & Foreyt, J. P. (Eds.). *Handbook of Eating Disorders: Physiology, Psychology, and Treatment of Obesity, Anorexia and Bulimia*. New York: Basic Books.

Swift, W.; Andrews, D. & Barklage, N. 1986. The relationship between affective disorder and eating disorder: A review of the literature. *American Jour*

nal of Psychiatry Vol. 143(3): 290–299.

Vaillant, G. 1981. Dangers of psychotherapy in the treatment of alcoholism. In: Bean, M. & Zinberg, N. (Eds.). *Dynamic Approaches to the Understanding and Treatment of Alcoholism*. New York: The Free Press.

Viesselman, J. & Roig, M. 1985. Depression and suicidality in eating disorders. *Journal of Clinical Psychiatry* Vol. 46(4): 118–124.

Weiss, S. & Ebert, M. 1983. Psychological and behavioral characteristics of normal-weight bulimics and normal-weight controls. *Psychosomatic Medicine* Vol. 45: 293–303.

LANAHAN NOTES

Substance Abuse, Eating Disorders, and other Impulse Control Disorders

——◄◦►——

SUBSTANCE ABUSE DISORDERS

Substance abuse constitutes major public health problems in the United States and Western Europe:

— billions of dollars in costs (lost productivity, wages, treatment)

— implicated in about half of criminal acts (higher in violent crimes).

— causes many deaths (vehicular accidents, crimes, illnesses like cancer).

— increases suicide risk.

Substance use has long history in virtually every culture (mentioned in Old Testament)—tolerance for use waxes and wanes across time and cultures.

Major controversy: Is substance abuse a medical "illness," a "social disease," or a moral weakness? How much is personal responsibility involved?

Drugs of abuse listed in the DSM-IV:

1. Alcohol
2. Amphetamine or amphetamine-like ("speed," "uppers")
3. Caffeine
4. Cannabis (marijuana)
5. Cocaine
6. Hallucinogens
7. Inhalants
8. Nicotine
9. Opioids
10. Phencyclidine or phencyclidine-like (PCP)
11. Sedative, Hypnotic, Anxiolytic (prescription medications)

Types of drug-related syndromes:

Abuse: maladaptive pattern of use

Dependence:
> maladaptive pattern, plus tolerance (need for markedly increasing amounts)
>
> withdrawal (physical and mental symptoms that occur when the use is abruptly stopped)
>
> inability to stop or reduce, or control use despite attendant problems

Substance-related organic syndromes (eg., intoxication, delirium, dementia, mood disorder, psychotic disorder)

Who is vulnerable?

—Hard to tell since so many substances are included and the line between use, abuse, and dependence is not always clear.

—Estimated that 6 to 8 percent of Americans have serious alcohol problem.

—Rates vary widely from culture to culture.

—Polydrug use is now the rule rather than the exception.

—Gender is a definite risk factor: men have higher incidence than women.

—Antisocial personality disorder is a risk factor.

Causes — biopsychosocial model clearly appropriate:

Biological/Genetic vulnerability: demonstrated for alcoholism

Psychodynamic perspective: drug use compensates for defective ego development and the ability to manage painful emotions.

Learning Theories:
> Opponent-process theory: in early stages, users seek affective pleasure while in later stages they seek to avoid the pain of withdrawal.
>
> Positive reinforcement models: drugs produce changes in brain that are powerfully reinforcing.
>
> Classical conditioning: drug-related stimuli induce craving and trigger relapse.

Sociocultural factors: peers, family, ethnic group, and religious orientation all affect norms and expectations about substance use.

Treatment:

Detoxification: gets the person off the substance and treats any withdrawal symptoms.

Education about addictive processes: helps break down psychological mechanism of denial and engages the person in treatment.

Cognitive-behavioral methods: skill-training, cognitive restructuring, lifestyle intervention—help prevent relapses.

Twelve-step programs (based on Alcoholics Anonymous): provide group support, enhancement of self-esteem, mutual learning, and additional cognitive-behavioral techniques.

Psychotherapy: helps repair self-esteem, develop awareness of conflicts and emotions that precipitate substance use.

Note: Psychodynamic psychotherapy can worsen substance abuse if it reinforces drinking, e.g., "I drink because I have psychological problems; I'll stop when my problems are solved." It is generally not used until the person has achieved stable sobriety.

Medication: used to treat co-existing depressive or anxiety disorders—although care must be taken not to substitute one addiction for another.

1. Antabuse inhibits alcohol use by making the person sick if he/she drinks.
2. Naltrexone blocks opioid transmission in the brain and reduces craving.

EATING DISORDERS

Discomfort with body weight, dieting, and occasional bingeing are common in our culture. Eating disorders are diagnosed when these patterns become dysfunctional and out of control.

Types:

Anorexia: Refusal to maintain body weight at minimally acceptable levels; may involve starvation, vomiting, laxative or diuretic abuse, compulsive exercise; dangerous—causes heart irregularities that may be fatal.

Bulimia: pattern of bingeing and purging; may use laxatives, vomiting, diuretics, exercise; tend to have body weight in normal range.

Who gets eating disorders?

About 2 out of every 100 females

Very rare in males (only about 5 percent of cases)

Onset is usually in early to late adolescence.

Severe trauma (e.g., sexual abuse) and depression may be risk factors.

Causes:

Biological: may be variants of mood disorder (family history of mood disorder)—although whether depression is cause or effect of starvation is not clear.

Psychological: deep need for autonomy—some important aspect of life is out of control (e.g., overcontrolling family environment, or history of abuse) so weight becomes the one thing that can be controlled.

Social: cultural pressures—for women, thin = beautiful = successful

Note: data suggest that African American women do not feel the same pressure; they have better body image, fewer eating disorders.

Treatment—Same range of options as in substance abuse:

Psychotherapy: generally plays some part in the treatment; usually long-term.

Cognitive-behavioral orientation: identifies and changes distorted cognitions about food and eating; helps patient identify environmental triggers for bingeing.

Psychodynamic orientation: identifies underlying autonomy issues; helps individual find healthier ways to achieve independence.

Group therapy (sometimes modelled after AA): can be very helpful.

Family therapy: used especially when the person is young adolescent.

Medications: antidepressants have been shown to be helpful for some.

Hospitalization: used when the person is dangerously thin.

Prognosis:

Like substance abuse, many improve, but relapse is common; "denial" makes treatment difficult—may refuse to admit they have a problem.

OTHER IMPULSE CONTROL DISORDERS

Types include:

Kleptomania: compulsive stealing
Pyromania: compulsive fire-setting
Pathological gambling

Trichotillomania: compulsive hair or eyebrow pulling

Explosive disorder: occasional violent outbursts

These can be considered addictive-equivalents—causal models and treatments are similar.

Note: Trichotillomania is probably a variant of Obsessive-Compulsive Disorder and can often be treated successfully with medication.

CHAPTER EIGHT

Neurocognitive Disorders

————◄○►————

L ike the last chapter, this one collapses several separate DSM-IV categories. Neurocognitive disorders include delirium, which is an acute disturbance of consciousness and cognition; dementias characterized by more chronic disturbances in memory, language, and thought; amnestic disorders in which memory loss can be accounted for by specific organic causes; and other mental disorders that can be attributed to medical conditions. As an example of these disorders we have included a case of dementia resulting from Acquired Immunodeficiency Syndrome (AIDS), and a first-person account written by a man whose wife had Alzheimer's disease.

Tic disorders, of which Tourette's disorder is one example, are classified in the DSM-IV as childhood disorders because they tend to be apparent at a young age. However, research suggests that they are neurologically based (although they may have profound psychological consequences), so we have included them here. Tourette's, in which the sufferer experiences a wide range of involuntary vocalizations and/or motor behaviors, has been detected by pediatricians with increasing frequency in recent years, perhaps because our ability to treat it has advanced significantly at the same time. The case we present is from Oliver Sacks' book, *An Anthropologist on Mars*. It is particularly fascinating because the sufferer is a surgeon who is only affected by his tics when he is *not* doing surgery. It is interesting to note that stuttering, another disorder first diagnosed in childhood that persists into adulthood, also disappears under certain circumstances—for instance, when the sufferer sings rather than speaks. Like tic disorders, stuttering may need to be reclassified as a neurocognitive disorder in DSM-V.

34

——————◄○►——————

AIDS-RELATED DEMENTIA:
THE CASE OF SAMUEL G.

LIEUTENANT JUNIOR GRADE SAMUEL G. was a twenty-seven-year old African American man on the threshold of a successful Navy career. A bright young man, the oldest of three sons in a middle-class family, Samuel made up for his smallish stature with aggressive, tenacious competitiveness. As a youngster, he did well in school, ran track, and practiced martial arts. He also was an accomplished pianist who took satisfaction in besting his father by learning all of the Bach *Inventions* by heart. At his summer job in the county youth department, he was known for being an efficient, no-nonsense guy who also had a quick wit and an ability to get along with almost everybody.

Samuel went to Catholic school and then on to a private college from which he graduated in 1978. Jobs were scarce so Samuel joined his younger brother, who had just graduated from high school, in enlisting in the United States Navy. He easily passed the examination for officer's candidate school and, as an ensign, was assigned to the personnel office on an aircraft carrier. Again, his job performance was exemplary, and he was reassigned to surface warfare school, where he was to be trained for service on a destroyer as a full lieutenant. It was then that his problems began.

Samuel appeared not to be responding well to the stress of his new academic responsibilities. He began to have a series of viral infections that left him weak and tired. Several times he fell asleep during class. His mood began to change. This once aggressive officer became listless and apathetic. He suffered from insomnia, anxiety, and depression. His self-esteem seemed to wane, as did his weight. He was unable to concentrate, and his grades slipped drastically.

At around the same time, his parents, living on the opposite coast, began to be concerned about him. They noted, in retrospect, that he seemed to be confused. He kept getting digits of phone numbers scrambled, so that they had trouble reaching him. His voice had become harsh from a seemingly never ending sore throat, and he seemed depressed and unwell. He complained to his parents that he was being harassed by the Navy. His inability to concentrate or even to stay awake, had prompted them to suspect him of drug use, and he had undergone a series of drug tests. Of course, the tests were negative, but his feelings of "harassment" continued. In January of 1984, his commanding officer wrote a report that reads, in part, as follows: " . . . low motivation, inadequate study habits, and the poor example this 'fleet JG' set for many Ensigns in the class. . . . He repeatedly fell asleep at his desk or in class and had to be often told not to read unofficial material at his desk. The few satisfactory tasks he did perform came only when PXO gave him highly structured and elaborate guidance. . . . Shows no initiative and appears content to simply sit at his desk until asked to do something. . . . In sum, LTJG G. is more of a liability to this unit than an asset. Because of his documented performance alone, I feel his selection for SWOS Department Head School should be reappraised." At the same time, his promotion to full lieutenant was put on hold.

Finally, in February of 1984 Samuel was admitted to the psychiatric unit of the Naval hospital for evaluation and treatment. Embarrassed and ashamed, he told his parents that he was being admitted because of concerns that he might have cancer of the liver. Once in the hospital, he was diagnosed as having an adjustment disorder with depressed mood. He seemed to improve while on the unit, and was discharged with the recommendation that he continue counseling on an outpatient basis.

Shortly thereafter, his condition seemed to worsen. His parents were informed by a physician who had been involved in his care that Samuel might have a condition called Acquired Immunodeficiency Syndrome, a rare but serious autoimmune disease. At the time, fewer than five thousand cases had been diagnosed in the United States, so knowledge was scarce. If Samuel had AIDS, he would likely also have a rare tuberculosis of the bone with which it seemed to be associated. Testing for this tuberculosis would take three months.

In the meantime, Samuel's behavior became more and more erratic. He got married—briefly. The marriage only lasted two weeks. He bought four buildings in the inner city and hired a manager to collect rents. But, he never made a mortgage payment, despite having the money to do so. Apparently, he thought the money that his manager sent him represented his net profits after the mortgage had been paid. In April, he wrote an articulate and heartbreaking letter to President Ronald Reagan, which ended as follows: "Mr. President, I am a very patriotic man. I have always wanted to be a naval officer, and now because of one man's insensitivity towards a person suffering of mental duress, my career is all but over. I implore you to intervene on my behalf."

In June, the diagnosis of tuberculosis of the bone was confirmed. The physician sent Samuel's parents a copy of an article recently published in the *New England Journal of Medicine* about AIDS. Confused and frightened, his parents sent him a ticket to come home for a visit. What they saw horrified them. His clothes hung on his gaunt frame. In the oversided fedora which came down over his ears he looked unkempt and bizarre. His color had darkened and his eyes were deep-set. Within minutes he was talking about having a cosmic relationship with Michael Jackson. But worst of all were his rantings about women. He called them, among other things, "nasty, greasy bitches." He was vile and hateful, and completely uncontrollable.

After two harrowing weeks, Samuel returned to the naval base where, in July he was readmitted to the psychiatric unit, this time with the diagnosis of narcissistic personality disorder. By this time he had virtually no sense of anybody else's needs. He was demanding, hostile, and completely self-centered. His attention span was continuing to decrease and his confusion was continuing to increase. On the day of his discharge, while driving back to his apartment from the base hospital, he got into four automobile accidents—the last of which totalled his car.

His parents hurriedly flew out to California, again having trouble finding him because of his inability to get numbers or directions straight. When they got to his apartment, they found it empty. Three hours later, Samuel returned. He had taken a neighbor to the hospital and gotten lost on his way home. He looked awful, having lost more weight in the short time since his parents had last seen him. They took him to a restaurant where he ordered fifty dollars worth of lunch . . . but ate none of it. He was so weak he could not walk to the car, but had to lie down on a couch in the restaurant's lobby for a while. His parents say that this was the first time they realized that their son was going to die. They made arrangements to have him discharged by mail from the Navy and took him home.

For three months his parents cared for Samuel. In his lucid moments, he told his father that he was gay, that his marriage (to a gay woman) had been "for show." He expressed sadness about his illness and about the stress he was creating for his family. He seemed particularly pained by his inability to read music or play the piano any more.

But he was not always lucid. Often he was quite demented. His recent memory deteriorated, and he made things up to cover the gaps. He wanted to become an astronaut, to buy a Mercedes. He ordered thousands of dollars worth of merchandise from the television, ultimately maxing-out his credit card. His social skills continued to deteriorate—in restaurants (until his parents stopped taking him), he would wander around, telling all of the patrons about his having AIDS, or about there being ice in the urinals in the men's room. Most heartrending for his parents was watching him stare into the mirror, talking about how handsome he was.

In November, Samuel developed a blood infection and his kidneys failed. He suffered a series of violent seizures and died before Christmas.

His bereaved and angry father decided that his son had deserved his promotion, so he decided to promote him, himself. In his obituary and at his funeral, full Lieutenant Samuel G. was properly memorialized.

Thinking About the Case

When Samuel G. was alive, neurological complications of Human Immunodeficiency Virus (HIV), the virus that causes AIDS, had not yet been identified. It is now known that approximately 40 percent of AIDS patients have observable neurological disorders. Upwards of 80 percent have neuropathological findings at autopsy.

Many patients, like Samuel G., exhibit symptoms that are particularly suggestive of frontal lobe damage. These include marked personality change, loss of social judgment accompanied by disinhibition resulting in socially inappropriate behavior, decreased volition and motivation, and difficulty placing events in temporal sequence. The earliest symptoms of AIDS-related dementia are typically depression, forgetfulness, and poor concentration, with the more serious cognitive deficits showing up somewhat later.

There is no treatment for AIDS-related dementia, although medications can sometimes be helpful to treat specific symptoms like depression or anxiety. Supportive psychotherapy to help with the reactive components of the problem—including the individual's reaction to the stigma associated with AIDS—family, social, or financial problems that may arise, and coping with impending death, may also be useful. Professional support for family members to help them anticipate, understand, and manage cognitive and emotional changes associated with AIDS is invaluable. Here, the focus is on assisting caregivers to support the patient, as well as on bolstering their own resistance to the often devastating emotional effects of the caregiving burden.

The question of whether or not individuals with AIDS-related complex (ARC), who have not yet developed AIDS, show cognitive deficits cannot yet be answered with certainty. Gross impairment is not observed, but studies indicate that subtle disturbances in memory and fine motor coordination may exist.

Questions to Consider

1. Do you think that neurological disorders like AIDS-related dementia and Alzheimer's disease should be included in the DSM categories? Why or why not?

2. Which of the symptoms exhibited by Samuel G. are similar to those of Alzheimer's patients? Which are different? Do these patterns tell you anything about the localization of certain functions in the brain?

3. The (mis)diagnosis of adjustment disorder with depressed mood in this case is easy to understand. However, there were clues that the diagnosis of narcissistic personality disorder was incorrect. What were they?

35

————◄○►————

TOURETTE'S DISORDER: A SURGEON'S LIFE

Tic disorders, including Tourette's, are listed in the DSM-IV under Disorders of Childhood and Adolescence because their onset is usually quite early. We have included them here though, because of their clearly neurological roots. What follows is an account by famed neurologist Oliver Sacks of a Canadian surgeon who is virtually consumed by compulsive tics of all sorts—except when he is operating. Sack's two books, *The Man Who Mistook His Wife for a Hat*, and *An Anthropologist on Mars*, are highly readable and full of accounts of strange and wonderful neurological anomalies: retarded individuals who can play complex sonatas on the piano, an autistic woman who designs cattle enclosures, people who can understand words but not facial expressions, a man with no memory. Read them if you get a chance, but in the meantime, imagine what it would be like to be operated on by Dr. Carl Bennett.

I first met Dr. Carl Bennett at a scientific conference on Tourette's in Boston. His appearance was unexceptionable—he was fiftyish, of middle size, with a brownish beard and mustache containing a hint of gray, and was dressed soberly in a dark suit—until he suddenly lunged or reached for the ground or jumped or jerked. I was struck both by his bizarre tics and by his dignity and calm. When I expressed incredulity about his choice of profession, he invited me to visit and stay with him, where he lived and practiced, in the town of Branford, in British Columbia—to do rounds at the hospital with him, to scrub with him, to see him in action. Now, four months later, in early October, I found myself in a small plane approaching Branford, full of curiosity and mixed expectations. Dr. Bennett met me at the airport, greeted me—a strange greeting, half lunge, half tic, a gesture of welcome idiosyncratically Tourettized—grabbed my case, and led the way to his car in an odd, rapid skipping walk, with a skip each fifth step and sudden reachings to the ground as if to pick something up. . . .

When Bennett first came to Branford, he was regarded, he thought, with a certain suspicion. "A surgeon who twitches! Who needs him? What next?" There were no patients at first, and he did not know if he could make it there, but gradually he won the town's affection and respect. His practice began to expand, and his colleagues, who had initially been startled and incredulous, soon came to trust and accept him, too, and to bring him fully into the medical community. "But enough said," he concluded as we returned to the house. It was almost dark now, and the lights of Branford were twinkling. "Come to the hospital tomorrow—we have a conference at seven-thirty. Then I'll do outpatients and rounds on my patients. And Friday I operate—you can scrub with me." . . .

In the doctor's common room, Bennett was clearly very much at ease with his colleagues, and they with him. One sign of this ease, paradoxically, was that he felt free to Tourette with them—to touch or tap them gently with his fingertips, or, on two occasions when he was sharing a sofa, to suddenly twist on his side and tap his colleague's shoulder with his toes—a practice I had observed in other Touretters. Bennett is somewhat cautious with his Tourettisms on first acquaintance and conceals or downplays them until he gets to know people. When he first started working at the hospital, he told me, he would skip in the corridors only after checking to be sure that no one was looking; now when he skips or hops no one gives it a second glance.

The conversations in the common room were like those in any hospital—doctors talking among themselves about unusual cases. Bennett himself, lying half-curled on the floor, kicking and thrusting one foot in the air, described an unusual case of neurofibromatosis—a young man whom he had recently operated on. His colleagues listened attentively. The abnormality of the behavior and the complete normality of the discourse formed an extraordinary contrast. There was something bizarre about the whole scene, but it was evidently so common as to be unremarkable and no longer attracted the slightest notice. But an outsider seeing it would have been stunned.

After coffee and muffins, we repaired to the surgical-outpatients department, where half a dozen patients awaited Bennett. The first was a trail guide from Banff, very western in plaid shirt, tight jeans, and cowboy hat. His horse had fallen and rolled on top of him, and he had developed an immense pseudocyst of the pancreas. Bennett spoke with the man—who said the swelling was diminishing—and gently, smoothly palpated the fluctuant mass in his abdomen. He checked the sonograms with the radiologist—they confirmed the cyst's recession—and then came back and reassured the patient. "It's going down by itself. It's shrinking nicely—you won't be needing surgery after all. You can get back to riding. I'll see you in a month." And the trail guide, delighted, walked off with a jaunty step. Later, I had a word with the radiologist. "Bennett's not only a whiz at diagnosis," he said. "He's the most compassionate surgeon I know."

The next patient was a heavy woman with a melanoma on her buttock, which needed to be excised at some depth. Bennett scrubbed up, donned sterile gloves. Something about the sterile field, the prohibition, seemed to stir his Tourette's; he made sudden darting motions, or incipient motions, of his sterile, gloved right hand toward the ungloved, unwashed, "dirty" part of his left arm. The patient eyed this without expression. What did she think, I wondered, of this odd darting motion, and the sudden convulsive shakings he also made with his hand? She could not have been entirely surprised, for her G.P. must have prepared her to some extent, must have said, "You need a small operation. I recommend Dr. Bennett—he's a wonderful surgeon. I have to tell you that he sometimes makes strange movements and sounds—he has a thing called Tourette's syndrome—but don't worry, it doesn't matter. It never affects his surgery."

Now, the preliminaries over, Bennett got down to the serious work, swabbing the buttocks with an iodine antiseptic and then injecting local anesthetic, with an absolutely steady hand. But as soon as the rhythm of action was broken for a moment—he needed more local, and the nurse held out the vial for him to refill his syringe—there was once again the darting and near-touching. The nurse did not bat an eyelid; she had seen it before and knew he would not contaminate his gloves. Now, with a firm hand, Bennett made an oval incision an inch to either side of the melanoma, and in forty seconds he had removed it, along with a Brazil-nut-shaped wedge of fat and skin. "It's out!" he said. Then, very rapidly, with great dexterity, he sewed the margins of the wound together, putting five neat knots on each nylon stitch. The patient, twisting her head, watched him as he sewed and joshed him: "Do you do all the sewing at home?"

He laughed. "Yes. All except the socks. But no one darns socks these days."

She looked again. "You're making quite a quilt."

The whole operation completed in less than three minutes, Bennett cried, "Done! Here's what we took." He held the lump of flesh before her.

"Ugh!" she exclaimed, with a shudder. "Don't show me. But thanks anyway."

All this looked highly professional from beginning to end, and, apart from the dartings and near-touchings, non-Tourettic. But I couldn't decide about Bennett's showing the excised lump to the patient. ("Here!") One may show a gallstone to a patient, but does one show a bleeding, misshapen piece of fat and flesh? Clearly, she didn't want to see it, but Bennett wanted to show it, and I wondered if this urge was part of his Tourettic scrupulosity and exactitude, his need to have everything looked at and understood. I had the same thought later in the morning, when he was seeing an old lady in whose bile duct he had inserted a T-tube. He went to great lengths to draw the tube, to explain all the anatomy, and the old lady said, "I don't want to know it. Just do it!"

Was this Bennett the Touretter being compulsive or Professor Bennett the lecturer on anatomy? (He gives weekly anatomy lectures in Calgary.) Was it simply an expression of his meticulousness and concern? An imagining, perhaps, that all patients shared his curiosity and love of detail? Some patients doubtless did, but obviously not these. . . .

Friday is operating day for Bennett, and he was scheduled to do a mastectomy. I was eager to join him, to see him in action. Outpatients are one thing—one can always concentrate for a few minutes—but how would he conduct himself in a lengthy and difficult procedure demanding intense, unremitting concentration, not for seconds or minutes, but for hours?

Bennett preparing for the operating room was a startling sight. "You should scrub next to him," his young assistant said. "It's quite an experience." It was indeed, for what I saw in the outpatient clinic was magnified here: constant sudden dartings and reachings with the hands, almost but never quite touching his unscrubbed, unsterile shoulder, his assistant, the mirror; sudden lungings, and touchings of his colleagues with his feet; and a barrage of vocalizations—"Hooty-hooo! Hooty-hooo!"—suggestive of a huge owl.

The scrubbing over, Bennett and his assistant were gloved and gowned, and they moved to the patient, already anesthetized, on the table. They looked briefly at a mammogram on the X-ray box. Then Bennett took the knife, made a bold, clear incision—there was no hint of any ticcing or distraction—and moved straightaway into the rhythm of the operation. Twenty minutes passed, fifty, seventy, a hundred. The operation was often complex—vessels to be tied, nerves to be found—but the action was confident, smooth, moving forward at its own pace, with never the slightest hint of Tourette's. Finally, after two and a half hours of the most complex, taxing surgery, Bennett closed up, thanked everybody, yawned, and stretched. Here, then, was an entire operation without a trace of Tourette's. Not because it had been suppressed, or held in—there was never any sign of control or constraint—but because, simply, there was never any impulse to tic. "Most of the time when I'm operating, it never even crosses my mind that I have Tourette's," Bennett says. His whole identity at such times is that of a surgeon at work, and his entire psychic and neural organization becomes aligned with this, becomes active, focused, at ease, un-Tourettic. It is only if the operation is broken for a few minutes—to review a special X-ray taken during the surgery, for example—that Bennett, waiting, unoccupied, remembers that he *is* Tourettic, and in that instant he becomes so. As soon as the flow of the operation resumes, the Tourette's, the Tourettic identity, vanishes once again. Bennett's assistants, though they have known him and worked with him for years, are still astounded whenever they see this. "It's like a miracle," one of them said. "The way the Tourette's disappears." And Bennett himself was astonished, too, and quizzed me, as he peeled off his gloves, on the neurophysiology of it all. . . .

Friday afternoon is open. Bennett often likes to go for long hikes on Fridays, or cycle rides, or drives, with a sense of the trail, the open road, before him. There is a favorite ranch he loves to go to, with a beautiful lake and an airstrip, accessible only via a rugged dirt road. It is a wonderfully situated ranch, a narrow fertile strip perfectly placed between the lake and mountains, and we walked for miles, talking of this and that, with Bennett botanizing or geologizing as we went. Then, briefly, we went to the lake, where I took a swim; when I came out of the water I found that Bennett, rather suddenly, had curled up for a nap. He looked peaceful, tension-free, as he slept; and the suddenness and depth of his sleep made me wonder how much difficulty he encountered in the daytime, whether he might not sometimes be stressed to the limit. I wondered how much he concealed beneath his genial surface—how much, inwardly, he had to control and deal with.

Later, as we continued our ramble about the ranch, he remarked that I had seen only some of the outward expressions of his Tourette's, and these, bizarre as they occasionally seemed, were by no means the worst problems it caused him. The real problems, the inner problems, are panic and rage—feelings so violent that they threaten to overwhelm him, and so sudden that he has virtually no warning of their onset. He has only to get a parking ticket or see a police car, sometimes, for scenarios of violence to flash through his mind: mad chases, shoot-outs, flaming destructions, violent mutilation, and death scenarios that become immensely elaborated in seconds and rush through his mind with convulsive speed. One part of him, uninvolved, can watch these scenes with detachment, but another part of him is taken over and impelled to action. He can prevent himself from giving way to outbursts in public, but the strain of controlling himself is severe and exhausting. At home, in private, he can let himself go—not at others but at inanimate objects around him. There was the wall I had seen, which he had often struck in his rage, and the refrigerator, at which he had flung virtually everything in the kitchen. In his office, he had kicked a hole in the wall and had had to put a plant in front to cover it; and in his study at home the cedar walls were covered with knife marks. "It's not gentle," he said to me. "You can see it as whimsical, funny—be tempted to romanticize it—but Tourette's comes from deep down in the nervous system and the unconscious. It taps into the oldest, strongest feelings we have. Tourette's is like an epilepsy in the subcortex; when it takes over, there's just a thin line of control, a thin line of cortex, between you and it, between you and that raging storm, the blind force of the subcortex. One can see the charming things, the funny things, the creative side of Tourette's, but there's also that dark side. You have to fight it all your life." . . .

It is difficult for Bennett, and is often difficult for Touretters, to see their Tourette's as something external to themselves, because many of its tics and urges may be felt as intentional, as an integral part of the self, the personality, the will. It is quite different, by contrast, with something like parkinsonism or chorea: these have no quality of self-ness or intentionality and are always fatal as diseases, as outside the self. Compulsions and tics occupy an intermediate position, seeming sometimes to be an expression of one's personal will, sometimes a coercion of it by another, alien will. These ambiguities are often expressed in the terms people use. Thus the separateness of "it" and "I" is sometimes expressed by jocular personifications of the Tourette's: one Touretter I know calls his Tourette's "Toby," another "Mr. T." By contrast, a Tourettic possession of the self was vividly expressed by one young man in Utah, who wrote to me that he had a "Touretized soul."

Thinking About the Case

Tourette's, named after its discoverer, the Frenchman Gilles de la Tourette, used to be nicknamed "the cursing disease" because many of its sufferers were plagued by the uncontrollable urge to curse or blaspheme, much to their own shame and embarrassment. Emerging generally before the age of fourteen, and three times more prevalent in boys than in girls, Tourette's syndrome typically involves uncontrollable head movements, accompanied by sounds, such as grunts, yelps, clicks, or words. Dr. Bennett's symptoms are particularly severe, including, as they do, movements of the limbs and torso as well as the head.

A generation ago, Tourette's was thought to represent a deep-seated psychological problem with managing hostility, and some of Dr. Bennett's experiences seem to support this hypothesis, but recent evidence suggests that the disorder is primarily neurological in origin. Perhaps the part of the brain that generates and modulates anger plays some role in Tourette's.

Still, as Sack's description makes clear, there are psychological aspects to the disorder. For one thing, why are certain words, often those which are socially unacceptable, "chosen" for tics and not others? Why are Tourette's patients often obsessively attentive to detail and order? What are the factors that make some tics feel like part of the self while others feel alien? Why are tics worse when the individual is tired or anxious? Answers to these questions are likely to come from the "psychological" rather than the "neurological" domain, if, indeed, such distinctions have real meaning after all.

Modern treatment for Tourette's is primarily biological. Medication often helps decrease the frequency and intensity of tics. Supportive psychotherapy and patient education can help the person cope with the impact the disorder may have on self-esteem and life goals. Reading about Tourette's or joining a self-help mutual support group may be of value to the individual and family.

Many tic disorders are less complicated than Tourette's, may have more situationally specific symptoms, and may yield to one or another form of behavioral therapy. One such therapy directs the person to repeat the tic behavior over and over. While this procedure often does decrease the frequency of the problem, it is not clear what mechanism is responsible. Perhaps the response satiates, or perhaps it is brought under voluntary control by repeated practice. General anxiety reduction strategies (like relaxation training or meditation) and even assertiveness training can be useful in the treatment of simple tics.

Questions to Consider

1. What personality characteristics would lead a person with Tourette's to become a surgeon? Assuming Dr. Bennett's Tourette's disorder emerged in childhood, as most do, what factors in his character or environment could account for his unusual success?

2. Tourette's disorder often co-occurs with obsessive-compulsive disorder. It is also associated with various learning disabilities and with attention deficit hyperactivity disorder (although the medication used to treat ADHD makes Tourette's worse). What do you make of all this?

3. Some people question the inclusion of neurocognitive disorders like Tourette's, dementia, and delirium in the DSM-IV. How do you think we should set the boundary between psychological and neurological disorders? Or, is a boundary necessary at all?

36

————◄o►————

No chapter on neurocognitive disorders would be complete without a selection on Alzheimer's disease, a progressive deterioration in cognitive functions that tends to afflict elderly people. Alzheimer's has drawn more and more attention lately, as the baby boomer generation ages. Since the incidence of Alzheimer's increases with age—approximately 5 percent of people age sixty-five are afflicted, while five times that many have Alzheimer's by age eighty—an aging population means that treatment and care of Alzheimer's patients will be a major public health concern over the next decade.

We have chosen to excerpt a book, called Ginny: A Love Remembered, *written by a man whose wife ultimately died of Alzheimer's. The excerpts record her progressive loss of function as well as how her condition affected those who loved her.*

FROM GINNY: A LOVE REMEMBERED

G. Robert Artley

IT IS HARD TO PUT A DATE ON WHEN the insidious disease that stole the mind and vibrant spirit away from Ginny first began to show itself. As we look back, we can now detect, from the perspective of what has transpired over time, different isolated episodes or incidents of peculiar behavior that were manifested perhaps as far back as 1978.

In 1980 Jeannie first noticed something being wrong when we were visiting her in Washington, D.C., when little Jennifer wanted to play the game of "Clue" with her grandmother and Ginny could not manage it. But those of us who had been around her more back home had been noticing other disturbing things about her behavior before then.

When the children, all gone from home, would come back for a visit, they would take me aside and ask, "What's the matter with Mom?" I, trying to deny my own fears, would be almost angry in replying, "What do you mean, what's wrong with Mom?" It was almost as if I considered them disrespectful of their mother. However, deep inside, I knew that their questions were legitimate, that there *was* something wrong. . . .

. . . [T]he last year the Print Shop was in business, an increasing number of printing jobs had to be done over because of some unexplainable errors that showed up in the finished work. This could prove quite costly, an expense that, of course, had to be borne by the Print Shop. Ginny felt terrible about these "goofs" for which she was responsible, and in my blindness I became impatient with her.

"Why in thunder did you do that?" I'd ask in exasperation. "I don't know *why* I did it!" she would reply, nearly in tears.

Little by little, the Print Shop seemed to be getting to be too much for her. The work was making her nervous and tired her more than before. Finally, we decided that, if we couldn't sell the shop as a going business, we would simply close it up, sell off the equipment, and put the building up for sale.

It was a relief, once we'd made up our minds, to finally deliver our last printing job. Yet with a feeling of sadness, too, we closed another chapter on our life together.

Unfortunately, we could not enjoy Ginny's retirement as we'd hoped. Her mental problems gradually became more evident. She would forget things that I, in my chronic forgetfulness, had depended on her to remember for me. She became easily confused, whereas she had been the one of us who knew what the score was. Ginny had been the one to take care of the monthly bills, write the checks, keep track of appointments and, in general, keep her home, husband, and business running on track.

Sometimes she did inexplicable things that were foreign to her usual way. On one occasion, putting on a new pair of pants for the first time, I discovered the button missing that would have fastened the little tab and held the front closed before pulling up the zipper. I asked Ginny to sew on the button when she had time, and I wore another pair that day. To my chagrin, when next I put on the new pair of pants, I discovered that, instead of the button being sewed on, the tab had been cut off, thus eliminating the need for the button.

This discovery was quite a shock. It bothered me to the extent that I never mentioned it to Ginny. Knowing that such behavior was not akin to Ginny's nature, I didn't want to confront her with it. I simply wore the new pants sans tab, with no one being the wiser. But every time I put them on, I saw Ginny's handiwork and was reminded that something *was* wrong . . . not only with the pants.

Other aberrations began to appear more and more often. When Ginny and I were visiting with friends, she would suddenly interject a thought that was entirely foreign to the topic of our conversation. This broke the thread of our intercourse and caused puzzled embarrassment to all of us, especially to Ginny, who realized she'd said something wrong.

Through the years, even though she was naturally shy and had a tendency to hold back, Ginny had always made worthwhile and even witty contributions to a discussion, so this verbal misstep was but further evidence that something was not right with her mental process. Sometimes she would use wrong words in a sentence. This could be humorous, and we all, including Ginny, would laugh at it. At first we poked good-natured fun by calling her Mrs. Malaprop, a character in a play who makes ludicrous blunders in her use of words. But, after a while, instead of laughing at these malapropisms of Ginny's, we'd try to overlook them, realizing that she was not *trying* to be funny.

One evening Ginny had invited friends for supper. As the time for their arrival drew near, Ginny, who loved to have people in for meals, seemed ill at ease and reluctant. As I helped her with the last-minute details, when it was necessary to rearrange some of the table settings, it seemed almost too much for her.

The meal was fine and our guests seemed to enjoy it, but Ginny seemed to not be really with us—to be somewhat in a fog. Years later, after Ginny's condition had been diagnosed, our friend, referring to that supper, confessed she had thought maybe Ginny was a closet alcoholic.

During the early stages of Ginny's mental problem, before a name had been put on it, these strange behavior patterns were stressful for all of us—certainly Ginny, because, as yet, she was still aware that she was apt to say or do something "stupid," and this only compounded her sense of insecurity and her suffering. . . .

The rest of that autumn and into December, Ginny was functioning about as she had been in Adrian. But there was increasing evidence that she had a health problem. She still drove the car occasionally but began to show signs of confusion and even got lost once or twice in our small town. Without making an issue of it, I gradually took over all the driving, until her Minnesota driver's license was no longer valid. However, she did ask me to pick up an Iowa driving test booklet for her to study in preparation for taking the test. She tried valiantly, for she had every intention of passing the test to get her Iowa driver's license. She spent hours going over all the driving rules and regulations and traffic sign recognition. Then she asked me to quiz her. However, those sessions were not successful at all and only caused her further frustration.

It was sad to see one who had always been so diligent in her studies and able to absorb facts, who had put me to shame with her ability to memorize, now not able to remember the simplest things in the book. When she would miss a question, she'd ask to take the book and study it again, but to no avail. Finally, she would put the book aside, determined to go at it again when "my mind is clearer."

This went on for quite a while. Ginny had always liked to read in bed; now, if she retired before I did, I'd come in later to find her asleep with the Iowa driver's license booklet propped up on her chest. As I'd always done, I would carefully remove her glasses and book and lay them aside. And, as always, if she was not in a deep sleep, a faint smile would flicker across her face.

So the weeks went by, with Ginny always preparing for the test that was given at the courthouse every Saturday morning. But, as Saturday arrived each week, I helped her forget the appointed time. I felt guilty in this subterfuge, but I had no intention of letting her suffer through the humiliation of trying to take a written test she was bound to fail miserably. Nor, for that matter, did I want her to attempt to drive again with her obvious state of confusion and erratic behavior. After a while, she forgot about taking the test, and I sadly put the little booklet away, realizing this to be but another part of Ginny that was in the past. . . .

As time went on, social exposures became more difficult, and we withdrew more and more into our shell. One time when I realized that Ginny's condition had brought us to this stage was at a function to which we had been invited at the Methodist church. It was a buffet supper with the food laid out on tables before the call to start the line. As we waited, Ginny and I were visiting with someone when I suddenly realized she was not beside me. Instead, she was at the food table, going from dish to dish, picking up and sampling morsels of food. As discreetly and quickly as possible, I went to her side and gently moved her away to where, hopefully, we could melt into the background. . . .

As time went on and Ginny's condition deteriorated perceptibly, people made allowances for her strange behavior or her inappropriate or incomprehensible speech. Even the Hampton police were aware of our problem and kept an unobtrusive watch over her. They were actively involved a couple of times.

Usually, when working at my drawing board, I would hear her moving around on the floor above me, going from room to room in a restless state. Sometimes, if I didn't hear her, I'd go up to find her lying on the couch or sitting quietly in a chair. At other times, she might have gone outside. This, of course, was my constant concern.

One time, as I was working in my basement studio, the phone rang, and a woman, whose voice and whose name I did not recognize, said that Ginny had come into her house and seemed confused, not knowing where she was or how to get home. I was shocked, for I had not even been aware that she was out of the house.

Just as I arrived at the home of the woman who had made the call, about three blocks from our place, a police car pulled up. The officer said that he had received a call, too. I assured him that I would take care of the situation and thanked him for his concern. When the woman of the house let me in, she said that Ginny was in the kitchen. I went there to find her standing in the middle of the room, quietly crying. Taking her in my arms, I kissed her, thanked the lady for her kindness, and we went home — Ginny in confusion and humiliation and I in sadness for my dear wife. I realized anew how vulnerable we were.

Some months later, Ginny again slipped out without my knowledge. Again I was alerted by a phone call. This time she was at a convenience store and gas station at the intersection of highways 3 and 65, about two blocks from our home. I took the car, and as I drove up to the store, I saw Ginny standing by a police car, talking to the officer inside. My nephew, George, was standing beside her.

It seemed that when Ginny had appeared in the store, quite confused and not able to make much sense to the clerks, someone called the police. When they had realized that she was Mrs. Artley, they had phoned my brother Dan's house. George, being the only one at home, had jumped in his car and come to see what help he could be to his Aunt Ginny.

Ginny's tendency to slip out of the house and wander away kept us all on the alert and on edge. . . .

Although all of this wandering about and suddenly appearing un-announced could in itself be disruptive and disturbing to those being visited, Ginny never did anything that was in any way antisocial or unfriendly. She was, as she had always been, soft-spoken and kind-ly disposed toward people. Thus, rather than antagonizing her sur-prised hosts, she elicited from them sympathy and concern for her well-being. . . .

There were countless stressful, embarrassing situations brought about by Ginny's growing confusion and memory loss, which, had it not been for the kindness and understanding of those around us, could have be-come even more painfully complicated. One such time was when the minister of our church surreptitiously handed me a check Ginny had given her — written for an amount much larger than we had been giving. I don't recall how I handled that situation, but I appreciated the minister's understanding, and the incident served as a flag, alerting me to keep track of the checkbook . . .

If Ginny's mental deterioration had happened all at once, as with a stroke, I think it might have been easier for us. Of course, there would have been the initial devastating shock, but later, faced with the reality of the thing that had happened, we would have resigned ourselves to the fact that all we could do was adjust to it.

But such is not the case with the insidious nature of Alzheimer's disease. Instead, especially in the early stages, one is not quite sure whether there is something wrong or not. It teases, and even, at times, dangles false hope before one. There were times when I would tell myself that Ginny was seeming better and that she was going to beat this thing that was destroying her while we who loved her stood by helplessly. Then there would be a cruel relapse and I knew the nightmare was real. . . .

I will not soon forget the first time I experienced Ginny's not knowing me. She had gone to bed, and after my usual nighttime rounds, locking the front and back doors, checking to see that the fire was okay in the fireplace and that Simon and Kelly (our cat and dog) were in the basement, and turning off the lights, I went into our bedroom to get ready for bed. As I entered, Ginny, with an expression of alarm on her face, said, "What are *you* doing here?"

Perplexed, I told her I was going to bed.

"Not in *here*, you aren't!" she said, and drew the bed clothes up tight around her. . . .

Never in all our married life, up until that fateful night, had I been denied entrance to our marriage bed. Thus, this harsh order from the lips of my loving Ginny struck me to the heart in total disbelief. Even though I knew that "this was not Ginny," still I felt profoundly betrayed and hurt.

After getting an extra blanket from the closet, under the stern, watchful eye of a Ginny I did not know, I retreated to my recliner in the darkened living room, wallowing in self-pity and with a sense of great loss of the closeness we had always shared.

At a very late hour, after Ginny had finally gone to sleep, I crept quietly back to our room and very carefully, so as not to jiggle it, lay down on my side of the bed. When morning came, at long last, Ginny had apparently forgotten about the "strange man" who had tried to invade her privacy and seemed to accept my presence for whomever she might think I was.

Another time when the chagrin of being perceived as a stranger by my loving wife was brought home to me, I was working in my studio, thinking Ginny was upstairs, when the phone rang. It was Rob, saying that his mother was there and for me not to worry, that she was fine but maybe, after a while, I should come for her. Then he went on to explain: Ginny had appeared at their door, about two blocks from our house (across busy Highway 65) to say that there was a strange man at her house and that she wanted her children to know that she was "not *that* kind of woman." . . .

In 1984 she began to have hallucinations. This didn't get to be a real problem in Ginny's case, but she would occasionally indicate that she saw something or someone in our house that none of the rest of us could see. But what she "saw" did not frighten her or cause her any concern. Here, too, we did not tell her she was "only seeing things" or try in any way to dissuade her. Instead, we either ignored her remark or acted as if we too saw what she saw. This could make for some fun in which Ginny seemed to enter.

Ginny and I usually walked about a mile every day — sometimes more. We most often took the same circuitous route, going south from our house and returning from the north. (I had calculated this way to be about a mile.) It took us through residential areas, past some homes of people we knew, past two school yards and the old Waterworks Park. It was a pleasant walk and we sometimes, if I felt up to it, took Kelly, our rambunctious Irish setter, along on a leash. But most of the time, it was just Ginny and I, walking briskly.

We walked mostly in silence, as Ginny's speech was increasingly becoming incoherent muttering. But sometimes, as we approached a fire hydrant, she would say to me in confidence, "Isn't he cute!" and then say "Hi" to it as we walked by. Eventually, if there was no one else nearby, I, too, not wanting to be left out of the camaraderie, would also greet the little iron fellows. We even stopped, sometimes, to briefly visit with these friendly fire hydrants that we were getting to know on our daily walks.

This all seemed to please Ginny. Now I look back, with a mixture of humor and longing, on those walks as another phase of our togetherness.

Accompanying Ginny's restless wandering was her inclination to pick things up and put them elsewhere. During this period, she was constantly rearranging and stashing items about the house. Maybe one shoe would be missing, or something from the kitchen would show up in the bedroom. I opened the refrigerator door one day to find the electric iron sitting on a shelf next to the butter dish.

Her diamond ring came up missing and we both searched throughout the house without success. I kicked myself for not being on top of the situation and not having put it away for safekeeping. Months later, when we moved from our house in town to the farm, one of the women helping us found it while wiping a cleaning cloth along the top shelf of the kitchen cupboard. Evidently, Ginny had *herself* put it away "for safe-keeping." . . .

The strange behaviors of some people suffering from dementia include disrobing—sometimes in public. Thankfully, Ginny was spared that humiliation. Instead of taking *off* her clothes, she *added* to what she already had on, layer upon layer.

At such times, when she would slip out of the house for one of her wanderings, she was literally overdressed. This gave her a ludicrous appearance, like a circus clown before he takes layer upon layer off in his comic act. I felt embarrassed for her to be seen this way before I could get her back into the house, but I was thankful I didn't have to rush out with a blanket to cover her nudity. However, one time I *did* rescue her before she went out the front door with an extra bra over her blouse.

One night during this period of overdressing, I went to help her get ready for bed and found her to have on three or four blouses and a like number of skirts, as well as underwear and stockings, one over the other. After peeling off her things, a layer at a time (similar to what the circus clowns did) until I got down to the real Ginny, I helped her get into her nightgown and into bed. Then I went into the bathroom to prepare myself for bed. I couldn't have been gone for more than three or four minutes, but when I returned I found Ginny out of bed and almost completely dressed again . . . with all her layers. In exasperation I blurted out, "Ginny, what are you doing?" and set about to get her ready for bed again.

Apparently, Ginny saw the humor in this situation (not far different from what she might have pulled on me as a trick in former years) for she burst out laughing, her familiar joyful laugh. We ended up by falling across the bed in one another's arms, in a paroxysm of laughter—the kind of deep, joyful laughter we had shared many times in our years together, but something we had not enjoyed for a long time. . . .

Another time, when some unexpected guests dropped in for a short time on their way through town, Ginny startled the man by suddenly bringing in from the kitchen and presenting to him a tray on which was a spatula, a serving spoon, and some other kitchen utensils. This, too, was her attempt to be the gracious hostess she had always been. The incident, like many situations brought about by the disease, was not without humor, yet not without pathos for the sensitive victim. . . .

[T]he family had finally persuaded me that, in view of Ginny's steady decline, I should begin planning for her to enter a care facility. For economic reasons, as well as the need for specialized care for Alzheimer's victims, we decided to check out the Iowa Veterans Home in Marshall-town, which we had heard was an excellent care facility and also included a new Alzheimer's unit. . . .

As we drove toward home in the gathering darkness late that afternoon, I was glad to be in the back seat among the shadows. Rob and Kris tried valiantly to bolster my spirits by recounting the attractive features of the place and "how good it will be for Mom"; how it was designed to give the residents freedom to do their restless wandering without being in danger; how it was made so as to minimize those things in their environment that might aggravate their confusion; how the decorator had used calming, harmonious colors that were nevertheless cheerful; how the television was fixed so that only the staff would be able to operate it so that they could select programs that would not agitate.

They reminded me how, mounted on the walls along the hallway between the rooms, were knobs that could be turned or moved to various positions through slots by the Alzheimer's patients in their constant need to be doing something; and how, for their safety, the doors in and out of the unit were secured by making passage possible only by a key carried by staff members at all times; and how sensitivity to the patients' needs had been shown by the planners, in providing that one door opened onto a porch from which patients could walk along walkways through an attractive, fenced-in garden area that included a gazebo, where on mild days they could sit on benches and listen to piped-in music; how even the flowers, shrubs, and trees of this garden were selected for their nontoxicity, in case they would be ingested.

By reminding me of all these features designed for the welfare and comfort of the residents who would be living there once it was open, Rob and Kris were trying to make me glad for the action we had taken that day. But I could not be glad. My heart was heavy and full of dread.

Such had been my mood as we came home that winter evening, as it would be for much of the time from then on until Ginny was actually admitted. And now, with the disturbing (to me) message from Marshall-town giving a specific date, March 2, 1987, when they would be ready for Ginny, the timer had been set. Each day ticked off, relentlessly bringing closer that fateful day when Ginny would no longer be at home. There was a conspiracy, I felt, that Ginny, in her trusting, loving, nature, would never have suspected—and I, of all people, was a part of it!

I don't recall any two months passing as quickly as January and February. Our time was active and full, with family and friends doing their utmost to help us in our helpless situation, but even though Ginny's condition continued to decline, she, as always, seemed pleased when folks came calling.

One time, when some friends were leaving after a pleasant afternoon visit, Ginny, who had sat quietly in our midst (a welcome change from her restless pacing) apparently enjoying the sound of voices around her, unexpectedly said with a warm smile as they were leaving, "You must come again." Even though this warm, gracious gesture, sincerely spoken directly from the heart and appropriately timed, was typical of Ginny, we were all startled, because for a long time most of her utterances, if there were any, had been unintelligible.

With the exception of a rare moment, now and then, the Ginny-that-had-been became further buried in the debris of a deteriorating mind. As the fateful day of her entrance into the Iowa Veterans Home drew ever closer, in spite of my dread, I was coming to realize (in my more rational moments) that she would no doubt be ready. Along with increasing confusion and other evidence of mental decline, there were beginning to be instances of incontinence. She was increasingly requiring constant supervision and more vigilance on the part of her caregivers, including me when those I'd hired were off duty. . . .

There were times when I thought I would collapse under the burden, and I longed to be able to share it with her, the one who had been my strength and comfort in times past—in all the crises we had gone through together. But *this* one, our greatest ever, she would not even be able to comprehend. I thanked God for a loving, supportive family.

LANAHAN NOTES
Neurocognitive Disorders

————◦————

Definition:

Organic brain disorders caused by three different factors:
1. pathological processes associated with aging
2. alcohol and drugs
3. physical disease or injury (tumor, blow to the head)

Types:

Delirium: confused or clouded awareness of the environment: attentional and cognitive difficulties; acute onset and fluctuating course

Dementia: memory and other cognitive deficits (language, recognition of objects, ability to carry out organized behaviors); can be accompanied by delirium, delusions and/or depression.

Amnestic (memory) Disorders

Three Sources of Data Used to Establish Organic Origin:

1. Detailed case history—pattern of onset of symptoms
2. Symptoms consistent with pattern expected from damage to particular neural structure
3. Physical findings like C.A.T. or P.E.T. scan (if available)

Neurological disorders have secondary psychological effects—on self-esteem, social relations, mood.

Treatment:

Remove (if possible) medical source of problem.

Retraining and rehabilitation of skills are sometimes possible.

Supportive psychotherapy to help person (and family) cope with deficits

Sometimes medication if genuine depressive disorder develops

Social Issue: As population ages, economic and social costs of Alzheimer's disease and other dementias of aging will increase. What to do?

CHAPTER NINE

Personality Disorders

————◄o►————

Some people seem to make the same mistakes over and over and over again. One person seems to distrust everybody he meets, leading people to behave towards him in distant, distrustful ways in return. Thus, he creates a self-fulfilling prophecy that only strengthens his views of others. Another seems to overreact emotionally—he falls hopelessly in love, demands absolute devotion and attentiveness, only to become suicidally depressed when his lovers inevitably run from his smothering affection. His life seems to be a screenplay for a grade-B movie. Yet another seems stubborn and unmotivated, sabotaging her chances for career improvement by never seeming to get things done on time, forgetting important meetings, and resisting suggestions. She lacks assertiveness in personal relationships as well, frustrating those who might become her friends by finding ways to get out of taking her share of responsibility for the relationship. These people, and many others like them are said to have personality disorders—longstanding, pervasive, and entrenched patterns of perceiving, thinking about, and relating to the world that result in impaired functioning and/or subjective distress.

In the DSM-IV the personality disorders, unlike those we have studied thus far, are listed under Axis II (along with mental retardation), meaning that they generally begin in childhood or adolescence and are relatively unchanging throughout life. They are grouped into clusters based on similarities in the symptom picture. Cluster A includes disorders marked by odd or eccentric behavior. Cluster B disorders are characterized by dramatic, impulsive, and erratic behavior. Cluster C is marked by anxiety and fearfulness. Many individuals fit the criteria for more than one personality disorder, and many of the people who carry an Axis I diagnosis also qualify for one or more personality disorders.

For this chapter, we have chosen one disorder from Cluster A (#37), two from Cluster B (#38 and #39), and one from Cluster C (#40). Since the Cluster B disorders are particularly vivid and can result in enormous difficulty for those who come in contact with people who have them, the readings have been chosen to expand on our understanding of the two Cluster B disorders we illustrated with cases: Antisocial personality disorder (previously called psychopathy or sociopathy) and borderline personality disorder. These disorders raise fascinating and important questions about distinctions between "bad" and "mad," and when people are or are not responsible for their behavior.

37

———◀◦▶———

PARANOID–SCHIZOTYPAL DISORDER:
THE CASE OF PETER N.

PETER N. IS A FORTY-FOUR-YEAR-OLD MAN who lives alone in a run-down trailer several miles outside of a small New England town. His appearance is decidedly odd. He is a small, emaciated man who has a full beard and wears old, often torn, clothing. He smells awful, as if he hadn't bathed in months. Townspeople give him a wide berth, not only because of his odor, but because he has flown off the handle at shopkeepers and bank tellers, yelling and cursing at what seem to be imaginary insults and slights. Everyone recognizes him, and while some people feel sorry for him, most are afraid of him. The sheriff's deputies are also familiar with Peter. Most of them have been on duty when he has created a scene in the community, or they have been to his trailer in response to neighbors' complaints that he threatened them or frightened them.

The appearance of Peter's trailer is also decidedly odd. His bedroom is covered with scraps of newspaper articles dabbed with blue paint. The articles are about the mental health system at which he is currently quite angry. Blue is his special color, reflecting, he says "the deepest parts of my personality." Blue paint is everywhere, on furniture, cooking utensils, even his shoes.

Also everywhere are the strange objects that he collects for his "projects." These projects always have to do with shielding himself or his possessions from harm. One of these projects, for example, involved using lime to clean lead which he then intended to melt down and coat other metal objects to protect them. He spent the better part of his welfare check to purchase huge bags of lime which sat around until his attachment to this particular project was supplanted by another project, as it always was. Then he returned the lime. Often, he was unable to return supplies, even when he berated the shopkeeper, so his stock kept gradually increasing. The trailer, both inside and out, exudes chaos. Weeds choke out grass. Clutter overwhelms order.

Peter doesn't work. Over the years, he has tried one job or another, but he has never been able to tolerate being involved with others for more than a few days. Invariably, he would become convinced that people were plotting to ensure that he would never have a relationship with a woman, that he didn't deserve such a relationship. He believed that other people thought that he was homosexual. He was enraged to think they believed this of him. On occasion, he would confront someone about this plot and get escorted off the premises. He hasn't tried to work in years now, and seems offended if anyone suggests that he should earn a living. This strong sense that he is entitled to be supported and to get what he wants when he wants it is a consistent thread in his view of himself in the world. Rather than work, Peter's habit is to spend intensive time on one of his projects for weeks or months, then impulsively go on a trip. While away, he lives in cheap, dingy single rooms. Nobody really knows how he spends his days while he's gone.

Sometimes he house sits for his parents. Generally, he arrives a day or so before they leave, and he leaves shortly after they return. He looks forward to seeing them, but can't stay in their presence for more than a few hours without getting into a noisy argument. Mrs. N. often gives him small gifts of money so that he can keep his truck going or buy a pair of shoes. Her husband objects because he feels that Peter should be supporting himself, but to no avail.

Peter is the second son, born to first-generation Jewish immigrants. His father is an accountant and his mother is a homemaker. Little information about his childhood is actually available, since his distrust makes communication with others, particularly about personal matters, difficult. Apparently, his older brother had an uneventful childhood and is now married, a father, and employed. Peter, on the other hand, seemed to have difficulties from the start. What seems clear is that he exhibited school refusal and other oppositional behaviors from an early age. His parents found him more and more difficult to manage and placed him in a residential treatment setting when he was ten or eleven. He hated it there because most of the children had severe behavioral problems and he was often targeted for batterings by more aggressive youngsters. He blamed his parents, especially his mother for "dumping" him there.

Although quite intelligent, Peter was in and out of school over the next several years, often running away for weeks at a time. It is unclear whether he actually graduated from high school—sometimes he talks about dropping out, while in other conversations he mentions having attended some community college classes.

Peter has been involved with the mental health system since he was a child and, at one time or another, has been on the receiving end of nearly every kind of service available—residential treatment, outpatient treatment, rehabilitation training programs, psychotherapy, and pharmacotherapy. None of these has seemed to have much impact, although, to be fair, it is hard to assess what his life would have been like without these interventions. His mental health connections seem to afford him his only safe human contact (outside of his parents, to whom he remains ambivalently attached), a tenuous but sufficient connection with the real world. He has lived like this for over twenty years, and may well do so for forty more.

Thinking About the Case

Psychiatric diagnosis is an inexact science. Nowhere is this more apparent than in the area of personality disorder where an indivdiual's symptoms may range across diagnostic categories within one of the clusters, and even between clusters. The case of Peter N. is a good example of this kind of diagnostic overlap. He certainly exhibits the pervasive distrust and suspiciousness that is the hallmark of paranoid personality disorder, and would probably be classified as such by many clinicians. He also meets the diagnostic criteria for schizotypal personality disorder: ideas of reference (thinking that others are talking about or laughing at him), odd beliefs inconsistent with cultural norms (the idea that painting things blue will protect him in some way), odd thinking and speech, suspiciousness, paranoid ideas, inappropriate emotions, behavior and appearance that is peculiar, a lack of close friends, and excessive social anxiety associated with paranoid fears.

To complicate matters, an argument could be made that Peter's symptoms almost meet the criteria for the Cluster B disorder, antisocial personality disorder. He fails to conform to social norms, is irritable and aggressive, and is irresponsible in terms of working for a living—three rather than the four necessary symptoms. Clearly he exhibits the sense of entitlement that invariably accompanies this disorder. Finally, his behaviors are also indicative of avoidant personalty disorder, a Cluster C diagnosis. He shows the characteristic pattern of feelings of social inadequacy, avoidance of social interactions and hypersensitivity to negative evaluation at a level that would clearly be sufficient to meet the criteria for this diagnostic category. However, his thinking and behavior are so bizarre, and his social avoidance so clearly related to paranoid ideas that this diagnosis seems inadequate to capture the flavor of the case. According to the DSM-IV, multiple diagnoses can and should be given if appropriate, so Peter would probably receive the diagnoses paranoid personality disorder and schizotypal personality disorder, with avoidant and antisocial features.

Many clinicians would entertain the possibility that Peter actually has schizophrenia. However, while he has fleeting delusional ideas (although not really a well-formed delusional system), he does not report hallucinations nor has he ever exhibited the gross disorganization of speech and behavior that characterize the acute phase of schizophrenia. Rather, the syndrome he exhibits has the characteristic childhood onset and unchanging course that is typical of personality disorders.

Questions to Consider

1. Do Peter's symptoms meet the criteria for any of the Axis I disorders discussed earlier in the book? Consider specifically social phobia and depression. If not, what criteria are not met?

2. What do you make of the fact that Peter's brother appears to have developed normally both as a child and as an adult? What factors could explain the differences in how the brothers turned out?

3. What are the implications of the fact that an individual like Peter can meet the criteria for several personality disorders at once? What does this say about our present diagnostic system?

38

——◄○►——

ANTISOCIAL PERSONALITY: THE CASE OF WILLIAM HARDIN

GANGS HAVE BECOME A UBIQUITOUS and frightening feature on the American landscape. In a society in which familial and cultural institutions have broken down, gang norms and relationships can replace those that are no longer available elsewhere. One particularly horrifying gang activity is known as "wilding." This is savage violence without comprehensible motive like robbery or personal antagonism, perpetrated on victims seemingly chosen at random. Wilding crimes, like the widely publicized near fatal attack on a jogger in New York's Central Park which occurred in the spring of 1985, seem to be engaged in for fun and amusement. Most gangs are not organized around violence as a central principle, nor are most incidences of gang violence examples of wilding. Rather, violence occurs more often in the service of economic, turf-protection, or group cohesion reasons. Similarly, many gang members are not primarily antisocial in orientation. They are capable of love, loyalty, and conformity to rules—the rules of the gang rather than the rules of the larger society. However, wilding gangs tend to be loose-knit groups composed of more isolated, disturbed youngsters. Many of these fit the classic profile of the individual with antisocial personality disorder.

William Hardin is a real person. His case history is drawn from *Gangs* written by two sociologists, Scott Cummings and Daniel J. Monti (New York: State University of New York Press, 1993). In April 1983 he was found guilty of capital murder in the beating deaths of three elderly residents of Rosedale Heights, an urban community of about ten thousand people located in the Greater Fort Worth, Texas, metropolitan area. He was also linked to several rapes, street robberies, and residential burglaries. Most of the victims were between seventy and eighty-five years of age. See if you think he meets the criteria for antisocial personality disorder.

William was twenty years old when he was arrested for murder. By that time he had already been involved in many incidents of burglary, petty theft, and car theft. Money from these crimes usually went to buy drugs. He was a fairly heavy alcohol user, and also used marijuana, hashish, and cocaine. He had one child, age three, whom he never saw and whom he did not support. He had no girlfriend, but rather a series of casual, emotionally unattached sexual connections. He happened to be working at the time of his arrest, in a job that paid $4.00 per hour. He had never held a job more than a few months at a time.

William was the fourth of seven siblings. He had never met his father and knew him only by name. He had brothers and sisters by different fathers. His mother had been absent from the home for several years, and William had lived with an older brother, who had tried, unsuccessfully, to parent him, and an older sister with whom he was living at the time of his arrest. He seemed emotionally unconnected to his siblings.

William had a brief and unrewarding school experience. His tested intelligence was lower than average and he had limited verbal skills. By the time he was in fifth or sixth grade, he was out of school more than he was in, often leaving in the middle of the day to go have sex with one or another girl. He was expelled for truancy on at least one occasion, and finally dropped out of school altogether in seventh grade.

From the age of fourteen on, William was on the streets. He was not associated with a formal gang, but rather seemed a marginal character in the neighborhood dramas, joining in when the impulse moved him. He liked getting high and he liked sex. Other than that, he seemed unmoved by anything or anybody.

Thinking About the Case

Criminal behavior, impulsivity, aggressiveness, and lack of remorse—core features of antisocial personality disorder, and core features of William Hardin's personalty. Do all people who are habitual criminals have antisocial personality disorder? The answer is clearly "no." People who steal or deal drugs because they have few legitimate opportunities to make a living may be capable of self-restraint, planfulness, committed relationships, and strict adherence to a code of behavior. These individuals may exhibit antisocial behavior (by the standards of the larger society), but not signs of antisocial personality disorder. Antisocial personality implies that the individual's behavior arises, to at least some extent, out of conditions that are beyond his or her control. The behaviors are thought to be compelled rather than chosen.

People with this disorder are distinguishable from ordinary criminals in three ways. First, their crimes are impulsive and often irrational (although they may be capable of more rational crimes as well). Second, they lack a conscience, guilt, and the ability to care deeply about others. Finally, they seem unable to experience strong, sustained emotions. Rather, they seem possessed of violent, brief feelings that quickly give way to new ones. Only a small percentage of people who are incarcerated are antisocial personalities. Further, many people with features of this disorder are not behind bars.

Clearly, the ability to control one's behavior and connect emotionally with others is a continuous, not a discrete variable. How much lack of control, impulsivity, or self-centeredness is enough to qualify an individual for a diagnosis of antisocial personality disorder? The line is arbitrary. This represents a problem with the diagnostic system in that it introduces a strong element of subjectivity in what should, in principle, be an objective process.

To what extent are antisocial behaviors the result of some individual psychopathology and to what extent can they be attributed to social and economic forces? In *Gangs* the authors suggest that in certain circumstances "crime becomes a rational response to the absence of tangible opportunities" (p. 70), and that wilding gangs "are aberrant and antisocial adaptations to the cycle of poverty and racism prevalent within urban ghettos like Rosedale" (p. 70). Like the other disorders we have studied, a biopsychosocial explanation seems applicable. Studies suggest that there may be inherited dysfunctions in normal arousal mechanisms in people with antisocial personality disorder. However, brutality and extreme conflict in the family have also been implicated. Many antisocial sons have antisocial fathers, leading to the possibility that modeling may also be a contributing factor. In any case, we are likely many decades away from being able to pinpoint the causes or cures of this disorder from which so much misery springs.

Questions to Consider

1. The incidence of antisocial personality disorder is about 4.5 percent in men and less than one percent in women. Why might this be so?

2. Why might the average age of onset of this disorder be earlier in men than in women?

3. Symptoms associated with antisocial personality disorder seem to improve spontaneously as the individual reaches his thirties and forties. What are some reasons why this might be so?

4. Can you design a study to tease out biological from social factors in the development of antisocial personality disorder? After you have done so, play devil's advocate and critique your own study.

5. What aspects of our society might nurture the development of antisocial personality disorder? What steps might be taken to reduce the incidence of this disorder?

39

——————◄○►——————

BORDERLINE PERSONALITY DISORDER:
THE CASE OF ROBERTA F.

"I'd like to make an appointment, please," she murmured softly into the telephone.

"Certainly. May I have your name, please?"

"No, I'd rather not . . . "

"I'm sorry, but we need your name in order to schedule you with a therapist."

"I don't see why that's necessary. Don't you people have some kind of thing about confidentiality?"

"Yes, we don't give out information about our clients without their written permission. Still, we need to have your name in order to set up an appointment."

"I suppose if I had the money to pay for a private therapist, I wouldn't have to go through all of this. My name is Roberta."

Roberta arrived fifteen minutes late for her first appointment. Her therapist, Dr. T., was impressed with how thin and gaunt the young woman appeared. When he inquired as to why she had requested counseling, she said that her boyfriend had told her to come—the choice was his, not hers. She didn't feel she needed any help. Dr. T. asked her why she thought her boyfriend had decided she needed counseling. She replied, "because of these," and rolling up the right sleeve of her white blouse, she revealed a line of small circular burn marks that started about three inches above her wrist and meandered up her inner arm with an inch or two space between each burn.

"Are those cigarette burns?" Dr. T. asked.

"Yes," she whispered.

"Where else do you have them?"

Silently, she touched her chest and her belly and then drew her fingers lightly up the inside of her left arm.

Dr. T. paused and then said, "Your boyfriend thinks you should get help to stop burning yourself, but you're not at all sure that you agree. Is that right?"

"Very perceptive, doctor."

Noting the sarcasm in Roberta's voice, Dr. T. knew that his next comment would have to be chosen carefully. In an instant, he decided against commenting upon her apparent anger and said instead, "perhaps we could explore together the meaning and value that the burning has for you so that you can become clearer in your own mind about whether you'd like to give it up. Would that be okay?"

Roberta considered before replying, "maybe. We'll see."

Over the next seven months, Dr. T. met with Roberta twice a week. Their sessions were unpredictable and stressful for the therapist. Sometimes Roberta was almost mute, seemingly too depressed (or sometimes too angry) to speak. At other times she was sarcastic and demeaning towards everybody and everything, including Dr. T. Occasionally she seemed lively and energized, quite normal in fact. Her warm, engaging behavior in these sessions bordered on the seductive. Even then, she could turn in an instant, becoming angry or hurt. Through the storms and the silences, Dr. T. learned some of Roberta's history.

Roberta was the third child, and only girl, in her family of four children. Her father ran an automobile scrap business in the small midwestern town in which they lived. Her mother kept the business's financial books but otherwise did not work outside the home. While the family was not exactly poor, neither were they financially comfortable. They had ample food and warm clothing (often passed down within the family) but little in the way of luxuries.

Roberta's father worked long hours, spending his free time hunting and fishing with his friends and sons. Her mother worked hard as well and often seemed tired and edgy. While Roberta's parents didn't argue much, she discovered when she was about eleven that her father had been having a long-term affair with a woman from a neighboring town. Apparently, her mother had decided for reasons of her own not to confront or leave him, but rather to suffer his separateness in silence. Roberta remembers that dinnertimes were eerie, with conversations that kept to "please pass the potatoes," and "this meatloaf isn't as good as the last one you made." She sometimes felt that she lived in a household of strangers.

"Roberta was a shy, clingy child from the start," her mother would later say. She had been easily upset by loud noises and changes of routine. The tumult and disorder created by her two older brothers seemed to overwhelm her. Mrs. F. often felt smothered by Roberta, whose needs for soothing and reassurance seemed endless. What Roberta remembers is that "my mother was never there for me. My father spent time with my brothers. Nobody spent time with me."

Mrs. F. has heard these complaints from Roberta many times over the past ten years. Her reaction is mixed, composed of equal parts astonishment, resentment, and guilt. Looking back, she doesn't see how she could have done more, as busy as she was and as isolated as she felt, but Roberta's blaming seems always to hit home anyway.

Roberta's early school years were uneventful from her parents' perspective. She attended regularly and got acceptable grades, unlike her brothers whose academic performances were marginal and whose social behavior at school left much to be desired. Mr. F., himself a bit of a "hellraiser" in his own youth was tolerant of his sons' misbehaviors, despite his wife's silent disapproval. Still he and his wife were both grateful that Roberta seemed to be achieving some measure of success without the constant surveillance their sons seemed to require.

Roberta's own recollections of these years belied the surface calm. "I always got picked on," she told Dr. T. bitterly. "The kids didn't like me because I wore my brothers' clothes. At lunch I sat by myself. That's when I learned the difference between the 'haves' and the 'have-nots.' Even the teachers pushed me away, despite my doing everything they asked me to do."

In fourth grade, something even worse happened. Roberta's oldest brother, Sam, turned fifteen and began babysitting his younger siblings two evenings a week while his mother went to Bingo and his father was out with "the boys." On one of these evenings, a few weeks after he'd started babysitting, Sam decided to "help" Roberta with her bath. Overriding her protests with the statement that he was in charge while their parents were gone, he demanded that she stand naked in front of him so that he could "make sure I was clean." Gradually, over the next several months, Sam's demands escalated. He watched her undress. He watched her urinate. By spring he had begun to masturbate as he watched her.

Roberta hated Sam for what he was doing. His behavior embarrassed, shamed, and sickened her. But she was also afraid of him. She knew from her own experience that he would slap or even punch her if she were uncooperative. Sam said, and she agreed, that her parents would blame her if she told them what he had been doing. So she cooperated, and in doing so came to feel even more worthless, dirty, and unlovable than she had felt before.

Not until the next winter did the situation gradually change. Sam got a girlfriend who often kept him company while he babysat. On these evenings he left Roberta alone. More and more often, Sam himself went out, leaving Roberta and her younger brother in the care of Steve, the second oldest brother, who basically ignored her. By summer, when Sam was almost eighteen and Roberta was fourteen, the abuse had virtually stopped.

Still, the prolonged trauma had taken its toll. Roberta, feeling desperate for attention and acceptance, and having been taught how finally to get it, became sexually active at age fifteen. She had believed her boyfriend really loved her, and she was emotionally devastated when he dropped her after going to bed with her twice. It was then that Roberta first burned herself—in response to overpowering feelings of self-loathing and fury.

Thus began an addictive pattern in which Roberta responded to painful feelings with self-destructive behavior that produced immediate relief but, in the long run, contributed to her self-hatred. She burned herself whenever she felt mistreated, isolated, or depressed. She told Dr. T. that she usually felt a lot better after she did it, but that the peaceful feeling gradually eroded over the course of a few weeks, giving way to increasing emotional discomfort as she absorbed innumerable slights, insults, annoyances, hostilities, smirks, sneers, and snubs from her co-workers at the supermarket, where she now worked as a checkout clerk, and from her brothers.

Externally, Roberta was living a fairly normal life as others saw her. She still lived at home—an attempt to share an apartment with an acquaintance right after high school hadn't worked out. She had a social life of sorts—an ever-changing assortment of people to do things with, but she declined to call any of them friends.

She even had a boyfriend. Richard, a twenty-five-year-old high school drop-out, was both possessive and abusive. He and Roberta went to bars on weekends and both invariably drank to the point of drunkenness. Typically, under the influence of alcohol, he'd get angry at Roberta for some real or imagined flirtation and was not above slapping or shoving her against the wall. Roberta felt that Richard both loved and needed her. Abuse was far preferable to neglect.

Lately, Roberta had become increasingly concerned about her weight. She'd seen Richard staring at other women, and she was convinced that he thought she was fat. When she looked in the mirror, her thighs looked huge and her waist appeared thickened. She reported to Dr. T. that she had recently lost twenty-three pounds by exercising and severely restricting her food intake, but still she felt fat. Whenever she got on the scale and discovered that she had lost another pound or two, she experienced the exhilaration and relief that burning herself produced, but the feeling never lasted very long. Lately, she often felt dizzy and weak from lack of food, but she found this strangely comforting. "At last," she thought, "I'm really doing it."

Aside from getting some sense of her history, Dr. T. made little progress during the therapy. Roberta seemed unable to maintain a comfortable distance from him, vacillating between feeling uncomfortably dependent and completely unconnected and untrusting. She confided once that frequently she spent hours prior to a therapy session thinking about what she would tell him and how he would react. Often she made up things just to see what he would say. She continued to express a great deal of self-loathing and the frequency of burning remained essentially the same. Dr. T.'s suggestions that Roberta try a medication that might help with her depression and her impulsively self-destructive behavior were met with complete resistance. She seemed to take these as attempts to get rid of her—"you just want to give me pills, because you can't stand to talk to me."

After a while Roberta's boyfriend tired of her alternating moods and her ceaseless demands for attention. Upon discovering that he had been seeing another woman behind her back, she became enraged and impulsively swallowed all the pills in her medicine cabinet—a combination of aspirin, cold medicine, and muscle relaxants. A few minutes later, she called and left Richard a message on his answering machine, telling him what she had done. Luckily, he came home shortly thereafter and called 911. Later that day, after getting her stomach pumped, Roberta was admitted to the psychiatric unit of her local hospital.

During the two weeks she was in the hospital, Roberta was seen daily by a psychiatrist. She also attended a therapy group where she was angrily mute. Attempts to get her to participate in occupational therapy or other ward activities were unsuccessful. Shortly before her release, Dr. T. visited Roberta to help prepare her for the transition back to outpatient therapy. During that visit, she confided that she was still suicidal, and, in fact, intended to kill herself as soon as she was released. This placed Dr. T. on the horns of a difficult ethical dilemma. On the one hand, his duty was to protect Roberta from harm. On the other, he was bound by the obligation to keep Roberta's communications confidential. Further, he knew that Roberta had set him a test, but he was unable to figure out what decision would constitute the right one. He suspected that he had been put in a lose-lose situation.

Dr. T. decided to notify the ward staff of Roberta's intentions. His decision enraged Roberta, who berated him for violating her confidentiality and for trying to interfere with her right to make an independent decision whether to live or die. Dr. T. spoke with the nurse in charge of the unit, and left with the sounds of Roberta yelling and cursing at him reverberating in his ears. The next day, the hospital psychiatrist called Dr. T. and suggested that he not visit again, since his visit the preceding day had obviously upset Roberta. The following morning Dr. T. received a letter from Roberta, firing him as her therapist. Despite his attempts to follow-up, he did not hear from her again.

Thinking About the Case

What is "borderline" about borderline personality disorder? It was originally conceived of as a disorder that had elements of both neurotic (in touch with reality) and psychotic (out to touch with reality) functioning, and was therefore on the hypothetical "borderline" between the two states. Our current classification system characterizes it as an Axis II disorder, an enduring behavioral predisposition that increases the likelihood of and exacerbates a host of Axis I conditions like depression, anxiety disorders, somatization disorders, dissociative disorders, substance abuse disorders, and eating disorders.

Roberta's behavior patterns fit the criteria for borderline personality disorder. She is impulsive, self-destructive and moody. Her relationship with Dr. T. mirrors other significant relationships in her life in its intensity and instability. Roberta alternates between idealizing those she cares about and devaluing them. She is intensely frightened of losing them, yet she pushes them away. She can't seem to maintain a comfortable emotional distance from others. Her primary emotion seems to be anger, although she is prone to feelings of emptiness and depression.

Conducting therapy with people with this disorder is challenging in the extreme. Because of their difficulty maintaining a consistent level of attachment, individuals with borderline disorder have enormous trouble establishing a truly therapeutic relationship—one in which they feel valued and safe. It is not uncommon for them to behave in ways which provoke inappropriate behavior from people trying to help them. Therapists may find themselves uncharacteristically uncertain about boundary issues, tolerating gradually increasing demands for time and attention, or becoming unduly rigid. They may struggle with strong feelings of fury, attraction, or loathing for their client. Genuine violations of the therapist-client relationship, like sexual contact between client and therapist, while rare in general, are more likely to happen when the client has borderline personality disorder than when he or she has most other disorders.

Borderline disorder has become highly controversial on at least three counts. First, it is diagnosed much more often in women than in men. This might reflect a genuine difference in prevalence, or it might reflect gender-based bias in diagnostic practices. Second, the diagnosis tends to carry a strongly pejorative charge. Clients with this diagnosis are avoided by many mental health professionals because their care is so often unrewarding. They are unlikely to be grateful and they often fail to improve. Third, studies indicate that a large percentage of women diagnosed with borderline personality disorder have a history of prolonged childhood trauma—often in the form of physical or sexual abuse.

Dr. Judith Herman, an expert in traumatology, suggests that borderline personality disorder is really a stigmatizing way of describing a kind of chronic post-traumatic stress syndrome. One of her patients, quoted in her book, *Trauma and Recovery* (Basic Books, 1992, p. 128), describes her own experience this way:

> Having that diagnosis resulted in my getting treated exactly the way I was treated at home. The minute I got that diagnosis people stopped treating me as though what I was doing had a reason. All that psychiatric treatment was just as destructive as what happened before.
>
> Denying the reality of my experience—that was the most harmful. Not being able to trust anyone was the most serious effect. . . . I know I acted in ways that were despicable. But I wasn't crazy. Some people go around acting that way because they feel hopeless. Finally I found a few people along the way who have been able to feel OK about me even though I had severe problems. Good therapists were those who really validated my experience.

Dr. Herman points out that adult abuse survivors show symptoms similar to those shown by other survivors of chronic trauma, namely Vietnam veterans who engaged in prolonged combat or were prisoners of war. She feels that the common component is psychological or physical captivity. Her ideas are currently under study by the working group for the *DSM-V*. This group, composed of both clinicians and researchers, is considering the inclusion of a new diagnostic category, tentatively labeled "disorder of extreme stress not otherwise specified" to unify the complex and disparate effects of prolonged trauma. To be included, the disorder must be demonstrated to be reliably diagnosable from clinician to clinician, and to be reasonably distinct from the other disorders already defined in the manual. Until then, borderline personality disorder will likely remain among the most controversial and challenging disorders to understand and to treat.

Questions to Consider

1. Speculate about biological factors that might be relevant to the development of Roberta's disorder. How might these interact with environmental factors to produce her symptoms?

2. What do you think of Dr. Herman's hypothesis that prolonged captivity and abuse lead to the development of borderline personality disorder? How might you explain the presence of the disorder in a person with no apparent history of that sort?

3. Why do you think borderline personality disorder co-exists so often with other psychiatric disorders? How would you expect its presence to affect the outcome of treating the other co-existing disorders?

4. Design a study (or series of studies) to decide whether borderline personality disorder truly occurs more often in women or whether there is some sort of diagnostic bias operating.

5. Roseanne Barr, the television comic actress, has written an autobiography, *My Lives*, (New York: Ballantine, 1994). Read it and consider whether she might have borderline personality disorder. Would other psychiatric diagnoses apply to her?

40

——◄o►——

AVOIDANT PERSONALITY DISORDER:
THE CASE OF CARL S.

CARL S., AN EIGHTEEN-YEAR-OLD COLLEGE freshman, had been in psychotherapy off and on since he was nine. He was first referred by his mother, a psychologically-minded public school teacher, who felt he was overly shy, socially isolated, and unhappy compared to his peers. Carl's father, a successful attorney, was less convinced that Carl had a problem warranting outside intervention. He, too, had been shy as a youngster (still was, although he hid it better now) and had done alright in the world. He and Carl's mother had been divorced for two years by the time Carl was first seen, and disagreement seemed to be their primary mode of interaction.

At nine, Carl was a short and chubby child who only reluctantly agreed to accompany the therapist to her office. Once there, he hopped up onto the seat she pointed to, each hand clutching an armrest, and looked anxiously around the room. His formidable intelligence was immediately apparent. His vocabulary and sentence organization was advanced, and his capacity to talk about computers, his singular passion, was astonishing.

Carl described himself as "somewhat" lonely at present, because his best (and only) friend had moved out of town a year ago. He didn't seem to have much in common with other boys, he felt. They were into sports and he was the least athletic kid he had ever known. "I can't throw or catch a ball, and if I try to kick it, I fall on my face," he related wistfully. Gym class was a torment for him. He felt himself to be a huge liability to any team he was assigned to, and he was embarrassed by his weight and his lack of skills. Kids did tease him some, but even when they didn't he felt awful. Often, he had stomachaches before gym class, and twice he had even vomited while suiting up and had spent the period in the nurse's office.

Carl did play in the marching band, a fairly popular activity, but no one spoke to him very much, and when they did, he didn't know what to say. His social awkwardness seemed to put other children off and for the most part, he was left alone. In the school lunchroom he ate alone. He walked to and from school alone. He wanted friends, he told the therapist, but he didn't think he was "made to have friends." He had long since given up trying. For several years now, he hadn't spoken to people outside of his family unless he was spoken to first.

Carl's life was not altogether unhappy, though. His teachers loved him. He was bright, diligent, and eager to please. He worked well on an independent basis and never participated in class shenanigans. His home life was pretty peaceful (except for the verbal wars between his parents which mostly went on outside of his earshot). When he was at his father's, he played chess with his dad or computer games most of the weekend. At his mom's house (his primary residence), he felt "sometimes good and sometimes bad." While he loved spending time with his older sister and his mom, he was acutely uncomfortable with his new stepfather who had sons of his own with whom he engaged in the kind of rough-and-tumble relationship that Carl couldn't seem to do right. He felt awkward and inadequate around his stepfather. He didn't know what to say to him at the dinner table. When his stepbrothers came to visit, Carl generally went to his dad's. This was fine with him because sharing a room with them made him really anxious. He knew they thought he was a wimp, and for some reason, he always acted "even stupider" when they were around.

Carl's therapist did not think that he was clinically depressed. While he did seem sad, he was eating and sleeping okay, his concentration was fine, and he seemed able to have a good time when not in a socially stressful situation. Carl said that he was interested in feeling better, but he vehemently denied wanting to make friends. He was fine, he said, with his family and his computer. The idea of trying to talk to children he didn't know was just too painful to entertain.

His therapist decided to try cognitive therapy to help Carl think about his social interactions in a new way. She had two major goals. The first was to help Carl stop "mindreading" other people—assuming that he knew what they were thinking about him. The second was to help him "decatastrophize," so that he wouldn't feel awful every time he perceived himself to have made a social blunder. Since Carl was verbal and loved academic tasks, she decided to use a chalkboard as a therapy tool. Together, she and Carl embarked on examining what he told himself about various situations. First, he identified a thought like "all the kids think I'm a total geek and I can't stand it." Then, writing it on the chalkboard, he learned to identify the "illogical" components of the thought with his therapist's help. "How do you know that 'all' the kids think you're a geek," she asked. "Do you mean that they're thinking about you all the time, and they think you're a geek all the time?" "Isn't it possible that you only act in a geeky way some of the time?" "What do you mean by 'I can't stand it?'" "Haven't you 'stood it' up until now?" "Don't you really mean that you don't like it?" Finally, he constructed more "logical" sentences: "It's possible that some kids think I act in a geeky way some of the time. It's also possible that some kids admire my brains or want to get to know me better. Even if some kids think I'm a geek, it doesn't make me one. And even if some people think I'm geeky, I can still be happy and successful."

Carl enjoyed the verbal sparring with his therapist. He enjoyed writing on the chalkboard and modifying the sentences to his therapist's satisfaction. She gave him an assignment to identify irrational sentences he found himself thinking while at school, and he enjoyed reporting back to her about what he had discovered. Over the course of twelve sessions, his mood improved substantially. By that time, school had come to a close and Carl's mother and the therapist agreed to terminate his treatment, at least for the summer.

Carl returned to the therapist's office two years later. He had asked his mother to set up a visit, because his father had remarried and he was having difficulty feeling comfortable around his stepmother. Now eleven, Carl was still a social isolate. Academically, he continued to perform in the superior range. He had quit the marching band because watching the other kids interact with each other at practices had been too painful for him. He continued with private trumpet lessons, which he enjoyed. He had found the Internet and had developed a number of long-distance relationships. When people couldn't see him and when he had time to construct his responses, he worried somewhat less about what they might think of him. The Internet brought him a great deal of pleasure, but also further distanced him from face-to-face interpersonal contact.

Carl's father and stepmother were willing to participate in therapy, so the therapist conducted several family therapy sessions in which she attempted to find some common ground between Carl and his step-mother, Mary. Mary appeared to be a shy and awkward person herself. She had been an only child and didn't have any experience living with a pre-teen boy. She wanted to be a good stepmother to Carl and seemed willing to work at it. When Carl heard his stepmother describe her own adolescence, he realized that her behavior towards him did not reflect her evaluation of him, but rather her own shyness. Using the "sentence-modifying" skills he had learned in his previous therapy experience, he was able to reduce his fear that Mary didn't like him and wished he weren't there. Together he and Mary practiced asking each other questions about how their respective weeks had gone until they were able to have brief conversations together. This gave them both more confidence, and therapy was once again terminated by mutual consent.

When he was fourteen, Carl and his parents returned for a consultation. Over time, their post-divorce relationship had mellowed so that they were increasingly able to cooperate when it came to Carl's and his sister's well-being. Now, they were thinking seriously about sending Carl to a Catholic school about fifteen miles away from the town in which he lived. Not unexpectedly, he was strenuously resisting this effort, as the thought of being with all new people terrified him. His parents felt that if he were in a school in which students valued intellectual strengths and talents as well as athletic prowess, he might have a more successful high school experience. They also wanted him to have the best possible education, and they felt that the rural school in which he was currently enrolled could not offer that. The therapist saw Carl's parents alone for the first session, Carl for the second, and all three of them for the third. The family was able to reach an agreement that Carl would attend the Catholic school for one year, at the end of which he would decide whether to continue there. While Carl wanted to be able to transfer back after one semester, his therapist convinced him that since it took him a long time to get comfortable in new social situations, three months would not give the Catholic school a fair chance. Reluctantly, he agreed.

A year-and-a-half later, Carl returned, this time self-referred. As expected, he did feel better at the Catholic school. The work was much more demanding, and he found the teasing much diminished. In fact, an atmosphere of mutual caring existed. Still, he felt completely on the margins of the school's society. As an adolescent, his isolation was becoming ever more painful. He now felt he wanted to work on making friends, even if the idea was very frightening. He still felt like a "geek" and couldn't imagine that anyone would want to be friends with him, but he was now willing to try.

He saw his therapist every few weeks for about a year. Continuing to use the cognitive techniques they had worked with years before, they now added specific behavioral assignments. The first was to make eye contact and smile at two people in the hallway each time he changed classes. When he was able to do this successfully, he took on the task of saying "hi" to at least one of these people each time. Gradually, the tasks increased both the duration and intensity of interaction. By the end of this course of treatment, he was eating lunch with a regular group of acquaintances each day, was able to call other students to discuss assignments, and engaged in casual conversation before and after classes. His final triumph before terminating was going on a school trip in which he had to room with three guys he didn't know for two nights. Choosing to go on the trip was itself an act of courage, and while he didn't actually make friends, he was able to interact with the other students, and he found to his surprise that he "wasn't miserable all the time." Even though he had not yet reached his goal of having friends with whom he felt comfortable doing things outside of school, he felt able to progress on his own from this point on.

The summer before college, he returned to his therapist's office once again, this time to discuss the transition ahead of him. He was worried about how he would fare with a roommate, whether he would be miserably lonely, how he would survive his father's directive that he should not return home to visit until Christmas, so he wouldn't be tempted to "retreat" into the comfort of his family. He still hadn't developed any personal friends. Virtually all of his socializing, what little of it there was, was done with his sister and her friends. He had had, however, a very successful experience working part-time at a computer supplies store. After some months, he had finally become reasonably comfortable with his coworkers and had felt valued, although "not for myself, but for what I know." The store had a branch near the university he was planning to attend, and his boss had offered to make sure he would be hired there.

At this point, therapy was mostly supportive, reminding Carl that he had developed a set of skills designed to help him meet and interact with new people and reinforcing his self-esteem. He went off to college with some trepidation, but also with some hope that he might not be "a complete and total isolate like I was before."

Thinking About the Case

Carl's problems fit the criteria of avoidant personality disorder quite well. He is socially inhibited, feels inadequate, and is exquisitely sensitive to criticism or negative evaluation by others. Notice that the criteria for social phobia are also met. These include marked fear of one or more social or performance situations related to concerns that the individual will be embarrassed or humiliated. Social phobia is diagnosed alone when the number of situations that stimulate the symptoms is relatively circumscribed or when the problem began sometime later than early adolescence. Avoidant personality disorder is more pervasive, earlier to develop, and generally carries with it a more extreme deficit in self-esteem.

Notice also that many of Carl's symptoms can occur in a normal condition that we call "shyness." Like the other personality disorders, this one appears to be an extreme variant of a normal personality dimension—in this case, extraversion-introversion. In order to qualify as a personality disorder, the condition must cause clinically significant distress or impairment in social, occupational, or other important aspects of functioning. Clearly, the cutoff point is a matter of subjective judgment.

This case is also noteworthy in that several kinds of therapy are employed: cognitive, behavioral, and supportive techniques, parent consultation, and family therapy. This eclectic approach is more common in day-to-day clinical practice than is dogmatic adherence to a single type of intervention. In fact, studies indicate that therapists with different theoretical orientations become more similar to each other in their actual behavior as they gain experience.

Finally, while Carl had a lot of therapy—off and on for nine years—his gains were modest. This is also not uncommon, particularly with respect to the personality disorders that are considered difficult to treat. In general, the more specific and limited (both in duration and pervasiveness) the disorder, the greater the chances of significant change with one or more psychotherapeutic approaches. More longstanding, generalized problems are more difficult to modify.

Questions to Consider

1. Do you favor nature, nurture, or a mixed model to explain this case? What evidence are you relying on?

2. What do you think of the therapist's decisions about choice of techniques and duration of treatment? Might you have made different choices at some point or another? Why or why not?

3. Do you consider Carl's therapy a success? Why or why not?

4. Why might experience change therapists such that they behave more alike over time, despite differences in theoretical orientation?

5. What Axis I disorders (besides social phobia) might commonly co-occur with avoidant personality disorder? Why?

41

——◄o►——

"Psychopath" is an old word for what is now called "Antisocial Personality Disorder." For about thirty years, Dr. Robert Hare, a psychologist at the University of British Columbia in Canada, has been studying these individuals who seem to have no conscience regarding their actions. In the brief article that follows, he summarizes what is known about this condition. Consider, as you read it, whether the behaviors he describes constitute a "disorder."

PSYCHOPATHS:
NEW TRENDS IN RESEARCH

Robert D. Hare

PUBLIC CONCERN ABOUT CRIME has never been greater. Perhaps most troubling are seemingly senseless and dispassionate acts of violence, particularly those committed by young people. In a frantic search for understanding, we readily blame upbringing, poverty, flawed environment, or an ineffective criminal justice system. All these may be important, but we tend to ignore another part of the picture: the enormous social, economic, and personal suffering inflicted by a few people whose antisocial attitudes and behavior result less from social forces than from an inherent sense of entitlement and an incapacity for emotional connection to the rest of humanity. For these individuals—psychopaths—social rules have no constraining force, and the idea of a common good is merely a puzzling and inconvenient abstraction.

Psychopaths use charm, manipulation, intimidation, and violence to control others and satisfy their own selfish needs. Lacking in conscience and in feelings for others, they cold-bloodedly take what they want and do as they please, violating social norms and expectations without the slightest guilt or regret. Although their numbers are small—perhaps 1% of the population—psychopaths account for a large proportion of the serious crime, violence, and social distress in every society. Psychopathic depredations affect people in all races, cultures, and ethnic groups, and at all levels of income and social status. As many as 15% or 20% of prisoners are psychopaths; the disorder is common among drug dealers, spouse and child abusers, swindlers and con men, high-pressure salesmen and stock promoters, gang members, mercenaries, corrupt politicians, unethical lawyers and doctors, terrorists, cult leaders, and black marketeers. In societies undergoing a chaotic breakdown (today, for example, in Rwanda, the former Yugoslavia, and the Soviet Union), psychopaths often emerge as "patriots" and "saviors." Wrapped in the flag, they enrich themselves by callously exploiting cultural or racial tensions and grievances.

Despite many years of debate, our understanding of the disorder is still surprisingly limited, but there are signs that the situation is beginning to change. Researchers are paying increased attention to the diagnosis and measurement of psychopathic traits. The mental health and criminal justice systems are considering new options for evaluating the risk of recidivism and violence, and new approaches to treatment and prevention. Theories and procedures derived from cognitive neuroscience are being adapted to study the causes of psychopathy.

Scientific progress depends heavily on the availability of generally accepted techniques for measuring key variables. Until recently, theory and research on psychopathy were seriously hampered by the lack of such tools. Different clinicians and researchers discussing the subject were often not talking about the same thing in practice. Today three diagnostic systems are commonly used to describe psychopaths: (1) the international classification of diseases (ICD-10) definition of dyssocial personality disorder; (2) the APA's DSM-IV definition of antisocial personality disorder; (3) the Psychopathy Checklist-Revised (PCL-R), a list of symptoms. ICD-10 and the PCL-R define psychopathy with reference to both behavior and inferred personality traits; DSM-IV emphasizes mainly behavior. ICD-10 and DSM-IV employ categorical diagnoses (the disorder is classified as either present or absent); the PCL-R instead provides a numerical score reflecting the degree to which a person's symptoms match the traditional clinical conception of psychopathy. This score can be statistically analyzed into two factors, one covering attitudes and feelings, the other covering socially deviant behavior.

Making a Diagnosis

These diagnostic systems sometimes have different theoretical and practical consequences. For example, the DSM-IV diagnosis of antisocial personality disorder, since it reflects mainly behavior, applies to most prison inmates and many offenders with mental disorders. Thus it is not very helpful in distinguishing those who are likely to commit further crimes after release. What differentiates psychopaths from other criminals is their egocentricity, shallow affect, manipulativeness, and lack of empathy or remorse—a point acknowledged in DSM-IV but not explicitly reflected in its diagnostic criteria. Here the PCL-R is useful. Almost two dozen studies have found that offenders with high scores on this rating scale are more than twice as likely as other prisoners to commit further crimes. The PCL-R score is especially useful for predicting violent and sexual offenses. It predicts recidivism and violence well even among young offenders, for whom a diagnosis of antisocial personality disorder is considered inappropriate.

Many criminal justice and mental health personnel know little about psychopathy or have obsolete and inaccurate ideas about it. Some persist in believing that it is a myth, or that all psychiatric categories are useless. Many are as confused and misled by psychopaths as their victims are. How often we have heard, after a violent criminal is released and commits another crime, that "he didn't present as a serious risk," "his therapist said he had made remarkable progress," or "he found religion and turned himself around."

Working the System

Psychopaths are often passed through a variety of treatment programs without success. In one study, for example, they were almost four times more likely to commit a violent crime after release from an intensive therapeutic community program than were other patients. In fact, treated psychopaths were more likely to commit a crime after release than untreated psychopaths who were otherwise similar. They had learned enough psychiatric and psychological jargon to convince therapists, counselors, and parole boards that they were making remarkable progress, but they used that knowledge only to develop new rationalizations for their behavior and better ways to manipulate and deceive. Court-mandated therapy programs for spouse abusers are equally ineffective for the 25% to 35% of their participants who are psychopaths.

The trouble with all these cognitive or insight-oriented treatments is that they are designed for people who recognize that they have a problem and want to change. Psychopaths enter therapy only because of a court order or to gain early release from prison. They see no reason to change their attitudes and behavior to conform to social standards that they regard as irrelevant.

Since even a modest improvement would be of great benefit to society, we must seek new ways to change psychopaths. There hae been some recent developments along these lines. An international panel of experts commissioned by the Canadian government has designed an experimental program for psychopaths and other offenders at high risk for violence. Antisocial and violent acts are conceived as potentially preventable endpoints in a chain of events. The program makes no attempt to train the offenders in empathy, put them in touch with their feelings, or help them develop a conscience. The view that they have simply gone off the track and need re-socialization is rejected. The aim is to make them accept responsibility for their behavior and persuade them that changing it is in their own long-run interest. The program tries to help them use their abilities to satisfy their needs in socially tolerable ways. The criminal activity of psychopaths often falls off with age; efforts are made to speed up that process. Tight control and supervision and clear and certain punishment for transgressions are essential, both during the program and after release from prison.

This kind of program requires continual evaluation to determine what works and what does not for particular individuals; for example, some components of it may be effective for psychopaths but not for other offenders, and vice versa. It is an expensive program and will constantly be in danger of erosion by changing institutional needs, political pressures, and community concerns. The results are likely to be modest. But the alternatives—to bear the enormous cost of keeping psychopaths in prison or run the enormous risk of simply letting them out—are even less attractive.

The Psychopathic Brain

Recent findings of cognitive neuroscience may throw some light on the causes of psychopathy by establishing a neurophysiological basis for the characteristic lack of empathy or guilt, shallow emotions, and cold-blooded cruelty. In one study, for example, subjects were instructed to determine as quickly and as accurately as possible, by pressing a button, whether a string of letters flashed on a computer screen formed a word. Most people, even non-psychopathic criminals, make these decisions more quickly, with larger and more prolonged recorded brain electrical potentials (brief changes in the EEG), when the words are neutral (e.g., table) than when they are emotionally charged (e.g., cancer). Psychopaths respond to all the words as if they were neutral. Other studies indicate that it is not only the linguistic processes of psychopaths that are devoid of affect. For example, normal people are more likely to blink in response to a startling noise while they are viewing an unpleasant slide than while they are viewing a pleasant slide. In psychopaths there is no difference.

Results of this kind may suggest why psychopaths willingly cause so much pain and suffering. They know how much it hurts only in an abstract intellectual sense; they are apparently unable to construct an "emotional facsimile" of others. A recent brain imaging study suggests a possible neurophysiological basis for failure to appreciate the emotional significance of words and images; the brain mechanisms that normally impart affect to cognitive processes may be inefficient or inoperative in psychopaths. Research in which psychopathology is integrated with cognitive neuroscience offers exciting prospects for improving our understanding of this devastating disorder.

42

———◄o►———

No other mental health diagnosis has raised as much recent contro-
versy as borderline personality disorder. Is it just a pejorative way
to describe and dismiss the difficult behavior of certain people (gen-
erally women)? Is it really a variant of post-traumatic stress disor-
der? Of affective disorder? Are people with borderline disorder
really ill, or just manipulative and demanding? The following arti-
cle, reprinted from American Health, *offers a good overview of*
what is known and not known about this puzzling condition.

THE HEMOPHILIACS OF EMOTION

Hal Straus

AFTER 18 YEARS OF DIFFERENT PSYCHOTHERAPISTS, diagnoses and unsuccessful treatments, "Alicia," a 45-year-old nurse, learned from a psychiatrist that her wild mood swings and broken relationships were caused by
borderline personality disorder (BPD). "For the first time," she says,
"someone else really understood what I was feeling."

"Bonnie," a 33-year-old telephone company clerk, had been tormented for years by her own impulsive behavior and short-lived, hot-
and-cold romances. "One day," she says, "I woke up suicidal, but I didn't
know why." After several hospitalizations for drug overdoses, doctors
finally put a name to her bewildering problem: BPD.

It's not surprising that Alicia and Bonnie—even therapists—had trouble pinpointing the cause of their turmoil. Identifying BPD is so tricky
that even the American Psychiatric Association didn't come up with a
definition until 1980. Its dizzying array of symptoms include wide, unpredictable mood alterations, erratic behavior, chronic feelings of emptiness, a confused sense of identity, and a long pattern of intense and
unstable interpersonal relationships. Depression, drug abuse, eating disorders and suicide attempts often punctuate the borderline's distress.

Scientists continue to debate whether BPD is caused by social influences—a traumatic childhood, the high divorce rate, changes in sex

roles—or by biological ones, such as genetics. Many think both are involved. However, all agree that BPD is a major mental health problem. . . . Alicia and Bonnie are lonely, but not alone: About 25% of those who seek psychiatric help—perhaps 10 million Americans—may have BPD.

Recent studies indicate that women borderlines outnumber men 2.5 to 1, or more. Some researchers think rapidly changing female roles are responsible. Others say borderline males are more apt to wind up in jail than in treatment.

For these millions of BPD victims, their families and friends, life is a relentless emotional roller coaster ride. "When you were a kid, did you ever close your eyes and go around in circles until you got real dizzy?" asks Bonnie. "So much of the time I feel like that, trying to cope with one mood after another."

Living on the Border

"Borderline" was coined in the 1930s to describe patients who seemed more ill than neurotics yet less so than psychotics. Their symptoms also "bordered" on those of other disorders, such as manic depression. "BPD has been to psychiatry what the virus has been to general medicine," says Dr. Jerold Kreisman, director of the comprehensive care borderline unit at St. John's Mercy Medical Center in St. Louis. "It's an inexact term for a vague but pernicious disorder that is difficult to define, frustrating to treat, and almost impossible to explain adequately to the patient."

The baffling world of the borderline, like that of a baby, splits into absolutes: ecstasy and misery, heroes and villains, being and nothingness. This fragmentation results from the borderline's lack of identity. Asked to describe herself, she'll paint a contradictory self-portrait—in contrast to neurotic patients, who have a clearer sense of who they are. Much like the title character in Woody Allen's film *Zelig*, she can adapt like a chameleon to the environment or companions of the moment.

"Borderlines don't follow Descartes' 'I think, therefore I am' principle," says Kreisman. "A borderline might say instead, 'Others act upon me, therefore I am.'" The borderline sees his good qualities as tenuous accomplishments to be re-earned continually. Based on a recent IQ test, he may view himself as intelligent, but as soon as he makes a "dumb" mistake, he's "stupid."

Emptiness is the borderline's chronic state. "Borderlines, particularly when they are alone, may actually lose the sensation of existing," says Kreisman. To prove to himself that he's alive, the borderline may commit impulsive or self-destructive acts: drug and sex binges, gambling and shopping sprees, gorging and fasting, self-mutilation and suicide attempts.

Bereft of the stabilizing sense of identity that steadies others, the borderline's mood changes come swiftly. She can move from the heights of joy to the depths of depression in minutes. Filled with anger one hour, she's calm the next. Her inability to understand her mood swings brings on depression and self-loathing.

"Borderlines suffer from an 'emotional hemophilia,'" says Kreisman. "They lack the clotting mechanism to measure out their spurts of feeling. Stimulate a passion, and they emotionally bleed to death."

"Good" and "Evil"

For those involved with the borderline, life is frustrating. "If you live with a borderline, your behavior is extremely influential on his moods and actions," says Dr. John Gunderson, Harvard professor of psychiatry and the primary formulator of the disorder's diagnostic criteria. "You feel like you're walking on eggshells. Borderlines are bewildering. You may feel that nothing you do seems to work."

A healthy person can handle contradictory feelings such as being angry at someone she loves. Because she's an infant emotionally, the borderline can't tolerate such apparent inconsistency: A person is either "good" or "evil."

Lovers, friends and therapists may be worshipped one day, totally devalued the next. When the person he idealizes inevitably disappoints, either the borderline must revile his idol or, to preserve the other's "all-goodness," reject himself. This defense mechanism, called "splitting," is the borderline's shield against contradictory feelings and images. Splitting ensures that his romantic attachments are highly charged and last days or weeks rather than months or years.

Real intimacy is almost impossible. The borderline fears abandonment, so she clings; she fears engulfment, so she pushes away. She winds up manipulating—and ultimately repelling—those she most wants to connect with.

"Part of me hates men with a passion," confesses Bonnie, "but another part is very promiscuous. I go from one extreme to the other." "All I know is that BPD has forced me to cut everyone out," says Alicia. "I've been engaged a couple of times, but I've had to break them off."

Though borderlines have extreme difficulty managing their private lives, some function productively in structured situations, like the workplace. Bonnie has held her job with a phone company for 15 years. "A part of me works there," she explains, "while the other parts stay away." A highly competitive or unstructured job, on the other hand, can open a Pandora's box of chaotic passions, anger and hypersensitivity to rejection.

Psychic Battlefields

BPD is probably the result of a combination of emotional, biological and cultural stresses. Psychological explanations focus on the early stages of a child's development, when identity—one's "separateness" from the rest of the world—is formed.

The normal two-year-old with healthy parents enjoys a strong bond with them—and also learns to separate temporarily from them. He develops an enduring sense of self, love and trust for his parents, and a balanced view of others' strengths and flaws. In contrast, the future borderline's mother fears intimacy. She can't allow her child to be close, but she can't let him separate, for fear of being alone. As a result, the child never grows into a secure, separate individual, but forever searches for a psychic "twin" to complete his identity.

Case histories of borderlines often describe desolate psychic battlefields. Their stories are strewn with broken homes, chronic child abuse and emotional deprivation. Their parents often suffer from BPD, depression, alcoholism and other emotional disturbances.

Alicia's parents were divorced when she was an infant, and she was raised by her alcoholic mother. At seven, she was shipped off to a series of boarding schools and convents. She was sexually abused as a child, she says, and raped in adulthood. Bonnie's background was similarly ripped by trauma. "When I was sixteen," she remembers, "I slashed my wrists. I told my mother I was going to do it, and she told me to shut up and go to bed."

"Child neglect and abuse may increase the likelihood of this illness," says Rex Cowdry, a psychiatrist at the National Institute of Mental Health. "That not everyone who is subjected to even the most profound abuse develops disorders like borderline suggests some kind of biological predisposition."

"We'll probably find that certain people have a nonspecific genetic vulnerability that could predispose them to different mental problems," says Harvard's Gunderson. "Whether one is borderline as opposed to, say, manic-depressive or healthy, will have to do with shaping factors in childhood and the environment."

Vulnerable Women

Though today's culture may not directly cause BPD, doctors think it at least exacerbates the illness. Our fast-paced, fragmented society is especially difficult for borderlines, who have immense problems creating structure for themselves. "I have no reason to doubt that increased divorce rates, greater mobility, and fewer extended-family networks would encourage a higher prevalence of borderline personality," says Gunderson.

BPD cuts across all socioeconomic classes, but financial stresses and a lack of good prenatal and child care seem to cause a higher incidence among the poor. They haven't been diagnosed borderline in greater numbers because they rarely have access to mental health care.

Women's higher rates of BPD hint at cultural causes. Some researchers point to the higher frequency of sexual abuse of female children. Others blame women's shifting social roles, which stretch from traditional homemaker to single careerist.

"Women in their teenage years experience terrible conflict," says Dr. Marsha Linehan, a psychologist at the University of Washington in Seattle who treats borderlines. "It's clear what males are supposed to do, but not very clear what females are supposed to do." This increases women's vulnerability to BPD, which centers on confusion over identity and roles.

Many psychologists, however, dispute the "woman's illness" statistics on BPD. In his study of children and adolescents, Dr. Paul Andrulonis, director of child and adolescent psychiatry at the Institute of Living in Hartford, CT, found as many male borderlines as females. "They fulfilled the same psychiatric criteria, but more females seek psychiatric care or attempt suicide," he says. "The males tend to act out violently. They are diagnosed as sociopathic and/or go through the criminal justice system."

Linehan points out that while men are generally more aggressive than women and have higher suicide rates, women *attempt* suicide and self-injury more often. She feels that for BPDs of both sexes the key issue is poor emotional control, which can lead to violence and many other behaviors.

A Tiger by the Tail

Therapists who treat borderlines often feel they have a tiger by the tail. "A typical phone message from a patient is, 'I took all the pills. Call me—if you want,'" says Kreisman. Not surprisingly, for years many therapists used "borderline" to label irritating patients who responded poorly. Because likable borderlines tend to do better in therapy, says Linehan, she has developed techniques to help therapists avoid "blaming the victim" for unpleasant BPD symptoms.

Psychotherapy for BPD usually requires several years. More than half the patients drop out. Sessions are apt to be stormy. Some psychiatrists have successfully treated borderlines with traditional, intensive psychoanalysis. But a more immediate, directive approach seems to work best— one focused on the external, practical problems of everyday life rather than volatile feelings. "After learning some coping skills," says Linehan, "the borderline is much more capable of handling past and present trauma."

Though no medications have proved generally effective for treating BPD, tranquilizers, antidepressants, antipsychotics and antiseizure medications like carbamazepine can help ease certain symptoms. Despite consequent improvement in mood or behavior, however, the patient's underlying personality disorder usually remains unresolved.

"Research on borderlines is in its infancy. As we learn more, our approaches will become less competitive and more integrated," says Gunderson. "Today, individual therapy is the backbone of most treatment. With severe cases, hospitalization is frequently necessary, particularly if substance abuse or suicide attempts are involved."

Most psychiatrists agree that BPD will continue to plague society until some fundamental changes are made. In today's demanding, fractured world, a large-scale effort to foster greater emotional stability in children is a crucial first step.

"We have to accept that growing up is much more difficult today," says Andrulonis. "We've got to recognize our kids' emotional problems early on and realize they're not always going to outgrow them. Some need treatment. We need to put more money into good day care and preschool programs. The first five years of life are critical in avoiding severe psychological disorders like BPD."

Until psychological and social stresses are reduced and breakthroughs in the treatment of BPD occur, early diagnosis and long-term custom-tailored therapy offer patients their best chance of improvement. Bonnie, like many borderlines, has come to accept that recovery is a slow process. "I feel like getting well is going to take a long time," she says. "I believe I can get better, but then, I *have* to believe it, don't I?"

LANAHAN NOTES
Personality Disorders

——◄◦►——

Questions:

1. Are personality variables continuous or do discrete "disorders" exist?
2. When people commit crimes and break rules, how do we decide whether they are "bad" or "mad"? Are people with personality disorders responsible for their behavior?
3. Are these disorders really distinguishable from each other? Why so much diagnostic overlap?

Definition of Personality Disorder: Patterns of Maladaptive Behavior That

appear early in life (late childhood to early adolescence).

are longstanding (possibly lifelong).

are pervasive (show up in lots of different situations).

result in significant social and/or occupational dysfunction.

Note: These are diagnosed on Axis II (along with pervasive childhood disorders). This means they can co-occur with and modify the prognosis for all of the Axis I disorders.

Types — Grouped into Three Clusters:

Cluster A — odd, bizarre, or eccentric behavior:
  — Paranoid: pervasive distrust and suspicion
  — Schizoid: social detachment and a restricted range of emotional expression
  — Schizotypal: extreme social isolation, cognitive oddities, and behavioral eccentricities

Cluster B — dramatic, overly emotional, and/or erratic behavior:
  Antisocial: violation of societal rules and expectations
  Borderline: marked instability in mood and personal relationships; often accompanied by impulsive and self-destructive behavior
  Histrionic: excessive emotionality and attention-seeking
  Narcissistic: grandiosity, excessive need for admiration, and lack of empathy

Cluster C — anxious or fearful behavior:

Avoidant: social inhibition, hypersensitivity to criticism, feelings of inadequacy

Dependent: excessive need to be taken care of

Obsessive-Compulsive Personality Disorder: overly orderly, rigid, perfectionistic

Who Gets Personality Disorders?

Actual numbers uncertain because diagnosis is so subjective but

Antisocial and narcissistic — more males;

Histrionic and borderline — more females.

Question: Is this diagnostic bias or true difference in prevalence? (Probably some of both.)

Causes — uncertain but probably include some combination of the following:

Neuropsychological Factors:

Antisocial: may have impaired ability to concentrate, plan, or inhibit behavior. Or, they may be deficient in anxiety — unable to learn through the results of negative behavioral consequences.

Cluster C may spring from an inherited tendency towards heightened autonomic nervous system reactivity that is experienced as anxiety or timidity.

Schizotypal (and maybe schizoid): Genetically related to schizophrenia?

Psychological Factors: psychodynamic theorists speculate, for example, that borderline personality disorder arises because of a failure of mother–infant bonding, and obsessive-compulsive traits reflect an individual's attempt to control shameful or upsetting thoughts.

Environmental or Social Factors: important role of trauma in borderline disorder: prolonged and severe physical (and particularly sexual) abuse can produce lasting changes in "personality" characteristics (like prevailing mood, ability to modulate emotions, self-concept).

Modeling effects: antisocial personality disorder arises in context of chaotic and abusive backgrounds. Social role expectations encourage dependent and histrionic behaviors in women but not in men.

Treatment — generally thought to have a low to moderate probability of success: improvement rather than "cure."

Psychotherapy: emphasizes interpersonal relationships, particularly the therapy relationship (transference and countertransference).

Cognitive/behavioral therapy: some success with helping patients with borderline disorder control self-destructive behavior, reduce anxiety, and avoidance in Cluster C disorders.

Medications: sometimes used as adjunct to psychotherapy (antidepressants, anti-anxiety medications, anticonvulsants to help with impulse control, antipsychotics with some Cluster A's).

CHAPTER TEN

Disorders First Manifest in Childhood or Adolescence

————◄○►————

U nderstanding the psychological and behavioral problems of children presents special problems. First, distinguishing between genuine disorders and simple lags in development may not be easy. For example, most children have temper tantrums, some go through a stuttering phase, and virtually all experience stranger anxiety in late infancy (around nine months). Second, children may not be able to communicate about their difficulties in words—instead, distress may generate maladaptive behavior. It is difficult for adults to know when to intervene and when to simply allow time to pass.

Interest in the specific psychological disorders of childhood did not really emerge until the early twentieth century. Prior to that time, children were thought of as miniature adults. Little attention was paid to problems specifically associated with developmental changes or those that appear to be relatively specific to childhood. Even now, resources for disturbed children are underrepresented in our overall mental health system, despite estimates that from 12 to 20 percent of children suffer from moderate to severe psychological difficulties.

The DSM-IV lists almost forty disorders of childhood. They can be loosely grouped under four categories: disruptive behavior disorders (like attention deficit hyperactivity disorder and oppositional defiant disorder), emotional disorders (for example, phobias and reactive attachment disorder), habit and eating disorders (like anorexia nervosa, bedwetting, and stuttering), and developmental disorders (including mental retardation and autistic disorder).

We have chosen to include a case of attention deficit hyperactivity disorder (#43) to exemplify the disruptive behavior disorders, because it is frequently diagnosed and a source of some significant controversy. Some child advocates suggest that it is overdiagnosed, inappropriately labeling exuberant or poorly-parented children as having a disorder, and that it is overtreated by fairly powerful psychostimulant medications like Ritalin. The second case in this chapter (#44) examines the multiple roots of school phobia, one of the most common emotional disorders of childhood. Finally, autistic disorder, our example of developmental disorder, is profoundly impairing and difficult to treat successfully. Case 45 illustrates how difficult it is for parents to get an accurate diagnosis and compassionate care.

The reading in this section describes how children with learning disabilities cover up and compensate for their problems in a school setting.

43

————◄o►————

ATTENTION DEFICIT–HYPERACTIVITY DISORDER: THE CASE OF MICHAEL C.

This case is contributed by Stephen A. Karl, M.S.W., a colleague who has had substantial experience in working with adolescents in an agency where a multiplicity of professionals and programs are available. Working together, psychologists, psychiatrists, nurses, occupational therapists, social workers, and others provide a combination of individual, group, residential, educational, and support services to youngsters with serious emotional and behavioral problems. The case illustrates how treatment of a youngster often involves more than one-on-one psychotherapy. It also makes clear that sometimes the best laid treatment plans are scuttled by outside events beyond a therapist's control. Good communication with the important people in a child's life, his parents, teachers, and doctors, among others, is essential, but not sufficient for progress to be made. Here is Michael C.'s case.

I MET MICHAEL C. FIRST WHEN HE WAS FIFTEEN, along with his mother, Linda, his stepfather, Dave, and his nine-year-old sister, Cindy. The thin, awkward boy had recently left his biological father, John, to re-establish residence with his mother. They all resided in a middle-class suburb adjacent to a moderately large city. Linda brought Michael for psychotherapy because she wanted to ensure that he would do well in school, and to avoid his becoming emotionally and physically abusive, isolated, and unemployed like his biological father, John. Michael C. freely admitted his frustration with himself and the failure he perceived in most parts of his life.

Michael's biological parents had separated when he was six. Linda had begun an affair with Dave shortly before she separated from John. Dave had provided the means for Linda to escape an increasingly abusive husband. The level of early attachment between Michael and his mother may have been limited by his mother's preoccupation with surviving the abuse dealt out by her husband and by the time and energy taken up by her affair with Dave. Also, she had a negative, although unconscious, emotional reaction to Michael, most likely because of his similarity in appearance, mannerisms, and behavior to his father.

At the first interview, the family revealed several prior attempts to obtain mental health treatment. At age three, Michael had been taken to a psychologist because he was waking several times a night, rarely sleeping more than three or four hours at a time. He was also difficult to manage during the day. He required constant monitoring to prevent him from jumping off high places or engaging in other, equally dangerous, activities. Linda reported that Michael wouldn't allow her to cuddle him or read to him. He couldn't seem to stay in one spot for more than a few minutes at a time. She felt worn out and frustrated.

After his parents separated, Michael's impulsivity in first grade increased to the point where his peers began rejecting him. He was teased or avoided by classmates who appeared to find his impulsive statements and aggressive acts intolerable. When Michael was eight, a psychologist diagnosed him as having attention deficit–hyperactivity disorder (ADHD) and recommended that his pediatrician prescribe a drug called Ritalin, a stimulant medication used to increase attention span. Linda reports having seen some improvement in Michael's behavior with this intervention, but his father was adamantly opposed to Michael's taking medication. He felt that Michael's problems were the result of Linda's poor parenting. Despite being separated from John at the time, Linda went along with his request to stop Michael's medication in order to avoid further conflict.

Dave, Michael's stepfather, had become part of the family when Michael was seven. A family therapist was engaged at about the same time that the Ritalin was started to help with the transition into a step-family. Linda told the therapist that since Dave had moved in, Michael had been crying at night and had developed a pattern of alternately engaging Dave then rejecting him. Michael appeared to become more cooperative and engaged with family members as a result of the family therapy. At the same time, the therapist worked with the school to provide tutors to assist Michael with his school work. This intervention helped Michael to focus and complete tasks.

Michael's parents commenced divorce proceedings when Michael was nine. The divorce process was difficult and drawn out for the family. Frequent accusations and court proceedings involving allegations of neglect and abuse between Linda and John persisted, and visitation and custody battles for both children continued long after. The ongoing power struggle between Linda and John seemed to result in a family that lived from one crisis to another.

Even though Linda was the main caregiver for Michael throughout most of his childhood, John had gained sole custody of Michael for two years (from age thirteen to fifteen). Michael had repeatedly voiced a desire to live with his father and the never-ending battle in the family had finally convinced Linda to let him try it. She and Dave felt they needed a break. However, they recently re-established custody of Michael because they suspected that John had been abusing him, both emotionally (frequent yelling, unpredictable expectations, irrational demands) and physically (slapping, verbal threats, and an incident of being threatened with a gun). Child Protective Services had investigated and had determined that the allegations were grounded in fact, so that custody was again awarded to Linda with paternal visitation allowed.

My evaluation began soon after Michael's return to Linda and Dave's home. His history seemed consistent with the original diagnosis of ADHD. In addition to the core features of inattentiveness, impulsivity, and hyperactivity, he also exhibited the commonly associated behaviors of defiance and aggression.

I suspected that Michael's father also had ADHD. John received Social Security Disability payments for an unspecified disability rather than seeking work. He had few meaningful relationships and a history of interpersonal conflict. He also exhibited antisocial behavior including verbal and physical aggression, frequent lying and stealing, irresponsibility, and poor financial management. These behaviors are often exhibited by adults with untreated ADHD. I felt that the following risk factors, which might predict Michael's ADHD, were in place: (1) probable family history of ADHD, (2) the likelihood of a critical maternal attitude, (3) early and excessive physical activity by the fetus while still in the uterus as reported by the mother, and (4) parental (paternal) psychopathology.

Michael's school history was also consistent with a diagnosis of ADHD. Despite having above average intelligence, he had experienced increasing difficultly in school as he went along. Prior to junior high school he had exhibited low frustration tolerance, often lost things, was impulsive and mouthy with teachers and his parents, and was fidgety and distractible, but his grades were good. Bright children like Michael are often able to keep their grades up until increased organizational skills are required in junior and senior high. By junior high, Michael's coping strategy of waiting until the end of the semester, cramming, and doing well on exams was proving increasingly less effective. Hoping that a more structured environment would benefit him, Linda and Dave enrolled Michael in a parochial school beginning in eighth grade. Between eighth and tenth grade Michael attended three different parochial schools. He failed in each of them despite average test scores because he was insolent, stubborn, and wouldn't do his homework. Not surprisingly, his teachers and parents increasingly thought of him as a lazy, procrastinating, unpleasant youngster.

Since mood disorders are frequently associated with ADHD, I requested a psychiatric evaluation to assess the possible presence of depression. Sure enough, the psychiatrist agreed that Michael was suffering from clinical depression and prescribed an antidepressant medication.

The first psychotherapy task was to engage with Michael, repair his damaged self esteem, and help his parents understand and cope with his disorder. I noticed that the family frequently displaced anger towards John at Michael, who, at fifteen, increasingly resembled his father. A Gestalt therapy technique of introducing an empty chair into the session, representing the absent father, allowed the family to vent or redirect their frustration towards John and away from Michael. I frequently referred to the empty chair when disproportionate anger was expressed towards Michael's behavior. I also tried to teach the family to recognize when Michael did something well. Children with ADHD frequently have histories of getting overwhelmingly negative feedback from others which, over time, damages their self concept and contributes to depression.

The interventions were only marginally successful. Typically, the family reported less conflict for two days after sessions and then returned to previous levels of conflict that came to include Linda's threats of violence toward Michael. After several months of increasing risk of domestic violence between Michael and his parents, Linda requested a foster care placement. Instead, I made a referral to an intensive in-home crisis intervention program in the hopes of preventing yet another residential disruption. The five-week, ten-hour-per-week intervention appeared to reduce family conflict and induce a sense of hopefulness. It also provided new coping strategies for Michael's parents, including improved communication skills, the ability to contract for desired behaviors, and the provision of immediate, logical consequences if Michael messed up. Additionally, I provided written and oral information about coping with ADHD in the family.

This intervention, along with medication and an alternative high school placement with special teachers who were knowledgeable about ADHD and behavioral management techniques, together with regular communication among providers, facilitated a ninety-day period of marked improvement. Michael showed less defiance and improved academic performance. His scores on a scale designed to measure ADHD behaviors were reduced and his relationships improved.

However, over the next three months, the loss of a girlfriend, the increased presence of John in Michael's life, and a reduction of Linda and Dave's use of appropriate behavioral techniques appeared to contribute to a worsening in Michael's behavior. He began to abuse marijuana and alcohol, increased the frequency of stealing from home, and was defiant of family norms.

Finally the increasing disillusionment and emotional disengagement by his mother and step-father resulted in Michael's return to John's home once again. Linda felt that Michael had indeed, become like his father. Her attempts to prevent it had been exhausting and unsuccessful. Her wish to protect and nurture Michael had been replaced by her wish for some peace and stability for herself, her husband, and her daughter. Although medication and specialized academic placement continue, Linda's disengagement, John's lack of cooperation, and Michael's increasingly antisocial behavior make the prognosis less than hopeful.

Thinking About the Case

The diagnosis of attention deficit/hyperactivity disorder is a controversial one. Some people feel it is diagnosed much too often, resulting in the labeling and medicating of children who are simply rambunctious or poorly parented. Parents and teachers apply the label, it is argued, to justify use of a "chemical straitjacket" for children who are hard to handle. According to this view, attentional capacities and activity levels fall along a continuum, where the cut-off point for defining a "disorder" is entirely subjective and open to misuse. The disorder, critics say, lies in the eye of the beholder.

However, others feel that ADHD is a true disorder which, if left untreated, often results in snowballing difficulties for children as they encounter ever more challenging life tasks. Many parents and teachers will attest to the startling change in a youngster's behavior and goal attainment when properly treated for ADHD. One mother described it this way: "It's like he can finally be who he really wanted to be. Before, he kept trying and trying, and we knew he didn't want to be like he was, but he just couldn't help it. Now, he can." Proponents of the diagnosis argue that even if the continuum idea has merit, children whose functioning is seriously impaired should have access to remediative treatments.

Unfortunately, there is no laboratory test that can detect the presence of ADHD. Instead, it is diagnosed on the basis of reports about the child's behavior. Most clinicians will gather data from parents, teachers, and even the child. If possible, classroom and/or home observation will be made. When the bulk of the data point to the possible presence of ADHD, a treatment plan is developed. This plan generally includes a trial of stimulant medication that improves attention span and fine motor control, education and support for family members and teachers, and training in behavioral management techniques. It may also include a specialized educational environment with a specially trained teacher and a smaller class size. Since specific learning disabilities are often associated with ADHD, additional educational services may be necessary.

The outcome for children with ADHD is extremely variable. Some respond well to treatment and learn to make adjustments in how they operate in the world to compensate for their inattentiveness and impulsivity. Their parents learn to cope with their deficits and value them for who they are. Others respond less well, live in a less supportive environment, or are perhaps less well treated. These may develop behavioral problems like Michael. In the worst case scenario, ADHD is associated with conduct disorder in adolescence and antisocial personality disorder in adults. Early detection and multimodal intervention are key to a successful outcome.

Until recently, it had been thought that children "grew out" of ADHD in mid-to-late adolescence. Typically, medication was stopped at some time during the teen years. It is now believed that ADHD is a life-long disorder and that some adults with it could benefit from treatment with stimulant medication, while others can proceed successfully without medication, using the coping strategies they have learned during their school years. Efforts are being made to reconsider the history of adults who have problems holding jobs, exercising adequate social judgment, and containing impulses to see if they might have undiagnosed ADHD. The outcome of treatment of these adults is currently under study.

Questions to Consider

1. What were the factors that contributed to the poor outcome of treatment in Michael's case? What might clinicians have done differently along the way?

2. Can you think of a way to determine whether medication was really helping a child with presumed ADHD? If you were a parent, how would you decide whether or not to accept a recommendation for medication?

3. Some researchers have discussed the concept of "goodness of fit" to describe the relationship between a child's innate temperamental traits and the expectations of the environment in which he lives. According to this model, if a child is lucky enough to have traits that "fit" his environment, he will do well, but if not, he will fare poorly. Can this concept be applied to Michael's case? Is this idea an alternative to the notion that ADHD is a true "disorder?"

44

⸻◦⸻

SCHOOL PHOBIA: THE CASE OF TIMMY R.

TIMMY HAD BEEN DEALT A VERY bad hand in life. He was born with spina bifida, a disorder in which the spinal column is incompletely formed and nerve damage of various sorts results. For Timmy this meant that he had no control of his bladder or bowel functioning. At six years of age and in first grade, he also walked with a slight limp and his speech was difficult to understand. The latter was not much of a problem, however, because Timmy rarely spoke. He stayed to himself and, according to his teacher, didn't seem to be interested in the other children in his class. She said that he reminded her of Tiny Tim in *The Christmas Carol*—small and thin, with a "pinched little face."

Timmy's father was a binge drinker and heroin user who had difficulty holding a job. The family lived in poverty and despair. They rented a trailer in a run-down park. Much to the park owner's consternation, the R.'s had several vehicles (or parts of vehicles) littering their small yard. Inside, they had mattresses on the floor rather than beds, but it didn't matter much—Timmy said that people in his family rarely went to bed. Instead, they tended to fall asleep watching television at night.

Mrs. R. was a thin, worn-looking woman. Missing her two front teeth and dangling a cigarette from her mouth, she looked two decades older than her actual age of thirty-two. She worked a part-time job making minimum wage and had her hands full at home. Timmy required lots of care and she didn't get much help from her older daughter, Cheryl, age twelve, who had lots of needs of her own. Still the house, though dreadfully furnished, was clean and neat, at least when the school's counselor made a visit.

Cheryl, a spare child with a pasty, acne-ridden complexion, had needed special education services throughout school. Often coming in just to talk, she liked to spend time with the counselor, who found her to be a needy, affectionate youngster. However, her speech was decidedly odd and difficult to follow. She switched referents in the middle of sentences so you could never really know what she was talking about. She drifted from topic to topic, getting distracted by a detail that took her in a new direction altogether. She talked a lot about animals, but her stories about them always revolved around injury or death. Her cat got hit by a car; a neighbor's gerbil was found dead in its cage; a friend's dog was poisoned. Her other main topic centered on her own illnesses and injuries. Her teacher said, "if she had half the things wrong with her that she says, she'd be the sickest kid on the planet." She talked about her neck "splitting" and bleeding. She had "locked" intestines. She had pain in her knees. She also saw and heard things that nobody else perceived. Despite being approached several times, Mrs. R. was resistant to having Cheryl evaluated by a mental health professional. Her own mother had had voices and visions, she said. It was no big deal. Cheryl was fine. It was Timmy that she had to worry about.

The counselor never met Mr. R., but her contacts with the three other members of the family left her with the feeling that they all felt that the family had been singled out for misfortune. Their sense of burden, mistreatment, and misery were almost palpable.

Despite his disabilities, Timmy had seemed to make an adequate adjustment to his half-day kindergarten when he was five. He had had some initial problems adjusting, but seemed to make out okay. He got along fairly well with the aide who was assigned to change his diapers and assist him in accomplishing his tasks.

However, he began to miss a lot of school in first grade. A new aide had been assigned who neither he nor his mother liked very much. He began throwing fits in the mornings, and his mother didn't seem to try very hard to make him go to school. He insisted on walking to school, refusing the several rides that were usually offered. It seemed as if he was purposely trying to make the ordeal as hard on himself (and his mother) as possible. On days when he did get to school, he spent most of his time making up illnesses and insisting that his mother had to be called.

At first his teachers ignored his constant complaining, gently refocusing him back on the task at hand. Then he escalated—pretending to throw up in the boys' room. He disrupted the class every ten to fifteen minutes with a physical complaint, a request that he be sent to the nurse, or that his mother be called. Finally, when they could stand it no longer, his teachers started sending him to the front office several times a day.

Mrs. R. reluctantly attended a school conference only after she was threatened with legal action if she did not. At the conference, she was informed that she was legally obliged to get Timmy to school and that he could be removed from home if she did not. A deal was cut: Mrs. R. would get Timmy to school if they would refrain from calling her during the day about his complaints. The counselor recommended that Timmy receive mental health therapy from the local mental health center, but Mrs. R. seemed uninterested in the suggestion.

For a while after that, things seemed to improve. Timmy got to school almost every day. His complaints and interruptions diminished under a behavioral plan devised by the counselor and administered by his teachers. According to this plan, Timmy earned a gold star for every fifteen-minute interval during which he did his work and did not interrupt the teacher. Ten stars earned him ten minutes of play time with the counselor.

All seemed to be getting better. But, unfortunately, in the spring of his first grade year, Timmy had to have surgery to attempt a partial repair of his spina bifida. He was out of school for some time, receiving in-home tutoring services to keep him up with his class. When he returned to school after six weeks of recuperation, his behavioral problems escalated again. His mother reported that he would become so upset at the idea of coming to school that he would hold his breath until he passed out. This frightened and dismayed her, and she didn't know how to respond. Getting him to school was just not worth the battle.

Individual sessions with the school counselor, now provided daily, didn't seem to improve the situation any. Timmy asked to have his sister come in to the sessions with him, but this, too, seemed to go nowhere. While he was content to play quietly in the counselor's office, he balked at going back to class, and the counselor found that she, like Timmy's mom, did not have the energy to resist his vociferous demands.

School officials were between a rock and a hard place. They could ask the family court to remove Timmy from his home to a foster care or residential setting in the hopes that this might improve the situation, or they could provide home tutoring on a long-term basis. As of this writing, Timmy is being tutored at home.

Thinking About the Case

School phobia can be an instance of separation anxiety disorder, which is marked by developmentally inappropriate and excessive anxiety concerning separation from home or from major attachment figures (usually the mother), or it can be an instance of simple phobia, when the child is able to be away from home or mother without anxiety in places other than school. The physical complaints, temper tantrums, and extreme distress that Timmy exhibited are common symptoms of both disorders, and, in fact, without knowing more about how he behaved outside of school, we cannot decide which diagnosis is more appropriate for him.

School phobia occurs in approximately one out of every hundred children. Younger children with school phobia tend to be less impaired and more responsive to treatment than children whose disorder has later onset, perhaps because of the decreased amount of control that parents can exert when the youngster reaches adolescence. Children who exhibit school phobia are at risk of developing psychological disorders in adulthood, including agoraphobia and personality disorders.

School phobia is distinct from truancy in that the child who is truant is not responding to anxiety about school, but avoids it because it seems boring or annoying. A truant child generally does poorly academically and may show other antisocial behavior as well. School phobics, on the other hand, may do well in school and may wish that their anxiety did not prevent them from attending. It is common for school phobia to emerge or be exacerbated by a break in schooling due to vacation, accident, or illness, as was true in Timmy's case. It appears as if the child has to get used to the situation all over again.

School phobia can have many causes. Some children have unrealistically high expectations (sometimes shared by parents) that can make school an emotionally threatening environment. Others are afraid to be away from their parents, or their parents are afraid to let their children be away from them. Others may be fearful of interacting with other children. Some of these may have actually experienced bullying or humiliating attacks by peers, while others may have a social phobia and fear embarrassment. Treatment can include: 1) operant conditioning designed to increase the payoff for school attendance (like the star system used with Timmy), 2) cognitive and behavioral techniques aimed at helping the child learn how to reduce or manage anxiety, 3) verbal or play therapy in which the underlying fear motivating the school refusal can be identified and worked through, 4) parent consultation to assess the possibility of parental contribution to the problem and to advise the parents on how they can be most helpful in its management, 5) family therapy to elucidate and rectify intrafamilial problems that may be contributing to the problem, and 6) antidepressant or antianxiety medication. Generally, a combination of methods is undertaken depending on the clinician's understanding of the problem based on the initial assessment. Early and vigorous intervention appears to be fairly critical for success. The longer the child is out of school, the less likely that he or she will return successfully. This is not surprising in view of what we know from learning theory: avoidance behavior (not going to school) is powerfully reinforced by the reduction in anxiety that it brings.

Questions to Consider

1. Why do you think Mrs. R. was so resistant to getting outside help for her children? Do you think she played a role in the development of Timmy's school phobia? If so, what was it? What might have been done differently to develop a more cooperative alliance with her?

2. What do you think were the contributions of Timmy's family environment to the development of his school problems? Do you think his physical handicap also contributed? In what way?

3. Develop a comprehensive treatment plan for Timmy, choosing any or all of the six treatment options listed in our discussion above. Justify your choice. How successful do you think your plan would be in this particular case? Why?

45

———◄○►———

AUTISTIC DISORDER:
THE CASE OF AMY P.

At two, Amy was not yet talking, and her parents were beginning to worry. She had begun to speak at thirteen months, right on time, but had stopped soon after. Mr. and Mrs. P. had brought their daughter, a beautiful, curly-mopped little girl, to a friend, a psychologist who studied language development, for an informal evaluation.

The family history was unremarkable. Amy's parents were a young married couple who doted on their only child. Mr. P. was a physics professor at a local university who, although deeply engaged in his research and in the struggle to achieve tenure, played with and read to his daughter each evening. His wife, although college-educated, had elected to stay home until Amy reached school age. They seemed a warm and engaging couple. There had been no history of mental illness on either side of their family, nor had there been any complications of pregnancy or birth. Amy had breezed through the early developmental milestones— holding her head up, rolling over, sitting, standing, walking—at an average or quicker than average pace.

The psychologist videotaped a play session with Amy and her mother, and in reviewing it, this is what she saw: Amy was a child who was fascinated with things, but virtually uninterested in people.

Amy's way of playing with toys was decidedly odd. She would pick up a toy, examine it visually and with her hands, then throw it down and pick up another. Her play was manipulative, rather than symbolic. That is, she never used the toys to create a pretend scenario as most children do. In fact, she didn't seem to understand what toys were for; she was interested only in their shapes, colors, and textures.

During the play session, Amy's mom sat or laid on the floor with Amy, talking to her and trying to engage her. Not only did Amy not speak, but she acted as if her mother were not there. She never looked at her, nor did she respond to her mother's questions, comments, or suggestions. It was clear that she could hear, because she noticed noises in the hall, and music coming from a radio in the next room. She simply did not respond to any language input.

The psychologist was struck by one other curious phenomenon. At one point in the session, Amy was drawn to the hallway by a noise. Arriving at the doorway, she stared, rapt, down the hall for four or five long minutes. The hallway was empty of people or objects. All the psychologist could see was the pattern made by the lights on the ceiling— light, dark, light, dark. When she mentioned her observation to Amy's mom, Mrs. P. related that Amy often stood, entranced in the same way, in front of a poster she had in her room at home. Trying to shift her attention would generally result in a tantrum. She herself could never understand Amy's particular fascination with this poster, but, interestingly enough, it too had alternating areas of darkness and light.

Amy's parents had not really thought of her behavior as disturbed. They attributed her lack of interaction to her lack of speech. They assumed that, once she learned to talk, everything would be fine. In the meantime, they treated her like a normal child.

The psychologist suggested to Amy's parents that the problem might be more pervasive than they thought, and that a psychiatric consultation might be of use. With some trepidation, they accepted a referral to a child psychiatrist who diagnosed Amy as having childhood schizophrenia. He told the dismayed parents that something traumatic must have happened to Amy to induce her profound emotional separation from others and urged them to search their memories for situations that might qualify. The only thing they could come up with was that Mrs. P. had gone away overnight to visit her parents when Amy was eight months old. The psychiatrist felt that this separation from her major attachment figure might indeed have been so awful for Amy that she developed the isolation as a psychological defense against any future loss of a love object. He further implied that perhaps Mrs. P.'s choice to leave Amy overnight at such a "sensitive" age was an indication of a more general lack of sensitivity to the nurturance needs of her child.

Mrs. P. was devastated by the psychiatrist's pronouncement. She had never meant to hurt her child, but here was an expert saying that she was responsible for inflicting serious, possibly permanent, damage on Amy's psyche. Mr. P. had a host of conflicting feelings. He loved his wife and he felt protective of her. He wanted to support her, but, on the other hand, if she had damaged his daughter, he couldn't help but be furious.

The P.'s continued to see the psychiatrist for several more sessions, but, at the same time, they began to read all that they could find about childhood schizophrenia. In their reading, they stumbled across an article about childhood autism that seemed to describe Amy's behavior perfectly. They were particularly struck by the description of how autistic children require ritualistic sameness in their environment. Amy listened to the same piece of music hundreds and hundreds of times. She would eat only a small number of foods, prepared in only one way. At the moment, she was into bologna sandwiches on white bread with the edges cut off, mayonnaise only on one side, and cut crosswise into quarters. If any of the steps were missing or wrong, she pitched an enormous fit, throwing herself around, and screaming until another sandwich was made, exactly as she wanted it.

They were also struck by the article's description of "autistic aloneness." Amy seemed to fit exactly—she seemed totally walled in. She existed in a world of things where no one else was invited. She didn't dislike people, she simply ignored them. She wouldn't sit on her mother's lap or cuddle. She didn't follow her parents around, even with her eyes.

Mr. and Mrs. P. decided to seek a second opinion regarding Amy's diagnosis and treatment. They took her to a program for autistic children where a multidisciplinary evaluation by a psychiatrist, a psychologist, a speech pathologist, and an occupational therapist confirmed the diagnosis of autism.

Most treatment programs for autistic children follow a strictly behavioral model in which youngsters are rewarded (for example, with candy) for behavior that brings them into contact with others. First eye contact is rewarded, then touching and speaking. The goal is to gradually shape interactional behaviors. At the same time, autistic behaviors, like tantrums or self-mutilative behavior, might be punished. Since autistic children are not innately rewarded by social contact, the use of "time out," which usually works well for normal children, cannot be used with autistic children. In some programs, mild electric shock has been found effective, although its use has been controversial.

The program in which Amy was enrolled was modeled on the principle of "gentle teaching." Instead of a regimented, rewards-and-punishments system, therapists and teachers allowed themselves to be led by the child's own behavior, commenting on the child's choices as the day progressed. While rigorous scientific studies have not yet been done, anecdotal evidence suggests that such an intervention might be a possibly successful alternative to behavioral treatment. Amy's parents are hopeful that she might improve, but they know that they must wait and see. In the meantime, they are learning all they can about autism. They have joined a support group composed of other parents of autistic children. Here they can grieve the loss of the person that Amy might have become and gain strength to accept the person that she is.

Thinking About the Case

Autism is one of several pervasive developmental disorders in which profound impairments in social development and communication skills are prominent. It is about as common as deafness, occurring in approximately four out of every ten thousand children. Amy's case is fairly typical: early disruption of speech, lack of relatedness with others, and ritualistic and stereotypic behavior patterns.

Some individuals with autism (called "autistic savants") display marked intelligence, even brilliance in certain areas. For example, some can replicate on the piano any musical piece, no matter how complicated, having heard it only once. Yet, they are unable to play even the simplest melody from written music, or to compose even the most elementary tune. Others are numbers whizzes. They are able to perform instant calculations of very large numbers. Yet, these same people often cannot make change at the grocery store. Some have amassed huge bodies of knowledge about a small area of information. For example, one child could recite all of the bus routes across the country. By now you have guessed the flipside: this same youngster was unable to find his way to the corner store and back home.

The cause or causes of autism are not yet known. The hypothesis put forth by the first psychiatrist who evaluated Amy was common at one time. Parents of autistic children were once thought to be cold, aloof, and unable to create a warm connection with their children. However, the fact that most autistic children have perfectly normal siblings made such a hypothesis unlikely to be true and, in fact, research efforts have been unable to demonstrate any patterns of parental behavior or characteristics that are related to autism. Since not all mental health professionals are equally conversant with the latest research in every area, parents would be well advised to seek a second opinion as well as to do some research on their own, like Amy's parents did.

Researchers, today, are looking more at possible biological underpinnings and are finding some things. First, autistic individuals have higher rates of abnormal brain wave patterns than non-autistic controls. Second, a variety of other functional and structural differences in the brain exist between autistic and non-autistic individuals. Third, there is a higher than expected incidence of seizure disorder as autistic youngsters reach adulthood. Further, obstetrical and perinatal complications are found more often in the history of autistic individuals than in controls. Twin studies indicate a possible genetic link as well, although the vulnerability appears to exist for a variety of cognitive impairments, rather than for autism alone.

Even with these findings, the prognosis for autism is still quite poor. Over half of the children diagnosed with autism are unable to function as independent adults. Some children who receive intensive behavioral treatment (over forty hours a week lasting several years) appear to have some promise if treatment is instituted very early and if parents can be enlisted to carry on the treatment at home, even after professional treatment is completed. Still, fewer than 5 percent of individuals with childhood autism are indistinguishable from "normal" individuals at adulthood.

Questions to Consider

1. What are some reasons why early intervention might be important in the treatment of autism?

2. Assume, for the moment, that some specific brain abnormality will be found in persons with autism. Would you still consider it a psychological disorder? Why or why not?

3. If you were the parent of an autistic child, what information would you want in order to decide which treatment program to place your child in? How would you go about getting this information?

4. What effect might the presence of an autistic child have on the life of a family? How might it affect the parents' relationship? How might it affect the siblings as they face their own developmental tasks? How might it affect the relationship between the parents and the well siblings?

46

——◄○►——

In reading over the childhood cases, we can begin to get a sense of what it might feel like to experience certain problems. In this article, the author describes the various ways in which learning disabled children respond to the stigma and self-esteem problems associated with their problems in learning. She describes these as "masks" that children wear to hide their difficulties. As you read through them, see if you can identify any of the psychological defense mechanisms that Freud described. For example, which "mask" describes "reaction formation?" Might these masks create difficulties of their own? Of what sort?

THE MASKS STUDENTS WEAR

Sally L. Smith

LEARNING DISABLED ADULTS ARE telling educators what learning disabled children can't. What we learn from these adults can improve the teaching of children and the training of teachers.

There are many types of learning disabilities including auditory, vision and language disabilities. And students can have combinations of different learning disabilities.

One of the most important messages learning disabled adults are giving is that the greatest challenge learning disabled children face is the battle for self-esteem. These adults say they felt stupid and were treated in school as though they were. They felt defeated, worthless and "dumb." Over the years, these adults learned to mask their hurts.

"I learned to act a certain way so I couldn't be teased. I would appear bored, tired, eager to be of help, all-knowing or funny, depending upon what was going on. In other words, I would do anything but let them know I couldn't read the material," confesses one learning disabled adult.

"I faked my way all through school," says another. "I had the gift of gab and an excellent memory."

Unfortunately, many dyslexic and learning disabled adults started to develop masks in first or second grade when they could not read what others could. Few ever received special education. They were not identified as learning disabled or dyslexic. Instead, their teachers often labeled them "lazy," "willful," "poorly disciplined" and "spoiled" when actually they were trying their hardest.

These students were called "retarded" if they had any speech and language problems and "disturbed" if they were hyperactive, impulsive or had any of the behavioral manifestations of a learning disabled child. Often these children were gifted, above average in intelligence, and unable to bear their inability to accomplish the simplest academic task.

Think of the energy many learning disabled students spend hiding their disabilities and masking the feeling of being stupid. The masks are an elaborate subterfuge that make students feel worse about themselves. The masks protect the students from being thought of as "stupid," but isolate them from others. Often the masks interfere with students' ability to learn.

Recognizing the masks learning disabled students sometimes wear to hide their inabilities will help you take action to have the problem treated. Masking behavior comes in many variations. The following types are among the most common masks students wear.

The Mask of Super Competence

"Easy!" "Oh, sure! Everyone knows that!"

With a great deal of bravado, this student tries to make everything look simple. He knows he can talk his way through anything. His logic is impeccable. He's good with people, numbers, problem solving and trouble shooting.

Gen. George S. Patton, a dyslexic, assured his daughter that Napoleon couldn't spell, either, and quoted Jefferson Davis as saying, "A man must have a pretty poor mind not to be able to think of several ways to spell a word."

The Mask of Helplessness

"I don't know." "I don't understand." "I can't do anything."

Through pity, this person gets everyone around to help her do her work and assume responsibilities so she never fails. She refuses to risk failure, but feels even worse because she knows she didn't do any of the work.

The Mask of Invisibility

"I would hide in my shell, hold my neck in like a turtle, almost pleading with the teachers not to call upon me."

By looking frightened, whispering to teachers and acting terrified with peers, this person gets everyone else to do his work for him.

The student realizes he can get through school by not talking, just repeating when necessary, taking a low profile, and making no waves. With his head down and sitting quietly for a long time, nobody bothers him. He has the talent of melting into the crowd. Teachers and supervisors later realize they never got to know this student or acknowledge he was there.

The Mask of the Clown

"Isn't that a riot!" "Ha, ha, ha." "What a joke!"

Everything is funny when this student is around. Laughter, however, hides the real issue—a learning disability.

Cher, the Academy Award-winning actress/singer, admits she was the "class clown" to divert attention from her inability to read, write or do arithmetic in school. Despite her problems, she was exceedingly verbal and outstanding in the arts. A teacher proclaimed that she was not working hard enough. Feeling stupid, she dropped out of school at 16 and wasn't tested for learning disabilities until after she was 30.

The Mask of the Victim

"It's not fair." "Everyone picks on me." "There's no justice anywhere."

Injustice is a basic theme with this person. Often called a "jail-house lawyer" because he has an argument for everything, this student feels victimized and takes on a "poor me" attitude. He assumes no responsibility for anything. He angers others around him.

The Mask of Not Caring

"I don't care." "Nothing matters." With this mask, the student is never vulnerable, and risks no failure. If she tries to succeed and fails, she says she never tried and it doesn't matter. The mask is a way of keeping others at a distance, making her feel woefully inadequate. If nothing matters, it's very difficult to change or motivate this person.

The Mask of Boredom

"This is boring!" Yawn. "What time is it now?" Yawn.

With big yawns, loud sighs, tapping fingers and toes, this person lets the teacher know how bored he is. This behavior puts the teacher on the defensive. Usually this person is not bored, but frustrated, and can't do what he's been asked to do.

Thomas Edison was kicked out of schools for not following instructions. He probably did not understand the instructions due to his auditory problems. Severe learning disabilities prevented him from being able to write what he was told.

The Mask of Activity

"Gotta run." "Sorry, I'm in a hurry, I can't talk." "I'm busy now, I'll do whatever you want later."

This student is always on the move. Standing still may bring her close to others, and she precludes any intimacy. Constant activity wards away others and keeps her from having to perform.

The Mask of Outrageousness

"I'm way out." "I don't like being a conformist." "I believe in individualism to the extreme." Through wild clothing, hair style and color, wigs, extraordinary glasses, stockings, boots, and so on, this student projects eccentricity and hides his problems.

Robert Rauschenberg, a famous artist who had extreme difficulty with math and spelling, did outrageous, unheard of things in school and in his career. Many artists feel he expanded the definition of art for a generation of Americans by daring to innovate.

The Mask of the Good Samaritan

"Let me help you." "What can I do for you?"

This student wants to please at any cost. Frequently, she is too nice and too accommodating. She will echo what you say, work longer hours than necessary and be overly helpful to get out of doing what she can't do.

The Mask of Contempt

"They don't know how to teach." "This whole place sucks."

Negativity encompasses this mask. This joyless student has a negative word for everything. If it's sunny out, it could be sunnier. He wears out the people around him because nothing is ever good enough. He takes no pleasure in small successes. He's angry at the world for making him feel stupid and believes the world owes him something. He puts everyone around him on the defensive.

The Mask of the Strong Silent Type

"I'm Joe Cool." "Nobody comes too close to me, but they follow me everywhere." "Get out of my face. Nobody moves on me." "Every sport is for me. I live for sports."

Personified by a sleek body and prowess in sports, this student is revered by many and endowed, in her own mind, with every fine feature.

Bruce Jenner, Olympic decathlon champion who is dyslexic, says sports gave him his self-esteem. Jenner says reading aloud in the classroom was much harder and more frightening for him than competing in the decathlon.

The Mask of Perfection

"If they don't recognize my talents, that's their problem." "Good artists don't have to read really well, anyhow."

Proclaiming loudly that there are machines to spell and write, secretaries to take dictation and lawyers to read for him, this student presents himself as perfection. He tolerates no mistakes in himself or others. He often carries an impressive book or magazine he can't read and saunters into a room looking completely pleased with life. He makes everyone around him miserable.

The Mask of Illness, Frail Health and Vulnerability

"My head." "My stomach." "My side." "My bladder." "My migraine."

To receive extra attention and get out of the work she can't do, this student calls in sick, leaves sick, constantly pretends to be sick and talks about her frailties.

Given something to read, she uses her illnesses and frailties as an excuse or cries if necessary. Expecting special attention, special privileges, while avoiding what she can't do, this student confuses everyone around her and usually gets by with this behavior.

The Mask of Seduction

"Hey, woman, write this down for me. Men don't write." The "macho man" often gets a female to do for him what he can't do. He hides behind his macho mask, making himself appear sexy.

"Math is men's work, girls can't do it." The "helpless female" asks a "macho man" to do what she can't do and hides behind her female mask to make it appear sexy.

The Mask of Being Bad

"Don't mess with me. You'll be sorry." "I threw the book at him, so what?" "I'd rather be thought of as bad than dumb."

Losers at school often become winners on the street. This student feels stupid, powerless and useless at school and often directs his frustration and anger towards his teachers. His peers enjoy his bad behavior and encourage more of it.

Billionaire Dallas real estate manager Rick Strauss changed schools several times, always suffering the humiliation of not learning to read or write due to his severe dyslexia. He compounded his problems by cutting up. Doing so diverted his teachers' attention away from his poor work. It wasn't until he was a high school senior that he learned that his inability to read and write resulted from his learning disabilities.

The Mask of Fantasy

"I'm going to be a millionaire by the time I'm 30!" "The world will understand me soon." "I'll have a PhD. once I learn to read."

Characterized by a fertile imagination and a great deal of creativity, this student tends to live more in her hopes and fantasies than in reality, which is filled with daily frustrations.

Hans Christian Andersen didn't learn to read and write, even with the help of 10 royal tutors of the Danish Court. He dictated his wonderful fairy tales to a scribe. His mask of fantasy protected him from the pain of facing reality, even though glimpses of his suffering appear in some of his stories, such as "The Ugly Duckling."

Removing the Masks

The masks can be removed when students reach a certain comfort level. This usually happens when a student realizes he is not stupid, but suffers from a learning disability. The student experiences enormous relief when he discovers why he has been having difficulties learning.

What learning disabled adults have to say about the masks they wore in school alerts educators to the need to reach children in their early years, identify those children who have trouble learning before they begin to wear the masks, and teach them in ways that will help them succeed.

LANAHAN NOTES

Disorders First Manifest in Childhood and Adolescence

⸺◄◦►⸺

COGNITIVE DISORDERS OF CHILDHOOD

Mental retardation (coded on Axis II): diagnosed by psychological tests; ranges from mild to profound (cutoff for services arbitrary); can be familial (generally mild) or illness/injury (more severe).

Learning, Motor Skills, and Communication Disorders

Pervasive Developmental Disorders (like childhood autism): tend to be severely incapacitating.

— All are lifelong, although severity of impairment varies.

— Modern methods emphasize community-based treatment and normalization.

— Behavioral techniques, special education, and parent consultation most helpful.

ATTENTION DEFICIT AND DISRUPTIVE BEHAVIOR DISORDERS

Note: all of these are more common in boys than girls (why?).

Attention Deficit–Hyperactivity Disorder (can be inattentive or hyperactive/impulsive type):

— tends to run in families (generally father to son).

— treated with a combination of stimulant medication and behavioral therapy.

— now being diagnosed and treated in adults (used to be thought that children grew out of it).

Conduct Disorder — breaking societal rules:

— precursor to adult antisocial personality disorder

— tends to have poor prognosis — not responsive to known treatment methods.

— runs in families — probably combination of genetics and modeling (Question: what is inherited?)

— also related to social class, family chaos, strong or inconsistent discipline.

—often occurs in children diagnosed with attention deficit disorder—may be predisposed to impulsivity.

Oppositional/Defiant Disorder: intolerant of authority but less disturbed than youngsters with conduct disorder.

   —genetic roots not as strong

   —more responsive to treatment: behavioral and/or family systems

Feeding and Elimination Disorders of Early Childhood

   —includes eating weird things, regurgitating and refeeding, or failure to eat enough (in children too young for anorexia nervosa).

   —also includes incontinence of urine (enuresis) and feces (encopresis).

   —when physical problems are ruled out, parent-child bonding issues are usually relevant and can be treated with therapy for the parent.

   —incontinence is also treated with behavioral therapy.

OTHER DISORDERS

Separation Anxiety Disorder: child cannot bear to be separated from parent.

Selective Mutism: child refuses to speak.

Reactive Attachment Disorder: child can't properly attach to caretakers.

Note: These three tend to be psychological in origin and generally require treatment of the caretaker (usually the parents) as well as the child. Often psychodynamic and/or family systems approaches are applied.

Stereotypic Movement Disorder: child rocks, head-bangs, etc.

Note: Children can also get many of the same disorders adults get, including Anxiety Disorders, Depression, and Psychosis. About 25 percent of children meet criteria for some psychological disorder. Of these, the majority have multiple disorders.

Part Two

———◦———

ABNORMALITY AND SOCIETY

CHAPTER ELEVEN

Psychotherapy

————◄○►————

All societies, from the most primitive to the most advanced, have had psychological healers. In many cultures, these are religious figures—shaman, witchdoctor, priest. In others, they are secular figures—physician, counselor, therapist. In the United States, one in five people will seek the advice of one of these healers, and fully half of those will be experiencing psychological or behavioral problems that are quite serious and painful.

How effective are we at alleviating psychological distress? This is not an easy question to answer since criteria for "success" are subjective; many people improve over time without therapy; and the mere expectation of receiving help often results in a decrease in symptoms (the "placebo effect"). One of the simplest, although perhaps least scientific, ways of addressing the question is to ask a large number of people whether therapy was helpful to them. *Consumer Reports* did just that, and the results of their survey are included here (#47). For a look at the other side of the coin, see "The Overselling of Therapy" (#48), a sobering reminder that our expectations for therapy ought to be relatively modest. In the next article, Albert Ellis, the founder of Rational-Emotive Psychotherapy (one type of cognitive psychotherapy), looks at the pros and cons of self-help methods as an alternative to formal psychotherapy. Finally, Stanley Sue addresses the question of whether there are special issues involved in the treatment of ethnic minority clients.

47

————◄◦►————

There are many ways to think about the question of whether or not therapy is useful. In order to design a study, we would have to answer several questions. First, what does "useful" mean? For example, do we mean that it produces behavior change, or that the client reports feeling better, or that the therapist believes that personality reconstruction has taken place? Second, we would want to know if the intervention is useful compared to something else—perhaps no formal treatment at all, a placebo, or some other therapy.

Surveys, as a method, have several drawbacks. First, they only examine the subjective response of the responders. There is no independent verification from family or friends regarding any outward manifestation of improvement. Second, they cannot control who chooses to respond (perhaps only those people who improved will fill out the survey). Third, there is no control group; perhaps many of the people would have felt better over time even without any therapeutic intervention.

Still, the survey excerpted here, first published in Consumer Reports, *is noteworthy in that it is the largest study sample ever gathered. The sheer number of the participants helps to support the conclusion drawn: that the majority of consumers of mental health services get substantial relief from their subjective suffering. Would this study convince you to seek help if you had a psychological problem? Why or why not?*

MENTAL HEALTH: DOES THERAPY HELP?

Staff, *Consumer Reports*

COPING WITH A SERIOUS PHYSICAL ILLNESS is hard enough. But if you're suffering from emotional or mental distress, it's particularly difficult to know where to get help. You may have some basic doubts about whether therapy will help at all. And even if you do decide to enter therapy, your health insurance may not cover it—or cover it well.

As a result, millions of Americans who might benefit from psychotherapy never even give it a try. More than 50 million American adults suffer from a mental or addictive disorder at any given time. But a recent Government survey showed that fewer than one-third of them get professional help.

That's a shame. The results of a candid, in-depth survey of *Consumer Reports* subscribers—the largest survey ever to query people on mental-health care—provide convincing evidence that therapy can make an important difference. Four thousand of our readers who responded had sought help from a mental-health provider or a family doctor for psychological problems, or had joined a self-help group. The majority were highly satisfied with the care they received. Most had made strides toward resolving the problems that led to treatment, and almost all said life had become more manageable. This was true for all the conditions we asked about, even among the people who had felt the worst at the beginning.

Among Our Findings

People were just as satisfied and reported similar progress whether they saw a social worker, psychologist, or psychiatrist. Those who consulted a marriage counselor, however, were somewhat less likely to feel they'd been helped.

Readers who sought help from their family doctor tended to do well. But people who saw a mental-health specialist for more than six months did much better.

Psychotherapy alone worked as well as psychotherapy combined with medication, like Prozac or Xanax. Most people who took drugs like those did feel they were helpful, but many people reported side effects.

The longer people stayed in therapy, the more they improved. This suggests that limited mental-health insurance coverage, and the new trend in health plans—emphasizing short-term therapy—may be misguided.

Most people who went to a self-help group were very satisfied with the experience and said they got better. People were especially grateful to Alcoholics Anonymous, and very loyal to that organization.

Our survey adds an important dimension to existing research in mental health. Most studies have started with people who have very specific, well-defined problems, who have been randomly assigned to a treatment or control group, and who have received carefully scripted therapy. Such studies have shown which techniques can help which problems . . . but they aren't a realistic reflection of most patients' experiences.

Our survey, in contrast, is a unique look at what happens in real life, where problems are diverse and less well-defined, and where some therapists try one technique after another until something works. The success of therapy under these real-life conditions has never before been well studied. . . .

Like other surveys, ours has several built-in limitations. Few of the people responding had a chronic, disabling condition such as schizophrenia or manic depression. We asked readers about their past experiences, which can be less reliable than asking about the present. We may have sampled an unusually large number of people in long-term treatment. Finally, our data comes from the readers' own perceptions, rather than from a clinician's assessment. However, other studies have shown that such self-reports frequently agree with professionals' clinical judgments.

Who Went For Help

In our 1994 Annual Questionnaire, we asked readers about their experiences with emotional problems and their encounters with health-care providers and groups during the years 1991 to 1994. Like the average American outpatient client, the 4,000 readers who said they had sought professional help were mostly well educated. Their median age was 46, and about half were women. However, they may be more amenable to therapy than most.

Many who went to a mental-health specialist were in considerable pain at the time they entered treatment. Forty-three percent said their emotional state was either very poor ("I barely managed to deal with things") or fairly poor ("Life was usually pretty tough").

Their reasons for seeking therapy included several classic emotional illnesses: depression, anxiety, panic, and phobias. Among the other reasons our readers sought therapy: marital or sexual problems, frequent low moods, problems with children, problems with jobs, grief, stress-related ailments, and alcohol or drug problems.

The Results: Therapy Works

Our survey showed that therapy for mental-health problems can have a substantial effect. Forty-four percent of people whose emotional state was "very poor" at the start of treatment said they now feel good. Another 43 percent who started out "fairly poor" also improved significantly, though somewhat less. Of course, some people probably would

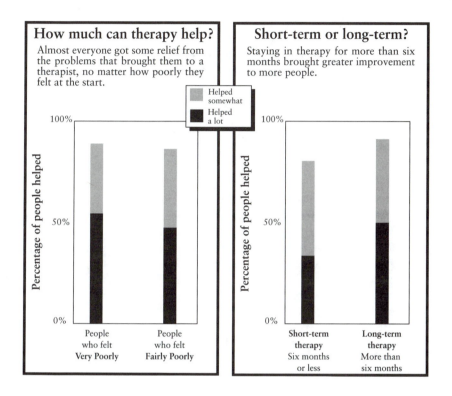

How much can therapy help?

Almost everyone got some relief from the problems that brought them to a therapist, no matter how poorly they felt at the start.

Helped somewhat
Helped a lot

Percentage of people helped

100%

50%

0%

People who felt **Very Poorly**

People who felt **Fairly Poorly**

Short-term or long-term?

Staying in therapy for more than six months brought greater improvement to more people.

Percentage of people helped

100%

50%

0%

Short-term therapy
Six months or less

Long-term therapy
More than six months

have gotten better without treatment, but the vast majority specifically said that therapy helped.

Most people reported they were helped with the specific problems that brought them to therapy, even when those problems were quite severe. Of those who started out "very poor," 54 percent said treatment "made things a lot better," while another one-third said it helped their problems to some extent. The same pattern of improvement held for just about every condition.

Overall, almost everyone who sought help experienced some relief— improvements that made them less troubled and their lives more pleasant. People who started out feeling the worst reported the most progress.

Among people no longer in treatment, two-thirds said they'd left because their problems had been resolved or were easier to deal with.

Whom Should You See?

In the vast field of mental health, psychiatrists, psychologists, and clinical social workers have long fought for turf. Only psychiatrists, who are medical doctors, can prescribe drugs and have the training to detect medical problems that can affect a person's mental state. Otherwise, each of these professionals is trained to understand human behavior, to recognize problems, and to provide therapy.

Historically, social workers have been the underdogs and have had to fight for state laws requiring insurance companies to cover their services. But many of today's budget-minded insurers *favor* social workers—and psychiatric nurses—because they offer relatively low-cost services.

In our survey, almost three-quarters of those seeking professional help went to a mental-health specialist. Their experiences suggest that any of these therapists can be very helpful. Psychiatrists, psychologists, and social workers received equally high marks and were praised for being supportive, insightful, and easy to confide in. That remained true even when we statistically controlled for the seriousness and type of the problem and the length of treatment.

Those who went to marriage counselors didn't do quite as well, and gave their counselors lower grades for competence. One reason may be that working with a fractured couple is difficult. Also, almost anyone can hang out a shingle as a marriage counselor. In some states the title "marriage and family therapist" is restricted to those with appropriate training. But anyone can use other words to say they *do* marriage therapy, and in most places the title "marriage counselor" is up for grabs.

What About Doctors?

Many people are more comfortable taking their problems to their family doctor than to a psychologist or psychiatrist. That may work well for some people, but our data suggest that many would be better off with a psychotherapist.

Readers who exclusively saw their family doctor for emotional problems—about 14 percent of those in our survey—had a very different experience from those who consulted a mental-health specialist. Treatment tended to be shorter; more than half of those whose care was complete had been treated for less than two months. People who went to family doctors were much more likely to get psychiatric drugs—83 percent of them did, compared with 20 percent of those who went to men-tal-health specialists. And almost half the people whose doctors gave them drugs received medication without the benefit of much counseling.

The people who relied on their family doctors for help were less distraught at the outset than those who saw mental-health providers; people with severe emotional problems apparently get themselves to a specialist. Even so, only half were highly satisfied with their family doc-tor's treatment (compared with 62 percent who were highly satisfied with their mental-health provider). A significant minority felt their doctor had neither the time nor temperament to address emotional issues. In general, family doctors did help people get back on their feet—but longer treat-ment with a specialist was more effective.

However, if you begin treatment with your family doctor, that's where you're likely to stay. Family doctors referred their patients to a mental-health specialist in only one out of four cases, even when psycho-therapy might have made a big difference. Only half of those who were severely distressed were sent on, and 60 percent of patients with panic disorder or phobias were never referred, even though specific therapies are known to work for those problems.

Other research has shown that many family doctors have a poor track record when it comes to mental health. They fail to diagnose some 50 to 80 percent of psychological problems, and sometimes prescribe psychiat-ric drugs for too short a time or at doses too low to work.

The Power of Groups

It was 60 years ago that a businessman and a physician, both struggling with alcoholism, realized they could stay sober by talking to one another. They talked to other alcoholics, too, and eventually worked out the system of long-term recovery known as Alcoholics Anonymous, or AA. Today there are over a million active AA members in the U.S., and attending an AA group is often recommended as part of professional treatment. The AA format has also been adopted by dozens of other self-help groups representing a wide spectrum of dysfunctional behavior, from Gamblers Anonymous to Sex and Love Addicts Anon. Support groups also bring together people who are dealing with medical illness or other trials.

One-third of our survey respondents went to a group, often in addi-tion to individual psychotherapy. Overall, they told us, the groups seemed to help.

Readers who went to AA voiced overwhelming approval. Virtually all endorsed AA's approach to treatment, and most said their struggle with addiction had been largely successful. In keeping with AA's principle that recovery is a lifelong process, three-quarters of our readers had been in the group for more than two years, and most were still attending. Most of those who had dropped out said they'd moved on because their problems had improved.

Certainly, not everyone who goes to AA does as well; our sampling method probably over-represented long-term, and thus successful, AA members. AA's own surveys suggest that about half of those who come to the program are gone within three months. Studies that follow people who have undergone treatment for alcoholism find that AA is no more or less effective than other programs: A year after entering treatment, about half the participants are still in trouble.

Nevertheless, AA has several components that may maximize the chance of success. In general, most alcoholics do well while they are being actively treated. In AA, members are supposed to attend 90 meetings in the first 90 days, followed by three meetings a week for life.

Drugs, Pro and Con

For decades, drug therapy to treat problems such as depression carried a raft of unpleasant, sometimes dangerous side effects. Then came Prozac (fluoxetine), launched in 1988. Safer and easier to take than previous anti-depressants, Prozac and other drugs in its class—including sertraline (Zoloft) and paroxetine (Paxil)—have radically changed the treatment of depression. Along the way, people have claimed that Prozac seems to relieve a growing list of other complaints—from eating disorders to shyness to, most recently, premenstrual syndrome.

In our survey, 40 percent of readers who sought professional help received psychiatric drugs. And overall, about 60 percent of readers who took drugs said the medication helped a lot.

However, many of our readers did well with psychotherapy alone; in fact, people who received only psychotherapy improved as much as those who got therapy plus drugs.

For many people, having the option of talk therapy is important because every psychiatric drug has potential side effects that some individuals find hard to tolerate. Almost half of all our respondents on medication reported problems with the drug. Drowsiness and a feeling of disorientation were the most common complaints, especially among people taking the older antidepressants such as amitriptyline (Elavil).

Although the problems associated with psychiatric drugs are well-known, 20 percent of readers said their provider never discussed them—a disturbing lapse in communication. Equally disturbing was the finding that 40 percent of the people taking antianxiety drugs had done so for

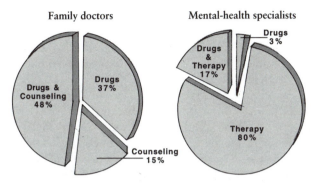

Talk or Drugs? Family doctors were much more likely to dispense mostly medication or a mix of drugs and talk. Very few mental-health therapists relied mainly on drugs; the vast majority provided psychotherapy.

more than a year—25 percent for more than two years—even though long-term use results in habituation, requiring larger and larger doses.

Antianxiety medications such as Xanax and Valium can provide relief if used for a short time during a particularly stressful period, such as the death of a parent. But they haven't been well tested for generalized anxiety—a kind of chronic, excessive worrying combined with physical and emotional symptoms—and therapists have found them only erratically effective.

Xanax is approved by the U.S. Food and Drug Administration for panic disorder, which causes repeated bouts of unbearable anxiety; studies show that it acts quickly to reduce panic attacks. But after two months, Xanax apparently performs little better than a placebo. (See *Consumer Reports*, January 1993.) The reason many people take antianxiety drugs for so long is that they're extremely hard to kick; if the drug is stopped, symptoms return in full force.

How Long Will It Take?

When a person needs psychotherapy, how much do they need? That has become a critical question—both for clinicians and for the insurers that pay for therapy. And it's a hard one to answer.

Nationally, most people who get therapy go for a relatively short time—an average of four to eight sessions. It's not clear, however, whether people stop going because they have been helped enough, because they don't think the therapy is working, or because they've run out of money. Controlled studies of specific kinds of therapy usually cover only 12 to 20 visits. While brief therapy often helps, there's no way to tell from such studies whether 30 or 40 sessions, or even more, would be even more effective.

For the people in our survey, longer psychotherapy was associated with better outcomes. Among people who entered therapy with similar levels of emotional distress, those who stayed in treatment for more than six months reported greater gains than those who left earlier. Our data suggest that for many people, even a year's worth of therapy with a mental-health specialist may be very worthwhile. People who stayed in treatment for more than two years reported the best outcomes of all. However, these people tended to have started out with more serious problems.

We also found that people got better in three distinct ways, and that all three kinds of improvement increased with additional treatment. First, therapy eased the problems that brought people to treatment. Second, it helped them to function better, improving their ability to relate well to others, to be productive at work, and to cope with everyday stress. And it enhanced what can be called "personal growth." People in therapy had more confidence and self-esteem, understood themselves better, and enjoyed life more. . . .

Our findings complement recent work by psychologist Kenneth Howard of Northwestern University. By following the progress of 854 psychotherapy patients, Howard and his associates found that recovery followed a "dose-response" curve, with the greatest response occurring early on. On average, 50 percent of people recovered after 11 weekly therapy sessions, and 75 percent got better after about a year.

Recommendations

Emotional distress may not always require professional help. But when problems threaten to become overwhelming or interfere with everyday life, there's no need to feel defeated.

Our survey shows there's real help available from every quarter—family doctors, psychotherapists, and self-help groups. Both talk therapy and medication, when warranted, can bring relief to people with a wide range of problems and deep despair. . . .

48

————◄○►————

This article, by Neil Jacobson, a psychologist who has been study-ing therapy outcome for decades, suggests that we should not jump too quickly to the conclusion that psychotherapy works. He sug-gests that its effects, while perhaps statistically significant, may be relatively modest in size. After reading it, do you find yourself thinking differently about the Consumer Reports *study? Why or why not? This article first appeared in the* Family Therapy Net-worker *and is copied here with permission.*

THE OVERSELLING OF THERAPY

Neil Jacobson

WHEN MONIQUE, A FIRST-YEAR LAW STUDENT, began psychoanalysis with a prominent analyst in 1982, she complained of pervasive sadness, hopelessness, fatigue, difficulty concentrating and loss of appetite. She regularly woke up in the middle of the night, unable to go back to sleep. She had been plagued by these problems for most of her adult life and met the diagnostic criteria for "major depression." During the entire eight years that Monique was in psychoanalysis, she remained depressed. Despite her lack of improvement, Monique's psychoanalyst never changed treatments, never suggested alternative approaches and never consulted with colleagues about her case.

While shopping at a pharmacy one day, Monique noticed a self-help book about cognitive therapy. After reading it and doing some investi-gating, she discovered that there were a number of brief psychotherapies that had some success in helping people with depression. Monique also learned of several antidepressant medications that were often effective. Needless to say, she was disturbed that her analyst had never told her about these options, let alone offered them to her. For all Monique knew when she began treatment, psychoanalysis was the treatment of choice, indeed the only viable treatment, for major depression.

Monique found a cognitive therapist, started taking an antidepressant and recovered from her depression within six weeks of terminating her analysis. By now a practicing attorney, she considered it unconscionable that her analyst had allowed her to suffer for eight years while continuing unsuccessfully with psychoanalysis. Drawing an analogy to physicians who are expected to provide clients with all available treatment options and to outline their costs and benefits, she was astonished to find that it was not common practice among psychotherapists to do the same. Monique believed that her analyst was guilty of malpractice, but, in the end, she was so delighted to be feeling better that she didn't pursue litigation.

There are aspects of this case that are all too familiar to most mental health professionals. It is not uncommon for therapists to keep clients in therapy long after it is obvious that little or no progress is being made. Nor is it unusual to encounter therapists who are either unaware of or do not present their clients with a range of treatment options or discuss the existing scientific knowledge of their relative efficacy. Indeed, numerous surveys of mental health professionals indicate that even those trained in research do not keep up with the research literature, which itself seems to have little influence on clinical practice. Instead, the practice of psychotherapy seems to be influenced primarily by tradition, current fads and fashions and the persuasiveness of charismatic workshop leaders and book writers.

As a clinical scientist, a psychotherapy researcher and the former director of a doctoral program in clinical psychology, I have been training therapists and practicing psychotherapy since 1972. It is clear to me that, as an instrument of human change, psychotherapists have been overselling their product since the days of Freud. If the media and even some of our social science colleagues are beginning to criticize psychotherapy, it may be in part because the culture is beginning to come to this same realization. How bad is the problem? Is there anything that can be done?

While lobbying hard for a piece of the health care reform pie, advocates for the mental health professions have presented psychotherapies (and pharmacotherapy) as proven treatments for a variety of mental health problems, citing positive research findings, whenever possible, to support their claims. Where research findings don't exist, they cite opinions, which often amount to nothing more than an endorsement of long-established, unsubstantiated clinical traditions. For example, one common unsubstantiated assumption is that brief therapy may be sufficient for relatively circumscribed problems, such as phobias or panic attacks, but long-term psychotherapy is necessary for lifelong, serious problems, such as personality disorders. This position is not based on any evidence of efficacy, but simply on the *belief* that brief therapies do not work with certain problems. Some proposals by state psychological associations have actually requested insurance reimbursement for up to 150 therapy sessions per year for serious problems, even though there is no empirical basis that would justify such coverage.

Of course, advocates for psychotherapy are no different from advocates for other health care providers, who also practice many unproven techniques with impunity and receive reimbursement for them from insurance companies. In some respects, health care reimbursement has been based on the professional qualifications of the *provider* rather than on the efficacy of their chosen *treatment*. Physicians are prone to practicing unsubstantiated techniques and requesting that the government pay for them, as are mental health lobbyists. For example, until recently, ulcers were treated as psychophysiological disorders, without any empirical basis for this assumption. It has since been discovered that ulcers are infectious diseases that have little or nothing to do with stress, and can be treated quite effectively with antibiotics if discovered early enough. Still, at least some medical treatments offered by physicians make a clinically significant difference in the quality of life of the patients even if they do not "cure" the condition. Can the same be said of psychotherapy?

There is substantial research apparently demonstrating that psychotherapy actually does work. The increasing sophistication of research methodology has made it possible to pool together large numbers of therapy outcome studies and, through a statistical technique called meta-analysis, come to general conclusions about therapy's efficacy. *The Benefits of Psychotherapy*, by Mary Lee Smith, Gene V. Glass and Thomas I. Miller, perhaps the most extensive meta-analysis of therapy research, has been widely cited as providing incontrovertible evidence that psychotherapy helps people. Indeed, the authors conclude, "Psychotherapy is beneficial, consistently so and in many different ways. Its benefits are on a par with other expensive and ambitious interventions such as schooling and medicine . . . The evidence overwhelmingly supports the efficacy of psychotherapy. . . . Indeed, its efficacy has been established with monotonous regularity."

In the widely used textbook on psychotherapy research, *Handbook of Psychotherapy and Behavior Change*, edited by Sol Garfield and Allen Bergin, the chapters are filled with explicit and implicit conclusions that the outcome question has been resolved. Even Robyn W. Dawes, in his muckraking critique of professional psychology, *House of Cards: Psychology and Psychotherapy Built on Myth*, concludes that "Psychotherapy works overall in reducing psychologically painful and often debilitating symptoms. . . . In fact, it is partly because psychotherapy in its multitude of forms is generally effective that I am writing this book."

Unfortunately, these conclusions are premature. For one thing, critics point out that such generalized assertions about psychotherapy's efficacy are meaningless, because they provide no information about what treatments provided by which therapists work for what problems. In other words, just because psychotherapy in general has a positive effect, we cannot infer that a particular treatment will work for a particular type of client treated by a particular therapist. For example, is psychotherapy of any value in the treatment of depression and, if so, what types of treatments are likely to work? Are certain types of therapists more likely than others to be effective with depressives? This sort of question tends not to be addressed in reviews that examine hundreds of studies with diverse client populations, diverse modalities of treatment and diverse types of therapists.

There is, however, a more fundamental problem with any conclusions about psychotherapy efficacy based on statistical comparisons between treatment groups. Suppose you are comparing an experimental treatment for obesity with a control treatment. If the average weight loss in the experimental treatment is 10 pounds and the average weight loss in the control treatment is zero, the size of the statistical effect could be immense. Yet, if the clients entered treatment weighing 300 pounds, an average weight loss of 10 pounds would not make a clinically significant difference in their lives. In other words, the size of a statistical effect tells you little or nothing about its clinical significance.

Statistical comparisons bear no necessary relationship to the clinical significance of the treatment under consideration. Clinical significance refers to the extent to which clients feel that therapy has given them something approximating what they came for or has made a meaningful difference in their lives. But what does this mean in terms that can somehow be measured? Although the concept of clinical significance has taken on increased importance among psychotherapy researchers, there is little consensus as to how it should be defined. My colleagues Dirk Revenstorf, William C. Follette and I have developed a set of statistical techniques that provide a definition of clinical significance in terms of recovery. We reasoned that if clients make clinically significant changes during the course of therapy, by the end of therapy they should resemble their "functional" counterparts more than their "dysfunctional" cohorts on whatever problem they entered therapy to solve.

For example, if clients enter therapy complaining of depression, by the end of therapy they should score within the normal range on measures of depression in order for their improvement to be clinically significant. Thus, a client who leaves therapy less depressed than when he or she entered, but who still has significant depressive symptoms, would be considered to be improved but not recovered. We have developed statistical techniques to determine whether the magnitude of change is substantial enough to place the client within the normal range by the end of therapy. Generally, consumers of therapy expect that the problem they came in with will be resolved. It is of considerable interest to know how often clients get what they came for, and it is important to recognize that clients enter therapy with little regard for statistically significant improvement—they simply want to feel better, which they believe will happen as soon as therapy eliminates the problem as they define it, whether or not the therapist deems that belief realistic.

Using these statistical techniques, we have discovered that when psychotherapy outcome is examined under the microscope of clinical significance, its effects appear to be quite modest, even for disorders that are thought to be easily treated and even when so called "established" techniques are used. For example, it is often said that there are many effective treatments for major depression. Biological psychiatrists consider it proven that various forms of antidepressant medication work. A number of brief psychotherapies—most notably Aaron T. Beck's cognitive therapy and Gerald Klerman and Myrna Weissman's interpersonal psychotherapy—have ostensibly received considerable empirical support.

Yet, when the actual outcomes of these treatments are examined in terms of their clinical significance, the results are disturbing. Consider the federally funded, multisite investigation conducted in the 1980s known as the Treatment of Depression Collaborative Research Program (TDCRP), designed to compare the effectiveness of psychotherapies versus antidepressant medication. It is difficult to study depression because it tends to be episodic; that is, most depressives recover within a year even without therapy, and most who recover eventually have another episode of depression. Thus, it is relatively easy to attribute to therapy what may have transpired even without therapy. The TDCRP is widely considered to have achieved the highest degree of methodological rigor of any large-scale outcome study yet conducted, and thus has produced results that are more believable than those from many other trials of dubious design quality.

From the standpoint of clinical significance, the question is, "What percentage of clients stay in treatment, recover from their depressive episode and stay recovered for a reasonable period of time following termination?" In this particular study, where expert therapists were used and millions of dollars were spent to ensure quality control, the proportion of clients who completed the 12-week, 20-session treatment, recovered from their depressive episode, and stayed nondepressed for 18 months ranged from 19 to 32 percent across the three active treatments (imipramine, cognitive therapy and interpersonal psychotherapy). Thus, only a minority of patients recovered and stayed recovered for more than a year. Even the placebo treatment did as well (20 percent). Neither pharmacotherapy nor psychotherapy led to lasting recovery for the great majority of cases.

These findings are not atypical, either for major depression or for other mental health problems. In a series of studies of clinical significance, our research group has examined conduct disorders in adolescents, couples seeking therapy for marital distress and people with anxiety disorders. We have found the recovered patient (the one who shows few or no signs or symptoms of the initial complaint and believes him- or herself to be "cured") to be the exception rather than the rule for every type of disorder examined and for every type of therapy that we have looked at—psychodynamic, behavioral, cognitive and family therapy. When one considers even more intractable problems, such as addictive behaviors, schizophrenia and personality disorders, the clinical significance data are even more bleak. The only exception we have found thus far to these modest recovery rates is the cognitive behavioral treatment of panic disorder, developed by David Clark at Oxford University and David Barlow at the State University of New York in Albany.

This is not to say that psychotherapy never produces recovery or that some therapies are not more effective at inducing recovery rates than others. Rather, it simply attests to the relatively modest average recovery rates shown by psychotherapy when examined under the microscope of clinical significance.

It is important to note that there are numerous psychotherapy researchers who dispute my gloomy interpretation of the psychotherapy research literature, arguing that "statistical significance" is a sufficient criterion for determining that a form of psychotherapy is effective. If a treatment works better than nothing, exceeds the outcome of a placebo, or adds to the effectiveness of alternative treatments, they argue, then the effect is worth talking about, however modest it might be. These critics point out that even small changes can enhance the quality of a client's life. They may be right. However, I do think it is important to maintain the distinction between statistical and clinical significance to make sure clients are not misled into expecting the latter when, in all likelihood, they must settle for the former.

Other critics argue that the measures outcome researchers use are too crude to adequately evaluate the changes occurring in psychotherapy. For example, measures of depressive symptoms may not reflect the full impact of therapy on a client's overall sense of well-being, self-confidence and the like. It is hard to know how to answer these critics. If a depressed person *still* feels depressed after therapy, what is the significance to him or her of being able to sleep through the night? What is the meaning of "overall well-being"? At the very least, we know that by currently available measures, the average outcomes of most psychotherapies are modest. Whether outcomes will look better with improved measures remains to be seen. I actually believe that there are a variety of excellent measures of psychotherapy outcome. Asking someone how they feel, which is essentially the basis of most self-report measures of change, is about as direct as one can get. If anything, clients are prone to exaggerate how much better they feel rather than to minimize their improvement, since the desire to please the therapist is a well-established psychological phenomenon.

There are other researchers who criticize randomized clinical trials because they inevitably involve samples of clients who are unrepresentative of those seen in clinical practice. Nobody in their right mind would volunteer for a randomized clinical trial, these critics assert, where they may end up in a control group, especially when they could see a therapist who will focus on their individual needs rather than on the requirements of an experimental design. Yet, there is good reason to believe that the effects of psychotherapy found in randomized clinical trials *overestimate* the positive effects found in the world of clinical practice, because patients who are selected typically have discrete, encapsulated problems, and complicated cases involving, for example, dual diagnoses are typically excluded. Also, therapists are scrutinized much more carefully during a clinical trial than they are when left to their own devices in private practice: the sessions are taped, rated and regular supervision meetings are held. In fact, there is actually some empirical support for the notion that the psychotherapy works better in efficacy studies than it does in clinical practice. In a landmark study published in the *American Psychologist*, John Weisz reported that child psychotherapy shows a statistical advantage over no treatment only when conducted in research settings. In naturalistic practice settings, child psychotherapies appear to be ineffective, not just from the standpoint of clinical significance, but of statistical significance as well. They apparently are *not* better than no therapy at all!

But perhaps the toughest challenge for those who believe that research underestimates the effectiveness of psychotherapy is the overwhelming evidence that, on the average, psychotherapy outcome is not improved by either years of clinical experience or by professional training. In a famous 1979 study, in which Hans Strupp and his colleagues compared psychodynamic therapists with an average of 25 years of experience to college professors with no therapy training, experience or supervision in the treatment of anxious and depressed college students, the professors did as well as the experienced therapists. The question of whether experience or training enhances outcome has been studied extensively, reviewed exhaustively and meta-analyzed to death. Skeptics have looked at the data in all sorts of ways, trying to find a way to challenge the devastating conclusions of these hundreds of studies. No matter how determined the advocate, no matter how the data are analyzed, no one has been able to find that either the amount of clinical experience or the degree of professional training enhances outcome. In one of my studies, I found that novice clinical psychology graduate students with no prior experience outperformed licensed psychologists in doing marital therapy.

Much as we would like to believe that we are better therapists now than we were before we started our training, the research literature tells us that, on the average, we aren't. The only advantage that experienced therapists have over inexperienced ones is that they have a lower drop-out rate, an accomplishment that may be of dubious value given the modest effects of psychotherapy, showing that clients valiantly hang in there even when it's not doing them any reasonable good. A substantial body of research tells us that sometimes people recover during the course of therapy, but, more often they do not. Neither the level of experience nor the degree of training influences the likelihood of change.

To make matters even more troubling, it is not even clear that contact with a live therapist is necessary for a positive outcome. Although the research on self-administered treatments (self-help books, inspirational tapes, meditation, adult education courses) and peer support groups is not definitive, the studies completed so far show no advantage for clinical work with a therapist over a self-administered treatment. Moreover, when peer support groups have been examined rigorously (for example, in the treatment of obesity), they appear to perform as well as psychotherapy conducted by a professional.

There is no particular school or modality that is uniquely subject to the criticism that therapy has a limited impact. Cognitive and behavior therapies, as well as specific forms of psychotropic medication, have received more attention in clinical trials than other approaches, and thus can claim at least some support, whereas the same cannot be said of the vast majority of approaches to psychotherapy. However, with few exceptions, the therapies examined all seem to be wanting in terms of clinical significance. Therefore, "empirical validation" too often means only that a form of treatment has been studied in a controlled setting, and has been shown to have some positive effects, however weak they may be.

While family therapy has been shown to do about as well as individual psychotherapy, it is not demonstrably superior to individual psychotherapy for any clinical problem (with the possible exception of schizophrenia). My own research shows that, on the average, when marital discord coexists with major depression, couples therapy does as well as—but no better than—individual psychotherapy. Moreover, this research investigated behavioral marital therapy, not exactly a popular theoretical approach within a field dominated by general systems theory.

Family therapy began with, and continues to be fertilized by, an exceptionally creative group of clinicians who have generated a great many viable and still untested hypotheses about family functioning and how it can be harnessed to generate change. Much of what family therapists write about constitutes an important phase—perhaps the most important phase—of the research process: the generation of hypotheses. The field is ripe with ideas waiting to be validated, confirmed, replicated or disconfirmed. Thus, it is all the more disappointing that family therapy is so guilty of making unsubstantiated claims of success. "This works, trust me!" has become the standard of proof on the family therapy workshop circuit, and the popularity of various approaches becomes a question of who is most persuasive, whose teaching tapes are most pristine, or even whose name is best known. The claims of astoundingly high success in an astoundingly few number of sessions made by some solution-focused therapists are particularly disturbing. Despite the assertion that these success rates are substantiated by research findings, nothing cited in the literature could conceivably be thought of as empirically valid clinical research.

False prophets are easy to recognize and need to be exposed. They expect you to trust their clinical judgment, while showing no signs of humility or doubts about the wisdom of what they are proselytizing. They show an indifference to independent tests of their ideas and sidestep the issue of research evidence. We have to ask our plenary speakers, theorists and workshop leaders questions such as, "How do you know this works?" We have to pin down 90-percent success claims with questions like, "How did you measure success?" "Was the *measurement* process independent of the *therapy* process, to ensure that it was not contaminated by the client's desire to make the therapist feel good?" Family therapists must face the challenge of building a knowledge base if we are to respond effectively to the criticism leveled at other forms of psychotherapy.

Today our field faces the challenge of making sure that therapy promises nothing it can't deliver and delivers the best, most honestly presented care of which clinicians are capable. Therapists can no longer afford to ignore the scientific foundations of their profession for, as Jay Efran and Mitchell Greene recently pointed out in the *Networker*, in the long run, science is all "that presumably distinguishes [therapists] from the expanding cadre of self-proclaimed psychics, new-age healers, religious gurus, talk-show hosts and self-help book authors." From a therapy researcher's viewpoint, there are a number of changes that need to be made in how our field operates.

First, therapists must treat only clients who have given truly informed consent, and must stop treatment when it is apparent that it is not working. Psychotherapists are obligated to be familiar with the research literature on whatever disorders they are treating, to present to their clients the full range of treatment options along with their costs and benefits—based on currently available information—and to refrain from overselling the brand they happen to be providing. In most cases, therapists should openly acknowledge that their treatments are "experimental," since the success rates of most commonly practiced models for most disorders are unknown. Where outcome evidence is available, it should be presented. Clients should be given the information they need to make informed choices before being asked to consent to treatment.

Therapy should never be interminable, as Freud once referred to psychoanalysis. Progress should be expected to occur in a timely manner, or alternatives should be discussed. Criteria for determining progress should be part of a dialogue initiated by the therapist and regularly assessed by both therapist and client. When therapy isn't working, the therapist has an ethical obligation to try something else — another form of therapy, a referral to another therapist, a psychotropic drug, a self-help book, meditation, yoga, gardening, exercise or something else. A disgruntled ex-client once said to me, "In retrospect, after spending $5,000 on unsuccessful psychotherapy, with no suggestion from the therapist that there was any alternative, it occurred to me that it would have been much more therapeutic to use that money to hire babysitters, a maid service, even a butler." Alternatives to psychotherapy may often be the best solution when timely progress is not evident.

Researchers themselves have been negligent in not focusing on the questions of most interest to psychotherapists. One of the primary reasons that psychotherapists so often operate in an empirical vacuum is that there is no alternative. Until recently, for example, there was no basic research on childhood sexual abuse, and there is still very little on repressed memories. Thus, when faced with these issues, psychotherapists have little scientific support in formulating their treatment approaches. Responding to this need for information, many organizations and interest groups have already developed "clinical digests" that summarize and disseminate research findings for practicing therapists, and these efforts should be applauded and expanded. Until research training receives more attention in all clinical training programs, psychotherapists cannot be expected to rely on primary sources for their information. Meanwhile, agencies that fund clinical research have to become more flexible in their definition of good science. Setting the rigors of randomized clinical trials as the gold standard for research discourages many investigators from exploring the questions most relevant to clinicians.

Managed care services are frequently criticized by psychotherapy advocates for denying coverage for adequate treatment. In fact, managed care providers are placing the burden of proof where it belongs: in the hands of psychotherapists. It is frustrating that we cannot justify long-term treatment, nor can we justify the choice of hiring an M.D. or a Ph.D. to provide services when masters- and bachelor's-level providers would, on the average, perform just as well. We may resent having to talk to case managers, request additional treatment sessions, and lower our fees, but the demands made by managed care bureaucrats follow from the psychotherapy research literature with a great deal more logic than do the criticisms directed at them by psychotherapy lobbyists.

This article has highlighted research findings that should make clinicians squirm. Carried away with our popular acceptance, we have promised far more than we can deliver. We need to take a close look at our excesses and our often tenuous relationship to scientific principles. But while research can tell us a lot about the impact of therapy, conclusions about its ultimate merits and its role in the culture cannot be made solely from outcome data. While the existing empirical evidence raises serious questions about the transformative power of the therapy experience, people clearly get *something* from it or they would not keep coming back for more. Consumer satisfaction measures are virtually always higher than outcomes based on measures of psychiatric symptoms. How are we to understand this?

It may be that for many people, the process of being in therapy is the whole point. The collaboration between therapist and client creates an experience of hope and optimistic possibility that many clients prize whether or not their specific presenting problems disappear. Not only does the process of being in such a relationship feel good to many clients, it may also have outcome benefits that have thus far eluded easy measurement. Even when the outcomes are not clinically significant, many clients are satisfied, and feel they have derived great benefit from the experience. They may not resolve their problem with one therapist, enter therapy with another, still not resolve the original issue, but nonetheless feel satisfied with both experiences of therapy! For many people, the process of treatment itself seems to provide some subtle but significant and meaningful benefits that have so far eclipsed our efforts to measure or even define them. The power of the therapeutic alliance and the availability of a person who, at the very least, is present and caring should never be underestimated.

For all our society's much-vaunted attention to the pursuit of happiness, the mass shuffle of a society dominated by vast, impersonal forces of consolidated power and privilege makes it harder and harder for many people to experience that happiness. In large part, that accounts for the mushrooming popularity of psychotherapy over the last 25 years. Where else, in an age that has seen the decline of family, church, school and community, and the widespread, creeping anxiety fueled by social violence and economic insecurity, can people find an authentic and personal experience of human connection and compassionate challenge to their own best possibilities? What other professional field has devoted so much intelligence, systematic study and toilsome labor to doing humane work in an inhumane world, trying to instill in people a vision of optimistic realism about their own lives that avoids false sentimentality on the one hand and deadening cynicism on the other? With all its flaws, for all its bumblings and stumblings, psychotherapy keeps some vital spirit alive in a culture that would be much the poorer and more desperate without it.

49

——————◄o►————

Self-help books and tapes constitute an enormous industry, as anyone who has browsed in a bookstore lately can attest. Learn to relax, become more efficient, have better sex, have more rewarding relationships, get relief from depression, anxiety, or even shyness. How effective are self-help methods in reducing psychological distress? While definitive studies have not yet been done, Albert Ellis, originator of Rational-Emotive Therapy (one of the earliest forms of cognitive therapy), discusses the benefits and pitfalls in this article.

THE ADVANTAGES AND DISADVANTAGES

OF SELF-HELP THERAPY MATERIALS

Albert Ellis

DO SELF-HELP MATERIALS REALLY help their users? Starker (1986, 1988a, 1988b, 1988c, 1992) found that nearly 90% of the psychologists he studied in Boston and San Diego considered self-help books helpful, and 60% encouraged their clients to read them. Only 4% found them unhelpful, and none considered how-to books harmful. Considerable evidence for the widespread use of self-help materials by therapists has also been presented by Atwater and Smith (1982), Pardeck (1991), and Pardeck and Pardeck (1984). Studies showing the effectiveness of these materials as a therapeutic method have been published by Barlow and Craske (1989); Carr (1991); Craighead, McNamara, and Horan (1984); Foa and Wilson (1991); Ogles, Lambert, and Craig (1991); Pardeck and

Pardeck (1984); Schrank and Engels (1981); Selmi (1991); and Starker (1992).

Although the articles and studies just cited largely favor the use of self-help materials, Rosen and his associates have done surveys that have pointed out many dangers and disadvantages of these materials and have called for some restrictions on them (Glasgow & Rosen, 1978, 1982; Rosen, 1976, 1977a, 1977b, 1990, 1993). I agree with Rosen that do-it-yourself therapy has distinct disadvantages, and his and others' criticism of it is important. But individual and group therapy also have their harmful aspects, as a number of critics have pointed out (Ellis, 1989; Mahoney, 1991; Strupp, Hadley, & Gomez, 1977; Yalom, 1985).

What are some of the main disadvantages and advantages of self-help materials? I may have difficulty objectively answering this question, as I am the author of several popular do-it-yourself psychotherapy books and cassettes; however, let me give my impressions, from over 40 years of personal involvement and from surveying the research in this field, and make some suggestions for minimizing self-help shortcomings.

Disadvangages of Self-Help Materials

1. Even where recommended by a therapist, self-help materials are a strange and varied lot and include some highly dogmatic, antiscientific formulations and advice. This is particularly true today, when articles, books, and cassettes espousing transpersonal psychology or New Age philosophy abound. These materials urge people to help themselves with large doses of shamanism, exorcism, astrology, psychic surgery, out-of-body experience, channeling, totemism, fortune telling, extrasensory perception, magic, witchcraft, miracles, demonism, and faith healing (Booth, 1986; Bufe, 1987; De Mille, 1976; Ferguson, 1980; Frazier, 1986; Peck, 1983). Devout belief in these kinds of occult phenomena may indeed help some disturbed people, but they may also encourage them to be more irrational, less self-helping, more dependent, and more rigid and bigoted than they were before being "helped" (Ellis & Yeager, 1989; Kurtz, 1986; Moore, 1991).

2. Self-help materials are subject to idiosyncratic interpretations, which vary widely. Thus, the Bible can easily be interpreted by some readers to promote tolerance and forgiveness of sinners (though not of their sins). But it also can be interpreted to uphold self-damnation and punishment of others (e.g., consignment to Hell). Because users of self-help materials are often severely disturbed individuals, they can easily read ideas and practice into these materials that the authors never intended to include.

3. Self-help materials, when unsupervised by a therapist, sometimes

give the impression that personal change is very simple and easy. Users may consequently be discouraged from doing the hard work and practice that is almost always required for profound and lasting change.

4. Many self-help products obviously have been designed for the main purposes of making money and enhancing the reputations of their authors (a great number of whom are not responsible professional therapists). Their "Pollyanna-ish" tone and content therefore frequently lead users to over-optimistically expect miraculous results and to later experience grim disillusionment (Moore, 1991; Rosen, 1990, 1993).

5. Even people who distinctly benefit from self-help books and cassettes could usually benefit additionally from individual or group therapy with a professional. But many materials promise so much from unguided self-help that they discourage readers and listeners from also going for therapy.

6. Disturbed individuals most probably have limited ability to diagnose themselves and therefore can easily treat themselves for the wrong problems unless they have a well-trained professional to guide them regarding which self-help materials to use.

7. No self-help materials can be arranged to be as specifically responsive or adaptive to each individual user in an ongoing and everchanging manner as would be the case if the user were having face-to-face therapy. This is true even in the case of computer-assisted self-help programs, no matter how well the individual has diagnosed his or her problem and no matter how appropriately he or she has selected the self-help materials. Thus, these materials can hardly cope with or protect a potentially suicidal or homicidal user and therefore have limited benefits for many "difficult" people, such as those who tend to be withdrawn, overly impulsive, assaultive, suicidal, borderline, manic-depressive, and psychotic.

8. A good number of users of self-help materials are withdrawn, asocial, depressed, lethargic, or otherwise inactive, and had better sometimes have an active, encouraging, accepting, supportive, and persistent therapist to help and prod them to be more engaged in life. Few self-help materials can fulfill these therapeutic functions! At the same time, some individuals are overactive, too volatile, and too eruptive for their own good and had better be monitored by a therapist or therapeutic group. Self-help materials will hardly restrain them and may actually encourage them to take foolhardy risks.

Advantages of Self-Help Materials

What are some of the advantages of self-help materials? Here are some benefits that I and other practicing psychotherapists have found.

1. Many people are literature-oriented and learn more by reading than by interaction with a therapist or group. They find that reading the same pamphlet or book many times helps them to be influenced therapeutically and to finally use a helpful idea, whereas many therapist sessions may not be as useful to them. I and several other therapists with whom I have talked have had many unsolicited letters from people who say that they were severely disturbed—for example, deeply depressed—and had several years of ineffective therapy with reputable professionals, only to become startlingly improved in a few months' time after reading two or three self-help books. Some of them have insisted that no amount of therapy would have helped them without this reading (Burns, 1989; Paul Hauck, Tom Miller, and Arnold Lazarus, personal communication, August 1985).

I think that I can safely say that the Judeo-Christian Bible is a self-help book that has probably enabled more people to make more extensive and intensive personality and behavioral changes than all professional therapists combined. So there is much evidence that self-help materials, with all their disadvantages, are often quite helpful to many people (Ellis, 1978).

2. Many individuals are "allergic" to bibliotherapy but sensitized to audio- and videocassettes. Thus, some clients who rarely read books and pamphlets report significant, and sometimes dramatic, change from listening and relistening to self-help audio- and videotapes.

3. Many clients appreciably hasten and deepen their improvement in therapy by simultaneously using self-help materials. My associates and I have for many years found that when our clients use pamphlets, books, and cassettes that we recommend at our psychological clinic, they often improve faster and better than when they do not use such materials. I have also seen a number of clients who, having had no therapy, read *Feeling Good* (Burns, 1980), *Your Perfect Right* (Alberti & Emmons, 1990), or other self-help books and were already half-cured when they came for their first session. I could see that they were much less anxious and depressed than they had been previously and that they required fewer sessions of therapy than they would have required had they not done this reading.

Scogin, Jamison, and Gochnauer (1989) reported that when elderly depressed individuals read self-help cognitive and behavioral books for 4 weeks, they significantly improved when compared with control groups who did not get the books. Six months later, their improvement was continuing. Scoggin, in another paper, reviewed more than 40 studies that compared using self-help books with actual psychotherapy and found that "By and large, the books worked very well. Psychotherapy had an advantage but only a slight one" (Goleman, 1989, p. B6; Scogin et al., 1990).

My associates and I at our psychological clinic have also noted that even when clients are allergic to reading books, and have avoided doing so for years, they will usually read the short pamphlets that we give to all clinic clients, and once again, this reading often helps them to understand some important therapeutic ideas better and to make faster progress in their individual and group therapy sessions.

4. Many people hate the exposure of regular therapy and refuse to continue it for any period of time even when they can afford to do so. They believe that they can get more help at less expense by reading and by listening to self-help materials; however, even if they are often wrong about this, they are often much better off with these materials than without them.

5. Similarly, a great many disturbed people refuse to go to therapy because they are ashamed to do so, because they belong to families or groups (such as certain religious groups) that oppose therapy, or for other reasons. Such people have self-help books and cassettes as one of their few viable options.

6. Self-help presentations offer a wide variety of methods that are not available to people in communities where there may be only one or two therapists available or where most of the therapists are of the same persuasion and where few innovative therapists practice. They therefore often offer people a much greater freedom of choice of therapies than they would otherwise have. I have heard from a number of people who had never known about cognitive-behavior therapy because practically all the therapists in their area were psychoanalytic, but when it was brought to their attention by cognitive-behavioral writings they first realized that suitable nonpsychoanalytic alternative existed. One women in a large city was referred to several analysts in a row for what she thought was ineffective treatment, begged for a different kind of treatment, but was unable to find it until she read *I Can If I Want To* (Lazarus & Fay, 1975) and *A New Guide To Rational Living* (Ellis & Harper, 1975). She now thinks that her physicians who kept referring her to analysts were highly unethical in failing to inform her of alternative forms of treatment.

7. Self-help materials are often ideal for people who are in isolated communities where no therapists exist and where they would have to travel considerable distances to see one. Thus, I have seen people from the Rocky Mountains, Alaska, Northern Canada, Africa, Asia, and Antarctica who were many miles away from therapists but who, by using books, pamphlets, and cassettes, and by seeing me personally a few times or by having occasional phone sessions, were able to make considerable therapeutic progress. Bereft of self-help materials, many of them would have been left in the lurch.

8. Self-help materials can be referred to many times until clients and other users finally absorb them (Barlow & Craske, 1989; Foa & Wilson, 1991). As several studies have shown, therapy gains are often dramatic at the start but fail to be maintained, especially after regular sessions have ended. Some clients solve this problem by recording their sessions and relistening to the recording months or years after our sessions have stopped. Many others, when they require therapeutic reminders, successfully reread or rehear self-help materials and thereby save themselves the trouble and expense of scheduling renewed sessions.

9. Many therapy "refuseniks," including some who have been turned off by previous treatment, read and listen to self-help materials and learn thereby that they can be helped and then start to come to or return to therapy. Thus, literature on alcoholism has led innumerable people to join Alcoholics Anonymous, Rational Recovery, and other self-help groups and to go for psychological treatment when, without this literature, they would never have sought therapeutic help (Alcoholics Anonymous, 1976; Bufe, 1991; Peele & Brodsky, 1991; Trimpey, 1989).

For the above reasons, and a number of others that could be added, self-help presentations, with and without regular individual or group therapy, can be of decided help to millions of disturbed people (Ellis, 1978; Fichtner, Jobe, & Barter, 1990; Hansen, 1984; Riessman, 1965; Skovholt, 1974). In fact, if we compare the number of troubled individuals in the United States who have been significantly helped by self-help books, pamphlets, and cassettes (not to mention workshops, courses, sermons, and radio and TV presentations) during the last 25 years to the number who have largely been helped by professional therapists, I would estimate that the former far outnumber the latter. If we include all the troubled people in the world who have recently been significantly aided by self-help materials or by regular therapy, I would guess that the former outweigh the latter by at least five to one.

The Feasibility of Testing Self-Help Materials

Rosen and others (1976, 1977a, 1977b, 1990, 1993; Glasgow & Rosen, 1978, 1982) have rightly pointed out that if self-help materials are to be published, especially when they are designed to be used without supervision by a therapist, it would be best to pretest them, in the usual control group manner, to see if they are reliable and valid instruments. That would be ideal and I hope this practice will be followed someday. However, unless the author of these materials is also the publisher (which is rarely the case), the present publishing system makes pretesting of do-it-yourself materials impractical. . . .

Conclusion

Self-help therapy books, cassettes, and other materials are an important part of our therapeutic culture and are doubtless here to stay. Many of them lead to wasteful or harmful results, but many are also quite useful both to people who do and do not take advantage of regular individual and group treatment. Pretesting and posttesting these materials to determine their reliability and validity would be highly desirable, but many obstacles to doing so, particularly on the part of publishers, now stand in the way of accomplishing this. Psychologists and their professional organizations could well give much more thought and active research to this important clinical and educational problem.

References

Alberti, R. F., & Emmons, M. L. (1990). *Your perfect right*. San Luis Obispo, CA: Impact.

Alcoholics Anonymous. (1976). *Alcoholics Anonymous*. New York: Alcoholics Anonymous World Services.

Atwater, J. M., & Smith, D. (1982). Christian therapists' utilization of bibliotherapeutic resources. *Journal of Psychology and Theology, 10,* 230–235.

Barlow, D. H., & Craske, M. G. (1989). *Mastery of your anxiety and panic*. Albany, NY: Center for Stress and Anxiety Disorders.

Booth, J. (1986). *Psychic paradoxes*. Buffalo, NY: Prometheus.

Bufe, C. (1987). *Astrology: Fraud or superstition?* San Francisco, CA: See Sharp Press.

Bufe, C. (1991). *Alcoholics Anonymous: Cult or cure?* San Francisco, CA: See Sharp Press.

Burns, D. D. (1980). *Feeling good: The new mood therapy*. New York: Morrow.

Burns, D. D. (1989). *Feeling good handbook*. New York: Morrow.

Carr, T. (1991). Cited in K. McAuliffe, Computer shrinks. *Self,* July 1991, p. 404.

Craighead, L. W., McNamara, & Moran, J. (1984). Perspective on self-help and bibliotherapy. In S. D. Brown & R. W. Lent (Eds.), *Handbook of counseling psychology* (pp. 878–929). New York: Wiley.

deMille, R. (1976). *Castaneda's journey: The power and the allegory*. Santa Barbara, CA: Capra Press.

Ellis, A. (1978). Rational-emotive therapy and self-help therapy. *Rational Living, 13*(1), 2–9.

Ellis, A. (1989). Ineffective consumerism in the cognitive-behavioral therapies and in general psychotherapy. In W. Dryden & P. Trower (Eds.), *Cognitive psychotherapy: Stasis and change* (pp. 159–174). London: Cassell.

Ellis, A., & Harper, R. A. (1975). *A new guide to rational living*. North Hollywood, CA: Wilshire Books.

Ellis, A., & Yeager, R. (1989). *Why some therapies don't work*. Buffalo, NY: Prometheus.

Ferguson, M. (1980). *The Aquarian conspiracy*. Los Angeles: Tarcher.

Fichtner, C. C., Jobe, T. G., & Barter, J. T. (1990). Self-help and the Chicago connection. *Chicago Medicine, 94*(7), 24–27.

Foa, E., & Wilson, R. (1991). *Stop obsessing!* New York: Bantam.

Frazier, K. (1986). *Science confronts the paranormal*. Buffalo, NY: Prometheus.

Glasgow, R. E., & Rosen, G. M. (1978). Behavioral bibliotherapy: A review of self-help behavior therapy manuals. *Psychological Bulletin, 85,* 1–23.

Glasgow, R. E., & Rosen, G. M. (1982). Self-help behavior therapy manuals: Recent developments and clinical usage. *Clinical Behavior Therapy Review, 1,* 1–20.

Goleman, D. (1989, July 6). Feeling gloomy? A good self-help book may actually help. *New York Times,* p. B6.

Hansen, F. W. (1984). Self-helping groups. In R. J. Corsini (Ed.), *Encyclopedia of psychology* (Vol. 3, pp. 291–292). New York: Wiley.

Kurtz, P. (1986). *The transcendental temptation.* Buffalo, NY: Prometheus.

Lazarus, A. A., & Fay, A. (1975). *I can if I want to.* New York: Morrow.

Mahoney, M. J. (1991). *Human change processes.* New York: Basic.

Moore, T. E. (1991, August). *Subliminal auditory self-help tapes.* Paper presented at the Annual Meeting of the American Psychological Association, San Francisco.

Ogles, M., Lambert, M. J., & Craig, D. E. (1991). Comparison of self-help books for coping with loss: Expectations and attributions. *Journal of Counseling Psychology, 38,* 387–393.

Pardeck, J. A., & Pardeck, J. T. (1984). *Young people with problems.* Westport, CT: Greenwald.

Pardeck, J. T. (1991). Using books in clinical practice. *Psychotherapy in Private Practice, 9,* 105–119.

Peck, M. S. (1983). *People of the lie.* New York: Simon & Schuster.

Peele, S., & Brodsky, A. (1991). *The truth about addiction and recovery.* New York: Simon & Schuster.

Riessman, F. (1965). The help therapy principle. *Social Work, 10,* 27–32.

Rosen, G. M. (1976). The development and use of nonprescription behavior therapies. *American Psychologist, 31,* 139–141.

Rosen, G. M. (1977a). Nonprescription behavior therapies and other self-help treatments: A reply to Goldiamond. *American Psychologist, 32,* 179–197.

Rosen, G. M. (1977b, August). *Nonprescription psychotherapies: A symposium on do-it-yourself treatments.* General statement. Paper presented at the Annual Meeting of the American Psychological Association, San Francisco.

Rosen, G. M. (1990, August 10). *The dangers of self-help materials.* Paper presented at the American Psychological Association Convention, Boston.

Rosen, G. M. (1993). Self-help or hype? Comments on psychology's failure to advance self-care. *Professional Psychology: Research and Practice, 24,* 340–345.

Scogin, F., Bynum, J., Stephens, G., & Calhoun, S. (1990). Efficacy of self-administered treatment programs: Meta-analytic review. *Professional Psychology: Research and Practice, 21,* 42–47.

Scogin, F., Jamison, C., & Gochneaur, K. (1989). Comparative efficacy of cognitive and behavioral bibliotherapy for mildly and moderately depressed older adults. *Journal of Consulting and Clinical Psychology, 57,* 403–407.

Selmi, P. M. (1991). Cited in K. McAuliffe, Computer shrinks. *Self,* July, 1991, pp. 103–104.

Skovholt, T. M. (1974). The client as helper. *Counseling Psychologist, 4,* 58–64.

Starker, S. (1986). Promises and prescriptions. *American Journal of Health Promotion, 1,* 19–24, 68.

Starker, S. (1988a). Do-it-yourself therapy: The prescription of self-help books by psychologists. *Psychotherapy, 25,* 142–146.

Starker, S. (1988b). Psychologists and self-help books. *American Journal of Psychotherapy, 42,* 448–455.

Starker, S. (1988c). *Oracle at the supermarkets: The American preoccupation with self-help books.* New Brunswick, NJ: Transaction.

Starker, S. (1992). Characteristics of self-help book readers among VA medical outpatients. *Medical Psychotherapy, 5,* 85–94.

Strupp, H. H., Hadley, S. W., & Gomez-Schwartz, B. (1977). *Psychotherapy for better or worse.* Northvale, NJ: Aronson.

Trimpey, J. (1989). *The small book.* New York: Delacorte.

Yalom, I. D. (1985). *The theory and practice of group psychotherapy* (3rd ed.). New York: Basic Books.

50

————◄o►———

It has sometimes been argued that psychotherapy is a white middle-class endeavor from which people of non-white ethnicity are less likely to profit. In fact, studies indicate that non-white clients are less likely to receive standard psychotherapy and are more likely to receive briefer, more directive psychotherapy and/or medication than white clients with similar presenting problems. It has also been argued that ethnic matching between client and therapist is essential for psychotherapy to be beneficial. One could imagine many reasons why this might be so, but is it really?

This article summarizes research into these issues and suggests that there is a difference between ethnic or racial matching and cultural matching. The former, Dr. Stanley Sue suggests, is an ethical or moral concern, while the latter is an empirical one. See if you agree with his conclusion.

PSYCHOTHERAPEUTIC SERVICES
FOR ETHNIC MINORITIES

Stanley Sue

ONE OF THE MAJOR GOALS OF American psychology has been to advance psychology as a science and profession in order to promote human welfare. In the past two decades, psychology and the mental health disciplines have engaged in a great deal of self-criticism over the effectiveness of psychotherapeutic services for ethnic minority groups. The criticisms have focused on prejudicial and discriminatory practices directed toward ethnic groups, therapists' lack of knowledge and understanding of sociocultural contexts of ethnic clients, inaccessibility or unavailability of services, and so on. Consequently, questions have been raised over the value of present approaches for treating ethnic minority populations. The criticisms have also stimulated studies examining ethnic or racial differences in the utilization of services, premature termination rates, client preferences for therapists, therapist prejudice, diagnosis and assessment, treatment strategies, and the process and outcome of treatment.

Under the assumption that therapy is often ineffective with ethnic minorities, I and other ethnic investigators have advocated changes in the way psychotherapy is conducted with different cultural groups. Yet, substantial controversy exists over the notion that ethnic individuals are shortchanged in psychotherapy and that an ethnically or racially dissimilar therapist–client dyad is undesirable. Despite the strongly held opinions over the problems ethnic clients encounter in receiving effective services, empirical evidence has failed to consistently demonstrate differential outcomes for ethnic and White clients. In the controversy, three positions have emerged. The first is that ethnic individuals frequently do not benefit from treatment and that many White therapists cannot work effectively with ethnic clients. The second position is that research findings support the null hypothesis (i.e., ethnic clients do not differ from Whites in treatment outcomes, and ethnic clients do not show better outcomes when seen by an ethnic rather than a White therapist). Finally the third and more cautious position is that the quality and quantity of research are insufficient to permit strong conclusions about the value of psychotherapy with ethnic minorities.

In this article, I examine these three positions, as well as some of the reasons for their maintenance. Although some investigators believe that opinions on the value of psychotherapy are divided according to ethnic lines, in the present article I argue that the issues of whether ethnic individuals benefit from treatment and whether Whites can effectively work with ethnic clients have been misconceptualized. The empirical issue of treatment effectiveness has often been confounded with moral and ethical issues involving the shortage of ethnic therapists and the resulting lack of freedom of choice in selection of therapists. Another problem is that treatment effectiveness and ethnicity are issues that cannot be meaningfully addressed by posing simple questions. It is proposed that ethnicity is quite distal to treatment outcomes and that the task is to examine more proximal variables. In this article, I do not intensively review all of the pertinent empirical studies on psychotherapy with ethnic minority groups. Excellent reviews have been conducted in the past (Dreger & Miller, 1968; Griffith, 1977; Griffith & Jones, 1978; Harrison, 1975; Parloff, Waskow, & Wolfe, 1978; Sattler, 1977; Siegel, 1974), including some updated ones (Abramowitz & Murray, 1983; Atkinson, 1983, 1985, 1986). Rather, I have devoted the present analysis to the conflicting conclusions drawn by reviewers and have suggested that the issues regarding ethnic outcomes in psychotherapy have been misconceptualized.

The Ineffectiveness of Psychotherapy
With Ethnic Clients

The President's Commission on Mental Health (1978) pointed to a number of problems encountered by ethnic minorities in the service delivery system:

> Racial and ethnic minorities . . . continue to be underserved. . . . It makes little sense to speak about American society as pluralistic and culturally diverse, or to urge the development of mental health services that respect and respond to that diversity, unless we focus attention on the special status of the groups which account for the diversity. . . . Too often, services which are available are not in accord with their cultural and linguistic traditions. . . . A frequent and vigorous complaint of minority people who need care is that they often feel abused, intimidated, and harassed by non-minority personnel. Like everyone else, minorities feel more comfortable and secure when care is provided by practitioners who come from similar backgrounds. (pp. 4–6)

Two types of difficulties can be distilled from the commission's report. One involves cultural and linguistic mismatches between clients and therapists and the detrimental effects that such mismatches have on therapy outcomes. Among the most frequent criticisms of psychotherapy with ethnic minority clients is the lack of bilingual and bicultural therapists who can communicate and can understand the values, life-styles, and backgrounds of these clients. For example, S. Sue, Wagner, Ja, Margullis, and Lew (1976) found that Asian Americans were more likely than Whites to believe that mental illness is caused by organic or bodily factors and that mental health is enhanced by will power and the avoidance of morbid thinking. These cultural differences in conceptualizations of mental health have important implications for psychotherapy. Clients may behave in accordance with cultural beliefs and values, but therapists may interpret the behavior solely as a sign of intrapsychic processes. For example, some therapists maintain that somatization and reluctance to discuss personal problems among Asians are indicators of deep and personal intrapsychic problems, such as repression. Without knowing the cultural basis for beliefs and behaviors of Asians, therapists can easily misinterpret the meaning of the behaviors. Similar analyses of the problems in therapist–client mismatches in culture or language have been made by other investigators for American Indians (Attneave, 1985; Trimble & LaFromboise, 1985), Asian Americans (Leong, 1986; D. W. Sue & D. Sue, 1985), Blacks (Jenkins, 1985; Snowden, 1982), and Hispanics (Acosta, 1984; Casas, 1985; LeVine & Padilla, 1980; Munoz, 1982).

The second difficulty is that therapists may hold stereotypes or biases concerning ethnic minority clients. These stereotypes or biases tend to reflect the nature of race or ethnic relations in our society. Kenneth Clark (1972) noted that the mental health profession has not been immune to the forces of racism in society and that racism may be reflected in diagnosis, assessment, and treatment. A. Jones and Seagull (1977) discussed these biases in terms of countertransference on the part of the therapist. Using less psychodynamic terminology, others have simply referred to the stimulus value of ethnic clients to therapists. Because the stimulus values of individuals are frequently influenced by societal values, ethnic clients may be victims of stereotypes. Ethnic clients may also have biases concerning the therapist, and transference/countertransference phenomena may occur regardless of the ethnicity of therapists or clients. Moreover, because of the changing nature of race or ethnic relations, it is difficult to specify what the biases are. Griffith and Jones (1978) stated that "descriptions concerning the effects of race in psychotherapy can do no more than capture a particular phase in time; they are by no means immutable and, in fact, are likely to change in important ways with the continued evolvement of the sociocultural context" (p. 228). In any event, it can be assumed that biases *per se* are likely to be detrimental to the therapeutic process. The consensus among the investigators cited above is that ethnic minority clients have a more difficult time than White clients in achieving good outcomes from treatment because of ethnic mismatches and therapist biases in treatment.

The Lack of Empirical Support for Differential Outcomes

It would be tempting to ask the question of whether psychotherapy is effective with members of ethnic minority groups. Such a question, however, would generate the same kind of debate that has existed in the field of mental health over the effectiveness of psychotherapy in general. This debate has stimulated the study of the meaningfulness of the question, methodological and conceptual approaches to psychotherapy research, and applications of meta-analyses and magnitude-of-effect techniques. Rather than dealing with the broader question of the effectiveness of psychotherapy with ethnic minority groups, I will examine a more specific issue: Is there evidence that ethnic minority clients have poorer outcomes from treatment than White clients? Because many ethnic clients are treated by White therapists, do ethnic clients fare worse when treated by White than ethnic therapists? The two questions are highly related because most ethnic clients are treated by White therapists, who may differ from the clients in cultural values and backgrounds.

Most treatment studies have failed to show differential outcomes on the basis of the race or ethnicity of clients. One of the first extensive studies of treatment outcomes for Black clients was reported by Lerner (1972). Based on her five-year work, Lerner investigated the effects of treatment on severely disturbed and predominantly lower class Black and White clients seen by White therapists. The vast majority of clients improved after treatment, and no evidence of a racial difference in outcome was found. In a 2 × 2 research design, Jones (1978) studied the effects of therapist and client race (Black and White) on the outcome of psychotherapy. Results indicated that the race of therapist and race of client had no effect on outcome and that Black and White clients improved equally. However, some process differences emerged when therapist–client interactions were tape recorded and analyzed using a modified Q-sort. Regardless of whether Black clients were seen by Black or White therapists, Black clients were more likely than White clients to express concerns involving racial issues. More erotic transference among clients was noted in Black therapist–Black client than White therapist–Black client dyads. Finally, Jones (1982) studied therapist ratings of treatment outcome with Black and White clients seen by Black or White therapists. Black and White clients benefited equally, and no differences were found between racially matched or mismatched therapist–client combinations. The studies of Lerner (1972) and Jones (1978, 1982) were presented because they are well cited and represent some of the most detailed and rigorous treatment studies involving Black clients. In his review of 10 actual treatment studies, Sattler (1977) adopted the position that Blacks and Whites benefit equally from treatment.

In the clinical analogue studies, individuals from different ethnic or racial groups can be asked to play the role of therapist or client in a simulated therapy session. In some cases, actual counselors or therapists may work with students who present "clinical" problems. The "clients" or "therapists" can be asked to rate the effectiveness (satisfaction, rapport, level of interaction, client preferences for ethnic therapists, etc.) of the treatment session, or the session can be rated by observers.

Evidence for a race effect is stronger in the case of the clinical analogue studies than in the actual treatment studies (Griffith & Jones, 1978). For example, Banks (1972) and Carkhuff and Pierce (1967) found that self-exploration was higher in same, rather than different, race dyads. However, many studies have also failed to show ethnic differences (Atkinson, 1986; Sattler, 1977). In the analogue studies, Blacks tended to prefer Black rather than White therapists, although this preference appears to be confined to Blacks rather than to other ethnic groups (Atkinson, 1986). One major limitation of most analogue studies has been the use of measures (e.g., client self-exploration, preference, and ratings of therapist's level of understanding) that do not directly assess client adjustment or well-being.

Methodological and Conceptual Limitations
in the Research

Several reviewers of the literature have been reluctant to draw strong conclusions, which is understandable. There is a lack of actual treatment studies. In 1978, Parloff et al. stated that almost no reported studies of "real" therapy could be found in which Black and White therapists were compared. In his 1986 review, Atkinson noted that the recent studies of ethnicity and treatment have produced conflicting findings, so that the effects of client and therapist race remain an open question. Another problem is that therapy investigations have had methodological and conceptual limitations, as follows:

1. Race or ethnicity of clients and therapists has frequently not been fully crossed. For example, in Lerner's study (1972), Black therapists were not included.

2. In many of the studies, clients are not randomly assigned to therapists. The investigation by Jones (1978) involved therapist ratings of clients who had already completed treatment. Although race of therapist and client was crossed, the assignment of clients to therapists was presumably based on institutional or routine practices and not on random procedures. In such situations, other factors can account for the results, and those therapists who see Black clients may be self-selected and more "liberal," skilled, or experienced with these clients.

3. Some studies have employed only a very small number of clients and therapists, which weakens the power of racial or ethnic comparisons.

4. Black or ethnic clients who enter treatment may be different from their respective counterparts who avoid treatment. They may be less skeptical or alienated from the mental health system. Ethnic differences may also exist in the propensity to seek treatment, so that outcomes may be influenced by these differences.

5. The different backgrounds (e.g., experience in treatment, social class, and attitudes and values) and characteristics (level of psychopathology among clients, sex, etc.) of therapists and clients may be confounded with race or ethnicity. Many of these factors have not been controlled.

6. The correlational nature of some of the studies has made it difficult to determine cause and effect.

7. Outcome measures may not have cross-cultural validity or may be insensitive to ethnic differences.

Clinical analogue studies have also suffered from methodological and conceptual problems. Because clients and therapists may be role playing, a whole host of problems can occur. Students or laypersons, rather than actual clients and therapists, have frequently been used. Individuals may see through the purpose of the study and respond in a socially desirable manner, and the experiment may be somewhat contrived, which weakens external validity. Outcome measures may be weak (e.g., client satisfaction) or confounded with process measures (e.g., self-exploration). Furthermore, ratings are usually conducted after one session, which may inaccurately reflect treatment outcomes that occur over a period of many treatment sessions. Most investigators have been fully aware of the problems in conducting such research.

Ethnic Outcomes From Treatment: Lack of Consensus

Given the discrepant findings, paucity of research, and methodological problems in previous studies, it is not surprising that opinions about the effectiveness of treatment with ethnic minority clients have varied considerably. In a sense, the research work has served as a projective stimulus in which investigators have been able to freely draw conclusions. Answers to the questions of whether psychotherapy is effective with ethnic individuals and whether ethnic clients receive positive outcomes when working with White therapists include "yes," "no," "maybe," "it depends," and "cannot tell." This is apparent in a sampling of the comments that have been made by the reviewers.

The Negative Position   The negative position has been stated by Sattler (1977) as follows:

> White therapists have been effective helping agents with a variety of Black clients. (p. 278)
>
> Therapist's race is for the most part not a significant variable in affecting the subject's performance and reactions. (p. 271)
>
> A comparison of the various types of preference studies covered in this section indicates that other things being equal many Black subjects prefer Black therapists to White therapists. However, a competent White professional is preferred to a less competent Black professional and the therapist's style and technique are more important in affecting Black clients' choices than the therapists' race. (p. 267)
>
> Black clients report that they have benefited from treatment received from White therapists, who have used, as far as can be determined, traditional forms of therapy. (p. 276)

The Positive Position   Griffith and Jones (1978) have presented the positive position as follows:

> The results of analog studies concerning black–white interactions in interviews simulating counseling situations support the conclusion that white therapist–black patient interactions are frequently ineffective. (p. 229)
>
> The few studies of actual psychotherapy of blacks, mostly involving

small samples, have produced somewhat more attentuated [sic] results than the analog studies but in the same direction. . . . Unquestionably, race makes a difference in psychotherapy. Still, this is not to say that the skillful and experienced white therapist cannot effectively treat the black client. Rather, the critical requisite is that the white therapist is sensitive to the unique ways in which his race affects the course of treatment. (p. 230)

The Neutral Position   A neutral position has been adopted by a number of researchers. For example, Parloff et al. (1978) stated,

This review of the research on race of the therapist does not provide much definitive information about the effects of race per se or of intra and interracial matching on the outcome of therapy. (p. 258)

The fact that almost no studies have been reported of "real" therapy comparing black and white therapists seriously limits the inferences to be drawn from this literature. In all likelihood, this limitation is due primarily to the shortage of black mental health professionals in many clinical settings. (p. 257)

Abramowitz and Murray (1983) wrote,

Those who would continue to press the charge of pervasive racial bias must explain why racial bias eludes detection when social class bias has been found. (p. 244)

Taking all of this together, it seems apparent that no definite conclusions can be drawn at this point. That is, no one really knows how prevalent race effects are in therapy as it is practiced today. (p. 248)

Atkinson (1985) stated,

To date, analogue and survey studies attempting to assess counselor prejudice and stereotyping directly have generally failed to establish the existence of these traits. (p. 150)

Analogue and survey studies examining counseling process variables have produced an almost even split between those finding and those not finding an effect attributable to race or ethnicity. . . . Archival documentation of differential treatment based on race or ethnicity is strong enough to warrant concern by the profession and continued monitoring by researchers. . . . Outcome research has failed to demonstrate that clients are better served by same race or ethnicity counselor–client pairings. The research in this area is so fraught with design limitations, however, particularly with respect to outcome criteria, that definitive conclusions are impossible. (p. 151)

The only real consensus among investigators has been over the state of the research: Not enough research has been conducted, and published research suffers from methodological and conceptual limitations.

Explanations for the Conflicting Opinions

In the systematic study of a research question, divergent answers are often expected to emerge. Indeed, divergence and conflict facilitate the progress of science. Issues are redefined, methodological advancements are made, opportunities for cross-validation of findings are stimulated, and theoretical formulations are developed. Yet, over the past decade or two, arguments over the effectiveness of treatment with ethnic minorities have remained remarkably unchanged, in that strong critics and proponents of psychotherapy with ethnic individuals can still be heard. Do we need to vary our forms of treatment when dealing with ethnic clients? Are white therapists likely to be culturally insensitive or biased when working with ethnics?

As mentioned previously, the conflicting positions are attributable, in part, to the lack of rigorous research in the area. Parloff et al. (1978) felt that the discrepancies may be due to investigators who rely on findings from different studies or who place differential weights on the significance of certain studies and outcome measures. The most controversial explanations of why investigators have differed in their interpretations have been proposed by Abramowitz (1978) and Abramowitz and Murray (1983). The two explanations are social-political in nature, with one involving the notion of "heart-pothesis" and the other having to do with the race of the investigator.

Abramowitz (1978) stated that

> the weight of those data repudiates the contention that black patients receive an appreciably less than fair shake from white therapists. . . . How is the persistence of formulations of white therapists' countertransference reactions to black patients to be explained in the face of substantial empirical disconfirmation?
>
> I propose to do so by introducing the notion of a "heart-pothesis." In contrast to mere hypotheses, which can be rendered mortal by data, heart-potheses are immune from them. In fact, whereas research is routinely done to confirm or disconfirm hypotheses, tests of heart-potheses often have a covert political function—bestowing scientific status on a personal conviction. (p. 957)

The view that critics of psychotherapy with ethnic individuals might merely be advancing personal convictions with political functions was perceived by some researchers as being distorted and one-sided. Fulton, Gad, and Sue (1979) responded by noting,

> We believe that the issues are far more complicated and cannot be so lightly dismissed. First, heart-pothesis is a double-edged sword. Some individuals may overestimate the degree of racism in specific situations, but there are also those who refuse to see discrimination when it is present. . . . Second, we believe that for the most part, therapists working with ethni-

cally or racially dissimilar patients do try to be fair and nondiscriminatory. . . . The responsiveness and effectiveness of treatment are the key issues. . . . The point is, and in this regard we agree with Abramowitz, there is a need for novel research strategies in examining complicated racial issues. (pp. 561–562)

Later, Abramowitz (Abramowitz & Murray, 1983) acknowledged that the heart-pothesis was not simply confined to critics of therapy with ethnic individuals: "Note that the notion of a heartpothesis does not imply the direction of the underlying political opinion; the conviction in some professional circles that black patients are most assuredly not given short shrift by white therapists qualifies as well" (p. 219). In the comprehensive review by Abramowitz and Murray (1983), another controversial issue was raised in trying to explain why opinions varied concerning the value of treatment, as follows:

The split is now clearly along racial lines. Sattler (1977), a white reviewer, saw little evidence that blacks get short shrift in therapy with whites; while Griffith and Jones (1978), black reviewers, found ample evidence that this is in fact so. . . . Black and white reviewers alike examined many of the same studies, and no new persuasive evidence has appeared in the interim. . . . In all likelihood, the empirical "truth" lies somewhere in between the polarized positions. (pp. 237–238)

There is no question that racial and ethnic issues have generated conflict and tensions, not only in the mental health profession but also in American society. However, the existence of personal or even political convictions in science is expected and, in many cases, beneficial in knowledge development (Rappaport, 1977). The convictions are problematic when they run counter to evidence and when they can never be disconfirmed. In the case of psychotherapy with ethnic minorities, although the bulk of the evidence may tend to support the null hypothesis, the quality and quantity of the research are insufficient to permit strong conclusions. Most disturbing is the notion that the convictions are divided according to racial lines. If Abramowitz and Murray's (1983) assertion of a racial split among reviewers was confined to the work of Griffith and Jones (1978) and Sattler (1977), the assertion loses meaning because only two works were involved. If it was intended to reflect a general phenomenon (i.e., Whites believe that race or ethnicity makes no difference in treatment, whereas ethnics hold the opposite view), then the assertion is incorrect. Many White investigators have argued that clients who are members of ethnic minorities or who are culturally different from therapists encounter difficulties in receiving effective treatment (e.g., Lefley, 1985; Klineberg, 1985; Pedersen, Draguns, Lonner, & Trimble, 1981; Triandis & Brislin, 1984). Sattler (1977) himself advocated that therapists gain experience in working with Blacks and attend to cultural and racial issues. Many ethnic psychotherapists have strongly endorsed the value of psychotherapy with ethnic individuals. For example, Evans (1985), a Black, stated that

> many more black and poor people are helped by the psychotherapies than is acknowledged by psychology trainees interested in minority mental health. The tendency for trainees to be oriented away from traditional (i.e., diagnostic and treatment) approaches with poor and black patients constitutes a bias contradicted by empirical data dating back to the early 1970s showing the efficacy of insight-oriented psychotherapy with black and poor patients. (p. 457)

Even Jones, who was part of the Griffith and Jones (1978) team, has more recently noted that "one cannot help but wonder whether those who continue to insist that it is only the rare black patient who is suitable for the psychological therapies remain under the spell of outmoded, stereotypic images, now rapidly being discarded" (Jones, 1985, p. 173). It is true that most ethnic investigators have advocated the consideration of the cultural background and experiences of ethnic clients. Here again, however, views have not been strictly polarized according to racial or ethnic lines.

If these explanations for the conflicting opinions are weak, why does the controversy persist? I believe that (a) the empirical issue of the effects of ethnicity is confounded with a moral/ethical issue and (b) the issue itself is misconceptualized and meaningless. That is, *ethnic* match is confounded with *cultural* match. The former is primarily a moral issue whereas the latter is more of an empirical issue.

Ethnicity of the Therapist: A Moral Issue

The question of whether therapist–client ethnic matches result in better outcomes than mismatches has obscured, and has appeared in the context of, another critical concern—namely, freedom of choice and access. Our mental health system has set high standards in the provision of care (President's Commission on Mental Health, 1978). Ideally, clients should have freedom of choice in the selection of therapists and should have access to therapists of their choosing (e.g., feminist therapists, gay therapists, or psychologists rather than psychiatrists). This is particularly true in our society, which is pluralistic and which values freedom and individualism. At present, there is a serious shortage of ethnic therapists to meet the demands of ethnic populations (Casas, 1985). This shortage is particularly acute for clients who want or need bilingual bicultural therapists. The view that ethnicity of therapists makes no difference in treatment may hinder efforts to diversify the field of psychotherapy.

Such a view has elicited strong emotions and perpetuates the controversy regarding ethnic issues. We need to affirm the commitment to an ethnically diverse mental health profession.

Ethnicity and Psychotherapy: Misconceptualizations of the Issues

The questions—whether ethnic clients are as likely as White clients to benefit from psychotherapy and whether ethnic matches are superior to ethnic mismatch between therapists and clients—have been framed as if simple answers can be provided. Such an approach is likely to produce heated and unresolvable debates. White and other therapists may be offended if informed that merely because of group membership, they are unable to conduct effective treatment with ethnics. Ethnic and cross-cultural therapists are angered if they are told that cultural differences and race/ethnic relations make no difference in treatment. Overlooked is the view of the trees from the forest.

For years, psychotherapy research has attempted to heed Paul's (1969) reformulation of the question "Does psychotherapy work?" with the question, "What treatment, by whom, is most effective for this individual with that specific problem, under which set of circumstances, and how does it come about?" (p. 44). In a previous article, Nolan Zane and I (Sue & Zane, 1987) argued that outcomes from treatment are likely to be linked to proximal rather than distal factors. For example, in the treatment of ethnic minority clients, a therapist's knowledge of the client's culture is *distal* to outcome in the sense that the cultural knowledge must somehow be translated into concrete behaviors in the therapy session. These culturally based behaviors may enhance the process of credibility (e.g., the client's belief that the therapist is understanding, knowledgeable, and competent), which is more *proximal* to therapy outcome and effectiveness. Distal variables are likely to exhibit a weaker relationship to outcome than are proximal variables.

Ethnicity of therapist or client and ethnic match are distal variables; consequently, weak or conflicting results are likely to be found between ethnic match and outcome. Ethnicity per se tells us very little about the attitudes, values, experiences, and behaviors of *individuals*, therapists or clients, who interact in a therapy session. What is known is that although *groups* exhibit cultural differences, considerable individual differences may exist within groups. Ethnic matches can result in cultural mismatches if therapists and clients from the same ethnic group show markedly different values (e.g., a highly acculturated Chinese American therapist who works with a Chinese immigrant holding traditional Chinese values). Conversely, ethnic mismatches do not necessarily imply cultural mismatches, because therapists and clients from different ethnic groups may share similar values, life-styles, and experiences.

Evidence for the importance of individual differences has come from a variety of studies. Atkinson, Maruyama, and Matsui (1978) found that Asian Americans vary in their ratings of credibility for an Asian American or Caucasian American therapist. After listening to an audiotape of a counseling session in which the therapist was described as being an Asian or Caucasian American, subjects were asked to rate the therapist on various factors, including therapist credibility. Asian American students assigned more credibility to the therapist who was described as an Asian rather than a Caucasian American. However, Japanese Americans from a young Buddhist association rated the therapists equally. Atkinson and his colleagues attributed the findings to differences among Asians: The Asian American students may have been less acculturated or more racially aware than the Japanese subjects because many of the students were recruited from a campus group concerned with racial awareness. Sanchez and Atkinson (1983) found that individual differences were important in preferences of Mexican Americans for an ethnically similar counselor. Subjects with a strong commitment to the Mexican American culture wanted to work with a Mexican American counselor. Those who had a commitment to Anglo-American culture, both cultures, or neither culture were less likely to prefer an ethnically similar counselor. In the case of Blacks, a number of investigators have formulated ethnic identity models and have tested Black client preferences for, or evaluations of, therapists as a function of identity (Atkinson, Furlong, & Poston, 1986; Cross, 1978; Morten & Atkinson, 1983; Parham & Helms, 1981; Pomales, Claiborn, & LaFromboise, 1986). All of these studies have recognized the importance of individual differences.

The emphasis on individual differences implicitly recognizes the complexity of the match issue. Other investigators have questioned whether mismatches are necessarily detrimental. Tyler, Sussewell, and Williams-McCoy (1985) have developed the Ethnic Validity Model in an attempt to specify the advantages and disadvantages that can occur in matches and mismatches. In this model, individuals have a conception of a reference group and of validity within that group. Ethnic validity for different groups may converge, diverge, or conflict. Convergence refers to patterns of interaction in which some or all of the criteria for well-being transcend culture, race, and ethnicity. Divergence is a situation in which the patterns of well-being are unique and reflect cultural or racial differences. Conflict occurs when the patterns in various groups not only differ but also clash. Ideally, the tasks are to enrich convergence (i.e., the commonalities) and divergence (e.g., pluralism), and to reduce conflict. The therapy encounter may serve to accomplish these tasks. Therapists and clients who match ethnically and culturally may relate well to one another and share experiences and perspectives. However, matches may not be conducive to transcending cultural biases and limitations. In mismatches, the advantage is that clients and therapists can learn about cultural diversity and confront conflicting validities. Problems can occur when cultural differences cannot be surmounted, and the capacity to communicate is limited. These ideas are intriguing, although it should be noted that Tyler et al. failed to clearly distinguish between ethnic and cultural matches.

The interest in individual differences as important mediators and the analysis of possible advantages and disadvantages in match and mismatch raise important questions. How do individual differences among ethnic individuals interact with type of therapist to affect outcomes? How can therapists who match or mismatch their clients achieve the tasks outlined by Tyler et al? These issues point to the fact that ethnic effects in treatment cannot be addressed by simple questions.

Summary and Research Directions

In summary, the evidence on ethnicity is not definitive, and the research work in the area is fraught with conceptual and methodological limitations. Nevertheless, available research has failed to systematically reveal outcome differences. By outcome, I am referring to measures of well-being and not to process measures or therapist preferences. Similarly, ethnic match has not been shown to consistently improve outcomes.

Is the failure to achieve definitive answers caused by the quality and quantity of research in the area? If it were possible, in fact or even in principle, to conduct a series of large scale, rigorous research, would answers be forthcoming? I believe not. Although it would certainly be desirable to have such research, my position has been that ethnicity and match/mismatch are distal variables. The simple relationship between distal variables and outcome is likely to be weak, and in many cases, meaningless.

This position can be easily misinterpreted. It seemingly argues that ethnicity is unimportant, that there is no reason to change therapeutic practices because ethnic individuals appear to benefit from treatment, and that the need for more ethnic therapists should be spurred by ethical rather than treatment considerations. I am *not* making such arguments. My point is that we have dwelled too long on questions that entail the use of distal variables.

Ethnicity is but one factor, embedded in many others, that may influence therapy outcomes. Furthermore, ethnicity has important aspects or components. Three aspects of ethnicity may influence psychotherapy. First, is the stimulus value of the therapist (or client). A Black or White therapist is a physical stimulus to the client, who may have expectations, transference reactions, and so on, based on race. Second, an ethnic therapist may be fluent in the ethnic language and relate to clients who primarily speak the language. Third, and most important, ethnicity may suggest something about one's culture, ways of behaving, values and experiences. These "meanings" of ethnicity are more important to study than ethnicity itself because they are less distal and are more likely to influence therapy outcomes. In addition, one cannot assume that each aspect is present in an ethnic therapist and absent in White therapists. It should also be noted that one's ethnicity is immutable; one's understanding of, and sensitivity to, different cultures are not immutable.

Cultural factors in the treatment of ethnic clients have commanded the greatest attention among ethnic therapists. Yet, research has been devoted to ethnic rather than cultural match, perhaps because of the difficulties in defining culture. If we are to understand treatment effectiveness with ethnic individuals, cultural match and its implications must be examined. As mentioned earlier, Sue and Zane (1987) have proposed that cultural match be operationalized into units that can be related to the therapy process. For example, cultural match between ethnic clients and therapists can be studied in terms of three variables—conceptualization of the ethnic client's problems, means for solving problems, and goals for treatment. These matched or mismatched variables can then be related to therapeutic processes (such as therapist credibility and rapport development) and outcome. In this way, knowledge may be gained regarding what aspects of match are important to therapeutic outcomes. The study of the actual behaviors in therapy may yield some insight into how matches or mismatches are reflected in treatment. Such a research approach can take into consideration individual differences, because ethnics themselves exhibit variability in cultural orientation and degree of acculturation. It can also provide a means of studying the advantages and disadvantages of match, as hypothesized by Tyler et al. (1985). Ethnicity is important, but what is more important is its meaning.

References

Abramowitz, S. I. (1978). Splitting data from theory on the black patient–white therapist relationship. *American Psychologist, 33,* 957–958.

Abramowitz, S. I., & Murray, J. (1983). Race effects in psychotherapy. In J. Murray & P. Abramson (Eds.), *Bias in psychotherapy* (pp. 215–255). New York: Praeger.

Acosta, F. X. (1984). Psychotherapy with Mexican Americans: Clinical and em-pirical gains. In J. L. Martinez & R. H. Mendoza (Eds.), *Chicano psychology* (2nd ed., pp. 163–189). New York: Academic Press.

Atkinson, D. R. (1983). Ethnic similarity in counseling psychology: A review of research. *The Counseling Psychologist, 11,* 79–92.

Atkinson, D. R. (1985). A meta-review of research on cross-cultural counseling and psychotherapy. *Journal of Multi-*

cultural Counseling and Development, 1, 138–153.

Atkinson, D. R. (1986). Similarity in counseling. *The Counseling Psychologist,* 14, 319–354.

Atkinson, D. R., Furlong, M. J., & Poston, W. C. (1986). Afro-American preferences for counselor characteristics. *Journal of Counseling Psychology,* 33, 326–330.

Atkinson, D. R., Maruyama, M., & Matsui, S. (1978). Effects of counselor race and counseling approach on Asian Americans' perceptions of counselor credibility and utility. *Journal of Counseling Psychology,* 25, 76–85.

Attneave, C. L. (1985). Practical counseling with American Indian and Alaska Native clients. In P. Pedersen (Ed.), *Handbook of cross-cultural counseling and therapy* (pp. 135–140). Westport, CT: Greenwood.

Banks, W. M. (1972). The differential effects of race and social class in helping. *Journal of Clinical Psychology,* 28, 90–92.

Carkhuff, R. R., & Pierce, R. (1967). Differential effects of therapist race and social class upon patient depth of self-exploration in the initial clinical interview. *Journal of Consulting Psychology,* 31, 632–634.

Casas, J. M. (1985). The status of racial- and ethnic-minority counseling: A training perspective. In P. Pedersen (Ed.), *Handbook of cross-cultural counseling and therapy* (pp. 267–274). Westport, CT: Greenwood.

Clark, K. B. (1972). Foreword. In A. Thomas & S. Sillen (Eds.), *Racism and psychiatry* (pp. 11–13). New York: Brunner/Mazel.

Cross, W. E. (1978). The Cross and Thomas models of psychological nigrescence. *Journal of Black Psychology,* 5, 13–19.

Dreger, R. M., & Miller, K. S. (1968). Comparative psychological studies of Negroes and whites in the United States. *Psychological Bulletin,* 70, 1–58.

Evans, D. A. (1985). Psychotherapy and black patients: Problems of training, trainees, and trainers. *Psychotherapy,* 22, 457–460.

Fulton, W., Gad, M., & Sue, S. (1979). "Heart-pothesis" is a two-edged sword. *American Psychologist,* 34, 561–562.

Griffith, M. S. (1977). The influence of race on the psychotherapeutic relationship. *Psychiatry,* 40, 27–40.

Griffith, M. S., & Jones, E. E. (1978). Race and psychotherapy: Changing perspectives. In J. H. Masserman (Ed.), *Current psychiatric therapies:* (Vol. 18, pp. 225–235). New York: Grune & Stratton.

Harrison, D. K. (1975). Race as a counselor-client variable in counseling and psychotherapy: A review of the research. *The Counseling Psychologist,* 5, 124–133.

Jenkins, A. H. (1985). Attending to self-activity in the Afro-American client. *Psychotherapy,* 22, 335–341.

Jones, A., & Seagull, A. A. (1977). Dimensions of the relationship between the black client and the white therapist: A theoretical overview. *American Psychologist,* 32, 850–855.

Jones, E. E. (1978). Effects of race on psychotherapy process and outcome: An exploratory investigation. *Psychotherapy: Theory, Research, and Practice,* 15, 226–236.

Jones, E. E. (1982). Psychotherapists' impressions of treatment outcome as a function of race. *Journal of Clinical Psychology,* 38, 722–731.

Jones, E. E. (1985). Psychotherapy and counseling with black clients. In P. Pedersen (Ed.), *Handbook of cross-cultural counseling and therapy* (pp. 173–179). Westport, CT: Greenwood.

Klineberg, O. (1985). The social psychology of cross-cultural counseling. In P. Pedersen (Ed.), *Handbook of cross-cultural counseling and therapy* (pp. 29–36). Westport, CT: Greenwood.

Lefley, H. P. (1985). Mental health training across cultures. In P. Pedersen (Ed.), *Handbook of cross-cultural counseling and therapy* (pp. 259–266). Westport, CT: Greenwood.

Leong, F. T. (1986). Counseling and psychotherapy with Asian-Americans: Review of the literature. *Journal of Counseling Psychology,* 33, 196–206.

Lerner, B. (1972). *Therapy in the ghetto: Political impotence and personal disintegration.* Baltimore: Johns Hopkins University Press.

LeVine, E. S., & Padilla, A. M. (1980). *Crossing cultures in therapy: Pluralistic counseling for the Hispanic.* Monterey, CA: Brooks/Cole.

Morten, G., & Atkinson, D. R. (1983).

Minority identity development and preference for counselor race. *Journal of Negro Education, 52*, 156–161.

Munoz, R. F. (1982). The Spanish-speaking consumer and the community mental health center. In E. E. Jones & S. J. Korchin (Eds.), *Minority mental health* (pp. 362–398). New York: Praeger.

Parham, T. A., & Helms, J. E. (1981). The influence of black students' racial identity attitudes on preferences for counselor's race. *Journal of Counseling Psychology, 28*, 250–257.

Parloff, M. B., Waskow, I. E., & Wolfe, B. E. (1978). Research on therapist variables in relation to process and outcome. In S. L. Garfield & A. E. Bergin (Eds.), *Handbook of psychotherapy and behavior change: An empirical analysis* (2nd ed., pp. 233–282). New York: Wiley.

Paul, G. L. (1969). Behavior modification research: Design and tactics. In C. M. Franks (Ed.), *Behavior therapy: Appraisal and status* (pp. 1–48). New York: McGraw-Hill.

Pedersen, P., Draguns, J. G., Lonner, W. J., & J. E. Trimble (Eds.). (1981). *Counseling across cultures* (2nd ed.). Honolulu: University of Hawaii Press.

Pomales, J., Claiborn, C. D., & LaFromboise, T. D. (1986). Effects of black students' racial identity on perceptions of white counselors varying in cultural sensitivity. *Journal of Counseling Psychology, 33*, 57–61.

President's Commission on Mental Health. (1978). *Report to the President*. Washington, DC: U.S. Government Printing Office.

Rappaport, J. (1977). *Community psychology: Values, research, and action*. New York: Holt, Rinehart & Winston.

Sanchez, A. R., & Atkinson, D. R. (1983). Mexican-American cultural commitment, preference for counselor ethnicity, and willingness to use counseling. *Journal of Counseling Psychology, 30*, 215–220.

Sattler, J. M. (1977). The effects of therapist–client racial similarity. In A. S. Gurman & A. M. Razin (Eds.), *Effective psychotherapy: A handbook of research* (pp. 252–290). Elmsford, NY: Pergamon.

Siegel, J. M. (1974). A brief review of the effects of race in clinical service interactions. *American Journal of Orthopsychiatry, 44*, 555–562.

Snowden, L. R. (Ed.). (1982). *Reaching the underserved: Mental health needs of neglected populations*. Beverly Hills, CA: Sage.

Sue, D. W., & Sue, D. (1985). Asian-Americans and Pacific Islanders. In P. Pedersen (Ed.), *Handbook of cross-cultural counseling and therapy* (pp. 141–146). Westport, CT: Greenwood.

Sue, S., Wagner, N. N., Ja, D., Margullis, C., & Lew, L. (1976). Conceptions of mental illness among Asian and Caucasian American students. *Psychological Reports, 38*, 703–708.

Sue, S., & Zane, N. (1987). The role of culture and cultural techniques in psychotherapy: A critique and reformulation. *American Psychologist, 42*, 37–45.

Triandis, H. C., & Brislin, R. W. (1984). Cross-cultural psychology. *American Psychologist, 39*, 1006–1016.

Trimble, J. E., & La Fromboise, T. (1955). American Indian and the counseling process: Culture, adaptation, and style. In P. Pedersen (Ed.), *Handbook of cross-cultural counseling and therapy* (pp. 127–134). Westport, CT: Greenwood.

Tyler, F. B., Sussewell, D. R., & Williams-McCoy, J. (1985). Ethnic validity in psychotherapy. *Psychotherapy, 22*, 311–320.

CHAPTER TWELVE

Abnormality and Social Institutions

————◄○►————

No examination of psychological disorders would be complete without looking at the interface between society and abnormal behavior. How does society define abnormality? How does it characterize its behaviorally disturbed citizens? How does it respond to them? What are the legal issues involved in protecting the mentally ill—and in protecting society from those with mental illness who might present a danger to others?

We have come a long way from the days when the mentally ill were chained to the walls of insane asylums. Still, individuals with psychological problems are stigmatized and discriminated against in our society. Studies indicate that most people would rather associate with known felons than with people who have been hospitalized for mental illness. Insurance coverage sets payment caps on treatment for emotional problems that is not set for treatment of "medical" problems. More research money is spent on tooth decay than on schizophrenia.

In this chapter we examine how the mentally ill are viewed and treated in late-twentieth-century United States. The first reading (#51) illustrates, through numerous examples, how the media portray mental illness. The next reading, (#52), explores the policy of deinstitutionalization. Begun in the 1960s, this sociopolitical movement was designed to transfer treatment of people with mental and emotional problems from large, impersonal, remote hospitals into the community. Intended both to increase the quality of life of patients and to reduce the economic burden of housing and caring for people with serious mental illness on society, deinstitutionalization has had both positive and negative consequences. In her reading (#53), Harriet Lefley, a psychologist and parent of a son who has suffered from schizophrenia for over thirty years, examines the question of involuntary treatment from the perspectives of the individual, the family, and society. The final reading (#54) highlights some of the ways in which public policy can affect the lives of citizens with mental illness. The moral of the story is that social policy can have a substantial impact on the lives of individual people. Decisions need to be made with care, with course corrections made when data suggest they are needed.

51

——————◄o►——————

Dr. Otto Wahl, a psychologist at George Mason University, has been studying how the media portray people with mental illness for twenty years. In this piece, drawn from a lecture he presented to the Alliance for the Mentally Ill of Virginia Beach, Virginia, in 1994, he summarizes the current situation. Consider, as you read it, how you would feel confronting the examples he gives if you or a family member had a serious mental illness. What would it do to your self-image? To your ability to relate to others? If you want to follow this topic in more depth, you might want to read his recent book, Media madness: Public images of mental illness *(New Brunswick, NJ: Rutgers University Press, 1995).*

STIGMA AND MASS MEDIA

Otto F. Wahl, Ph.D.

STIGMA IS DEFINED IN THE dictionary as "a mark of shame or infamy." It is a word with which those with mental illnesses and their loved ones are very familiar, for people with mental illnesses frequently find themselves viewed and treated differently—usually more unfavorably—than others, as if their illnesses were indeed a mark of shame or infamy.

Research studies have shown that a label of mental illness leads to negative expectations and reactions from others, including outright discrimination. Knowledge that one has had a mental illness substantially decreases the likelihood that he or she will be offered a job, accepted into a graduate program, be rented a room, or even be seen as an acceptable co-worker (Fink & Tasman, 1992; Melton & Garrison, 1987; Wahl, 1995). Resistance to group homes for those with mental illness is commonplace, and some estimate that as many as half of the attempts to establish such housing are defeated by community opposition fueled by misconceptions about mental illness (Piasecki, 1975).

Those who suffer the illnesses and who face the stigma, furthermore, are very aware of negative public attitudes. In one survey (Wahl &

Harman, 1989), 487 relatives of mentally ill patients were asked about their impressions of stigma. The vast majority (77 percent) indicated that they believed their mentally ill relative had been much or very much affected by stigma, with the most cited negative effects being lowered self-esteem, decreased ability to make and keep friends, difficulty getting a job, and reluctance to admit mental illness. It is no surprise, then, that, in an August 1991 survey of 250 members of a patient support group in Staten Island, New York, 89 percent reported that they had withheld information about their disorders for fear of possible negative reactions.

So where, we may well ask, do these negative attitudes toward mental illness come from? In fact, Wahl & Harman asked just that in their 1989 survey. The most cited contributors to stigma were mass presentations— movies about mentally ill killers, news coverage of tragedies caused by mentally ill individuals, casual use of slang and offensive terms referring to mental illness, and jokes about mental illness. That mass media— television, movies, newspapers—may play a significant role in the creation and perpetuation of stigma was supported also by the recent (1990) findings of a Robert Wood Johnson Foundation survey. Talking by telephone to 1,300 individuals representative of the U.S. population, they found that most people identified mass media as the primary source of their information about mental illness.

Unfortunately, the images of mental illness which fill these media tend to be inaccurate, demeaning, and stigmatizing. Media depictions, for example, convey that people with mental illnesses are fundamentally different from others. Content analyses of television programs (Wahl & Roth, 1982; Signorelli, 1989) reveal that the majority of mentally ill characters on television are shown as distinctly different from others in being without important aspects of social identity such as family or successful employment; their only identity is as mentally ill individuals. Many depictions suggest that persons with mental illnesses are even different from others in physical appearance, that they stand out and are easily identifiable by their odd and unusual physical characteristics. So crucial is the idea of physical distinctiveness to the portrayal of mental illness, in fact, that one of the reported starting problems for the 1975 Oscar-winning film, *One Flew Over the Cuckoo's Nest*, was finding enough competent actors who looked unusual enough to play mental patients in the film. There was even consideration of use of actual patients from Oregon State Hospital, where the movie was filmed, but such use was rejected because the real patients did not look distinct enough to depict mental patients on the screen.

Mental illnesses and mentally ill people are also treated in the media as objects of humor and ridicule. While it is rare to find other serious disorders being lampooned, there seem to be few inhibitions about poking fun at mental illness. Cartoons regularly convey that mental illness is laughable, while movies like *Crazy People*, *The Dream Team*, and *Mixed Nuts* rely on a parade of patients with humorous idiosyncrasies to amuse their audiences. *Newsday* even described the plot of *Dream Team* — "four acknowledged crazy people on their own in New York City" as "an innately funny premise" (Darling, 1989).

Lack of appreciation of the seriousness of mental illness and lack of respect for the sensitivities of mentally ill people and their loved ones is shown also by the continued widespread use in mass media of slang and offensive terms for mental illness and treatment. Articles and films about mental illness are typically peppered with disrespectful terms like "lunatics," "wackos," "crazoids," etc. From advertisements that exclaim, "To offer these deals, we'd have to be committed," to record promotions that have invited "neurotics, psychotics, schizoids, and music lovers at all levels of mental dysfunction" to come to scheduled locations and get their pictures taken in a straitjacket, to restaurants that advertise their seafood specials as "Lobster Lunacy," mental illness is trivialized for profit. The epitome of this may be the packaging and advertising of a Georgia peanuts product with the name "Certifiably Nuts." The gift bag of peanuts came packaged in a straitjacket with a "patient history" attached stating that the owner's family had been "nuts" for generations. If one pulls the small ring on the package, hysterical laughter is heard. The product won an advertising industry award (a CLIO) for creative packaging (Wahl, 1995).

As if the facets of media depiction of mental illness so far presented aren't bad enough, there is an even more prominent and damaging aspect to be considered. That aspect is the extraordinarily common and consistent portrayal of mentally ill people as violent, dangerous, and criminal. Although research has repeatedly demonstrated that the vast majority of those with mental illnesses are neither violent nor criminal, mass media continue to suggest otherwise (Monahan, 1992).

George Gerbner, for example, has looked at a number of different groups portrayed on television — males, females, African Americans, Hispanics, etc. — and noted how often each was portrayed as a villain and how often as a hero. Of all the groups he studied, only one group appeared more often as villains than heroes — those with mental illness (Gerbner, 1993). In addition, it has been reported that mentally ill characters are far more likely to be violent than any other type of character. Ratings of samples of prime-time television over many years revealed that 42 percent of the "normal" characters in prime-time drama were shown to be violent; but fully 72 percent of those characters labelled mentally ill were violent; 22 percent were killers (vs. only 9 percent of "normals"). This pattern was found to be true even for the gentler sex; although only 27 percent of all female characters were violent, 60 percent of female mentally ill characters were violent (Signorelli, 1989).

The clear message is that mental illness makes people—even ordinarily nonviolent people like females—violent and dangerous.

Mentally ill killers are certainly a common plot device for films, as well. So successful was Hitchcock's ground-breaking *Psycho* that Norman Bates returned for three sequels. Likewise, *Friday the 13th*'s Jason, *Halloween*'s Michael Myers, and *Nightmare on Elm Street*'s Freddy Kruger ("the most popular cinematic maniac since Darth Vader," according to one movie ad) have made multiple appearances. More recently, *Silence of the Lambs* and the popularity of the cannibalistic Hannibal Lecter has proven again that mentally ill killers attract large film audiences.

Serial and psychotic killers are likewise popular these days in paperback fiction. These novels include John Sanford's best-selling "Prey" series (*Rules of Prey*, *Shadow Prey*, *Eyes of Prey*, *Silent Prey*, *Winter Prey*, *Night Prey*, and *Mind Prey*), which features the same detective facing a new serial killer in each novel, and Rex Miller's novels (*Slob*, *Slice*, *Chaingang*, *Savant*, and *Butcher*), centered around a 400-pound brute, diagnosed with schizophrenia, who murders relentlessly and occasionally rips out and eats the hearts of his victims. These, and many other similar slice-and-dice thrillers, clearly communicate that violence, excessive violence in fact, is to be associated with mental illness (Wahl, 1992).

Even in less-expected places, one can find the image of murderous madmen. Cartoonist Shel Silverstein includes in his tongue-in-cheek *Uncle Shelby's ABZ Book* this entry: "S is also for Stanley. Stanley is a crazy murderer who likes to murder little boys and girls *early* Sunday morning," showing an ugly, ill-shaven man with blood dripping from a knife. And, in the otherwise delightful children's story *How to Eat Fried Worms*, there is a passage in which one child, seeing someone behaving strangely, warns his friends: "Don't let him see we're afraid. Crazy people are like dogs. If they see you're afraid, they attack." Children's media, in fact, are filled with images of mentally ill people as criminal and dangerous. Comic book villains, for example, often begin as well-intended scientists but become villains when, for one reason or another, they become insane. Toys and games similarly connect mental illness with criminality by making their villains—e.g., Batman's primary menesis, the Joker—insane (Wahl, 1995).

The daily diet of unfavorable and frightening images of mental illness to which the public is exposed through the mass media harms those with mental illnesses. They are harmed directly, by being offended, insulted, and undermined in their efforts to recover self-esteem, and indirectly, but significantly, by the perpetuation of public fears and disrespect of those with mental illnesses. The stigma of mental illness, in short, creates a heavy burden above and beyond that of the illnesses themselves, and the pervasive inaccurate images of our mass media contribute to that stigma and to that continuing burden.

References

Darling, L. (April 7, 1989). City as psych ward: Four crazoids hit the streets. *Newsday*.

Fink, P. J., and Tasman, A. (Eds.) (1992). *Stigma and mental illness*. Washington, D.C.: American Psychiatric Press.

Freedom from Fear (August 1991). *Public perceptions of people with mental illnesses*. Unpublished manuscript.

Gerbner, G. (June 1993). Women and minorities on television: A study in casting and fate. In *Report to the Screen Actors Guild and the American Federation of Radio and Television Artists*.

Melton, G. B., and Garrison, E. G. (1987). Fear, prejudice, and neglect: Discrimination against mentally disabled persons. *American Psychologist, 42*, 1007–1026.

Monahan, J. (1992). Mental disorder and violent behavior: Perceptions and evidence. *American Psychologist, 47*, 511–521.

Piasecki, J. R. (1975). *Community response to residential services for the psycho-socially disabled: Preliminary results of a national survey*. Philadelphia: Horizon House Institute.

Robert Wood Johnson Foundation (April 15, 1990). Public attitudes toward people with chronic mental illness. Unpublished manuscript.

Rockwell, T. (1973). *How to eat fried worms*. New York: Dell Publishing.

Silverstein, S. (1961). *Uncle Shelby's ABZ book*. New York: Simon & Schuster.

Signorelli, N. (1989). The stigma of mental illness on television. *Journal of Broadcasting and Electronic Media, 33*, 325–331.

Wahl, O. F. (1995). *Media madness: Public images of mental illness*. New Brunswick, N.J.: Rutgers University Press.

Wahl, O. F. (1992). Messages about mental illness from the serial killer novel. *Journal of the California Alliance for the Mentally Ill, 4*, 43–44.

Wahl, O. F., and Harman, C. R. (1989). Family views of stigma. *Schizophrenia Bulletin, 15*, 131–139.

Wahl, O. F., and Roth, R. (1982). Television images of mental illness: Results of a metropolitan Washington Media Watch. *Journal of Broadcasting, 26*, 599–605.

52

———————◄o►———————

In the 1970s and 1980s the population of state mental hospitals across the United States (and, indeed, public psychiatric hospitals throughout Western society) shrank dramatically. There were several reasons for this shift from institutional care to community care—what we call deinstitutionalization. First, newly discovered biological treatments were successful at reducing the most severe psychotic symptoms for many patients. Second, it was hoped that treatment in the community would help individuals with mental illness to maintain social skills and social ties. Third, treatment in the "least restrictive setting" was felt to be more humane and moral. Fourth, outpatient treatment was likely to be significantly less expensive so that the care of patients in the community rather than in the hospital would result in economic savings to society.

The outcome of deinstitutionalization has been mixed. Because the development of community-based treatment programs has lagged behind the closing of hospitals, many people have "fallen through the cracks," winding up homeless or in jail. Others, however, have achieved a decent quality of life with the help of medication, specialized work or educational opportunities, supervised housing, and counseling.

In the article that follows, a Harvard psychiatrist, Robert L. Okin, M.D., makes the case for deinstitutionalization, suggesting that we resist the pressure to re-open state mental hospitals. It would be preferable, he argues, to put our energy into improving the care and support available in the community.

THE CASE FOR DEINSTITUTIONALIZATION

Robert L. Okin, MD

FEW CONTROVERSIES IN PUBLIC PSYCHIATRY are as important—or as notorious—as the debate about deinstitutionalization. For a number of complicated reasons, state mental hospitals in the last 30 years have discharged many of their patients and restricted the admission of others before enough resources were available to care for them in the community. Even when the tragic effects became obvious, states failed to provide adequate funds, and services in many places are still incomplete, fragmented, and poorly monitored. Some authorities now say that in order to compensate for the deficiencies of the community system and deal with its casualties, we should return patients to state hospitals. I believe that instead we should extend and improve community care.

We need a wide range of services for both acute and chronic patients, including outpatient care, crisis intervention, day treatment, and psychosocial and vocational rehabilitation. A graduated series of residential settings should provide active treatment at one end of the continuum and asylum at the other. Responsibility for specific patients should be assigned through a case management system. Psychiatric units in general hospitals are needed to serve acutely disturbed patients who need inpatient care. As this full range of services is established, the role of state hospitals can be reduced until they are being used only for the most unmanageable patients. The mental health system of the future should be balanced, but clearly tilted in favor of treatment in the community whenever possible.

The Case for Community Treatment

Most of the mentally ill should remain in the community because treatment usually works best in an environment that minimizes coercion, encourages contact with family members and the rest of society, and makes demands for independent functioning to the extent possible for the patient. Besides, most patients will eventually live in the community, and should learn the needed skills in the place where they will be used.

Most acutely ill patients in need of hospitalization can be treated in general hospitals, which are well equipped to diagnose and treat the biological aspects of mental disorders and to handle the complicated medical problems that often accompany acute psychiatric illnesses. They are located in the patients' home communities, which encourages family involvement and ensures continuity of care when they are discharged.

Studies in 7 states over the past 15 years have demonstrated that 60 percent of state hospital patients could be cared for in the community if proper services were provided. That is true even in certain parts of California, where deinstitutionalization has already gone further than in most other places. A recent study revealed that almost two-thirds of the patients in Los Angeles state hospitals would not have to be there if adequate community treatment were available. A Boston study concluded that with satisfactory community care only 15 state hospital beds per 100,000 population would be required. Today there are more than 70 beds per 100,000 persons in the nation as a whole.

Studies also show that, given adequate services, many severely ill people prefer to live in the community rather than in state hospitals. Furthermore, most states do not allow involuntary hospitalization except for patients who are dangerous to themselves or others, or so gravely disabled that they cannot care for themselves. If states used their resources to improve the community system, fewer patients would be so seriously impaired, and therefore fewer could be legally committed.

Problems of State Hospitals

The arguments in favor of community care are paralleled by arguments against state hospital care. Reform is unlikely to remedy the basic deficiencies of these institutions. It is not just that most of them are antiquated and poorly staffed and provide only limited programs. Other problems are less easily curable. State hospitals must operate by inflexible bureaucratic procedures such as rigid civil service systems and line item budgets. This reduces their capacity to use funds efficiently and interferes with almost every aspect of their functioning; for example, they cannot adjust staffing to changes in the patient population, and cannot compete with the private sector for qualified staff.

A deeper problem is that state hospitals are isolated and isolating. It is hard to involve families in treatment and discharge planning. Patients have little access to the rest of the health care system. They do not receive continuous care, and hospital programs are often unable to prepare them for life on the outside. For most patients, state hospitals provide not just inferior treatment but the wrong kind of treatment. That would still be true even if they had larger and better-trained staffs, and more attractive and comfortable physical plants.

Counter Arguments

Mental health administrators are sometimes urged to expand the state hospital system because many patients need asylum—shelter from a world that is threatening and confusing to them. But because of the very problems I have described, state hospitals are not the only or even the best place for asylum. It is also argued that state hospitals are better than the substandard housing, low welfare payments, and insufficient medical and social services provided for many patients in the community. But hospitals could not be built large enough to accommodate all of the indigent mentally ill patients now living in the community. Instead of solving the economic problems of the mentally ill, state hospitals merely hide them from public view. It makes more sense to provide reasonable welfare payments and adequate housing.

Another argument is that mental patients allowed to live outside of hospitals burden their families intolerably. But long-term hospitalization is no answer to that problem. For one thing, it is illegal to hospitalize a patient involuntarily for the family's sake; the courts have correctly determined that the civil rights of the mentally ill take precedence. Furthermore, research has now shown that certain forms of family therapy (along with medication) can be enormously helpful to patients, and by implication probably reduce the burden on their families.

Opponents of deinstitutionalization also point out that many patients in the community fail to take their medications. But committing patients to state hospitals simply to make them take drugs is even less justifiable than involuntarily hospitalizing them just to make life easier for their families. No court would permit it.

One of the most common arguments in favor of an expanded state hospital system is the high rate of return by discharged patients under the current system. But there is no good evidence that longer hospital stays make for lower rates of rehospitalization. What *does* reduce recidivism is improved community care following discharge. Some patients will still have to spend time in hospitals periodically, but there is no reason why they should not be allowed to live in the community whenever their condition permits. Many of them will gradually become accustomed to community life and require less frequent hospital treatment.

Supporters of expanded state hospitals also complain that a comprehensive community system is expensive. But rebuilding, modernizing, and expanding state hospitals would be expensive too; care of high quality simply cannot be provided at low cost. Nor is society more likely to provide resources for state hospitals than for community services. If anything, the opposite is true. In the 150 years of their history, state hospitals have been used mainly to hide the mentally ill and their problems from view. In contrast, the plight of the mentally ill in the community is disturbingly visible; that is one reason for its emergence as a major political issue, which has led to substantial increases in mental health budgets over the last 20 years.

Community system versus state hospital system is not an either/or issue, but resource limitations force states to choose where to spend the bulk of their funds. Attempting to straddle the fence by providing a little more money to state hospitals and a little more to community care has proved historically to be the most expensive course of action, offering the least hope for significant improvement in either system. It would not even be advisable to enlarge state hospitals as a transitional measure while waiting for community services to improve. That would divert from community care the very resources needed to correct its deficiencies, and even more state hospital beds would be needed.

The clinical, practical, and legal arguments all lead to the same conclusion. The deficiencies of the community mental health system are best addressed directly. Most patients do not want to return to state hospitals, and they neither can nor should be forced to return. State hospitals could never be built large enough anyway; they would again become grossly overcrowded and could not fulfill the only function that justifies their existence: providing intensive care to the small minority of patients who cannot be treated anywhere else.

53

——◄o►——

Before you read this article, consider how you feel about involuntary treatment of people with severe mental illness. Under what, if any circumstances, should they be treated against their will? Now, imagine that you are the parent of a young adult person who is wandering the streets, running from imaginary pursuers, not eating, and sleeping in doorways. Have your views changed?

Dr. Harriet P. Lefley is a psychologist, but she is also the parent of a man who has been living with schizophrenia for thirty years. She is in a unique position to see all sides of the involuntary treatment issue, and she presents them here with admirable clarity.

INVOLUNTARY TREATMENT: CONCERNS OF CONSUMERS, FAMILIES, AND SOCIETY

Harriet P. Lefley

THE QUESTION OF INVOLUNTARY treatment embodies some of the most basic philosophical, clinical, and political issues in any society. Many of these are antinomies, or conflicts between principles that appear to have equal validity. These include the rights of the individual versus those of the group; the civil liberties versus the survival needs of persons with presumably impaired judgment; the rights of disabled individuals versus the rights of those on whom they rely for survival; the rights of dependent persons versus their responsibilities to lessen their dependency; the obligations of society to protect the individual from self-damage; and the rights of physicians to carry out their mandate to heal. These issues are framed within the meaning of mental illness at any given time in history, that is, whether it is viewed primarily as a biomedical disorder, a psychological condition, a label attached to deviant behavior, possession by evil forces, a desirable transcendent experience, or an undesirable condition that is experienced at all levels of the biopsychosocial continuum. These definitions largely determine how society views the control and accountability of a mentally ill person in crisis.

The spectrum of opinions ranges from a totally civil libertarian view that no one can be deprived of his or her liberty without due process and clear demonstration of a crime (not for imminent dangerousness), to the concept of the state as parens patriae, fulfilling a protective role for persons who are too disabled to function in their own best interests. Views on this issue range from total opposition to involuntary treatment under any conditions to approval of involuntary commitment as a treatment modality that simultaneously protects both the patient and society. Some practitioners even view involuntary treatment as therapeutic, as responding to a "call for help" from people who feel they are losing control. In this view, the availability of involuntary treatment provides reassurance that a person will not be allowed to do harm when he or she is in a psychotic state. Indeed, a substantial number of persons have expressed relief that at one time or another they were hospitalized against their will, and who recalling the events leading up to their hospitalization, have stated that in all likelihood they would have been dead or in jail if this social mechanism had not been available.

Other former patients, however, particularly those who view themselves as survivors, have stated that jail would have been a less dehumanizing alternative. It is difficult for most of us to understand why, for some people, involuntary imprisonment may be preferable to involuntary hospitalization. Jail often fulfills the most terrifying fears of the person in psychosis — that one has committed nameless crimes for which the most awful penalties must be exacted. Moreover, any jail experience with its potential for physical assault from criminal offenders is likely to be far more cruel and unusual punishment than involuntary hospitalization.

Why do some consumers (although by no means the majority) prefer jail to hospitalization? Perhaps imprisonment is less threatening to the self-integrity of persons who have felt humiliated and dehumanized by the treatment system. Jail suggests that the person was in control of what she or he was doing and was the architect of the consequences. Involuntary hospitalization appears to reinforce feelings of helplessness—the type of feelings that indeed may have stimulated the psychotic behavior that led to this unwanted end.

Most societies differentiate between socially deviant behavior that is criminal in intent and deviant behavior attributable to impaired mental capacity. Persons in the latter category often come under the protection of the state. In the struggle for self-affirmation, mental health consumers have long contested the paternalistic principle that other people have the right to determine their "best interests" without final decision making on their part. Yet, people with severe and persistent mental illnesses are usually dependent on other people—family, friends, kind strangers, or the government—for their sustenance. They are forced by circumstance to accept the entitlement benefits that enable them to survive but at the same time require their designation as mentally disabled persons. For many people, any tradeoff of autonomy for survival benefits—whether it is in the form of subsistence funds, medical care, or involvement in the treatment system—seems too costly.

But those who bear the burden of support also have rights. They feel they have the right to expect that people who are dependent will do everything in their power to reduce their dependency. They expect that people with mental illnesses will work toward recovery, aiming for clear judgment and a level of autonomous decision-making that is informed rather than capricious. Families, in particular, suffer greatly when a relative's concept of self-determination means rejection of treatment, noncompliance with medications, substance abuse, or even homelessness. They suffer when their relatives insist on a self-imposed isolation that rejects interaction with consumer groups as much as with mental health professionals. Families experience circularity in the trajectory of patients' rights. The argument of self-determination, that leads mentally ill persons to reject involuntary treatment as an abuse of their rights, can also be used to support the self-destructive behaviors that make such interventions necessary.

Concepts of Mental Illness and Appropriate Treatment

Participants in this discussion seem to take positions based on their fundamental view of mental illness. Those who view major psychiatric disorders as legitimate illnesses that are largely biologically determined, tend to accept involuntary treatment as an undesirable but necessary safety net. Opponents of involuntary treatment tend to characterize the behaviors preceding commitment as psychologically-based responses to overwhelming environmental stress.

The premise of advocates who oppose involuntary treatment is that most psychotic episodes are based on terrified perceptions of threat, and that these feelings can be abated through appropriate behaviors that convey a real understanding of the terror and reassurance that the person will not be harmed. Physical or chemical restraints, on the other hand, only reinforce the convictions underlying the terror. In this viewpoint, psychotic episodes are preventable and treatable if one is able to recognize the events that trigger the terror. Respite houses or mobile crisis teams may defuse a psychotic episode. Consumers, who have endured these experiences themselves, have an essential role in calming the person and assuring safety. Drugs may not be necessary and indeed, a medical ambience may exacerbate rather than reduce the person's fear.

Another view, however, holds that internal stimuli, whether triggered by street drugs or malfunctioning neurons, can also generate psychotic episodes that involve a threat to oneself or others. Essentially, this position holds that we do not know enough yet to be able to differentiate between psychological and biological precursors of psychotic behavior. We have few means of distinguishing between those crisis episodes that can be defused with appropriate calming behavior, and those that cannot be controlled under any circumstances without physical restraint. It is highly unlikely that command hallucinations to harm oneself or others, persistent self-mutilation, or a substance-induced psychosis can be talked away. In this model, medical oversight in a safe environment is essential, and anti-psychotic medications are usually required to return the person to rational functioning. Untreated, such persons may pose a severe danger to themselves or others.

Do We Have Any Answers?

Various models of alternatives to involuntary treatment have been postulated. Some of these involve programmatic alternatives to hospital treatment, such as mobile crisis teams or consumer-run alternative services. Other models focus on ways of transferring decision making control to the person themselves. Some consumers and family advocates have proposed advance directives in which a person with a stabilized mental illness may appoint a health proxy or give prior permission for treatment in the event of later incompetency. Rosenson and Kasten (1991) call this "autonomy based on enlightened self-interest." This definition views mental illness as cyclical, with intermittent periods of decompensation. In this model, patients take control of their destiny by planning ahead for a crisis. Consumers Rogers and Centifanti (1991) view this type of advance directive as "giving away our rights to choose and refuse in advance" and counterpose a more proscriptive model that enables a patient to reject certain types of treatment in the event of incompetency, and forbids others to override their wishes.

Some clinician-researchers such as Marvin Herz (1984), Robert Liberman (1987), John Strauss (Strauss, Boker, & Brenner, 1987) and many others have been working with patients in identifying their prodromal cues of decompensation as well as learning coping and competency skills for recovery. Techniques are learned so that patients themselves can take control when they recognize these precursor signals and possibly avert psychotic episodes. Other approaches recognize that excessive environmental stimulation and situations with high-demand characteristics, in the treatment system as well as in the home, may lead to decompensation and the need for involuntary hospitalization (Lefley, 1992).

These approaches recognize that the critical issue is not only finding alternatives to involuntary treatment, but recognizing and avoiding the terrible crisis situations that make this a need. If involuntary treatment itself is a self-perpetuating precipitant of attitudes and behaviors that lead to more crises, then we need to study and correct a potentially damaging social process. If families, professionals, and treatment programs have undue expectations or otherwise raise anxiety levels; or if consumers categorically reject treatment options without offering viable, demonstrable solutions for the sickest among them, then for all groups we need reeducation based on our current state-of-the-art knowledge base.

Civil liberties are the most treasured possession of a free society. Constraints on freedom are so alien to our sensibilities and create so much anguish and anger, that we need to discover and avoid as much as possible the conditions that require their infringement. As members of a free society, we recognize that we are engaged in a common enterprise in which our rights and our obligations to each other are intermeshed. In resolving the issue of whether and under what conditions people may be treated against their will, we need ongoing dialogues among present and former primary consumers, families, service providers, legal advocates, and representatives of the society in which we all live.

References

Herz, M. I. (1984). Recognizing and preventing relapse in patients with schizophrenia. *Hospital and Community Psychiatry, 35*, 344–349.

Lefley, H. P. (1992). Expressed emotion: Conceptual, clinical, and social policy issues. *Hospital and Community Psychiatry, 43*, 591–598.

Liberman, R. P. *Psychiatric rehabilitation of chronic mental patients.* Washington, DC: American Psychiatric Press.

Rogers, J. A., & Centifanti, J. B. (1991). Beyond "self-paternalism": Response to Rosenson and Kasten. *Schizophrenia Bulletin, 17,* 5–14.

Rosenson, M. K., & Kasten, A. M. (1991). Another view of autonomy: Arranging for consent in advance. *Schizophrenia Bulletin, 17,* 1–7.

Strauss, J. S., Boker, W., & Brenner (1987). *Psychosocial treatment of schizophrenia.* Toronto: Hans Huber.

54

——◄o►——

Everyone knows that the health care system in the United States is undergoing rapid change. Pressures to contain costs while continuing to provide quality care have led to the development of health maintenance organizations and other social experiments, while many voices speak to the need for a national policy on health care.

People with severe and persistent psychological disorders have been treated as "second-class citizens" with respect to health care. Monetary limits on care make ongoing management of these disorders difficult if not impossible.

In the article that follows, Stephen W. White outlines the public health implications of untreated mental illness. He also suggests some of the fundamental changes that society must make to address the problem effectively. As you read it, keep in mind the points made by the authors of the two previous articles. What would a good mental health system look like?

MENTAL ILLNESS AND NATIONAL POLICY

Stephen W. White

IN HIS FOREWORD TO THE 1991 BOOK *Psychiatric Disorders in America,* by Lee Robins and Darrel Regier, Daniel X. Freedman writes:

Less than a month after President Carter's 1977 inauguration, Rosalynn Carter was authorized to assemble a commission to examine the nation's needs for mental health services and new knowledge about disorders. Sitting with her in a basement office of the White House East Wing as the initial plans were made, one could not mistake Mrs. Carter's clear respect for and interest in sound information. Her questions were unerringly straightforward. How many are suffering from these illnesses, who are they, and how are they treated? Embarrassingly, equally straightforward answers could not be provided. The base of information about the scope and boundaries of mental illnesses was simply inadequate. Fifteen months later her commission had sparked a remarkable decade-long journey to this singular volume.

What Lee Robins and Darrel Regier discovered is disconcerting. Put bluntly, the authors report that "The figures of a 32 percent lifetime and 20 percent annual prevalence are the best current estimates of the prevalence of psychiatric disorder in America." [Follow-up estimates of prevalence rates are even higher. In a later article published in *Archives of General Psychiatry* (February 1993), Regier et al. note a 28.1 percent annual prevalence rate for mental *and* addictive disorders (44.7 million adults) or 22.1 percent annual prevalence rate for mental disorders alone (35.1 million adults).] These estimates are based on conclusions drawn from a decade-long study of mental illness in a designated ECA (Epidemiologic Catchment Area) covering five sites in New Haven, Baltimore, St. Louis, Durham, and Los Angeles. The good news about these figures is that they represent the entire spectrum of psychiatric disorder, not just severe mental illness. The bad news is that the magnitude of the numbers indicates a significant national crisis in mental health care, for we know that if the current population of the United States is 252 million (1991), then there are perhaps 50 million people with psychiatric disorders. And as we approach questions about reforming the health care system in the U.S., we know that the populations most likely to be overlooked will be those with mental illness, mental retardation, rare genetic disorders, etc. — in short, those with special needs.

A quick mathematical calculation would reveal that, in the area of psychiatric disorder alone, over 75 million people will be at some point in their lives affected directly by reform in mental health care (given a 32 percent lifetime prevalence rate for mental illness). And many more (friends and relatives) are potentially concerned that the structure for health care reform be carefully planned to ensure health coverage for the mentally ill. But before this nation will act collectively to do anything about its mentally ill, citizens will first have to be convinced that there is indeed a crisis. And there is.

Speaking before a conference of the National Alliance for Research on Schizophrenia and Depression (NAR-SAD) in Atlanta, Georgia, in 1992, Dr. Charles B. Nemeroff—the chairman of the Department of Psychiatry at the Emory University School of Medicine—called attention to a number of dramatic facts to underscore the potentially costly nature of untreated mental illness. Citing data from the American Suicide Foundation, Dr. Nemeroff pointed out that over 30,000 people in America killed themselves in 1991. This is a national tragedy. And over one-half million people attempt suicide every year. . . . To put this in context, Dr. Nemeroff poignantly added that almost as many people in the United States die in a two-year period from suicide (60,000) as died during the entire Vietnam conflict (47,355 battle deaths, 67,008 total war-related deaths). His citing these statistics made me ponder how different our responses have been to the two national crises of war and suicide. Suicide is the second leading cause of death among young people from fifteen to nineteen years of age, yet there is no chanting or marching in the streets for its victims.

When one considers that depression may be a leading cause of suicide, it is frightening to think, as Dr. J. Raymond DePaulo, Jr., points out, that "only about 20 to 30 percent of people with those disorders (like depression) are receiving drug therapy." And he adds, "If we are overselling biological treatments, we're not doing a very good job of it," for "medications are clearly helpful for . . . depressions." Perhaps a more tragic dimension of this "treatment gap" revolves around a fact that Laurie Flynn—the executive director of the National Alliance for Mental Illness (NAMI)—points out: Only 10 percent of those surveyed believe that "mental disorders have a biological basis involving the brain."

When one adds Dr. Kay Redfield Jamison's observation that "the list of writers and artists who ended their lives by suicide is staggeringly long," one must see the cultural, social, and economic—not to mention human—implications of untreated illness. Those who are clamoring for more health care, for more social services, for a truly "kinder, gentler America" that "puts people first" are neither bleeding hearts nor crusading alarmists. And suicide is only one tip of the very large iceberg of mental illness threatening to sink the "invincible" social and economic *Titanic*.

Next, we must accept the fact that social problems like homelessness and mental illness are immediately intertwined. As the architects of Senate Bill 2696 note, "approximately one-third of the nation's 600,000 homeless persons suffer from severe mental illnesses." Three factors account for homelessness among the mentally ill: deinstitutionalization, deliberate abandonment by the community mental health centers of their stated mission to serve the needs of deinstitutionalized patients, and the deliberate dismantling of sectors of the social-welfare support system.

By the early 1980s, as Judge Robert C. Coates, author of *A Street Is Not a Home*, observes, "The new American homeless were upon us. They had fallen upon the nation's cities like winter's first snow, unexpectedly, silently. We rubbed our collective eyes. Our communities went through convulsions of rationalization as we struggled to think about these new ghosts haunting our consciousness." Judge Coates continues, "severely mentally ill people have never before been permitted to roam the nation's streets unassisted, bringing their private (treatable) hells out in the open to haunt us and our cities." And in almost no other industrialized nation is this allowed to happen. As Dr. E. Fuller Torrey points out, "Homelessness is not only a personal tragedy for these individuals, but also a national scandal."

Homelessness and suicide are only two aspects of the mental health crisis. Another scandalous dimension involves confining the mentally ill to jails and prisons. As Fuller Torrey notes, "They are often charged by the police with petty crimes such as trespassing simply to get them off the street." Estimates suggest that as many as 37,500 to 150,000 people with mental illness may be inappropriately placed in the prison system.

If we have been slow to recognize the neurobiological basis of mental illness in adults, we have been even slower to recognize it in children, as Enid and Richard Peschel and their coauthors argue in *Neurobiological Disorders in Children and Adolescents*. The authors note that "Neurobiological research has documented that many disorders in children and youth—including autism and pervasive developmental disorders, bipolar and major depressive disorders, obsessive-compulsive disorder, Tourette's syndrome, attention deficit hyperactivity disorder, schizophrenia, and anxiety disorders—are characterized by demonstrable malfunctions or malformations of the brain, or both." If we assume that just 1 to 3 percent of our school population of 47 million children have a neurobiological disorder, the population to be served could be as high as 1.4 million. Yet, a cursory examination of school rolls will reveal that very few of these children are being served under the current Individuals with Disabilities Education Act. The systems which ought to be serving these children are ignoring them except when parents demand service, and when they do, the systems often refuse to acknowledge the latest findings of the neuroscientific revolution.

We will not resolve the crisis in health care for those with psychiatric disorders, especially the seriously mentally ill, until we alter the way we perceive mental illness. What must we do?

First of all, we must realize, as Frederick K. Goodwin of the National Institute of Mental Health stated at a Conference of the National Alliance for the Mentally Ill, that mental illness is not a myth. It names a real class of neurobiological disorders. Although thoughts don't have high temperatures, coagulate, grow lesions, or develop high serum cholesterol levels (a thought per se cannot be diseased), thoughts do become disordered, confused, unclear, predominantly bleak, manic, delusional, or paranoid often as a result of a brain disorder (read "neurobiological disorder"). So, while it may be linguistically correct to say that the "mind" does not become ill, the brain does; and it would be a human tragedy to deny treatment to people with severe neurobiological disorders. Those who think seriously about psychiatric illnesses have always suspected that these disorders were biologically based, but there has been so much diagnostic debris (mostly Freudian) in the way, that it has been difficult to see clearly.

We must strip away the stigma associated with neurobiological disorders. Increasingly, as we discover more and more biologically based interventions for treating these disorders, there will be less stigma attached to them. And because such well-known individuals as Patty Duke, William Styron, Rod Steiger, Dick Cavett, Lawton Chiles, Art Buchwald, Diane and Lisa Berger, et al. have had the courage to "go public" with their or their family members' histories of bouts with depression or manic depression, the battle against stigma is slowly being won.

However, perhaps the most important dimension of health care reform affecting the mentally ill may lie in funding for research in the area of biological psychiatry. We may never discover a Salk vaccine to *prevent* or a penicillin to *cure* neurobiological disorders, but we are already seeing the development of drugs capable of targeting specific mechanisms in the brain. As Dr. Sheldon Preskorn remarks, "the potential for advancing our ability to treat brain diseases is astounding."

We now know that mental illness is no respecter of individuals. It cuts almost equally across all divisions of society—rich and poor, male and female, young and old, all ethnic and religious groups, and all sexual preferences. Because of this, the solutions must be far-reaching, systemic, holistic. Reform in health care must be integrated with an emphasis on providing shelter and homes, jobs and job training, health care coverage, education, vocational training, medical intervention, and, yes, even community mentoring for those with neurobiological disorders in our society. For, as Dr. Alexander Vuckovic of the Harvard Medical School has said, "Unlike the majority of victims of other illnesses, the victims of major mental illness remain with us year after year, decade after decade. They are our sons and daughters, brothers and sisters, wives and husbands." As we move along in the 1990s—a decade Congress has designated as the Decade of the Brain—can we not clearly see that when we learn to care for those whose quintessentially human qualities have been stolen from them through biological mishaps, we will have discovered more about who we are—a truth which Robert Frost once said is "too sudden to be credible"?

Credits and Acknowledgments

———◀○▶———

Cover illustration by Ann Marie Rousseau. Reproduced by permission.

Numeral refers to case or reading numeral.

5. "The Auto Accident that Never Was," from *The Boy Who Couldn't Stop Washing* by Judith Rapoport. Copyright © 1989 by Judith L. Rapoport, M.D. Used by permission of Dutton/Signet, a division of Penguin Books USA Inc.

7. "The Devil is in the Details: Fact and Fiction in the Recovered Memory Debate" by Robert Schwarz and Stephen Gilligan, from *Family Therapy Networker*, March/April, 1995. Reprinted by permission of the *Family Therapy Networker*.

8. "Personal Responsibility in Traumatic Stress Reactions" by John Russell Smith, from *Psychiatric Annals,* 12:11/November 1982, reprinted by permission of Slack, Inc.

12. "Living and Working with MPD" by Anonymous, from *Journal of Psychiatric Nursing,* 1994, Vol. 32 No. 8, reprinted by permission of Slack, Inc.

15. From "Dealing with Cross-cultural Issues in Clinical Practice" by Harriet Lefley, in P. A. Keller and S. R. Heyman (Eds.) *Innovations in Clinical Practice: A Source Book* Vol. 10, 1991. Reprinted by permission of Professional Resource Press.

17. "Light and Biological Rhythms in Psychiatry" by Norman E. Rosenthal, from *The Harvard Mental Health Letter*, March 1995. Reprinted with permission from *The Harvard Mental Health Letter*, 164 Longwood Avenue, Boston, MA 02115.

18. "Depressive Realism: Sadder but Wiser?" by Lauren B. Alloy, from *The Harvard Mental Health Letter*, April, 1995. Reprinted with permission from *The Harvard Mental Health Letter*, 164 Longwood Avenue, Boston, MA 02115.

21. "First-person Account: Behind the Mask: A Functional Schizophrenic Copes" by Anonymous, from *Schizophrenic Bulletin*, Vol. 16, No. 3, 1990.

22. "The Outcome of Schizophrenia" by Courtenay M. Harding, from *The Harvard Mental Health Letter*, May, 1988, reprinted with permission from *The Harvard Mental Health Letter*, 164 Longwood Avenue, Boston, MA 02115.

27. "A Conceptual Framework for Understanding Sexual Abuse: The W.A.R. Cycle" in S. L. Ingersoll and S. O. Patton, *Treating Perpetrators of Sexual Abuse*. Copyright © 1990 Jossey-Bass Inc, Publishers. First published by Lexington Books. All rights reserved. Reprinted by permission.

30. Excerpt from *Eating Disorders* by Hilde Bruch. Copyright © 1973 by Basic Books. Reprinted by permission of BasicBooks, a division of HarperCollins Publishers, Inc.

31. "Half Steps vs. Twelve Steps" from *Newsweek*, March 27, 1995, © 1995, Newsweek, Inc. All rights reserved. Reprinted by permission.

32. "Planet Bulimia" by Susan E. Gordon, from *Family Therapy Networker*, January/February, 1995. Reprinted by permission of the *Family Therapy Networker*.

33. Excerpt from "Eating Disorders and Substance Abuse" by Joan Ellen Zweben, from *Journal of Psychoactive Drugs*, Vol. 19, Number 2, April-June, 1987. Copyright © 1987, by Haight-Ashbury Publications / *Journal of Psychoactive Drugs*. Excerpted and reprinted with permission. All rights reserved.

35. "A Surgeon's Life" by Oliver Sacks, from *An Anthropologist on Mars* by Oliver Sacks, Copyright © 1995 by Oliver Sacks. Reprinted by permission of Alfred A. Knopf, Inc.

36. From *Ginny: A Love Remembered* by G. Robert Artley, published by Iowa State University Press. Copyright © 1993 by Bob Artley. All rights reserved. Reprinted by permission of Iowa State University Press.

41. "Psychopaths: New Trends in Research" by Robert D. Hare, from *The Harvard Mental Health Letter*, September, 1995. Reprinted with permission from *The Harvard Mental Health Letter*, 164 Longwood Avenue, Boston, MA 02115.

42. "The Hemophiliacs of Emotion" by Hal Straus, from *American Health*, June, 1988. Copyright © 1988 by Hal Straus. Reprinted by permission of *American Health*.

46. "The Masks Students Wear" by Sally L. Smith, from *Instructor*, April, 1989. Copyright © 1989 by Sally L. Smith. Reprinted with permission of the author.

47. "Mental Health: Does Therapy Help?" Copyright 1995 by Consumers Union of U.S., Inc., Yonkers, NY 10703–1057. Reprinted by permission from *Consumer Reports*, November, 1995.

48. "The Overselling of Therapy" by Neil Jacobson, from *Family Therapy Networker*, March/April, 1995. Reprinted by permission of the *Family Therapy Networker*.

49. "The Advantages and Disadvantages of Self-help Therapy Materials" by Albert Ellis from *Professional Psychology: Research and Practice*, 1995, Vol. 24. No. 3, 335–339. Copyright © 1995 by the American Psychological Association. Reprinted with permission.

50. "Psychotherapeutic Services for Ethnic Minorities: Two Decades of Research Findings" by Stanley Sue, from *American Psychologist*, April 1988, Vol. 43, No. 4, 301–308. Copyright © 1988 by the American Psychological Association. Reprinted with permission.

51. "Stigma and Mass Media" by Otto Wahl. Copyright © 1994 by Otto Wahl. Reprinted by permission of the author.

52. "The Case for Deinstitutionalization" by Robert L. Okin, from *The Harvard Mental Health Letter*, October, 1987. Reprinted with permission from *The Harvard Mental Health Letter*, 164 Longwood Avenue, Boston, MA 02115.
53. "Involuntary Treatment: Concerns of Consumers, Families, and Society" by Harriet P. Lefley, from *Innovation and Research*, Winter, 1993. 2, 1, 7–9. Reprinted by permission.
54. "Mental Illness and National Policy" by Stephen W. White. Reprinted from *National Forum: The Phi Kappa Phi Journal*, Volume 73, Number 1, (Winter 1993). Copyright © by Stephen W. White. By permission of the publishers.